South African Review III

Edited and compiled by
SARS (South African Research Service)

Ravan Press   *Johannesburg*

Published by
Ravan Press (Pty) Ltd.,
P O Box 31134, Braamfontein 2017, South Africa

First Published 1986

Cover Design: Ingrid Obery

Typesetting: Sandy Parker
Set in 10 on 12pt. Times Roman

ISBN 0 86975 289 8

Printed by Galvin and Sales (Pty) Ltd, Cape Town.

Contents

for occupational diseases — Difficulties for workers in obtaining compensation — Conclusion.

SECTION 2: POLITICS: STATE AND CAPITAL

Usages and Abbreviations

In this *South African Review*, the term 'black' refers collectively to all racially oppressed groups, ie, Africans, Indians and coloureds. These racial categories reflect part of the reality of apartheid society, and their use is accordingly necessary in contemporary writings. But the editors of the *Review* reject the racism implicit in such categorisation.

Most abbreviations used in the text of the *Review* are spelled out in full on first usage. In the case of trade unions, a list of acronyms used appears at the beginning of the section on labour. Newspapers referred to in the text are abbreviated in the following way:

Argus	*Argus*
BD	*Business Day*
Cit	*Citizen*
CP	*City Press*
CT	*Cape Times*
DN	*Daily News*
EPH	*Eastern Province Herald*
FM	*Financial Mail*
FW	*Finance Week*
RDM	*Rand Daily Mail*
SE	*Sunday Express*
Sow	*Sowetan*
SStar	*Sunday Star*
ST	*Sunday Times*
Star	*Star*
STrib	*Sunday Tribune*

Preface

The areas surveyed in the third *South African Review* reveal the range of fields in which the massive clash of social forces is under way in the intensifying struggle to forge a new South African society. In ruling-class politics and popular resistance, in the fields of labour and Southern African relations, in the crisis-ridden economy, the conflicts of class and race are taking on new forms.

This constant flux makes South African developments difficult to review. No sooner are articles written and predictions made, than they are superseded by new developments. The pace of crisis, conflict and change has increased dramatically, particularly since the beginning of 1984. Nonetheless, the *Review* remains surprisingly topical and relevant. The trends and processes analysed, subjects targeted for treatment, analytical methods used and questions posed are pertinent and current. The contributors, many working collectively, have found the essential pulse of their topics, and their views and analyses reflect this.

South African Review is divided into four sections:
Labour;
Politics: State and Capital;
Politics and the Economy; and
South Africa and its Peripheries.

Each section contains contributions which describe and analyse some of the major trends and events in contemporary South Africa.

The *Review* is produced and edited by the Southern African Research Service (SARS). Glenn Moss coordinated the project for SARS, while Susan Brown undertook the bulk of editing. She was assisted by Judy Freidberg, Isobel Hofmeyer, Karen Jochelson, and Ingrid Obery who also designed the cover. Thanks is due to all those mentioned, as well as to the publishers and contributors, for their time, energy and creativity.

Contributors are responsible for the views expressed in their articles only, while SARS bears responsibility for the overall nature and form of the book.

Trade Unions and Federations:
A List of Abbreviations

ABWU	Amalgamated Black Workers Union
AEU	Amalgamated Engineering Union
AFCWU	African Food and Canning Workers Union
AMAWU	African Mining and Allied Workers Union
AZACTU	Azanian Confederation of Trade Unions
BAMCWU	Black Allied Mining and Construction Workers Union
BCAWU	Building, Construction and Allied Workers Union
BEEWU	Black Electronics and Electrical Workers Union
CCAWUSA	Commercial, Catering and Allied Workers Union of South Africa
CMBU	Confederation of Metal and Building Unions
CTMWA	Cape Town Municipal Workers Association
CUSA	Council of Unions of South Africa
CWIU	Chemical Workers Industrial Union
DWASA	Domestic Workers Association of South Africa
EAWU	Engineering and Allied Workers Union
EIWUSA	Engineering Industrial Workers Union of South Africa
FBWU	Food and Beverage Workers Union
FCWU	Food and Canning Workers Union
FEDCRAW	Federal Council of Retail and Allied Workers
FMU	Federated Mining Union
FOSATU	Federation of South African Trade Unions
GAWU	General and Allied Workers Union
GWIU	Garment Workers Industrial Union
GWU	General Workers Union
GWUSA	General Workers Union of South Africa
IMF	International Metal Workers Federation
MACWUSA	Motor Assemblers and Components Workers Union of South Africa
MAWU	Metal and Allied Workers Union
MGWUSA	Municipal and General Workers Union of South Africa
MICWU	Motor Industry Combined Workers Union
NAAWU	National Automobile and Allied Workers Union
NUDAW	National Union of Distributive and Allied Workers
NUM	National Union of Mineworkers

NUTW	*National Union of Textile Workers*
PWAWU	*Paper Wood and Allied Workers Union*
OVGWU	*Orange Vaal General Workers Union*
RAWU	*Retail and Allied Workers Union*
SAAWU	*South African Allied Workers Union*
SABMWU	*South African Black Municipal Workers Union*
SABS	*South African Boilermakers Society*
SACC	*South African Coordinating Council (of the IMF)*
SACOL	*South African Confederation of Labour*
SACTU	*South African Congress of Trade Unions*
SACWU	*South African Chemical Workers Union*
SALDWU	*South African Laundry and Drycleaning Workers Union*
SAMWU	*South African Mine Workers Union*
SASBO	*South African Society of Bank Officials*
SASDU	*South African Scooter Drivers Union*
SEAWU	*Steel, Engineering and Allied Workers Union*
SFAWU	*Sweet, Food and Allied Workers Union*
T&G	*Transport and General Workers Union*
TAWU	*Transport and Allied Workers Union*
TUCSA	*Trade Union Council of South Africa*
TWU	*Transport Workers Union*
UAMAWUSA	*United African Motor and Allied Workers Union of South Africa*
UMMAWSA	*United Metal, Mining and Allied Workers of South Africa*

Introduction:
Trends in Organised Labour

Alan Fine and Robyn Rafel

Some consolidation, and a good deal of change, have been keynotes in the labour field over the past year. Structures within the union movement have continued to be fluid since early 1984, with new alliances forming and old ones breaking up. By mid-1985 it appeared that union unity talks between leading emerging unions were finally about to bear fruit, though some of those previously expected to take part had withdrawn. The revival of the SA Coordinating Council of the IMF has had significant effects on union alliances and has already begun to play an important role in union relationships with employers.

A number of unions have suffered breakaways, sometimes with but often without serious consequences. MAWU faced the most serious crisis in losing a large part of its East Rand branch. NUM, CCAWUSA and SAAWU were also affected by the split syndrome. TUCSA, too, has faced a series of disaffiliations by, among others, some of its largest member unions.

On the legal front a controversial amendment to the Labour Relations Act was introduced in 1984, to be greeted with anger and confusion by unions and employers alike. The National Manpower Commission, for which the Wiehahn Commission had great plans, has yet to prove that it is anything more than an unwanted appendage to the Department of Manpower.

The rather unsatisfactory term 'emerging union' is used in this article to refer to those unions established since the early 1970s, but includes some older unions which have become part of those groupings. It refers also to the unions involved in the unity talks, including those aligned with the UDF, and to black consciousness worker organisations.

The unity talks

At present the most closely-watched moves in the labour field are the unity talks, which aim at a giant federation of emerging unions. This section traces the course of the talks from early 1984 until August 1985.

At a Johannesburg meeting in March 1984, a group of UDF-aligned unions — SAAWU, GAWU, MACWUSA, GWUSA and MGWU — withdrew from the talks under pressure from the other participants.

The main causes of conflict were the reluctance of the general unions to form industrial structures, allegations that they were attempting to recruit the memberships of the other unions in the talks, and their failure to provide detailed information about their organising activities. The UDF unions were given the option of accepting observer status or withdrawing from the talks completely. Not surprisingly, they chose the latter course.

Thereafter the feasibility committee coordinating the unity talks — now consisting of FOSATU, CUSA, GWU, CCAWUSA, CTMWA and FCWU — formed a sub-committee whose task was to draft a constitution for the new federation. Although its work took almost a year to complete, it proceeded relatively smoothly, and it seemed that the date of October 1985 planned for an inaugural conference was a realistic possibility. The only question mark concerned the commitment of some CUSA affiliates to the new federation, an issue discussed in more detail below.

A meeting scheduled for June 1985 was to be attended by the national executive committees of all 23 unions involved in the talks, including FOSATU's eight and CUSA's 11 affiliates. The meeting was to approve the draft constitution and arrange a date for the official launch of the new federation. But a month before it was held, these plans were altered when FOSATU proposed to other feasibility committee members that unions outside the talks should be invited to the June discussions.

Though FOSATU's motives for this initiative were not made

public, a number of interpretations have been put forward by observers. One suggestion points to the fact that the unions involved in the feasibility committee have been accused by exile organisations such as SACTU of dividing the emerging union movement. The 'feasibility unions' have therefore faced increasing pressure to open ranks to the mainly UDF-aligned unions, and thus need at least to show that they attempted to do so.

Another interpretation points out that FOSATU participated with the UDF and black consciousness unions in campaigns around May Day and the Raditsela funeral, and then came under rank-and-file pressure to include these unions in the federation. Certainly there are elements in FOSATU which believe that a good long-term relationship with the UDF is necessary. A further explanation points out that FOSATU suffered a setback during the March stayaway in the Eastern Cape. The stayaway was organised by UDF affiliates, while the feasibility unions operating in the region, of which FOSATU's NAAWU is the strongest, opposed it. There was a significant response to the stayaway call and this damaged FOSATU's standing, the theory goes, causing it to attempt rapprochement with UDF-aligned bodies.

Whatever the reasons, the June meeting was attended by representatives of almost the whole emerging union movement. They included the five which had withdrawn from the talks 15 months previously, the newly-formed black consciousness federation AZACTU, and a number of others which are generally aligned with the UDF. Among these were UMMAWSA, FEDCRAW, DWASA, OVGWU and two RAWUs.

The June meeting was unproductive. The nature of disagreements between feasibility committee members and unions which had previously withdrawn had not changed. Indeed, events since March 1984 had increased scope for ill-feeling on the latter's part. They still felt they had been shabbily treated in being forced to withdraw, and that the constitution had been drafted without any input from them.

Newcomer AZACTU was formed early in 1985 by a group of seven black consciousness unions. Its leadership claims a total membership of 75 000. Four of its affiliates are general unions. The best known AZACTU union is BAMCWU, which was involved in the Penge dispute, and has launched a campaign for the banning of asbestos. Another affiliate, BEEWU, came into the limelight briefly when it was involved in a dispute in Pietersburg.

AZACTU's participation in the unity talks was short-lived. At the June meeting, AZACTU representatives made clear their unhappiness with the non-racial principles and practices of the feasibility committee unions.

This was not unexpected. The surprise was that a number of CUSA union representatives came out in favour of the AZACTU line. While CUSA had always been part of the feasibility committee and has said that it favours the new federation in principle, NUM was the only CUSA affiliate to have made its commitment to the federation absolutely clear.

CUSA (excluding NUM, which by then had decided to disaffiliate from it) finally decided in early August 1985 to withdraw from the talks largely for this reason. CUSA's reaction must be seen in the light of a range of factors.

Firstly, CUSA's commitment to a policy of black leadership had always raised the question of its compatibility with the non-racial unions. Although CUSA recently made a policy statement to the effect that most of its unions are open to white workers, it still objects to white intellectual leadership.

Another point of friction is the long-standing conflict between CUSA and FOSATU affiliates. Their respective unions in the metal, food, chemical, transport and motor industries have a history of conflict — with FOSATU usually coming out on top. At present competition is most severe in the Pretoria area motor industry, as NAAWU chips away at UAMAWUSA membership. There have also been tactical differences between MAWU and SEAWU on the metal industrial council, and conflict continues between FOSATU's SFAWU and CUSA's FBWU. SFAWU broke away from FBWU when FOSATU was formed. There has been some cooperation in the chemical and transport industries, but long-held grudges are not easily forgotten.

An apparent breakthrough came at a meeting later in August. It was attended by the UDF unions and the remaining feasibility committee organisations. A date was set for the launch of a new 'superfederation' of trade unions which will represent more than 400 000 workers from almost every major industrial sector in South Africa, and all the UDF-aligned unions present committed themselves to participating. This includes the 11 affiliates of the 11 500-strong Natal-based National Federation of Workers.

Observers expressed surprise that the UDF unions agreed to unite with FOSATU and its allies, as well as some scepticism over whether the new-found unity between the two groupings can be sustained. But sources at the August meeting described discussions between the two groups as the 'most constructive ever'.

Two of the most controversial areas of disagreement between them were resolved at the meeting. It was agreed that the general unions will continue to set up industrial structures, and all unions present committed themselves to accelerating moves toward mergers of unions operating in the same industry.

Further, the UDF unions dropped demands that the federation's draft constitution be revised before the new organisation is established, agreeing instead that any proposed amendments be debated at the inaugural congress, now scheduled for November 1985.

The CUSA withdrawal was a blow to the unity talks, but certainly not a mortal one. TAWU and SACWU in particular would have been an asset to the new federation. FBWU and SEAWU both have substantial membership although they are not seen as dynamic organisations. But the remaining unions are clearly strong enough to form a powerful organisation without them.

The split union phenomenon

While inter-union unity in the emerging union movement is stronger than it has ever been, intra-union conflict has recently taken its toll of a number of important organisations. As already indicated, NUM, representing half of the total affiliated membership of CUSA, decided to disaffiliate because of CUSA's attitude toward the unity talks.

Earlier, three of the largest and fastest-growing mainly black unions — MAWU, CCAWUSA and NUM — suffered splits during 1984. The most serious division involved MAWU. As is inevitably the case in such circumstances, explanations of the split differed widely. Four MAWU officials, including ex-general secretary David Sebabi, were sacked for 'financial mismanagement' in July 1984. Together with FOSATU vice-president Andrew Zulu, they established UMMAWSA soon afterwards. At its launch UMMAWSA claimed that it stood for 'worker control, more political activism', (meaning alignment with the UDF) and 'less bureaucracy, and opposition to domination by white officials'. MAWU countered with accusations of anti-white racism.

There were also conflicting claims about the new union's following. It appears though that UMMAWSA took with it about 12 000 members from 30 East Rand factories. It also claimed to have membership at six mines. UMMAWSA has since organised some new factories, but has lost ground at others — it recently claimed a membership of 8 000, of which half is paid up.

The CCAWUSA and NUM splits were less serious. Two Transvaal Branch Executive Committee (BEC) members of CCAWUSA were expelled early in 1984 and, claiming that CCAWUSA was 'undemocratic and dominated by officials', went on to establish FEDCRAW. Both officials worked for the Edgars chain and retained the loyalty of about 500 Edgars group workers, about one-third of the total CCAWUSA membership at the company. But they have failed to make any further significant gains in the industry or in the company.

The NUM breakaway was lead by Vuyani Madolo, a disenchanted organiser in the western Transvaal who described NUM as a bosses' union. He established AMAWU and claims membership of 7 500. This, he says, includes most workers he organised for NUM at three Goldfields mines, Libanon, Venterspost and Kloof, among others. AMAWU has however not yet attained sufficient membership to be recognised at any of its organised mines.

The other significant union to have faced such upheavals is SAAWU. After its glory days in the early 1980s, it faced a series of setbacks — its top leadership has been detained numerous times, and membership has shrunk after several strike defeats. A long-anticipated clash between its East London branch on the one hand, and its Natal and Transvaal branches on the other, was precipitated by the expulsion of general secretary Sam Kikine and two other officials — Herbert Barnabus and Isaac Ngcobo — at a conference in April 1984. No official reasons, other than allegations from both sides of unconstitutional conduct, were given. There followed a messy court case over custody of union property and records. Both factions continued to operate under the name of SAAWU.

This was not the end of SAAWU's problems. In early 1985 Kikine fell out with his lieutenant, Transvaal branch official Herbert Barnabus, who decided to establish the National Federation of South African Workers. The Eastern Cape group, led by Sisa Njikelana and Thozamile Gqweta, meanwhile branched out into the Western Cape and the Transvaal, where it has established SAMWU together with GAWU. In early 1985 there were reports of a possible split within this faction of SAAWU as well. The problems of both SAAWU factions were compounded when Kikine, Ngcobo, Njikelana and Gqweta were arrested and charged with treason soon thereafter, along with a number of political activists associated with the UDF.

Conversely, union mergers are also on the agenda. FCWU and the FCWU (which have to all intents and purposes always operated as one entity, and have been referred to as a single entity here) decided to amalgamate. And there have been talks between FCWU and SFAWU with the aim of eventually forming a single organisation. CUSA's FBWU was also invited to participate, but did not respond.

The International Metalworkers Federation

In March 1984 ten metal industry unions, all affiliated to the IMF, reestablished the South African Coordinating Council of the IMF. The body had been dissolved in 1981 after heated clashes between emerging unions and the conservative CMBU. The possibility of a revival emerged with the expulsion from the IMF of the all-white South African Electrical Workers Association and the AEU.

The ten affiliates to the SACC still came from widely divergent backgrounds. They included TUCSA (the Radio, TV, Electronic and Allied Workers Union, and, at the time of the SACC's formation, MICWU and EIWU), CUSA's SEAWU, and FOSATU's MAWU and NAAWU. There were four independents — the SABS (which had left TUCSA the previous year), EAWU, the South African Tin Workers Union and the FMU.

Among the SACC's objectives are:

• to promote understanding and cooperation between all metalworkers, and between the organisations to which they belong;
• to strive for fair and equal employment, training and promotion opportunities for all metalworkers;
• to study and inquire into international labour relations so as to

improve the working conditions and welfare of South African metalworkers;
• to establish trade union educational programmes and sponsor seminars on national and international labour relations, economic and other problems;
• to compile and issue publications on matters concerning social and economic events and their effects on workers;
• to endeavour to resolve jurisdictional and demarcation problems between member unions;
• to work for the extension of trade union rights, in particular collective bargaining, to all South African workers; and
• to involve itself in any matters affecting the metalworkers and their organisations.

The SACC's most important task to date has been its involvement in the 1985 wage negotiations in the Metal Industrial Council. Its five affiliates party to the Industrial Council formulated joint demands, and caucussed together throughout the talks. But the outcome of the negotiations was not satisfactory to the IMF unions, and MAWU ultimately broke ranks with the others by refusing to sign the agreement. Nevertheless, the IMF connection has helped to develop a closer relationship between some long-established unions in the industry and their emerging counterparts. Three SACC affiliates have left TUCSA since late 1983 — SABS, MICWU and EIWU.

MAWU and SABS have worked particularly closely. In 1984 they decided jointly not to sign the metal industry wage agreement, which was not negotiated under the auspices of the IMF. A joint wage dispute with Highveld Steel followed. But this dispute showed that there was a long way to go before real unity among the rank-and-file was established. When a work stoppage was called, SABS' members failed to respond, despite the good intentions of leadership.

There is also little chance of the ex-TUCSA unions joining the new SACC in the near future. The SABS' multiracial, rather than non-racial, structure would be a hindrance, while MICWU and EIWU have expressed doubt about some of the militant methods of the emerging unions. Clearly, despite closer cooperation on specific issues, the IMF will be hard-pressed to eradicate completely the divide between old-style and emerging unionism.

The Trade Union Council of South Africa

TUCSA's standing as the most important trade union federation in South Africa has been waning for some time in the face of competition from the more dynamic elements in the emerging union movement. Nonetheless, to date it has at least been able to claim a larger membership than any other grouping. But even this distinction is likely to disappear soon. The formation of the new federation of emerging unions, and a run of TUCSA disaffiliations, will probably see to that.

During 1983, total membership of TUCSA affiliates was close to half a million. That was before it lost member unions with a combined membership of 200 000. The decision by the 50 000-strong SABS to withdraw from TUCSA in late 1983 started the ball rolling. SABS followed in 1984 by two other unions in the metal industry — MICWU (membership 24 000) and EIWU (26 000).

When it disaffiliated, MICWU said it opposed the uniracial policies of some TUCSA affiliates. EIWU expressed similar criticisms, arguing that TUCSA's whites-only and craft unions ignored the needs of unskilled workers. These disaffiliations coincided with the revival of the SACC of the IMF discussed above.

MICWU's and EIWU's leftward shift followed the departures in 1982 and 1983 of their respective long-serving and conservative general secretaries, both of whom were TUCSA loyalists. MICWU's Ronnie Webb, who was TUCSA president for two years in the late 1970s, became one of the first members of the President's Council, while EIWU's Archie Poole is now a member of parliament.

TUCSA has not only lost unions to the left. The conservative 10 000-member South African Footplate Staff Association withdrew in May 1984, citing a 60% hike in affiliation fees as its major reason. And in early 1985, SASBO (29 000 members), one of TUCSA's most right-wing members, disaffiliated. It argued that there was no advantage in TUCSA membership for white-collar workers.

Meanwhile, the 50 000-strong GWIU (Natal) seems to be deliberating about its TUCSA membership. It is unclear whether reports of its disaffiliation are accurate. But at the very least GWIU has applied to be exempted from payment of affiliation fees, on the

grounds that it faces financial difficulties as a result of payments to
members laid off from work.

Several smaller unions have also disaffiliated, and TUCSA
membership threatens to fall below 300 000. TUCSA's position in
the trade union movement was further threatened by the death of
its general secretary of nearly 20 years, Arthur Grobbelaar, in
August 1984. In an important sense, Grobbelaar was TUCSA. The
new incumbent will have great difficulty in holding the confederation together, not to mention leading it out of its downhill slide.

Perhaps the most vivid illustration of TUCSA's failing fortunes
relative to the emerging union movement was the decision at its
1984 conference to try to create links with the emerging unions.
After years of open warfare with them, TUCSA eventually
acknowledged that emerging unions were a legitimate part of the
union movement and announced that it would be approaching
them. TUCSA president Robbie Botha followed this decision with
a speech (to the Cape Chamber of Commerce, an unlikely forum)
in which he pleaded for cooperation 'for the sake of the workers'.

At its conference and in subsequent press statements, TUCSA
has also been taking a harder line on issues like rents and detentions
of unionists — a far cry from its lukewarm response to the 1982
death in detention of Neil Aggett. It has sent letters to a number of
emerging unions proposing meetings. But response to these efforts
has been minimal.

Legislation

The Labour Relations Act (LRA) of 1956 (formerly the Industrial
Conciliation Act) is the key regulator of industrial relations between workers and management in South Africa. Since 1979, when
its definition of 'employee' was finally extended to include African
workers, the Act, which is designed primarily to institutionalise the
inevitable conflict of interests between workers and management,
has been tested as never before.

From the government's point of view, the primary aim of the
LRA is to channel conflict. To do so, the Act promotes collective
bargaining and encourages employers and workers to settle
disputes by the negotiation and conclusion of agreements. And if
this is not possible, the Act sets out mechanisms for resolving

disputes — such as mediation, arbitration and the Industrial Court — to provide alternatives to that ultimate worker weapon, the strike. The Act is also designed to control the financial and administrative management of unions, and to control their political activities by denying them the right to affiliate to political parties.

The problem with the proposed system is that some unions have not been prepared to go along with it, hence the major debate on registration some years ago, when many unions refused to apply. Of course, there are penalties to be paid for non-registration. Unregistered unions cannot obtain stop-order facilities without the permission of the Minister of Manpower. At one stage they were barred from having their disputes referred to industrial councils and the Industrial Court, though this has since changed.

The government and employers have been anxious to eliminate this dualism in South African industrial relations. Over the years, amendments have been made to the LRA which have imposed more and more obligations on unregistered unions. This process has blurred the distinction between registered and unregistered unions on a number of administrative and technical points, but has not helped to deal with the other major difference between some unregistered and registered unions — namely, political involvement.

As a result, when the LRA Amendment Bill was tabled in parliament in early 1984, some of its provisions were widely interpreted as a move to tighten control over the more overtly political unregistered unions in the emerging union movement, SAAWU and its soulmates in particular.

The Bill aroused so much controversy that it was referred to a select committee straight after its first reading. Much of the controversy centred on its proposals for section 31(a). In essence, these made private agreements between trade unions and employers' organisations (or workers or employers who act together like such organisations) unenforceable in court, if they do not comply with certain provisions. Further, if parties to such an agreement did not comply with the Bill's provisions, they would commit an offence. The proposal excluded agreements concluded outside the ambit of industrial councils or conciliation boards.

The provisions placed obligations on unions or employer organisations:

• to supply the Industrial Registrar with a copy of their constitu-

tion, head office address, and the names of office-bearers and officials;
• to maintain membership registers;
• to submit membership returns annually to the Industrial Registrar;
• to keep proper books of account which must be audited annually;
• to table statements of income and expenditure at a general meeting at least once annually;
• to retain such documents for at least three years; and
• to maintain a head office situated in South Africa.

The emerging unions condemned the Bill. There was strong suspicion that the government had bowed to pressure from employers, and perhaps even from politically conservative union bodies like TUCSA, which had an antagonistic relationship with emerging unions. Further misgivings were expressed later in the year, when the government released a National Manpower Commission report that it had kept on ice since July-August 1983. This contained different provisions designed to deal with precisely the same issue.

Admittedly, the Bill was not as harsh as the majority NMC recommendation — that organisations failing to comply with similar provisions should not be allowed to operate. But a pertinent question was, why did the government decide to put forward legislation before it had released the NMC report for comment? The question developed barbs when some NMC members complained that they had not been consulted about the Bill.

Union registration has become a far less controversial issue than it used to be a few years ago. Nevertheless, it is still sensitive. This much is apparent even in the NMC report, which contained a number of minority recommendations on the subject. Some labour observers believe that the government was anxious to get the Bill, or some form of legislation, through quickly, and did so before the NMC report was issued because it was aware of the serious divergence of opinion on the issue.

As a result, Pietie du Plessis, who took over as Minister of Manpower at the beginning of 1984 after Fanie Botha's fall from grace, was expected to be a hard-liner. Yet the Bill could well have been a legacy of the Fanie Botha regime, as all major legislation is usually approved by the cabinet before September of each year. Against that, the Department of Manpower's admission in June — more than a year after the NMC report was released — that it was still having difficulty reconciling all the different views on offer, does seem to confirm that the government had acted hurriedly.

Despite strong objections from the Progressive Federal Party, the Bill emerged from the select committee with only minor adjustments, was passed by the House, and came into effect on 1 September 1984. It has not turned out to be the big bogeyman everyone expected; in fact, commentators have had a field day pulling it to pieces.

Even employers climbed in. Richard Schuster, industrial relations adviser of Barlow Rand subsidiary Reunert Ltd, made some scathing comments: 'No doubt the Department of Manpower's intention was to give employers a reason to refuse to contract with unions that do not comply with these provisions and thereby put pressure on them to comply', he wrote. But the new legislation could backfire if unions choose to renege on agreements by the simple expedient of deciding, say, to appoint a new officer-bearer and deliberately not informing the Industrial Registrar. Or the same technicality — if a union accidentally failed to notify the registrar of a new appointment — could make a bona fide wage agreement unenforceable.

A great deal of criticism has also been levelled at a new provision intended to ensure that employers submit copies of recognition agreements to the Department of Manpower. The amendment is so badly drafted that, read literally, it means that only legally unenforceable agreements need be sent. Obviously this was not the intention of the lawmakers, but that is what the law says. Schuster also spoke for many when he said that 'it is difficult to reconcile the Department's stated policy of non-interference in plant-level bargaining, with a provision which looks like a first step towards state involvement'.

Labour lawyer Halton Cheadle has highlighted other anomalies in the amendment which, he argues, undercut the Act's principal aim of promoting collective bargaining. In the *Annual Review of South African Law* he writes:

> The potential for one of the parties to avoid the obligations of an agreement will undermine an essential process in collective bargaining, namely, the conclusion of a binding agreement. The second mistake in princi-

ple is that the rendering of an agreement unenforceable in a court of law
encourages precisely what the Act is directed against: the proliferation
of unnecessary resort to industrial action. Indeed, it has been the credo
of English trade unions to have their collective bargaining agreements
with employers unenforceable in law in order to have a free hand in en-
forcing them by way of industrial action, and it has been the credo of
Conservative governments to have the opposite.

Cheadle makes another point. He argues that disputes arising out
of unenforceable agreements will now have to include a 'trial
within a trial' to determine whether or not the union or employers'
organisation complies with the Act's requirements. This, Cheadle
says, will entail discovery of material quite unrelated to the issue in
dispute. And when the documentation associated with an average-
sized South African union of 20 000 members is taken into consideration, the costs and time associated with such an exercise make
this form of regulation inappropriate:

> It would have been preferable, assuming that it is wise to interfere with
> collective bargaining in this way, to have given the registrar of trade
> unions the power to issues certificates of non-compliance, and on the
> basis of those certificates to determine the enforceability of such
> agreements.

Then there is the question of agreements with organisations that
pursue purposes 'similar to those of trade unions', which are unenforceable irrespective of whether or not they comply with the Act's
new provisions.

Cheadle says that given the present definition of 'trade union' in
the LRA, it is arguable whether unions themselves are included
within its terms: 'Certainly, federations of trade unions fall within
its ambit, and many trade unions federate for the limited purpose
of making a joint stand in collective bargaining'. He takes the example of the Council of Mining Unions' agreements with the
Chamber of Mines: 'Those agreements in all probability are now
unenforceable, whether or not the constituent trade unions of the
federation itself have complied with their obligations under the
Act. Does this represent the will of the legislators, or the hand of
the draftsman?'

Other provisions in the LRA are less controversial, but nevertheless quixotic. For example, in 1982 government transferred appeals against industrial council decisions from the Minister to the Industrial Court. These have now reverted to the Minister.

Amendments made to the LRA last year may at this stage not seem to be important. But it should not be forgotten that the Manpower Department is processing responses to the NMC's report, and that a White Paper has been promised. This will almost certainly contain some recommendations on registration. We may yet see stronger action against unions which do not maintain themselves in a proper state and those which are too 'political'.

The National Manpower Commission

Of all the cautious experiments the National Party government has conducted so far in its slow retreat from old-style apartheid, those in the labour field have been the most daring. However, now that the process has been set in motion it has a new worry: ensuring that labour relations stay on track — a matter of making sure that giving a finger does not mean losing an arm.

In 1979, the Wiehahn Commission laid the foundations for long-overdue changes to South Africa's industrial relations system. But a body was needed to deal with matters the commission left unresolved, and to continue formulating labour policy on an ongoing basis. That body is the National Manpower Commission (NMC); a tripartite think-tank where representatives of government, management and labour sit to advise the Minister of Manpower on all matters concerning manpower development and utilisation in South Africa.

The NMC, which was established in 1979, enjoys the status of a government-appointed commission of inquiry. As a permanent statutory body, it has the power to monitor progress on any recommendations it has made which have been accepted by government, and any other recommendations relating to labour made by other committees or commissions of inquiry. It is the only body in South Africa which does monitoring of this nature and which makes its findings public.

A great deal of the NMC's work has been defined for it in directives laid down in White Papers, or by the Minister of Manpower. But it has also initiated research programmes. Some subjects that have warranted the NMC's attention in the past are:

• high-level manpower in South Africa (published 1980);
• the closed shop (published 1981);
• labour relations training in South Africa and a levy system for the promotion and financing of industrial training (published 1982);
• the principle and application of a national minimum wage (published 1983);
• the levels of collective bargaining and works councils, the registration of trade unions and employers' organisations and related matters, and the Industrial Court (published 1984);
• in-service training (published 1984);
• the small business sector in South Africa, with specific reference to the factors that may retard its growth (published 1984); and
• a strategy for the creation of employment opportunities.

These are weighty matters; ones which, from the government's point of view, must be addressed practically as well as theoretically if South Africa is to prosper. There lies the rub. Two main problems have plagued the NMC: doubts about whether it has enough clout to fulfil its mandate, and its unwieldy size. There have been many complaints about dead wood on the commission.

The new NMC, appointed in June 1985, has 28 members, as opposed to 61 in the second and 41 in the first, appointed after the 1979 Wiehahn Commission report. The reduction in the number of commissioners has been widely welcomed.

The second NMC especially was criticised for being cumbersome. It had seven specialist sub-committees covering employment creation; industrial relations; education and training; employment services; conditions of employment and social security; productivity; and international labour affairs. They would present reports for debate by the whole NMC before recommendations were finalised. Some commissioners complained that when this was done, the presence of many people with no specialised knowledge of the issues hindered the achievement of consensus. In fact, it is commonly suggested that this accounts for the gap sometimes found between the logic of arguments contained in NMC reports, and its subsequent recommendations. One labour commentator has described the NMC's recommendations as 'muddy compromises'.

But perhaps the major criticism the NMC has had to face is the accusation that its views are not truly representative because the emerging union movement is not represented on it. Unionists who sat on the NMC are all drawn from TUCSA or SACOL, or from other established registered unions not affiliated to either of them.

Until the end of April 1985, when the third NMC was appointed, the emerging unions had never been invited to sit on the commission. Presumably this was because the authorities feared rejection. If so, their fears were probably well founded. The emerging unions have shown marked hostility towards participation.

Similar problems beset the Wiehahn Commission — and it misread some issues as a result. One of the commissioners has confirmed that he and his colleagues were firmly convinced that emerging unions would want to participate in industrial councils once access had been opened to them by changes to labour legislation. Events after 1979 proved them wrong. Now, even when some emerging unions have joined councils, they still do not regard them as ideal for collective bargaining and dispute resolution. The Wiehahn Commission got it all wrong, says the same commissioner, because it did not receive any input from the emerging unions.

The NMC has fallen prey to the same problem. Although some individuals appear to have private doubts about boycotting the NMC, thinking that perhaps they would be able to use it to their advantage, to date the emerging movement as a whole has rejected it.

The NMC did make efforts to redress the situation during 1985. NMC chairman Hennie Reynders says that invitations to sit on the third commission were sent to 'certain registered unions' in the FOSATU and CUSA camps. When the list of the commissioners on the third NMC was released, the government component had been significantly slashed, but unionists were again drawn from TUCSA, SACOL and the established registered unions. A new face is that of SABS president Ike van der Watt, whose appointment is an interesting development because his is the only established union to enjoy good relations with the emerging unions.

These unions themselves were not represented on the list, however. Reynders says that an extra commissioner representing them may be appointed at some time in the future. He will not, however, comment further. If the appointment obtains emerging union consent it would represent a significant shift in their thinking.

Other participants in the NMC have also criticised it — most notably TUCSA, a founder member. TUCSA's attitude was spelt out clearly in the September 1984 edition of its mouthpiece, *Labour Mirror*: 'Unless the composition of the NMC is changed to make it a forum for employers and employees, we can no longer lend it credibility'. *Labour Mirror* decried the fact that trade unionists and employers were in the minority on the second NMC. They had 13 and 12 members respectively, while the remaining 36 were drawn from 'government departments, the academic community, and even women's organisations'.

Academics on the NMC came in for particularly heavy attack. The same source quoted new TUCSA president Robbie Botha of the Mine Surface Officials' Association, who has replaced Grobbelaar on the commission: 'There is no place for academics who are either furthering their own studies or promoting their universities. There is no place for any of those who have only a secondary interest in labour. They divert the commission from its true purpose'. TUCSA's 30th conference passed a resolution calling for an NMC on which the state nominates the chairman and vice-chairman, with the remainder of the membership equally divided between employer and employee representatives.

As the term of the second NMC wore on, it seemed increasingly questionable whether it had genuine influence on the government. Such doubts sharpened when NMC members complained that they had not been consulted about the controversial Labour Relations Amendment Act tabled in parliament early in 1984. As the government had been sitting on NMC recommendations covering the same ground as the Bill's section 31(a) provisions since the middle of 1983, the complaints seemed well grounded. Certainly it appears that the government deliberately ignored the NMC, bowing to behind-the-scenes pressure instead. Nonetheless, Reynders has consistently claimed that the commission retains its influence.

The new NMC has retained some of the second NMC's standing committees, but the pattern now is for project committees to be appointed on an ad hoc basis. These committees, which can coopt outside experts to help in their deliberations, are dissolved once a particular project has been completed.

According to NMC sources, 11 project committees are operating at present. They are investigating: high-level manpower; middle-level manpower; vocational guidance; employment services; the levels of collective bargaining and the dispute settling machinery; International Labour Organisation (ILO) conventions; cyclical unemployment; labour-intensive production techniques; rural development; retrenchment; and labour shortage in critical occupations. The standing committees cover: manpower projections, strike analysis, and international labour affairs, while another coordinates general manpower research.

Comments from some commissioners indicate that they are hopeful that the new structures, and the reduction in the NMC's size, will make for more constructive debate and decision-making.

Two major NMC reports are due to be released during 1985. One covers recommendations on the regulation of working conditions of farm labourers and domestic workers, while the other takes a further look at aspects of the closed shop. Labour observers will be watching government's responses to them — and to the other work emanating from the new streamlined NMC. That will be the acid test of its relevance.

Stayaways, Urban Protest and the State

*Mark Swilling**
Labour Monitoring Group

The forceful reemergence of the stayaway tactic during 1984-85 raised key questions of strategy and tactics for popular and working-class opposition. These hinge on the nature of the relationship between community and class-based struggles in the context of escalating mass resistance. Is the stayaway merely a demonstration of protest, or can it be used to mobilise sufficient power to undermine the state? By participating in a stayaway, do trade unions subordinate themselves to multi-class organisational objectives? Since a stayaway requires people to remain in their homes and hence isolated from one another, does it not involve surrendering initiative to the state? Should trade unions participate in stayaways during a recession? What role should workers play in

* The bulk of the material for this article comes from research conducted by the Labour Monitoring Group (LMG) into the Transvaal and Eastern Cape stayaways. The LMG is an informal group of academics from the University of the Witwatersrand. It was established during the November stayaway and has continued to monitor labour and community politics. Its research, which is written collectively, is published in the *South African Labour Bulletin*. As a member of the LMG I am obviously indebted to the extensive discussions that it has had over the last year, but the conclusions reached in the article are my own. Articles published by the LMG are: 'Report: The November Stayaway', *South African Labour Bulletin*, 10(6), 1985; and 'The March Stayaways in Port Elizabeth and Uitenhage', *South African Labour Bulletin*, 11(1), September 1985.

organising community-based collective action? What relationship should there be between community and workplace organisations?

The stayaway tactic is a legacy of previous phases of popular and working-class struggle.[1] It has been used by oppressed communities to express protest by withdrawing their labour from production. The fact that such communities inhabit racially defined areas separate from white communities facilitated the organisation of stayaways as collective communal challenges to this division. But this communal determinant has not prevented various class interests from shaping the political objectives and organisational achievements of stayaways. The dynamic between community and class forces can be seen particularly clearly when one compares the factors giving rise to stayaways in the 1950s and 1980s.

The nature of the oppositional movement in the 1950s is the subject of considerable debate. Dan O'Meara argues that the militant trade union moment of the late 1940s gave the national democratic movement, led by the ANC, a firm proletarian base. This solidified the class alliance between different oppressed classes, and won the petty bourgeoisie over to anti-capitalist politics.[2] A similar interpretation is used to describe the present phase of national democratic opposition.

Legassick expresses a different view, arguing that working-class and petty-bourgeois interests participated in a contradictory alliance which was cemented by the non-class 'populist' discourses of African nationalism.[3] The stayaway, therefore, was for O'Meara the expression of a coherent class alliance, and for Legassick a petty-bourgeois populist tactic that tended to subordinate the working-class. Lodge in turn subjects both Legassick and O'Meara to a historical critique, and concludes that there were no coherent class interests in the 1950s that could have imposed a distinct class ideology on the oppositional movement. In this more historically sound view, political mobilisation during the 1950s tended to emerge from deeply oppressed urban communities within which there were no significant competing class interests.[4]

This does not mean that urban communities were not socially differentiated. Rather, patterns of differentiation were not predominantly class-based. Political consciousness tended to emphasise the national (or colonial) oppression of 'the people' over exploitative relations between classes. The politics of nation-building embedded itself in popular consciousness and became an important political tradition in organisations and struggles of the oppressed classes.

Over time this tradition came to be identified with an important collection of ideas, leaders, symbols and tactics. These include concepts of national democracy, non-racialism, the Freedom Charter, leadership figures like Nelson Mandela, boycotts — and the stayaway tactic. This tradition shapes and influences political strategies in the contemporary period. For example, when the KwaThema parent-student Committee was planning the local stayaway that preceded the Transvaal stayaway in November 1984, one of their meetings was punctuated by shouts of 'Azikwelwa' ('We shall not ride') — a slogan from the 1950s.

The national tradition and its tactics have been substantially modified and recast by the new class forces which have emerged since the early 1970s. These new forces, a product of changes in the South African political economy, are not simply reenacting previous phases of resistance, but are forging new traditions, new leaders, new symbols and, more significantly, new tactics.

The consolidation of monopoly capitalism has created a massive working class that has generated its own sub-cultures.[5] The ruling groups have encouraged development of a significant petty bourgeoisie to act as allies in a bourgeois reformist project. Urban communities have become much more heterogeneous, as a range of new interests emerged: radical and collaborative petty bourgeoisies, an expanding working class with substantial numbers moving into skilled and supervisory positions, upwardly mobile school-leavers, and a large impoverished group of unemployed people. These have given rise in recent years to powerful trade union, national democratic, and popular resistance movements.

Distinct class interests, particularly those of the organised working class, have shaped the ideological, political and organisational agendas of the popular and working-class opposition.[6] This underlies the important debates over, among other things, the role of the working class, the nature of democratic organisation, the relationship between the national and class struggle, and the problems of prefigurative social transformation which currently permeate the thinking of the oppositional organisations.[7]

The manner in which the stayaway tactic was deployed in November 1984 in the Transvaal, and in March 1985 in the Eastern Cape, is revealing. In both cases, the stayaway was the culmination of bitter struggles in community and workplace over the level of urban subsistence, the fiscal unviability of local government, state violence, and education. However, whereas the Transvaal stayaway made a substantive contribution to building a working-class politics, the outcome in the Eastern Cape was much less clear, especially in Port Elizabeth. By focusing on these differences, regional variations in the relationship between class and community-based forces, and the respective ideological traditions shaping collective action, can be thrown into relief. In the course of these struggles, organisations representing different class interests have begun to contest the form and content of the stayaway tactic.

Transvaal, November 1984

The successful two-day stayaway in the Transvaal on 5-6 November was not only a major protest against township conditions and apartheid education. It also initiated a new phase of resistance against apartheid, because it was the beginning of united action between organised labour, the student movement, and community organisations.

No previous stayaway had been supported on the same scale. The Labour Monitoring Group calculated that between 300 000 and 800 000 workers stayed away from work, and 400 000 students boycotted classes.[8] The organisations involved concur, believing that the stayaway mobilised over one million people.

The sheer scale of the stayaway must be understood in terms of the build-up of conflict and struggle in three key spheres in the Transvaal: the townships, schools and factories. Protest and struggle affected all strata of black society in 1984, causing both the state and liberal observers to comment that the situation was worse than in 1976.

The main cause of widespread political mobilisation in the Transvaal and Eastern Cape townships during 1984 and 1985 was the fiscal unviability and political illegitimacy of the black local authorities (BLAs) which were established towards the end of 1983. They were constituted in terms of the Black Local Authorities Act (Act 102 of 1982), one of the infamous 'Koornhof Bills' that embodied the logic of the Riekert Commission. The state's aim was to make the BLAs politically autonomous by giving them wider powers than their predecessors, and by making them self-financing, which would relieve the central state of the burden of financing black urbanisation.

The principle of fiscal autonomy forced the new BLAs to increase rent and service charges to finance township improvements. They had no alternative revenue sources, because there are no industries or substantial middle classes to provide a viable tax base. However, even these measures left many BLAs with a deficit. The Soweto Council, for example, budgeted for a R30-million deficit in 1985, which it hopes to reduce by R10-million by increasing rents and service charges, in some cases by 100%. Even the state now acknowledges that, in the words of a top official, 'If we had given the BLAs resources with magnitude we might now have had a viable and credible system. We might not have had so much of the current unrest' (*Star*, 08.06.85; *FM*, 03.03.85; *FW*, 19-22.05.85).

The political consequences of fiscal unviability were exacerbated by the political illegitimacy of the BLAs. The 15%-25% polls when they were elected in 1983[9] reflected the fact that Africans were not prepared to accept local political rights without central state representation. The BLA system is now in ruins as a result of mass resistance. In 1983, 34 BLAs were introduced; by the end of 1984 there were meant to be 104. By April 1985 only three were still functioning (*RDM*, 16.04.85).

In the Transvaal, the unviability of the BLA system generated powerful community organisations. Two types have emerged: the civics for residents, which take up subsistence issues like rents, transport, and housing; and the youth congresses which tend to mobilise around ideological and political principles, such as the Freedom Charter, political rights, and national democracy.

Most important mass-based community organisations are affiliated to the UDF. Excluding Soweto, where there has been very little resistance, leadership of these community organisations tends to be drawn from the working class and relatively well-educated unemployed youths. On the East Rand, for example, the East Rand People's Organisation (ERAPO) was founded by a MAWU official, and is dominated by UMMAWSA shop stewards. The Vaal Civic Association's leadership was composed of workers, unemployed youths and a few progressive priests.

In no case is there a significant petty-bourgeois presence.

Traders, businessmen, officials and professionals have tended either to remain politically inactive, or have supported the BLAs. Their attitude towards community organisations has been openly hostile, and councillors have supported the state's line that unrest is purely the product of agitators. So it is not suprising that community leaders in the civics and youth congresses frequently articulate the aims of community struggle in class terms.[10]

In the factories, despite the recession, there were more strikes than in any year since the Second World War. Whereas in 1982 and 1983 there were 394 and 336 strikes respectively, in 1984 there were 469. The number of working days lost increased by 200%, from 124 594 in 1983, to 378 712 in 1984 (*RDM*, 11.03.85). Industrial relations consultants were concerned that strikes were lasting longer and involving more workers than previously (*RDM*, 11.03.85). One personnel manager remarked prophetically in September 1984: 'We will be lucky if by the end of the year we only have a labour relations problem' (*STrib*, 09.09.84).

Contrary to what might have been expected, during the recession workers were using their organised power to resist unjustified retrenchments and unnecessary cuts in wages, as well as to challenge management's power in the workplace with regard to health and safety, arbitrary dismissals, and the very organisation and running of the production process.[11] The frontiers of management control have been rolled back at the point of production. This has given workers a crucial understanding of the advantages of collective action, reinforced by the democratic organisational practices of the independent union movement.

However, unions have tended to confine this new-found power to the workplace, on the grounds that before workers' organisations could take up political issues, a firm foundation should be constructed in the workplace. The formation of the UDF and NF rapidly eclipsed the possibility of forging a separate working class party — as implied in a speech delivered in 1982 by Joe Foster, FOSATU's secretary general.[12]

The intense politicisation of the townships in 1984 placed unions under tremendous pressure to involve themselves in political issues. As tensions mounted and the conflict intensified in the Transvaal with the entry of the SADF into the townships after the September Vaal uprising, these unions were catapulted into a central role in the stayaway. Misgivings were expressed about this development on the grounds that workers were pulled onto what Foster called a 'populist' terrain. An alternative view is that the shop stewards organising the action were responding to the demands of their children, and attempting to use the stayaway as a tool for furthering a working class politics beyond the point of production.

Beginning in Pretoria in January 1984, in the course of the year school boycotts spread across the Transvaal. By October, there were 200 000 students boycotting classes, primarily in the Pretoria-Witwatersrand-Vereeniging region. Throughout the year, the Congress of SA Students (COSAS) presented students' demands to the Department of Education and Training. These included establishment of democratically elected SRCs, abolition of the age limit, abolition of corporal punishment, and an end to sexual abuse of female students.

The initiative leading to the November stayaway came from students. The momentum of student protest was slowing down by the beginning of October for three main reasons: the failure of the state to respond adequately to student demands; students as a group, and particularly COSAS activists, were subject to detention, which weakened their organisations — 556 were detained in 1984 and in some cases students were killed;[13] finally, end-of-year examinations were approaching. School principals and particularly town councillors were campaigning to entice students back to school. Large numbers of boycotting students could be expected to return, unless the terrain of struggle was shifted and the support of broad social forces enlisted. To this end, COSAS called for the support of UDF organisations and the trade unions, and parent-student committees were established in a number of townships.

Momentum built up in three localised stayaways that took place in the Transvaal after September 1984. On 3 September, a successful stayaway was mounted in the Vaal to protest against a R5,90 rent increase — rents in this area were already the highest in the country. It was at least 60% successful, but ended in violence when 31 people lost their lives in clashes with the police. By July 1985, Vaal residents were still not paying rents, costing the state approximately R10-million. Two weeks later the Release Mandela Committee (RMC) called a stayaway in Soweto, in solidarity with the ongoing struggles in the Vaal. It was unsuccessful and led to considerable confusion, because the RMC's weak, populist form of organisation is not based on a firm grassroots structure in Soweto.

The third stayaway took place in KwaThema on 22 October. It was called by the local parent-student committee, made up of ten students and ten unionists, one of whom was FOSATU president Chris Dlamini. The stayaway, which was over 80% successful, was called in support of the school boycott and the student demands listed above. Other demands were for the removal of security forces from the townships, the release of all detained students, and the resignation of all councillors. The success of this stayaway, according to Chris Dlamini, guaranteed union support for the later call for a wider regional stayaway.

The stayaway committee

The momentum built up in the KwaThema stayaway prepared the way for wider regional action. On 27 October a crucial meeting took place in Johannesburg in response to the original COSAS appeal for worker support. The meeting was attended by 37 organisations, including representatives of FOSATU, CUSA and other unions, together with representatives of youth congresses, community organisations, and the RMC. COSAS called on unions to show solidarity with the student demands articulated earlier.

All organisations came prepared to take concrete action. The process by which FOSATU representatives reached this decision is illuminating. The federation's officials were already involved in the KwaThema campaign, and there was a groundswell of shop-floor support for students' demands — due in part to student solidarity with unions during the Simba Quix boycott launched in August.[14] At a public meeting in Johannesburg on 7 November, Chris Dlamini explained how dividing lines between student and worker struggles were increasingly becoming blurred; how SRCs were similar to shop stewards' councils; how age restrictions on students would force them onto the labour market during a period of high unemployment. Further, workers are parents who have to finance their childrens' education from their own pockets, Dlamini argued.

The central committee of FOSATU met on 19-21 October. Following reports from Transvaal locals on the crisis in the townships all Transvaal representatives on the committee, irrespective of political affiliation, felt some action was necessary.

A sub-committee made up of Transvaal members was established and given wide powers to monitor the situation and to take appropriate action where necessary. Chris Dlamini was chairman and Bangi Solo information officer. Both were detained after the stayaway. Meetings were held with students and student-parent committees.

FOSATU representatives arrived at the 27 October meeting with concrete proposals, and were empowered to take action. As far as can be ascertained, a debate over the length of the stayaway resulted in a compromise duration of two days. It was also agreed that demands be broadened to encompass those of trade unions and community organisations.

The representatives of the 37 organisations present formed a general committee (the Transvaal Regional Stayaway Committee, as it was dubbed by the press). A four-member coordinating group was elected to handle practical preparations. This core group consisted of Moses Mayekiso of FOSATU and MAWU, Themba Nontlane of MGWUSA, Oupa Monareng of SOYCO and the RMC, and Thami Mali of the RMC — that is, two union organisers, one unemployed worker from SOYCO, and one ex-detainee out on bail.

The UDF was not formally represented because it did not initiate the stayaway itself; because some organisations involved were not affiliates; and because it was felt that the presence of UDF affiliates made it unnecessary for the Front itself to be formally represented. It was also felt that since the struggle was specific to the working-class African townships of the Transvaal, UDF leadership was inappropriate.

Two days after the meeting of 27 October, FOSATU convened a meeting of Transvaal unions to coordinate action for the stayaway. This was followed by a series of meetings of unions, locals, and shop stewards to report back to members on the proposed demonstration. Decisions taken by the sub-committee were ratified by the full central committee when it met after the stayaway on 10 November. This meeting reiterated the central demands of the stayaway: the removal of schooling age limits; democratically constituted SRCs; withdrawal of the army from the townships and an end to police harassment; and the suspension of rent and bus fare increases.[15]

The initial pamphlet calling for a stayaway on 5 and 6 November issued the following demands: democratically elected SRCs; the abolition of corporal punishment; an end to sexual harassment in schools; the withdrawal of security forces from the townships; the release of all detainees; no increase in rents, bus fares, or service charges; and reinstatement of workers dismissed by Simba Quix. The last demand, a workplace issue, illustrates the continuity with previous campaigns. In the event, the Simba workers achieved their goal before the stayaway began.

The object of the stayaway was to articulate student, worker and civic grievances, and to put pressure on the state to redress them. Grievances included the punitive effects of recession and retrenchment, the education system, and state violence in the townships. Each organisation was given specific tasks in an attempt to mobilise non-unionised workers on the shop floor. Hostel dwellers, ignored in the past, were a main target. In contrast to 1976, many hostel dwellers were now unionised, particularly on the East Rand. In addition, 400 000 pamphlets were printed for distribution. Finally, COSAS specifically addressed its student constituency to guarantee the stayaway in the schools, while the unions undertook to ensure the stayaway from work.

Monitoring the stayaway

The stayaway from work

In monitoring the stayaway, the LMG's sample of factories was drawn exclusively from those organised by trade unions. Using the South African Labour and Development Research Unit's directory of trade unions as its data base, the LMG phoned every firm in the PWV area which had a recognition agreement with an independent union. Of 71 contacted, only six refused to comment. The findings were:

1. Unionised factories gave overwhelming support to the stayaway. Seventy percent of the sample had a stayaway rate of over 80%.
2. Unionised factories were concentrated on the East Rand and the Vaal — the areas where stayaway rates (as management bodies agreed) were highest. All establishments surveyed in the Vaal and far East Rand had over 80% participation, with 60%

of the near East Rand and 91% of Kempton Park/Isando also showing 80% participation. The poor showing in Pretoria reflects the limitations of the sample group. Secondary sources revealed that the stayaway in Atteridgeville was almost total, but commuters from the neighbouring 'homeland' came to work in Pretoria as usual. Similarly, in Brits, location dwellers supported the stayaway and commuters worked normally.

3. There was no weakening of the stayaway on day two, as was anticipated by some observers: 56% of establishments maintained the same level of stayaway for two days, 20% weakened and 24% actually intensified on day two. In the past, extended stayaways have failed: for example, a five-day stayaway called in November 1976 simply petered out.

4. All sectors where unions were present were equally affected. Mining was the exception, where lack of participation was probably due to workers' isolation from the townships, and to the aftermath of their own recent strike.

5. There seems to have been no significant difference in the participation of migrants and township dwellers. In nine of the 71 establishments surveyed, migrants were a significant proportion of the workforce. In these nine factories, there was a 90% participation in the stayaway. Secondary evidence later confirmed these findings.

6. None of the employers interviewed envisaged disciplinary action. The most common response was to deduct wages for the two-day absence. Some employers treated it as paid leave; others, more sympathetic, accepted employees' accounts of 'intimidation' and paid wages in full. There is later evidence of dismissals in smaller and unorganised factories.

7. Many employers commented that coloured and Asian staff worked normally.

According to press reports, some 400 000 students observed the stayaway. In the Transvaal some 300 schools were completely closed. The Minister of Law and Order put the number of boycotting students at 396 000.

The overwhelming majority of schools in the Vaal Triangle, East Rand and Atteridgeville regions were deserted. The Department of Education and Training claimed that in Soweto, school attendance ranged from 30% to 90%. However, LMG investigations indicate a much lower attendance level, although most matric students did write their exams on 6-7 November. Students at the University of the North observed the boycott.

The state and capital responded ambiguously to the stayaway. Although the security forces were too thinly spread to suppress it forcibly as they have done in the past, they did mount a counter-attack afterwards. The leaders of the stayaway committee were detained and charged under the Internal Security Act, and 5 000-6 000 SASOL workers were dismissed. However, there were indications that senior officials and cabinet ministers had reservations about the Department of Law and Order's hard-line tactics (*SE*, 18.11.84).

Organised commerce and industry expressed similar reservations after CUSA's Piroshaw Camay was detained (*SE*, 18.11.84). Representatives argued that the stayaway should be played down, and that the state should not overreact because this 'fuels an ever-increasing cycle of action and reaction' (*FW*, 15-21.11.84). In general, they wanted to protect their fragile relationship with the unions, rather than politicise it by overreaction. Further, after the stayaway, capital and advanced reformers in the state became much more vocal about the need to accelerate structural reform.[16] Tony Bloom of the Premier Group went so far as to say that '[t]here is an inherent inevitability about talking to the ANC' (*FW*, 15-21.11.84; *FM*, 15.11.84).

To sum up, although rising tensions in the community were the driving force behind the stayaway, working-class organisations tended to dominate the action, giving it a distinct character. However, it was the UDF's working-class affiliates — the civics and youth congresses in African areas — together with the powerful independent unions that made the stayaway a success.

The stayaway was most widespread in areas where strong union, student and community organisation coexisted. The fact that most of these organisations are mass based was an important factor. There is no evidence to support the view that the unions, which are in any case only a part of the working class, subordinated themselves to a populist petty-bourgeois programme. Indeed, it is hard to believe that the aggressive class consciousness forged in the crucible of factory struggles in recent years could simply dissolve when faced with a seductive populism.

Port Elizabeth-Uitenhage, March 1985

Between 18-22 March, more than 120 000 black workers stayed away from work in the Port Elizabeth-Uitenhage area for at least one day. A survey conducted by the LMG found that 90% of African workers in Port Elizabeth and 36% in Uitenhage responded (excluding those not working as a result of short-time). The Port Elizabeth Black Community Organisation (PEBCO) issued the call for a stayaway in response to the political and economic crisis in the region. Initially PEBCO identified the following issues: mass retrenchment, the AMCAR-Ford merger, and increased petrol prices. The last became the final focus of the stayaway.

All unions not affiliated to the UDF expressed reservations about the wisdom of staying away at that time. In particular, they were concerned that a call made by an African community organisation — PEBCO — would exclude coloured workers; that a local response to national problems was likely to be ineffective; that consultation with workers was inadequate; and there were fears about the effect of the stayaway on workers at smaller, unorganised firms.

These differences over strategy reflect deep divisions between community organisations and trade unions, between coloured and African workers, and (mainly in Port Elizabeth) between employed and unemployed workers. These divisions have hampered the development of an organised working-class politics in the region.

The working class in the Port Elizabeth-Uitenhage region is more or less equally composed of coloured and African workers.[17] In the 1950s, coloured and African communities tended to live in racially mixed residential areas, which provided a basis for joint political action.[18] This social solidarity was systematically undermined from the late 1950s onwards, as the apartheid state imposed its racial blueprint on the region.[19] Racially separate African and coloured residential areas were created, and coloureds were given better jobs in the workplace. By the late 1970s this process was complete in Port Elizabeth.

In Uitenhage, the same process has not been fully completed. As a result, Langa township, which still faces the threat of removal, is racially mixed, with 42 000 residents (*EPH*, 13.06.85) of whom approximately 3 000 are coloureds. These divisions influenced the outcome of the Port Elizabeth-Uitenhage strike wave of 1979-80.

In October 1979, 700 African workers walked out at Ford's Cortina plant in Struandale, Port Elizabeth, to protest the sacking of PEBCO president Thomazile Botha, a trainee draughtsman at the company. The United Automobile, Rubber and Allied Workers Union (UAW), a parallel union of the coloured National Union of Motor Assembly and Rubber Workers of South Africa (NUMAR-WOSA), had organised the neighbouring Ford engine plant, but at the time of the strike had only begun to organise at Cortina. Consequently, it was the PEBCO-linked Ford Workers Committee (FWC) which took the lead in mobilising against Botha's sacking.[20]

PEBCO had been founded just two weeks earlier at a mass meeting in New Brighton, as an umbrella organisation of the many residents' associations then organising in the Port Elizabeth African townships.[21] It had neither called for nor organised the actions at Ford, but as Botha was its president and most Cortina workers were members, PEBCO became centrally involved in the dispute. Volatile conditions in the townships, where residents were mobilising to protest rent increases, set the scene for events at Ford. The proximity of the plant to the township, the younger, more politicised workers at Cortina, and Botha's leadership all contributed to the close linkage between township and shop-floor grievances.

The strikes caused an important ideological and organisational rift. On the one side, PEBCO and the FWC began to articulate their aims in terms of the national democratic tradition, and concentrated on building mass-based community organisations. The FWC — which later became MACWUSA, and like PEBCO affiliated to the UDF — bitterly criticised UAW for neglecting the workers at Cortina. On the other hand, UAW and NUMARWOSA (which have since merged to form NAAWU, the most powerful FOSATU union in the region), distanced themselves from the PEBCO-MACWUSA style of 'community unionism' on the grounds that it was 'populist' and neglected workers' interests on the shop floor.

This division, which has been aggravated by personality differences over the years, persists today as a particularly virulent stand-off between the 'populist' community organisations and 'workerist' trade unions. The battle between these two groupings has exacerbated the structural division between home and work by preventing sustained union-community solidarity.

In Uitenhage, however, the outcome was different. Union shop stewards were leaders in the Uitenhage Civic Organisation. The Volkswagen strike in June 1980 occurred after employers refused to accept the union's demand for a living wage of R2,00 an hour, and the magistrate banned the union report-back meeting. Not only did both coloured and African workers at Volkswagen go out, but their action precipitated a general strike in the city.[22] Unlike the Ford factory at Struandale, the VW plant is located in a central industrial district, and draws its workforce from both the coloured and African communities of Uitenhage.

While the differing social geography of the two cities does not of itself account for the different outcomes, it certainly established the terrain on which the difficult relationship between trade union and township organising was worked through. Whereas in Port Elizabeth ideological differences between PEBCO-MACWUSA and NAAWU were reinforced by divisions between NUMAR-WOSA's coloured membership and MACWUSA's young militant African membership, similar sources of division were virtually absent in Uitenhage. Only in the unions has the division between coloured and African workers been overcome, and this non-racial working-class unity has remained confined to the workplace.

The strategies of union and community organisations have also been shaped by the different problems they face in the factories and townships respectively. The recession has hit the region particularly hard. The main manufacturing sector in the region, the motor industry, declined as demand contracted because of high interest rates, and factories began moving up to the Rand. Consequently, 11 000 motor workers and a further 20 000 in related industries have lost their jobs during the last three years.[23] NAAWU estimates that a further 10 000 workers will lose their jobs as a result of the AMCAR-Ford merger. Unemployment also increased as a result of the drought, which undermined what little subsistence base there was in the bantustans, and reduced job levels in the white agricultural sector.

The Eastern Cape has a strong union presence, won in a series of bitter factory struggles after 1980. NAAWU is in the forefront of the union movement, followed by the other FOSATU affiliates, GWU, CCAWUSA and FCWU. MACWUSA does not have a significant presence in the factories, because it believes that workers should be mobilised in the community. The main concern of unions at present is to consolidate their position, preserving their hard-won gains on the shop floor, and seeking to protect as many jobs threatened by retrenchment as possible. In the circumstances, they have tended to weigh up the costs of involvement in non-workplace issues extremely carefully. This concern reinforces a strong tendency in Eastern Cape FOSATU unions to avoid alliances with the community organisations — a particularly orthodox 'workerist' position.

In the townships, related problems have produced different effects. With unemployment as high as 35%,[24] and alarming levels of poverty,[25] militant community organisations with a substantial base among the young unemployed have emerged. Towards the end of 1984, the newly elected BLA tried to increase squatter rentals. The resulting outcry forced the BLA to back down, and saw the rebirth of PEBCO, which had been inactive since 1981. PEBCO's revival against the background of desperate subsistence struggles in the townships suggests that it and the national democratic tradition which it espouses strike a ready chord among these poverty-stricken urban dwellers.

The politicisation of the unemployed youth, a common feature of the 1985 township revolts, did not emerge spontaneously. At about the same time that PEBCO was revived, the Port Elizabeth Youth Congress (PEYCO) and the Uitenhage Youth Congress (UYCO) were formed by small groups of unemployed youths. By April 1985, PEYCO was a mass-based organisation drawing most of its support from the unemployed, particularly from squatter areas. It has well-developed organisational structures and provides PEBCO with most of its membership.

UYCO, on the other hand, has despite its name become a civic, with support in the employed and the unemployed working class.[26] Most of its leaders are workers and unemployed youths. It has developed a sophisticated democratic grassroots structure based on street and area committees. Whereas both UYCO and PEYCO have managed, in effect, to take control of the political life of the townships over the last few months, PEBCO has remained distinctly populist, relying on mass meetings rather than solid organisational structures to win support. This may be connected to the fact that its leadership has links with radical petty-bourgeois interests that are opposed to the BLA.

Momentum for the March stayaways built up during the schools boycott that began in October 1984. Conflict between COSAS and the authorities frequently resulted in running street battles between police and the community. This generated an atmosphere of tension and conflict that began to politicise wider sections of the community. Significantly, the schools boycott led to an alliance between COSAS and FOSATU in the Uitenhage Parents Committee, which was instrumental in resolving the schools conflict in January-February.

FOSATU was also involved in the Parents, Teachers and Students Association which was formed in February to take up educational grievances in Uitenhage coloured schools. However, a similar alliance was absent in Port Elizabeth's African townships.

By the end of February, rising tensions in Port Elizabeth townships were not accompanied by closer relations between unions and the main community organisations, as was the case in the Transvaal before November. Existing links between unions and student organisations did not influence the union's decision to oppose the stayaway, because educational demands were not given as a reason for calling it.

Further, COSAS is not nearly as significant or organisationally powerful in the Eastern Cape as it is in the Transvaal. Instead, the youth congresses played a central role in organising the stayaway. They were responding to the increasing militancy of the unemployed youth during the first months of 1985. At this time many of the youth attacked town councillors and black policemen, forcing them to resign or leave the township.

It is difficult to gain insight into the consciousness of these youths. They are unemployed, badly educated and younger than the average activist. They come mainly from squatter areas, and generally have not been adequately educated within political organisations. As the community organisations established dominance, the youth were drawn into political activity without substantially altering their position on the fringes of legality. Known in the townships as 'the guerillas' or 'amabuthu' (frontline warriors in the frontier wars), they confront all forms of authority without always getting approval from community organisations.

Meanwhile, PEBCO and the youth congresses were steadily building up their organisations by taking up civic and political issues like shacks, rents, and the illegitimacy of the BLAs. Regular mass funerals at weekends provided a platform for those who wanted to draw a broader spectrum of the community into more militant action.

The unions were not drawn into these struggles as they had been in the equivalent phase in the Transvaal. This cannot be explained in terms of their desire to avoid militant action, because they were, and have subsequently been, engaged in extensive strike action in a number of factories. Rather, the absence of a working relationship between the unions and community organisations, and a legitimate mistrust of the radical populism of the unemployed youth, lay behind union reluctance to support the stayaway.

The unions did not, however, suggest an alternative tactic. This omission prevented organised labour from playing a leading role in the stayaway; it also meant that burning working-class issues like the AMCAR-Ford merger were not articulated.

The stayaway

There are conflicting reports of the origins of the stayaway call. In November 1984 there were rumours of a stayaway to follow the Transvaal one. Though rumour linked the proposal to PEBCO and MACWUSA, both denied knowledge of it. There was a stayaway call in response to a rent increase designed to come into effect from 1 December, but this was rescinded following the Khayamnandi (Port Elizabeth) Town Council's resolution not to increase rent and service charges.

Meanwhile, a highly successful stayaway occurred in Grahamstown on 9 November. It was called by COSAS to coincide with the funeral of a 15-year-old unrest victim, Patrick Mdyogola. According to reports, 'only a handful of Africans turned up for work after a call for a mass boycott of work' (*EPH*, 10.11.84).

Chronology: Port Elizabeth

• End of January: At a PEBCO meeting at the Rio Cinema a stayaway was proposed, and PEBCO leaders decided to meet the trade unions to discuss the proposed action.
• 3 February: The press carried a report about the proposed stayaway before PEBCO met the unions. Shortly afterwards a FOSATU regional congress rejected the idea of a stayaway.
• 7 February: UDF organisations met the 'unity talks' (non-UDF) unions to discuss a stayaway. PEBCO identified three issues: retrenchments of workers which resulted in mass unemployment;

the AMCAR-Ford merger; and the increase in petrol prices. The unions expressed reservations about the wisdom of staying away but agreed to go back to workers for a mandate.

• 10 February: Another meeting was scheduled, but unions had not had enough time to go back to the factories.

• 10-17 February: Unions discussed the stayaway call with members on the factory floor. Union leaders indicated that workers did not support the stayaway call. PEBCO disputed the union statement arguing that the unions had never consulted the workers. It proceeded with planning of the stayaway.

• 16 February: GWU held a general meeting, at which workers rejected the idea of a stayaway, but because 'there was support for some sort of action', they decided to recommend a consumer boycott as an alternative. This proposal was never seriously entertained because of PEBCO's insistence that a stayaway should take place, nor was the proposal taken up by any of the other unions.

• 17 February: At a PEBCO meeting of 2 000 in Port Elizabeth, the unions' opposition to the stayaway was announced. A vote was taken in support of a stayaway. A stayaway committee was formed, and unions were invited to send representatives. They refused, and PEBCO decided to go it alone. The committee set the date for a Black Weekend — boycott of shops — and stayaway. Both were to apply to Uitenhage as well.

• 17 February-16 March: Unions concentrated on getting management to agree not to victimise workers who stayed away. During this time tensions mounted in the townships:

Vigilantes hired by the town councillors became more violent, and in turn were attacked and burnt;

Confusion developed in the schools boycott, which eventually fizzled out in February;

Increased frequency of clashes between police and demonstrators led to an increase in the number of political mass funerals;

Buses stopped coming into townships as youths took to stoning them;

PEBCO, PEYCO and UYCO began an extensive pamphleteering campaign and door-to-door organisation around the stayaway call;

The Port Elizabeth Chamber of Commerce, Port Elizabeth Afrikaanse Sakekamer, the mayors of Port Elizabeth and

Uitenhage and the police issued statements urging workers not to stay away (*EPH*, 15.03.85).

Unionists complained that militant youths were increasingly threatening reprisals against workers who did not stay away.

• 11 March: The unions held a meeting at which they decided not to support the stayaway, and informed PEBCO of their decision. 'PEBCO was reluctant to give an answer, but said the workers supported them and not the unions', CCAWUSA organiser Phindile Maneli subsequently said. A press statement was issued by the unions, publicly disassociating themselves from the stayaway and insisting that PEBCO had to bear the consequences of any dismissals. In contrast, the general secretary of MACWUSA, Dennis Neer, said: 'Workers represented by these unions had voted unanimously in favour of the stayaway call'.

• 13 March: Unions called a meeting with UDF and black consciousness organisations (the latter also opposed the stayaway) to reemphasise their reasons for wanting the stayaway called off:

1. The demands were national ones and should be made nationally. A local response simply exposed workers to attack;
2. It would affect some workers more than others, thus causing division: commercial workers would lose three days' pay and others only one day's pay;
3. The call was not made in the coloured areas, thus reinforcing division;
4. No provision had been made for workers who would lose their jobs, especially unorganised workers.

The unity unions did not propose any alternative action, and PEBCO simply rejected their objections. The unions released a press statement opposing the stayaway, but did not mobilise against it.

• 16-17 March: Black Weekend was supported in the African townships.

• 18 March: The stayaway was supported in the African townships.

Chronology: Uitenhage

• 28-29 January: A coloured schools boycott started, due to the management committee's attempts to establish a sports board in rivalry with the Uitenhage Sports Board.

- February: The schools' struggle intensified at schools falling under both the African Department of Education and Training (DET) and the coloured Department of Education and Culture. It spread to Port Elizabeth.
- 4 February: The Uitenhage Parents Committee (UPC) was established.
- 8 February: COSAS met the UPC to discuss student grievances.
- 9 February: At a UDF meeting, NAAWU and FOSATU were challenged to take up the case of Mncedisi Sithoto, a MACWUSA member who was dismissed from his job at Goodyear. Both the union and the federation were attacked.
- 11 February: UPC met the regional director of the DET, and students demands were presented and accepted.
- 18 February: The DET boycott ended on the understanding that the new academic year would begin on 18 March.
- 22 February: All coloured schools were closed by the Minister.
- 27 February: A Parents, Teachers and Students Association was established which included many FOSATU officials and shop stewards.
- 1 March: A mass meeting attended by more than 1 000 parents was held in Uitenhage to demand the reinstatement of teachers transferred from the area for political reasons and the removal of principals involved with the Labour Party.
- March: There were rumours of the impending stayaway, but unionised workers decided not to support it. Attempts by the unions to explain their position at community meetings were not permitted. The unions were accused of betraying the struggle.
- 16-17 March: Black Weekend. Two people died in township unrest. The magistrate banned funerals on all weekends and public holidays.
- 18 March: The stayaway was unevenly supported.
- 19 March: UYCO held a mass meeting to call for a stayaway on 21 March to bury the unrest victims. This call was supported by workers at meetings in some factories.
- 20 March: Unionists pressed managements to apply for lifting of the ban on weekend funerals. This was done that afternoon, and the funeral planned for the following day was banned by the magistrate at the behest of the local police.[27]
- 21 March: The Langa massacre and stayaway took place.
- 22 March: Stayaway.

• 25 March: 15-minute memorial stoppage in unionised factories.

Monitoring the stayaway

The LMG conducted a study among employers, unions, and community organisations in the area to ascertain the dimensions of the stayaway. In Port Elizabeth a random sample of 50 of the 235 firms listed in the Midlands Chamber of Industries Directory were interviewed. Seventy-five percent of industrial employers in Uitenhage were interviewed, along with a sample of employers in the commercial sector. All interviews with employers were conducted over the telephone. In-depth interviews were conducted with key activists in the community and the trade unions. The main findings of the telephone survey were:

1. Forty-three percent of black workers in Port Elizabeth and 62% of black workers in Uitenhage in our sample are on some form of short-time.

Table I: Short-time work in Port Elizabeth and Uitenhage

	Africans	Coloureds	All black workers
Port Elizabeth	40%	48%	43%
Uitenhage	65%	49%	62%

2. In Port Elizabeth 99,5% of the African worker force in the commercial sector heeded the call to stay away on 16 March, a Saturday morning shopping day. Workers classified as coloured came to work as usual, although many stores closed early. On Monday 18 March 90% of African industrial workers stayed away. Again few coloured workers participated. The situation in Uitenhage was less clear, as 69% of the companies surveyed employed African workers who were not expected to work that day because of some form of short-time. Of those meant to come to work on 18 March, 36% stayed away.

Table II: African industrial workers: percentage which stayed away

Date	18	21	22
Port Elizabeth	90%	—	—
Uitenhage	36%	98%	97%

3. In Uitenhage a further stayaway was called for 21 March, the anniversary of Sharpeville, so that all members of the community could attend the funerals of people killed by the police the previous weekend. The massacre at Langa on 21 March ensured that the following day was also a stayaway. Ninety-eight percent of the African workers stayed away on Thursday and 97% on Friday. The proportion of coloured workers staying away reached 16% on Thursday but dropped to 4% on Friday.

Low as coloured participation in the stayaway may seem, it was nonetheless high in comparison with that in the Port Elizabeth area. In certain factories the coloured stayaway was much higher than the mean. This reflects the fact that geographical and organisational divisions are not so clear cut in Uitenhage.

4. Sixty-one percent of the employers surveyed in Port Elizabeth, and 73% of those surveyed in Uitenhage held discussions with employees before the stayaway. All employers, regardless of whether they held such discussions or not, followed a policy of 'no work, no pay' as recommended by employer bodies. In some companies workers lost their attendance and service bonuses, and a few workers in unorganised firms were dismissed.

5. Of the employers, 71% of the sample in Port Elizabeth and 69% in Uitenhage predicted that stayaways would continue in the future. Only one employer thought stayaways would not continue. 'Stayaways', one employer remarked, 'have become a fact of life'. Most of our informants felt that the solution to stayaways lay either in quelling the unrest or employing coloureds instead of Africans in future.

The unions' opposition to the stayaway has been interpreted in different ways. The consensus among community organisations was that the stayaway was a resounding success, and that the unions had misjudged the level of support for it among workers. In the words of the PEYCO president: 'For the first time we have managed to draw our parents into the struggle'. As far as the unions were concerned workers stayed away because of intimidation. Although it is extremely difficult to ascertain the truth of the matter, there is evidence of substantial support among workers for some form of collective action, but there was also a feeling that workers feared the consequences of not staying away.[28]

Views of the political objectives of the stayaway also differed. The vice-president of FOSATU criticised the stayaway as not being in the interests of the working class. Instead, he argued, non-workers ultimately benefited: white chainstores registered record takings on the Friday before the Black Weekend; black traders and shebeen owners made a killing over the weekend; taxi drivers did extremely well because there were no buses; and it was only workers who lost out — they lost a day's pay, some lost their jobs, and they were left weaker and more divided than before.[29]

Community organisers judge success in very different terms. As they see it the stayaway demonstrated the level of resistance in the township, increased the organisational power of community organisations, and satisfied the demand by unemployed youths for more militant action.

These differences reflect the disharmony between unions and community organisations over the purpose of political mobilisation. To the unions, community-based action should not play into the hands of non-working class interests. That unions did not provide an alternative plan of action may reflect the impossibility of organising a pure working-class politics outside the workplace, especially when unions are preoccupied with defending workers on the shop floor during a recession.

To the community organisations, there is no real difference between the interests of the community and those of employed workers, many of whom are on short-time in any case. Therefore, they argue, the unions should follow where the community leads. This indicates that the political strategies of the community organisations are being shaped predominantly by community conditions and particularly by the highly politicised unemployed who bear the brunt of the depressed regional economy.

This kind of politics, however, runs the risk of intensifying divisions between unemployed and employed workers, especially if it is couched in populist ideology that does not recognise the leading role of the working class. All this reinforces the traditional ideologically-based divisions that have plagued union-community relations in the Eastern Cape in recent years.

Significantly, during the stayaways in Uitenhage on 21 and 22 March there was greater harmony than in Port Elizabeth between community and union organisations as well as between coloured and African workers. This was partly due to the strength of UYCO which, unlike PEYCO, has a substantial base among the older working-class members of the community,[30] and also because the unions did not oppose these stayaways. Hopefully this will provide the basis for greater unity in the future.

State, capital, and black petty-bourgeois responses

State, capital, and black petty-bourgeois responses to the stayaways cannot be divorced from the general state of crisis in the townships, of which the stayaways were the most organised and dramatic expression.

State response to the township crisis was to declare a state of emergency on 21 July 1985. This was widely interpreted as a swing to the right and hence away from reform. This is not true. A sustained period of reform, characterised by substantial departures from Grand Apartheid,[31] are part of the state's attempt to resolve the crisis of political legitimation and accumulation which has plagued South Africa since the mid-1970s. However, counterposed to state reforms were struggles in factories, townships, and schools. In these struggles subordinate classes attempted to resolve the crisis on their own terms.

The most significant state reforms in the townships are the proposed Regional Service Councils (RSCs). The RSCs are designed to redistribute substantial resources into township urban renewal programmes. But the level of support for popular protest posed a major threat to the implementation of these new federal-type structures. Many areas became no-go zones where police and army could appear only in force. State authority at local level was destroyed: 240 black local government officials resigned between September 1984 and July 1985, and 360 black policemen were forced out of the townships.

The state therefore faced a fundamental contradiction. It needed to press on with its new urban policy, but could not do so without regaining the strategic initiative necessary to impose its policies. In 1960, only after the state of emergency effectively crushed resistance could the state implement Grand Apartheid. Shortly before the 1985 state of emergency top military and police officials openly admitted to being unable to control township unrest. This then is why the emergency was necessary. If opposition is totally broken the emergency regulations will succeed in preparing the way for reform to restabilise South Africa's capitalist system.

The state is attempting to restabilise politically during the current endemic crisis in what Miliband terms a 'Bonapartist' manner. He says, '[W]here . . . the hegemony of a dominant class is persistently and strongly challenged, the autonomy of the state is likely to be substantial, to the point where, in conditions of intense class struggle and political instability, it may assume "Bonapartist" and authoritarian forms, and emancipate itself from constraining constitutional checks and controls'.[32] This is what PW Botha meant when he announced that he, as state president, was allowed to call a state of emergency if, in the words of the Public Safety Act (Act 3 of 1953) 'the ordinary law of the land is inadequate to enable the government to ensure the safety of the public, or to maintain public order'.

Organised capital understands this perfectly. Raymond Parsons, president of ASSOCOM, said the state of emergency provides a 'breathing space for reform'. However, organised capital is clearly also uneasy about supporting the state of emergency because of its politicising effect on trade unions. This fear is not unfounded. If opposition is to survive this period of repression, it will be because unions remain intact. This may prove to be the Achilles heel in the state's 'Bonapartist' project. This in turn reinforces the need for unions to play a leading political role, giving direction to the battered but still lively popular movement.

The black petty bourgeoisie has not opposed the state of emergency. Unfettered participation by coloured and Indian parliamentary parties, bantustan leaders, and urban councillors in any new reformist political solution is only possible if popular and working-class opposition is crushed.

In short, future reform initiatives depend on whether the 1985 state of emergency can destroy opposition in the same way as its 1960 precursor did. The coercive might of the state may make this possible. However, contemporary opposition is different from that mustered by popular forces in 1960. Firstly there is a powerful union movement emerging from a massive working class with well developed class consciousness. Secondly, community organisations have drawn large numbers of people into a political culture that is unlikely to disappear if leaders are removed.

Conclusion

A comparison of the Transvaal and Eastern Cape stayaways reveals the regionally specific determinants of mass political mobilisation.

The relationship between trade unions and community organisations is not marked by a history of antagonism in the Transvaal. Indeed, Transvaal unions have extensively debated the question of the relationship between unions and community organisations.[33] Nor have Transvaal unions, particularly on the East Rand, shied away from becoming involved in communities.

The same cannot be said for the Eastern Cape. Although unions did involve themselves in the boycott of elections for the tri-cameral parliament in August 1983, and in the school boycotts of 1984-85, this did not ease traditional antagonisms between PEBCO-MACWUSA and the unions. Furthermore the dominant union in the region, NAAWU, tends to adopt a particularly hardline 'workerist' position in the debate over union involvement in mainstream political movements.

The Transvaal economy is also far more complex and not nearly as depressed as the Eastern Cape economy. In the latter region, the state of the economy had a differential impact on unions and political organisations. Whereas unions were desperately trying to consolidate workers' jobs and wages in the factories, community organisations were being pushed into increasingly militant action by the particularly large number of politicised unemployed. Although similar pressures existed in the Transvaal, they were not as intense.

Community organisations in the two regions have a different class profile. The Transvaal civics are led mostly by workers and relatively well-educated unemployed youths, and have a fairly solid support base among residents. In Port Elizabeth, PEYCO is dominated by unemployed youths and has a large support base among the unemployed. PEBCO has definite populist tendencies, has no solid grassroots organisational structure, and is influenced by radical petty-bourgeois interests. It relies on PEYCO for its support base and on the UDF's national structure for legitimacy.

UYCO, on the other hand, operates effectively as a civic, is led by working class and unemployed people, and has massive support among the impoverished squatter populations. The high number of workers on short-time in Uitenhage narrows the gap between employed and unemployed workers. In short, although the Transvaal and Eastern Cape community organisations represent the poorer classes in the community, those in the Eastern Cape are far more receptive to the demands of the unemployed, which do not always coincide with those of the employed working class.

Another difference is that the Transvaal working class is not plagued by the division between coloureds and Africans. When the Eastern Cape unions objected to the stayaway on the ground that it would exclude coloureds, they were reflecting the real difficulties involved in building non-racial working-class unity outside the workplace in a region where apartheid has been particularly successful in dividing the working class. It remains to be seen whether the community organisations and unions will be able to overcome this obstacle.

The Transvaal stayaway grew out of the student struggle and was preceded by substantial cooperation between unions and student organisations. Although in the Eastern Cape the unions did have links with the student organisations prior to the stayaway, they were not sufficient to dissolve divisions between the unions and community organisations, mainly because educational demands played no role in the stayaway.

There is some force in the argument advanced by the Eastern Cape unions that the stayaway was called in support of demands that required national rather than local response to succeed. In contrast, the Transvaal stayaway demands did concern regional problems and were theoretically attainable. Realistic and attainable demands are essential to win union support when workers are faced with the threat of retrenchment during a recession. There is all the more reason for unions to engage in community politics in order to ensure this.

Clearly, distinct class interests have become crucial determinants of the form and content of mass political mobilisation. Regional variations depend on a range of social, economic and ideological factors. In the Transvaal it was possible for the organised working-class to take a decisive step towards building a working class politics by playing a leading role in the stayaway. In the Eastern Cape this process was hampered by numerous obstacles that both unions and community organisations still need to overcome. It is crucial that unions formulate a political strategy for organising beyond the workplace, rather than leaving this to the community organisations.[34]

The stayaway tactic remains a highly effective way of demonstrating mass opposition to oppression and exploitation. Judging from the experience of the Transvaal stayaway there does not seem to be any necessary reason why it cannot become an important weapon in the arsenal of a working-class political offensive. This stayaway demonstrated how the organised working class can begin to establish its control over the form and content of what some have called a populist tactic. Rather than sliding into populism, this form of politics may well transform the struggle for national democracy into a meaningful struggle for socialism.

Notes

1 E Webster, 'Stayaways and the black working class: evaluating a strategy', *Labour, Capital and Society*, 14 (1), April 1981, 11-38.
2 D O'Meara, 'The 1946 African mineworkers strike', *Journal of Commonwealth and Comparative Politics*, XII (2), July 1975.
3 M Legassick, 'South Africa: capital accumulation and violence', *Economy and Society*, 6 (3), 1974.
4 T Lodge, 'Political mobilisation during the 1950s: an East London case study', paper presented to the Conference on Economic Growth and Racial Domination, University of the Western Cape, September 1984.
5 M Swilling, 'The politics of working class struggles in Germiston, 1979-1983', paper presented to the History Workshop Conference, University of the Witwatersrand, February 1984.
6 M Swilling, 'Working class politics: the East Rand and East London in the 1980s', paper presented to the Association of Sociologists of Southern Africa Conference, University of the Witwatersrand, July 1984.

7 Swilling, 'Working class politics' and A Erwin, 'The question of unity in the struggle', paper presented to the Association of Sociologists of Southern Africa Conference, University of Cape Town, July 1985.

8 The conservative figure of 300 000 was obtained by multiplying the total number of blacks employed in private industry in the PWV area (374 313) by 60% (the consensus figure of how many stayed away) and then making allowance for retail and service sectors. The figure of 800 000 was obtained by multiplying 60% of the total number of blacks in paid employment in the PWV area (1 485 000) minus the number of mineworkers ($\pm$ 150 000).

9 J Grest and H Hughes, 'State strategy and popular response at the local level', *South African Review 2* (Johannesburg, 1984).

10 Discussions and interviews with ERAPO, Vaal Civic Association, and youth congresses held between 1983 and 1985.

11 E Webster, 'A new frontier of control? Changing forms of job protection in South African industrial relations', Second Carnegie Commission, paper 111, Cape Town, 1984.

12 See *South African Labour Bulletin (SALB)*, 7 (8), July 1982.

13 For example Benjamin Khumalo, Soweto branch secretary of COSAS, *SASPU Focus*, 3 (2), November 1984. All figures on deaths supplied by the SAIRR.

14 See *SALB*, 10 (2), 1984.

15 Details from official FOSATU press releases and statements by Alec Erwin, acting general secretary of FOSATU at the time.

16 See the article by W Cobbett et al, elsewhere in this edition of *South African Review*.

17 Labour Monitoring Group, 'The March stayaways in Port Elizabeth and Uitenhage', *SALB*, 11 (1), September 1985.

18 See T Lodge, *Black Politics in South Africa Since 1948* (Johannesburg, 1983).

19 For a detailed account, see Labour Monitoring Group, 'The March stayaways'.

20 P Bonner, 'Trade unions since Wiehahn', *SALB*, 8 (4), 1983, 23.

21 See articles in *SALB*, 6 (2 & 3), 1983; also C Cooper and L Ensor, *PEBCO: A Black Mass Movement* (Johannesburg, 1981).

22 Bonner, 'Trade unions', 28.

23 *State of the Nation*, May 1985.

24 A Roux, 'Unemployment and education in the Eastern Cape', Carnegie Commission, paper 120, Cape Town, 1984.

25 These conditions include: 120 000 homeless families; one-third of the

African population in Port Elizabeth lives in shacks; 60% of the shacks house ten or more people; 20% of the squatters earn R20 a month or less, while the average earns R240 a month; severe shortage of educational, recreational and health facilities. See Labour Monitoring Group, 'The March stayaways'.

26 This is because the civic, the Uitenhage Black Civic Organisation, which was originally controlled by FOSATU has remained inactive and has not played a role in the recent wave of resistance.

27 For the claims and counter-claims surrounding these events see D Pillay, 'The Port Elizabeth stayaway', *Work in Progress*, 37, 1985.

28 This emerged from interviews with unionists and prominent leaders of the community organisations.

29 *FOSATU Worker News*, 37, May 1985.

30 UYCO claims to have 8 000 paid-up members. In June a proper civic was founded to represent this large membership.

31 See Cobbett et al, *South African Review 3*, for an extensive treatment of the state's reformist initiatives.

32 R Miliband, *Class Power and State Power* (London, 1983), 68.

33 M Swilling, 'Workers divided: a critical assessment of the MAWU split on the East Rand', *SALB*, 10 (1), 1984.

34 See Erwin, 'The question of unity', for a useful indication of how this problem is being thought out in FOSATU circles. The congruence between this type of thinking and what some in the UDF are beginning to talk about is an extremely hopeful sign for what might happen in the future.

The Fight to Save Jobs: Union Initiatives on Retrenchment and Unemployment

Georgina Jaffee and Karen Jochelson

The past decade has seen deteriorating national economic performance, inflation and increased unemployment. These are features not only of the South African recession but of the current global crisis. South African capital is adjusting to economic decline in much the same way as capital in other industrialised countries, where the recession has led to permanent restructuring of the labour force through layoffs and retrenchments and the introduction of new technology and techniques to rationalise the labour process.

South Africa differs from other industrialised countries, however, when the responses of both organised labour and the state to the recession are considered. Countries with a longer history of industrial relations are modifying the system within already established parameters, while South Africa's industrial relations system is newly established. The present recession is defining for the first time some major issues for the unions. One such issue is the demand that employers negotiate fair dismissal procedures. Where this is denied, unions have made use of the Industrial Court, which has provided considerable opportunity to challenge and redefine management prerogatives.

Another important difference between South Africa and many other capitalist countries is that organised labour, management and the state in some European countries have joined forces in developing tripartite approaches to industrial relations in order to alleviate the crisis. Fiscal measures, social security benefits, increased public investment and improvements in the provision of social security were offered to workers and employers by the state in order to secure wage moderation[1] and to pacify militant demands. This has not been possible in the South African case, as the very nature of the apartheid state and the lack of social security for black workers preclude such collaboration.

Further, while the South African government has adopted policies similar to those of Britain and the United States to control inflation through budget cuts and monetarist techniques, it has not intervened directly to alleviate the effects of the downswing. The French and German governments, for example, have attempted to combat unemployment by instructing employers to reduce hours of work and shorten the normal working week, or by passing legislation to this effect. They have offered special subsidies to companies creating jobs for the youth and unemployed. This has not occurred in South Africa, which has none of the features of a welfare state.

Finally, in the current crisis unions in both Europe and the USA have become less militant and less prone to strike. In South Africa unions have continued to grow in numbers and militancy during the recession. According to figures released by the Department of Manpower, there were 469 strikes involving 181 942 workers in 1984. This marks a rise from the 336 strikes during 1983, which involved 64 499 workers. The Department of Manpower attributed the high level of strike action to sympathy strikes resulting from retrenchments and dismissals where employers had not gone through the correct channels.

The present trend involves the increasing politicisation of economic demands. Working-class response to the economic crisis is heightened by continued political exclusion of the black population, by the lack of adequate housing, medical, unemployment and welfare benefits, and by rising prices and rents. Linking of workplace demands with broader economic and political issues, and the consequent development of social movement unionism, is gradually confronting the limitations of the free enterprise system and undermining the legitimacy of state reform.

Over the past year, organised labour has managed to use the Industrial Court's procedural standards to intervene in the retrenchment process.[2] In some instances labour has faced management attempts to subvert the decisions of the court. Despite this, there have been definite gains in preventing arbitrary dismissal of workers. New trends are emerging in union-management negotiations on retrenchment — demands for the disclosure of information, reductions in the numbers of proposed retrenchments, negotiation of layoffs instead of retrenchments, and the development of preferential reemployment clauses.

Despite such gains, thousands of workers have been retrenched in all sectors. Central Statistical Services estimates that 8 000 jobs a month will be threatened during 1985, and it indicates that sectoral patterns of unemployment have not changed much since 1984. Some 23 000 jobs were lost in the general manufacturing sector alone betwen 1981 and 1984. About 7 000 jobs were lost in the clothing industry during 1983-84, and another 2 000 are threatened. Twelve hundred garment workers lost their jobs in February and March of 1985. The Steel and Engineering Industries Federation of SA (SEIFSA) estimates that 7 000 jobs in its sector were lost in 1984 (*ST*, 10.03.85), with a further 10 000 lost between the end of 1984 and the first quarter of 1985 (*BD*, 17.06.85). The building industry estimates that 6 000 general workers lost their jobs between September 1984 and January 1985. Total retrenchments in the construction and civil engineering sector could exceed 12 300 for the 12 months to January 1985 (*ST*, 10.03.85). In the motor industry, NAAWU lost 3 000 union members by the beginning of 1985.[3]

Unemployment levels are estimated to be between 25% and 30% of the economically active black population.[4] In a study of the Pilanesberg area Keenan calculated that the median time spent out of work was two years.[5] This is indicative of the trend towards permanent exclusion of increasing numbers of people from the workforce.

Unions and community organisations are now mounting initiatives to help the unemployed, and to put pressure on the state and capital to improve Unemployment Insurance Fund (UIF) benefits. As a result, unions and community organisations are developing demands which recognise the inability of the state and capital to lighten the effects of the crisis on the working class. These demands reflect the increasing attempts to articulate alternative economic strategies which expose the limits of the capitalist system.

Trends in the retrenchment process

The retrenchment guidelines adopted by the Industrial Court over the last two years include the following:

1. The employer must consider possible ways of avoiding retrenchment, such as transfers, eliminating overtime, and working short-time.
2. The employer has an obligation to consult with workers' representatives about the retrenchment, after having considered all possible ways of avoiding it.
3. The employer must consult with workers' representatives on criteria for selection of those to be retrenched, and these must be objectively checked against such things as attendance records, efficiency at the job or length of service.
4. The employer must give sufficient warning to employees and their representatives and must consult with the employees to be retrenched in the absence of a collective bargaining agent.[6]

In the last year most of these guidelines have been used by workers to challenge management decisions. The demand for disclosure of financial data is one which has emerged recently. Unions have asked management to furnish union accountants with relevant information to prove the necessity for retrenchment, and to show that all other alternatives have been considered. Disclosure of information played an important role in settling a retrenchment dispute between OK Bazaars and CCAWUSA in January 1985. The union accountant's report revealed that future trading prospects appeared dismal because of high interest rates and a drop in consumer demand. CCAWUSA agreed to a settlement in which workers were given a choice between layoff and retrenchment.[7]

   Unions are also negotiating to ensure that the minimum number of workers are retrenched, and insisting that management deal with the union to secure the best retrenchment package.[8] Negotiations between FBWU and Coca-Cola resulted in jobs being saved through reducing the number of retrenchments and by introducing a rolling-leave system. The company initially planned to retrench 104 workers, but reduced the number to 20, and the remaining workforce agreed to take unpaid leave every sixth week. The company also agreed to no new employment, no overtime, no casual labour, early retirement and a limited freeze on expenditure for capital equipment.

Unions are insisting that management consider all possible alternatives to retrenchment. Of particular interest is CCAWUSA's dispute declared in June 1985 with Foschini. The company decided to place 230 workers at Pages Stores on part-time work from 1 July 1985, and refused to consider the union's proposal for short-time. The company argued that the decision to put 29% of its workforce on part-time was their alternative to retrenchment. The union responded that short-time for the whole workforce was preferable, with all workers serving 40 instead of 45 hours weekly. All workers would then lose about R40 per month, instead of 230 workers losing R119 per month. Under management's plan, the part-time workers will get smaller pensions, UIF and workers' compensation, but will still have to pay the same travel costs to work while receiving less money. The union has argued that short-time work would save workers a certain amount in travel costs on the days when they do not go to work, and it calculates that short-time will save the company the same amount. The company responds that short-time is inflexible, and that the nature of the work, with its peak and low periods, is better suited to part-time employment.

The failure of employers to consult with workers prior to retrenching has generated many disputes, and generally results in the union bringing an application against management in terms of section 43 of the Labour Relations Act. This is an interim procedure to protect or restore the status quo while conciliation takes place or while awaiting a final determination by the Industrial Court.

In November 1984, Pretoria Precision Castings retrenched 32 workers, including two NAAWU shop stewards, thus breaking a commitment to negotiate with the union. Four months later, before the case came before the Industrial Court, the company settled. The settlement provided for the reinstatement of five workers and a cash payment for the others. Similarly, in the case of OK Bazaars in January this year the company finally entered into negotiations around retrenchment after CCAWUSA and NUDAW brought an application against it for implementing retrenchments without consultation with the union. In both cases the companies concerned were forced to negotiate with the workers' representatives who won much better severance packages and reduced retrenchments for their members. Most importantly, in the case of OK Bazaars the final agreement allowed workers to choose between layoff and retrenchment. The laid-off workers were guaranteed reemployment by August 1985. They won the right to remain on medical aid and the pension fund as well as to draw on the Unemployment Insurance Fund.

Criteria for retrenchment have also become a contentious issue over the past few years. In most instances, trade unions have advocated the principle of last in, first out (LIFO). Although employers are not obliged to adhere to it, if an alternative system is adopted the employer is obliged to prove the objectivity and fairness of this system.[9]

Of interest is the case of *Shezi vs Consolidated Frame Corporation*. The Industrial Court found that the company's use of efficiency as the criterion for retrenchment was not sufficient to ensure objectivity. The Frame Corporation had only used the LIFO principle in cases where employees had recently been transferred to new departments. This meant that some of those retrenched had up to 20 years' service with the company in other departments. The court found that length of service in all departments should be taken into account by the employer. The Frame Corporation is contesting the right of the Industrial Court to reinstate employees where the post had been abolished because of retrenchment.

Employers are currently on the offensive, challenging the Industrial Court's right to make such decisions. Many cases have been taken on appeal. Although arbitrary dismissal seems to have been prevented, management has now developed new quantitative techniques — such as testing workers for productivity or efficiency — in order to select for retrenchment. These are again being challenged by the unions. It appears that prior consultation with the union and fair selection criteria with justification for deviation from LIFO are now firmly established as principles of the Industrial Court. Where the employer deviates from LIFO, the unions have attempted to get the best possible severance package tied to service — which has the counterbalancing effect of forcing management to consider the cost of retrenchment.

Some unions are succeeding in inserting clauses in recognition agreements to prevent retrenchment for the duration of the agreement. In most cases where there are agreements management has been forced to stick by them. Agreements tend to be much tighter than in the past. For example, preferential reemployment clauses are now often written in. Accordingly, the name and address of the retrenched worker is kept by both management and the union to secure preferential reemployment. As a result, unions are playing a much more active role in the rehiring of workers. This is an important development, because workers who are retrenched will remain in closer contact with the union. Such gains have been won along with better severance packages for retrenched workers, and benefits for workers temporarily laid off.

In the motor industry, layoffs have been more common than retrenchment during the first half of 1985. This temporary suspension from the payroll in lieu of retrenchment is used along with putting workers on short-time work. According to NAAWU,[10] this development is due to motor plants reaching the lowest level at which they could still operate.

Negotiations have also concerned the closure of companies. NAAWU, for instance, made a number of demands over 2 500 jobs which were threatened by the Ford-AMCAR merger in January 1985. Demands included assurance of jobs in other Ford and Anglo American companies; that all employees aged 50 and over, and those with 20 years' service, be retired with normal pension benefits; that benefits include two months' salary for each completed year of service; that employers refund their own as well as workers' contributions to the pension fund; full gratuity; full service leave; and assistance for training.

Similarly, the NUTW negotiated over the closure of AA Fabrics. Initially the company did not offer severance pay but it eventually agreed to an amount equal to about 75% of each worker's wage per year of service. The workforce was predominantly migrant, and the union managed to get the company to agree to pay for workers to stay on in their hostels for an extra month, rather than being immediately evicted. The union was trying to get exemption from the East Rand Board for those workers who would have qualified for section 10(1)b rights had they not lost their jobs through closure.

The recession is leading to a permanent restructuring of some sectors of the economy. In the retail trade and service sectors there are attempts to introduce part-time and casual workers. In other sectors which are more mechanised it is more difficult to change a complex labour process. But managements are attempting to reorganise job categories and introduce work-study plans for inculcating efficiency in order to increase productivity. At the same time there are widespread attempts to increase the intensity of work, and to introduce new technology and systems of management.

Unions and the unemployed

Union gains in challenging the management prerogative to retrench unilaterally represent only the best possible deal negotiated from a position of weakness. Unions recognise that fighting retrenchment is only one strategy to adopt during a recession. Structural unemployment also holds potential for friction between those with and without work, as the threat of unemployment and ready replacement in the event of dismissal is used to discipline the workforce. Discussion within unions about unemployment is only just beginning and as yet there is no national strategy in the offing. Two tactics are being mooted: pressuring the state to improve its grossly inadequate social security schemes, and organisation of the unemployed.

Demanding social security: the UIF Benefit Charter

In July 1984, after many months of discussion between a range of service organisations including the Industrial Aid Society, the Black Sash, the East Rand Community Advice Bureau as well as a number of unions,[11] a memorandum detailing the shortcomings of the Unemployment Insurance Fund and demanding worker-orientated alternatives was submitted to the Minister of Manpower. A Benefit Charter was drawn up to popularise the demands of the memorandum.[12] At present, domestic, farm, seasonal and contract workers are barred from the UIF: the charter demanded the formation of a single fund for all workers. Another demand was that workers receive 60% of their last wage for one year rather than the current 45% for only six months. Employers were called on to make an equal contribution to the fund (at present employers contribute 3c of every 5c paid in by workers), while the state was urged to raise the present R7-m ceiling to its contribution and put in an amount equivalent to the joint contribution of workers and employers.

Another key demand was that the state establish a subsistence fund for people whose UIF benefits had lapsed, or were exhausted, or who had never been able to find work. Finally, the charter demanded that workers have more control over the fund, and that workers' representatives be appointed to the fund's board.

Allegations of corruption and maladministration of UIF are widespread. Though by no means all those entitled to unemployment benefits manage to claim them, UIF expenditure already exceeds income by between R1-m and R3-m monthly (*STrib*, 12.08.84). The government has not issued an official public response to the charter, but in letters to organisations involved in drawing it up the Department of Manpower has indicated it is still considering the proposals. There has been no response from capital.

Organisations involved in drawing up the charter are currently discussing ways of popularising it. Possibilities include using it as an educative document, setting up advice centres for unemployed workers, and offering training and education sessions on UIF to organisations for unemployed workers.

Union responses to unemployment

Most unions respond to unemployment by concentrating on the protection of the jobs and rights of their members. They admit that limitations of time, material and organisational resources force them to concentrate first and foremost on protecting the security of employed workers and negotiating the best possible retrenchment packages for members.

Only a few projects have been set up in response to widespread unemployment, and generally their organisational structures and aims are still tentative. Instances discussed below outline current ideas rather than long-established programmes.

Most unions have no formal structure to facilitate contact between the union and its unemployed members. Successful moves by unions such as T&G and CCAWUSA to insert a preferential rehiring clause into retrenchment agreements could potentially systematise contact between the union and its unemployed members. FOSATU-affiliated union constitutions prescribe that unemployed workers remain union members for six months following dismissal during which time they are not liable to pay dues. CCAWUSA is at present considering amending its constitution to allow unemployed workers to retain their membership for 12 rather than six months. This is related to the union demand that management maintain preferential rehiring agreements for a 12-month period.

Members of the FCWU, once unemployed, remain members for three months only, a period which orginally coincided with seasonal layoffs in the canning industry. SABS members are retained for six months, during which they may still collect death and sickness benefits even though their dues are suspended. CUSA workers remain members of the union for only 14 weeks while SAAWU members are retained as 'inactive members' indefinitely.

Social security and organising the unemployed are political issues, but the latter raises more serious questions about the forms and functions of such organisations. Should they be incorporated into existing community, youth or civic organisations, for example, or affiliated to a body that deals specifically with their problems? Should such a body be independent, or allied to the union movement?

The danger of competition between employed and unemployed when managements go union-bashing is palpably real. It poses the question of what strategy to adopt when workers are dismissed and an employer turns to the 'reserve army of labour' to recruit a more malleable and cheaper workforce. An additional problem: with whom would representatives of unemployed workers negotiate? In a factory workers have direct access to management, which can if necessary mediate with the state on certain issues. In a community, the focus of opposition is diffuse — issues can be passed on from one governmental department to another, from local to national level, to delay negotiation and frustrate opposition.

PWAWU argues that unions must adopt a new strategy to fight retrenchment. While union education stresses the broader political and economic context in which retrenchment and unemployment must be contested, union strategy does not. At present, retrenchment is fought on a factory-by-factory basis which inhibits union attempts to confront the causes of unemployment. Monetarist policy and the rationalisation of industry must be challenged on a multi-factory political basis and labour redirected into socially useful production.

T&G points out, however, that an organisation for the unemployed should be linked to unions to consolidate the unity of the working class as a whole, and to demonstrate its common interest. Unions can offer organisational experience, resources, and some bargaining leverage. Possibly unemployed workers could be organised on an area basis through shop steward councils.

Some unions have already taken steps to confront the issue of unemployment on a practical basis. Most initiatives to date are embryonic and their success is still in the balance.

At the SABS annual conference, the union stressed the need to examine possibilities of a minimum severance pay level. A resolution was passed recommending creation of an assistance fund for retrenched workers. Funds would be drawn from a dormant welfare fund which originally served as a strike fund. There is some debate within the union as to whether it is overreacting, with doubters suggesting that by the time the fund is established the retrenchment problem will not be so acute. SABS is anxious to ensure that administration of such a fund will not result in a burgeoning bureaucracy which absorbs all the money.

Another problem is determining criteria for eligibility. Ike van der Watt, general secretary of SABS, explained that while it is possible to establish that a worker applying for assistance has actually been retrenched, it is more difficult to prove that he is actively seeking reemployment: 'You always have a group of individuals who are found a job but continually lose it or leave it. You have to ensure that this type of person does not misuse the fund'. The union also runs an employment agency for members. Workers must furnish proof that they are members of the union to participate in the scheme. The union is in touch with numerous companies which inform SABS about vacancies, and it then selects applicants from its own ranks.

NAAWU argues that until the state assumes its proper responsibility in providing a sufficient number of jobs and an adequate social security system, the union will have to assist its unemployed members. In 1983 NAAWU introduced a retrenchment benefit scheme. Any union member in good standing is entitled to a payment of R25 per week up to a maximum of six weeks. In 1984 the union paid out R300 000 in retrenchment benefits.

A new assistance project was begun by NAAWU in 1985 at General Motors, where 461 workers were laid off in February. Almost 2 000 workers agreed to donate R2 per week to assist laid-off workers, making about R4 000 a week available to them.

CUSA too has set up a Steel and Engineering Fund to assist retrenched workers. Employed workers contribute 20c per month in dues to the fund. The union also operates a Solidarity Fund which draws on financial sources other than dues but is currently bankrupt. CUSA envisages unemployed workers in a particular area meeting to discuss projects they can undertake, while relying on CUSA to supply contacts with resource organisations. At present two such groups have been established — one a group of retrenched metal workers who are making burglar proofing, the other a car-washing group. The latter relied on CUSA for assistance in printing advertising leaflets.

Organising the unemployed has been on the SAAWU agenda since its 1980 annual conference, when it resolved to establish an unemployed workers' union. At present SAAWU boasts a blueprint modelled on typical union structure. A pilot study will be undertaken in the Eastern Cape, which SAAWU claims as its stronghold and where there is a high level of worker consciousness and rampant unemployment. But nothing concrete has been attempted. SAAWU explains that since 1980 the plan has been interrupted by government harassment, including the detention and trial of its leaders. Such measures had particularly severe effects since discussion of the unemployed workers' union was confined to national leadership level, and had not filtered down.

Other projects under discussion in SAAWU include literacy programmes, discussion groups on the plight of unemployed workers, and the Sithenga Sonke (We Buy Together) Communal Buying Scheme. The scheme organises families in particular areas to buy food in bulk and at cheaper prices.

Organising the unemployed[13]

CUSA, in cooperation with the IAS and other organisations including FOSATU and several independent unions, is planning a pragmatic programme to set up unemployed workers' committees (UWCs). Unions involved in the project[14] have committed themselves to establishing District Workers' Centres which will conduct projects through democratically elected committees of unemployed workers. Projects will be coordinated through regional or national offices. Unions involved have agreed to help the unemployed make representations on issues which directly affect them, and to provide counselling and educational and training assistance. UWCs may be organised around issues such as UIF, social security, buyers' and producers' cooperatives, education, skills development, recreation and community and trade union issues.

A common motivating theme is the need to build unity between employed and unemployed. It is proposed that the project incorporate both urban and rural regions and that finances be drawn from contributions by union and service organisations. CUSA and its partners in the UWC scheme have drawn up a draft list of demands which could be publicised by the UWCs.

UWCs are planned in the Springs township of KwaThema. In April a UWC was formed in Duduza, also on the East Rand. The four office bearers, unemployed workers, are changed every three months to ensure that it does not collapse should office bearers find a job and leave.

The group meets once a week in church halls, and at present consists of 150 workers. Members are recruited from queues outside the local labour office, and through personal contact. The group deals with common UIF, rent and pension problems. The Duduza Committee wrote a letter of complaint about difficulties in obtaining UIF to the Johannesburg and Pretoria Commissioners, and were informed that the matter has been referred to the divisional inspector of the Department of Manpower. Workers now go to apply for UIF in groups to defend themselves when they are given the wrong forms. They also want to open an advice office.

The committee has taken up the issue of unemployed workers evicted from their homes because they cannot pay the rent. A letter was sent to the Duduza township superintendent explaining their predicament and attempting to negotiate exemptions. Letters have also been written to furniture shops to negotiate delays for HP payments. The committee is considering a bulk-buying scheme and a home industry.

Lack of funds is a problem. The committee is considering soliciting contributions from unions and from overseas and community organisations. Its activists are well aware that education is not enough: the unemployed need material gain to survive. The project is still in its infancy and it is difficult to judge how successful it will be.

In the Brits industrial decentralisation zone, retrenched workers in an independent project have organised a small cooperative making bricks and clothes. It is made up of workers with no opportunity to find work as they are blacklisted at the labour bureau for union activities. The project is given some support by FOSATU. The venture is successful, but only involves 30 people.

Seeking an alternative economic strategy

There is growing awareness within both unions and community organisations that unemployment cannot be fought successfully at the point of production or by creating alternative projects for the unemployed. Both these strategies have limitations. Increasingly, demands put forward by labour organisations recognise that the economic crisis can only be alleviated through alternative economic policies; increasingly too, demands at the point of production are accompanied by wider political and economic demands.

For example, the May Day demands (drawn up by unions involved in the unity talks, those affiliated to the UDF and to AZACTU, and the Joint Union Education Project) dealt not only with factory floor issues, but called for the scrapping of racist legislation including influx control and the Group Areas Act, and the abolition of all discriminatory and intimidatory legislation and all existing parliamentary systems. There were also demands for adequate housing, transport, social security, a price freeze on basic commodities and no taxation for workers.

In general, unions and community organisations have attempted to explain the causes of the recession to their constituencies, and to demand a response both from capital and the state. In the first half of 1985, most union and community newspapers carried articles diagnosing the recession as unavoidable due to the nature of the capitalist system, with its processes of monopolisation and the introduction of new technology. But such articles simultaneously blame the government for a political system which spends billions of rand on the army and the police for the maintenance of apartheid, instead of creating jobs.

Increasingly systematic criticism of employers' policy and planning are reflected in the refusal of unions to accept arguments by management that retrenchments caused by mergers and closures are a result only of the recession. For example in NAAWU's newspaper the Ford-AMCAR merger into SAMCOR was explained in terms not only of economic necessity, but of 'poor management. Unions have rejected the idea that a company based in the Eastern Cape cannot be successful'.[15] Workers are demanding access to the company's sales forecasting.

Union demands also aim at forcing managements to consider alternative employment practices in a systematic response to unemployment. An instance is the demand to save as many jobs as possible by banning overtime and reducing working time from 45 to 40 hours a week. NAAWU's national policy is to cut the maximum working week down from 46 to 40 hours. The union argues that if the numbers of hours are reduced then more people will be employed. An additional 148 491 jobs would be created, cutting unemployment by 7,5%. It would also give workers more leisure time, an item needed by workers who spend up to four hours commuting to work each day. This demand has already been met in one instance — NAAWU and Willard Batteries in Port Elizabeth agreed that shift workers should go onto a 40-hour week.[16]

By far the most common demand is still for a 'living wage' and a wage increase equal to the consumer price index (CPI). This reflects workers' increasing difficulty in meeting food, rent and transport costs as these have escalated over the last two years. Unions have now begun to calculate a national minimum wage which is linked to inflation and the CPI. Unions also recognise that workers living in townships experience costs which are not calculated in the CPI, such as taxes on animals and fuel costs.

In the absence of a national social security scheme, and with the inadequacies of the UIF, managements face demands to assist in the provision of security to workers. For example, NAAWU has begun to demand that companies lay off workers for a period so that they can get access to UIF before actual retrenchment takes place. A similar demand is that instead of working a short week, workers be allowed to combine 'down' days into a longer layoff period. This would enable workers to have access to UIF payments after the initial seven-day period. Such proposals in turn are linked to the demand for control over investment of pensions, and that on retrenchment workers should be paid both the employer's and their own pension contribution, plus a competitive rate of interest.

The present recession and its severe consequences in terms of retrenchment and unemployment should increasingly press unions to develop stronger general strategies against management, and to evolve their own proposals for alternative economic systems. If a vision of economic alternatives is joined to organised labour's demands for democratic rights and worker control, the South African working class will become increasingly radicalised.

Notes

Information for this article was obtained from interviews with the following: CUSA, CWIU, CCAWUSA, FCWU, MAWU, NAAWU, PWAWU, SABS, SAAWU, T&G, the Industrial Aid Society, Johannesburg labour lawyer Halton Cheadle, Witwatersrand University industrial sociologist Eddie Webster, and an independent group which analyses alternative economic strategies. Their assistance is greatly appreciated.

1 International Labour Organisation, *Collective Bargaining: a response to the recession in industrialised market economy countries* (Geneva, 1984).
2 C Thompson, 'Retrenchments and the law', address to Institute of Industrial Relations seminar on retrenchment, Johannesburg, 26 April 1985.
3 Personal communication with NAAWU official Taffy Adler.
4 J Keenan, 'Free markets, ideology and control: the South African case' in J Clammer, ed., *Beyond the New Economic Anthropology* (London, forthcoming).
5 J Keenan, *The Pilanesberg Game Reserve: report on the socio-economic effects of the Pilanesberg Game Reserve on the surrounding population and the attitudes of the surrounding population to the Game Reserve*, Vol II, Department of Social Anthropology, University of the Witwatersrand, Johannesburg, 1985.
6 H Cheadle, 'The law and retrenchment', *South African Labour Bulletin*, 10(1), August-September 1984; Thompson, 'Retrenchments and the law'.
7 D Douglas, 'Retrenchments and accounting disclosure to unions', address to the Institute of Industrial Relations seminar on retrenchment, Johannesburg, 26 April 1985.
8 Thompson, 'Retrenchments and the law'.
9 Thompson, 'Retrenchments and the law'.
10 Personal communication with NAAWU official Taffy Adler.

11 Organisations endorsing the charter include the Industrial Aid Society, Black Sash, the Industrial Aid Centre, the East Rand Community Advice Bureau, the SA Institute of Race Relations, AFCWU, ABWU, CTMWA, CUSA, FCWU, GWU, MGWU, OVGWU, PWAWU, SABMWU, SASDU and the Teammates Workers Union.

12 G Jaffee, 'Unemployment and social security: the UIF investigation', *Work In Progress*, 33, August 1984; and G Jaffee, 'The retrenchment process', *South African Review 2* (Johannesburg, 1984); and 'UIF memorandum to the Minister of Manpower', *South African Labour Bulletin*, 10(1), August-September 1984.

13 Groups organising unemployed workers exist in Cape Town and Durban, but no further information could be obtained.

14 Unions and federations involved in the project include: AZACTU, CCAWUSA, GAWU, SASDU, UMMAWSA, BCAWU, FBWU, NAAWU, NUM, NUTW, National Union of Wine, Spirits and Allied Workers, PWAWU, SACWU, SALDWU, SEAWU, SFAWU, T&G, TAWU, TWU, and Vukani (a union of security guards). Service organisations include the Industrial Aid Society, Urban Training Project, Learn and Teach, and the English Language Project.

15 *NAAWU News*, 1(1), February 1985.

16 *NAAWU News*, 1(1), April 1985.

Organisation on the Mines:
The NUM Phenomenon

Jean Leger and Phillip van Niekerk

On 16 September 1984 — the date set by the National Union of Mineworkers for the country's first ever legal strike by black miners — more than 40 000 miners refused to work. Spreading to non-unionised mines during the rest of the week, the action was the culmination of two years of incredible union growth in an industry unpenetrated since 1946 and never systematically organised. During the next year the upsurge of union activity and industrial action continued. According to Andrew Levy, an industrial relations consultant, about 375 000 working days were lost on the mines through strikes in the first six months of 1985 alone.

Despite the fact that some 13 unions are known to be organising on the mines, and that the majority of black miners are still not unionised, most of the strikes in 1984 and 1985 involved NUM and few involved other unions. Before NUM made impressive gains, the conventional wisdom was that the industry, with its closed compounds and migrant labour system, would be virtually impossible to organise. To understand what has taken place it is necessary to look at the changing structure of the industry, the changing social environment and the particular nature of NUM. This review is mainly concerned with the gold mines, by far the most important sector both in the mining industry and in NUM's development to date.

Gold: the economic base

Gold is the foundation of the South African economy. Although only 15% of the local gross domestic product is directly and indirectly accounted for by gold mining, more than half of foreign exchange is earned by gold sales. After the creation of a free market in gold in 1968, the price of the metal took off in 1972. For decades before this, working costs had been artificially constrained by the fixed price of gold despite inflationary pressures.

Black miners bore the brunt of this pressure. Their wages declined in real terms from before the Boer War until 1972. By that year black wages on the mines were equivalent to only 30% of those in manufacturing. This was a decade after Harry Oppenheimer had announced the first in a series of 'new deals' and promised better pay and conditions of employment for black workers. In 1971 their average cash wage was R18 per month; the minimum underground wage was R11, while the minimum surface wage was less than R10.

The lift-off point for black wages on the mines was 1972. By 1984 the average wage had increased to R350 and the minimum underground wage to R166, a nominal increase of 1 900% and a 300% increase in real terms.

Three main factors underlay this process: the freeing of the gold price; a shortage of mine labour precipitated by the withdrawal of Malawian workers and the independence of Mozambique; and attempts to increase productivity starting in the early 1960s and gaining momentum in the 1970s.

Freeing of the gold price

During the 1970s the gold price soared from $35 to a peak of more than $700 an ounce in 1980. Whereas in 1971 the mining houses received an average of R28,64 for every ounce mined, in 1984 they received an average of R525, an increase of 1 830%. This provided the material means for wage increases. Super profits for gold resulted in the reopening of marginal mines and in massive development projects. The labour force rose from 412 000 in 1972 to 510 000 in 1984, an increase of 24% despite improvements in productivity.

Labour shortages

Prior to 1972 gold mines relied on foreign labour recruited from outside South Africa. Almost 80% was from Malawi, Mozambique, Lesotho, Botswana and Swaziland. Instead of paying wages competitive with the developing manufacturing industry in South Africa, the mining houses chose to recruit labour from those areas in Southern Africa where there was no competition for manpower.

In 1972 there were 109 000 Malawian workers on South African gold mines, the single largest ethnic component, more numerous than the total recruited from South Africa. Using the pretext of an air crash in 1973 in which 68 Malawian workers died, President Hastings Banda refused further recruiting of all Malawian nationals. Uncertainty arising from their isolation which was fuelled by violent conflicts on the mines in the mid-1970s, led thousands of Malawians to demand repatriation. Their numbers plunged to 494 by 1976.

The emergence of a socialist government in Mozambique in 1974 deeply disturbed mining bosses. The Chamber of Mines and the state feared the importation of an ideology that might lead to the organisation and politicisation of the workforce. Recruitment was drastically curtailed from 91 000 Mozambicans in 1975 to 35 000 in 1978.

The shortage of labour, experienced most acutely in the middle 1970s, led to an inevitable upward trend in wages designed to attract more local workers. However, attempts to recruit workers from the urban areas proved dismally unsuccessful. There was a major shift to recruiting labour from the bantustans. By 1983 almost 60% of the workforce came from black areas within South Africa, chiefly from the 'homelands'. This represented an increase of 160 000 workers.

Workers from the bantustans were within the inner ring of the South African political system and not subject to the volatility of African states on the periphery. Increased recruitment from the bantustans went hand in hand with a tightening of influx control and the rigid application of labour zoning. In 1968 Proclamation 74 had already classified workers from certain districts as miners for all time, preventing them from seeking work in any other industries. The application of this measure appears to have been stepped up after 1974. Meanwhile massive resettlement of black communities and the mechanisation of agriculture during the 1960s and 1970s greatly expanded the captive labour pool within the bantustans.

Stabilisation and productivity

The mining houses have long held the view that productivity on the gold mines is low. From the earliest statements of Harry Oppenheimer it is clear that wages were linked to productivity improvements. In an Anglo statement in June 1961 where Oppenheimer hinted at increases in mine wages, he had this to say:

> Anglo American will seek for ways of giving adequate recognition to higher skills and improving efficiencies among our native workers . . . . If we are to achieve higher levels of productivity greater attention must be given to the abilities, personal needs, inclinations and aspirations of individual Africans.

To understand restraints on the productivity of gold mines one has to understand the physical nature of the work. Underground work is extremely difficult to supervise. A typical gold mine has 250 working rockfaces, each 40 metres long. If all these workplaces were strung end to end, they would form a line ten kilometres in length. For management, a production line this long in a well-lit factory would be difficult enough to supervise. But in a mine where the working faces are scattered over many square kilometres, direct supervision is almost impossible.

Work at each rockface is dangerous, noisy and hot. While coercion is employed at times to ensure production in the face of these hazardous conditions, management must gain the cooperation of workers to obtain optimal production. Further, greater productivity requires a more skilled and experienced workforce — which in turn requires stability and relative comfort. The freeing of the gold price provided the material means for the application of the 'Anglo American philosophy', that is, the strategy for stabilisation/ productivity/wage increases indicated by Oppenheimer 15 years before.

A cornerstone of the strategy of stabilisation was the introduction of valid reengagement certificates and early return bonuses. For those migrant workers who did not return for their next contract before the deadline, it became increasingly difficult to obtain mine employment. The effect of this strategy is evident: the average length of service rose steadily from three years in the 1970s to over six years in 1981, and is still increasing.

The changing social climate

After the 1973 Durban mass strikes a new era of unionisation of
black workers dawned. Liberalisation of labour laws followed the
Wiehahn Commission in the late 1970s. By the early 1980s black
trade unions were largely accepted as an integral feature of the
South African economy, but this process had bypassed the mines.

The unnatural situation of mine compounds away from major
urban areas and tight compound security had made union organisation a daunting task in the past, and were the primary reasons why
unionisation on the mines lagged behind other sectors.

Despite improvements in wages and living conditions, the 1970s
were characterised by unprecedented worker resistance and unrest,
culminating in the 1982 wild-cat strikes. Some managements felt
that the way to contain this resistance and to further the process of
stabilisation was to set up better channels of communication with
workers. In the subsequent debate some mining houses began to
argue that this would be best achieved by representative trade
unions.

Limited unionisation was accepted in the sixth report of the
Wiehahn Commission tabled in 1981. But before this could be
implemented, the July 1982 strikes erupted, highlighting to the emerging union movement the existence of a large and extremely important
body of unorganised workers. Into this breach stepped CUSA, which
passed a resolution at its 1982 congress to form NUM.

The 1982 strikes also appear to have been a watershed in the
thinking of the Chamber of Mines, ending with the victory of the
'Anglo American philosophy'. Soon afterwards the Chamber signed
recruiting agreements with several unions, including NUM, allowing them access to mine compounds. Later the Chamber dropped
the demand that any union had to be registered to be recognised
and by June 1983 NUM had achieved its first recognition agreement.

The development of NUM

The specific nature of NUM and the factors which have made it
such a dynamic force need to be examined.

Solid infrastructure

The formation of NUM under CUSA in August 1982 provided the union with an advantage from its inception. CUSA, as an established federation, was able to divert manpower and financial resources into getting NUM off the ground with a number of full-time organisers in the field.

Early organising strategies

Instead of dissipating its forces, NUM concentrated on the large mines of the Free State gold fields. These were mainly owned by Anglo American, which had adopted a more tolerant approach compared to some other mining houses, and the workforce was largely Sotho and Xhosa.

Popular militancy against Leabua Jonathan's regime had spawned proto-organisational structures closely linked to the Basotho People's Congress. In 1975 the Lesotho government proposed legislation whereby 60% of Sotho migrant workers' wages would be paid directly to the Lesotho National Bank, sparking off much of the industrial action of the mid-1970s. While NUM had no party political affiliations, these informal structures were harnessed for union purposes.

Many of NUM's early leaders were young, educated men from the Eastern Cape and Lesotho, frustrated by the lack of job opportunities at home and prevented by influx control from moving into other industries. Politically, many of the workers from the Eastern Cape had been schooled in the 1976 education protests and subsequent community upheavals. They were ready to take up the cudgels.

The legal approach

NUM's initial battles were on legal terrain. The Hlobane inquiry, the 1984 legal strike and the subsequent action against the police (for alleged assaults at Western Holdings during the strike) were the most dramatic instances. By challenging the might of the mining houses and winning legal victories before a substantial membership had been created, the union shielded itself in the period of greatest vulnerability. This strategy was all the more effective because it coincided with the Chamber's vision of 'responsible unionism' and won it a good press among the public at large. At the same time the strategy publicised the union among black miners who flocked to an organisation that was seen to be effectively representing their interests.

Fighting in the interests of miners

Just as important as the organising strategies were the issues which NUM fought. The union won support from miners by tackling the issues closest to their concerns. This was not fortuitous, but arose from the democratic structures of the union. Initiatives and strategies evolved at individual mines. Head office, in a back-up role, was able to provide expertise and resources. Because of co-ordination and the exchange of information at a rate which outstripped the informal 'bush telegraph' of the past, these struggles spread rapidly to other mines. The most important issues taken up by NUM have included:

Arbitrary dismissals: While largely unpublicised, the union's day-to-day siege of management's power to dismiss individual workers over trivial issues has been crucial to miners' security and confidence in organisation.

Wages: Traditionally the major cause of strikes on the mines. NUM articulated worker demands as the first black union to bargain wages at industry level.

Exploitation by monopolistic businesses on the mines: Few issues have contributed so greatly to the success of NUM's recruiting campaigns as the boycotts of overpriced concession stores, taxis and mine liquor outlets. The importance of these battles, many of which have been won, is that workers in different mines in far-flung parts of the country have been alerted to the immediate gains of organisation. Starting at Hartebeesfontein mine in the Western Transvaal shortly after the 1984 strikes, the boycott strategy spread like wildfire to other areas.

Safety: The publicity surrounding the death of 68 miners in the Hlobane disaster, and the West Driefontein case, where workers refused to work in an area they considered unsafe, alerted workers to the advantages of unionisation. NUM emerged from these confrontations as the first mine safety watchdog acting in the interests of black miners.

Dignity of workers: Assaults by white miners, the piccanin system (which requires 'miners' assistants' to accompany white miners, carrying refreshments, tools and personal effects) and many other established racially discriminatory practices went virtually unchallenged before the emergence of NUM.

Job advancement: At its January 1985 congress, NUM made job reservation a priority issue in the year ahead. Here again, an imposition which had been legally entrenched since the early years of gold mining was for the first time being challenged systematically by workers.

Assessing NUM

Despite the astounding progress NUM has made, it is facing the most powerful and securely established grouping of employers on the continent of Africa. Fundamental restructuring of practices in the industry has hardly begun. Wage structures remain little altered by the bargaining process, the migrant labour issue has not even been tackled, and disputes are still frequently settled by police force and mass dismissals.

Cash wages of the lowest paid black miners — surface workers grade 1 — stand at R160 per month after the 1985 increases, still less than half the Bureau of Market Research's minimum living level. Only limited concessions were gained at the last minute during the 1984 negotiations though more substantial gains at three mining houses followed the 1985 wage negotiations. Anglo American, JCI and Rand Mines broke ranks with the other three mining houses and in a last minute settlement granted increases of up to 3% above the already-implemented July increases. While the July wage increases were not significantly above the inflation rate, they could have been substantially less had NUM not engaged in tough bargaining.

The 1985 showdown resulted in cracks within the Chamber widening under the pressure of the NUM's threatened national strike in the industry. While the Chamber's final offer showed up the differing philosophies of the Goldfields-Gencor and Anglo American-Rand Mines groupings, it posed fundamental problems for the union. The strike that eventually occurred took place on

NUM's weakest terrain — the Goldfields and Gencor mines. More than 80% of the union's membership are at Anglo American mines and thus the Chamber's split offer neutralised the union's major power base. In the future the union's priority should be to establish itself more firmly at those mining houses which are more hostile to unionisation.

The brutal show of force by Goldfields and Gencor in the 1985 strike exposed the extent to which industrial relations have not progressed on the mines. Since the union's first major industrial action in 1984 strikes have been frequently put down by strong-arm tactics — police teargassing and firing rubber bullets at workers and workers being forced to go underground at gunpoint. Goldfields is reported to have patented their own rubber bullet and during the 1985 strike the affected mines resembled the townships during severe protest with armoured cars patrolling the mine properties. During the 1984 strike ten workers were killed at non-unionised mines and more have been killed subsequently. Workers have brought a major legal suit — amounting to several million rand — against the police for alleged assaults during the 1984 strike but this has not proved a restraint on mine management's security-conscious approach to labour relations.

Apart from brute force the ability of mine management to fire workers has been a massive drawback to unionisation. The mass dismissals of 17 000 workers at Vaal Reefs and Hartebeesfontein were concrete evidence that management was prepared to use extremely tough measures to quell workers militancy. Selective reemployment after mass dismissals has cost NUM its most active and able leadership at some mines. For example at East Driefontein the union's recognition has lapsed since the strike and dismissal of the local leadership in February 1985. Up till now there has been little other than international opprobrium to restrain the virtually untrammelled power that management has to fire thousands of workers and replace them from the labour pools in the rural areas. The one significant outcome of the 1985 strike is the test case the union has brought to the Industrial Court challenging the right of an employer to dismiss workers during a legal strike after the union has painstakingly followed all the provisions of the Labour Relations Act.

NUM also faces internal hurdles. The exponential growth of the union — which now includes coal, diamonds and other mining sectors — has allowed little time to consolidate, despite attempts by NUM to firm its base. The formation of breakaway unions are a distinct possibility, as has occurred in other large independent unions. A threat to the unity of mine workers is posed by the decisions of a number of other unions to organise in competition with NUM, although the new federation with its policy of 'one union, one industry' should restrict this. Futhermore, some mine managements have displayed an open door policy to rival unions and encouraged splinter unions.

In the three years of its existence NUM has matured rapidly. In contrast to the farcical display of 1983 where the union accepted increases which the Chamber would have paid anyway, the 1985 negotiations revealed a sophisticated bargaining strategy. The union has waged a war of nerves with the Chamber, painfully drawing out the very real threat of strike action, but holding it as a last card. By keeping the strike within official channels, the union has used shrewd bargaining whilst keeping legal resources open.

For the future, new strategies of industrial action are being tested. The underground work stoppages at Vaal Reefs in April 1985, where workers demanded to be hoisted to surface after working for only four hours, overcame the vulnerability of workers in the compounds to police action. As organisation grows stronger, innovative forms of action such as this — which require stewards in every workplace — are likely to emerge. But in many cases the union does not yet have the necessary strength.

After almost three years of purely industrial activity, NUM began to adopt an increasingly high profile on political issues from mid-1985. The union's warning of national industrial action if state president PW Botha carried out his threat to repatriate foreign migrant workers was an important new development. The decision to boycott white shops in protest against the state of emergency showed NUM moving closer to community organisations. The political involvement of the union, which represents the largest and most strategic body of workers in South Africa, could have a major bearing on the future political direction of the country.

The full importance of a representative miners' union is yet to be felt in the economic and political life of the country. While NUM is firmly on the road, it is still a long haul from winning living wages, the right to live with family and the right to industrial action without the fear of mass dismissal and police action — rights taken for granted in other societies.

Trade Union Initiatives in Health and Safety

Jean Leger, Judy Maller and Jonny Myers*

An overview

In 1984-85 trade unions have been consolidating health and safety activities on the shop floor and shop stewards have won significant rights through negotiation with managements. It has also been a period of new initiatives. Of particular importance was the entry of mineworkers into the arena through the National Union of Mineworkers (NUM). Several NUM projects conducted throughout 1984 culminated in a highly successful health and safety conference for shaft stewards in 1985.

Earlier trade union initiatives resulted in a number of compensation claims for occupational diseases among mineworkers and workers in other industries. For the first time organisations of black workers are systematically making use of what benefits exist in terms of South African compensation law. The last section of this review will focus on recent events in the complex, confusing and shifting world of workmen's compensation.

Meanwhile, the Department of Manpower, the state compensation authorities and management have responded to labour's thrusts by way of conservative interpretations of the new health and safety legislation and by tightening up the compensation process.

What is certain is that things will never be the same again when it comes to health and safety at work. Many thousands of workers

---

* This contribution was coordinated by Jonny Myers.

have begun to take up their complaints and are defending their health rights with increasing effectiveness through trade unions that are becoming more and more concerned with and competent in health and safety issues.

Health and safety legislation

The Machinery and Occupational Diseases Safety Act (MOSA) was finally promulgated in October 1984. The Act provides a new structure to deal with health and safety in the workplace. Though it can be seen as a response by the state and management to the growth of trade unions and their increasing involvement in these issues, the Act is not entirely disadvantageous to workers. Some of its provisions, and particularly its regulations, confer important rights — most notably to information on work processes and substances used.[1] However, there are important rights that are not to be found in this Act. Some of these rights have already been won by workers at plant level, illustrating the necessity for workers to go beyond the meagre provisions of MOSA.

Some unions (eg FCWU) began organising health and safety training courses for their shop stewards or (eg GWU) for worker-elected safety representatives.

Employers began to appoint safety representatives and safety committees at work, mostly without the participation of workers. Employers have also tended to use the committees envisaged by the Act to bypass the negotiation process between themselves and shop stewards' committees.

Unions have begun to challenge these practices using different strategies. Some (NUTW, PWAWU and FCWU) have boycotted the proposed structures, which are seen as liaison-type committees, while others (GWU and MAWU) have demanded representation in the new structures to varying degrees. This has led to a spate of negotiations on health and safety agreements, protocols for safety representative training and protocols for medical screening at work. In summary, the process of organising a health and safety infrastructure in industry, as required by the new law, has got off to a slow and patchy start.

Union-commissioned surveys

In 1984-85 a number of unions were involved in surveys into accidents, noise-induced hearing loss, and heat stress on the mines (NUM); silicosis in foundries, lead poisoning among transport workers, asbestosis among asbestos-cement and transport workers (GWU); occupational asthma among grain workers (FCWU); and byssinosis and hazards of dyestuffs in textile factories (NUTW).

The advantages of unions becoming involved in activities of this nature are many. Apart from obvious preventive health benefits to members, sick workers are referred for medical attention, those with compensable conditions have claims submitted, organisation at the plant surveyed is enhanced, hazards at work are attended to, shop stewards learn new organisational and technical skills by participating in survey work, and new scientific knowledge about the hazards of work is produced.

Mineworkers organise around health and safety

One of the most significant events in the period under review was the first NUM national safety conference in March 1985, which was attended by 350 shaft stewards from all over the country. The full range of health problems and their organisational implications in the mining industry were vigorously discussed by union members. Up to now mine managements have had complete control over health and safety practices and research. At the same time the mining industry has an appalling health and safety record, being one of the major generators of death and disease in South African industry.

Mineworkers have since confronted management with demands for recognition of safety stewards and committees, the right to negotiate health and safety, improvements in working conditions, and better protective clothing. To date the Chamber of Mines has refused to negotiate over health and safety outside of an unrepresentative and bureaucratic forum — the Prevention of Accidents Committee. Now it would appear that individual mine managers, faced by militant workers, have shown a willingness to negotiate improvements. This represents an important organisational gain by a major union in an industry which has long been without any worker representation. It holds out exciting new possibilities for the prevention of accidents and illness in what is perhaps the worst workplace of all, with fair compensation and the provision of social security for the victims. NUM has also launched a concerted campaign against the Mines and Works Act. The union argues that the Act is meant to ensure safety, and that in reality management and white miners have used the law to sanction dangerous practices and managerial coercion.

BAMCWU launched a national anti-asbestos campaign in October 1984 as a result of their experiences at the Penge asbestos mine in the Transvaal, where there is a high rate of asbestos-related diseases among mineworkers and residents in the nearby community.

Workers' health and safety rights

Maternity rights

A number of trade unions won maternity rights during the period under review. South African law forbids the employment of women four weeks before and eight weeks after confinement. It does not protect against dismissal for pregnancy or guarantee reinstatement after the birth. The only financial provision made is through the Unemployment Insurance Act. If they are eligible, women may draw unemployment insurance (45% of wages) for the 12-week period specified by law. Women workers are extremely vulnerable, particularly unskilled workers, who are liable to lose their jobs once their pregnancy is obvious.

CCAWUSA has won important maternity rights at a number of chain stores, but their latest agreement with Metro Cash and Carry sets new precedents in South Africa.[2] The unusual features of this agreement are:

• the right to 12 months' maternity leave, the timing of which may be decided by the woman involved;
• the right to a wage, calculated to ensure that the woman receives an amount which, together with unemployment insurance benefits, equals her wage at the time her leave started;
• the right to attend ante-natal and post-natal clinics without loss of pay;

• the right to protection from hazards to pregnancy, including dangerous chemicals, physical work, continuous standing, carrying heavy objects, night work and overtime.

It is also significant that the company has accepted that male workers can take three days' paid paternity leave during or after the birth of a child.

Shift work rights

Shift work is a widely used system in South African industry, and can have ill effects for workers in the form of disruptions of normal bodily functions. Judging it impossible at present to argue for its abolition, unions have argued for improvements in the conditions of shift work, such as restroom and canteen facilities, as well as an allowance.

PWAWU has negotiated shift allowances in some companies. For instance, in one company this allowance amounted to 10% for night shift and 5% for the 'twilight' shift in 1984. In another company the allowances were 25% and 15% respectively, in 1985.

The right to union health and safety training

Some unions have managed to negotiate time off for training that meets management's requirements and goes further than MOSA. Such training has included teaching safety representatives how to monitor working conditions, how to recognise hazards, how to measure them, and how to decide on ways of improving work conditions. This has gone hand in hand with union insistence on worker election of the safety representatives who receive the training. Training courses for union safety representatives are now available in most large urban centres.

The right to information

One of the major stumbling blocks for unions challenging bad working conditions is their lack of access to information about work hazards and their prevention at work.

T&G members at Freight Services who were required to repair transport containers complained about health hazards connected with their working materials. The union needed exact information about these substances in order to make suggestions about removing the hazards. Workers taking labels with information about the materials and samples for laboratory analysis to the union were fired for theft. After a threatened Industrial Court action by the union the workers were reinstated. As a result the union has negotiated the right of access to information about materials at work on request.

Access by workers to their medical records

Important strides were made in ensuring the right of access by workers to results of medical tests and examinations performed on them by company doctors, and the right of access by doctors appointed by workers to these medical records for purposes of providing a second opinion.

In the asbestos-cement and transport industries initial refusals by company doctors to allow access by union-appointed (GWU) doctors to medical records held by them and paid for by the company gave way to reluctant cooperation. This followed union threats to take legal steps against company doctors and managements for violations of the law and professional ethics in preventing workers obtaining a second opinion.

Continuing struggles over basic conditions of employment

It should not be forgotten that many workers lack even the most basic protective devices and safe conditions in the workplace. This is well illustrated by struggles waged by workers in the steel and engineering and precast concrete industries, and by town council sewage and garbage workers (GWU). After protracted struggles these groups of workers were provided for the first time with overalls, safety boots, elementary washing and toilet facilities and other basic conditions laid down by the law.

Responses to serious or fatal accidents

Inquiries in factories (under MOSA)

Union representation at inquiries into deaths or serious injury has been increasing.[3] This participation has highlighted a number of problems:

• some workers present at the event have been induced by management to sign statements, later used against them, before they have had time to consult with their unions or lawyers;

• the factory inspectorate usually holds an initial investigation into an accident which is followed by an inquiry. Under the Machinery and Occupational Safety Act the decision to hold a formal inquiry is left to the discretion of the inspector. What often happens is that 'informal' inquiries are held instead directly after an accident. The injured workers are often not present because they are being treated. In addition, their unions or fellow workers have usually not had time to arrange representation.

Worker representation at inquiries is a significant advance, as it challenges dangerous working conditions. In the last year, a number of independent unions sought technical and legal representation at inquiries (SACWU, CWIU and GWU).

Last year an accident inquiry was contested and won by T&G following the death of an industrial tractor driver who was crushed by a large container. An informal inquiry was held immediately after the accident, but the findings were never made public. An on-site investigation of the accident was conducted by experts brought in by the union. Faults were detected in the tractor's brakes, gears and throttle. These findings were submitted at the inquest which found management negligent in not providing safe working conditions for the driver. A claim has subsequently been submitted for increased compensation for his family.

On the one hand union representation carries with it the potential for putting pressure on management to improve conditions of work. If negligence is proved at an inquiry, it is also possible to claim increased compensation. On the other hand inquests are held for only a handful of the very large number of serious and fatal accidents, and to date very few have led to conclusive findings in favour of workers. There is a tendency to become bogged down in a lengthy bureaucratic process which may be frustrating and disappointing for workers. There may thus be organisationally negative implications in tackling employer negligence exclusively in this way.

Inquiries in mines (under the Mines and Works Act)

Unions have been defending individual workers at mine accident inquiries. For example, the Hlobane explosion inquiry was the first time that deceased black miners were legally represented since the 1960 Coalbrook disaster.

In the 25 years since Coalbrook the death rate has not significantly improved. Between 800 and 900 miners die each year, making safety a crucial issue. Yet deaths are just the tip of the iceberg. Fatality statistics cannot convey the injuries, ills and fears that plague every worker.

In September 1983 a methane explosion at the Hlobane Colliery killed 68 workers. NUM gathered an impressive array of international mine experts to represent deceased miners at the inquest. The presiding magistrate found one of the deceased, miner TJ Bezuidenhout, immediately responsible for the blast. He was blamed for failing to detect a build-up of explosive methane gas. Although this finding was limited, the inquiry gave the lie to management's claims of safety consciousness. For example:

• evidence led by the mine inspectorate showed many safety regulations had been ignored at the mine;
• grave doubts were cast on the Chamber's safety system, the so-called 'International Mine Safety Rating System'. Hlobane had been rated a 'four star' mine — five stars being the highest rating;
• evidence of the overseas experts showed how local safety precautions and regulations have lagged behind international standards.

Now NUM and latterly BAMCWU regularly represent workers at fatal accident inquiries. Representation at inquiries is important for a number of reasons:

• deceased or fellow workers may unjustly be blamed for an accident;
• persons found responsible for an accident may be dismissed and have criminal charges laid against them;
• victims, or their families if they are deceased, can claim increased compensation if management is found negligent. In the case of Hlobane, NUM has lodged a claim of R6-million for 42 families and six injured workers;
• safety regulations are derived from the findings of inquiries. The evidence of NUM's experts at Hlobane has resulted in draft regula-

tions for methanometers to improve methane detection and self-contained air rescuers to assist workers in escaping the suffocating fumes of an explosion.

Despite the gains to be made, inquiries are of limited benefit because:

• the right of workers to lead evidence is restricted by the Mines and Works Act to those who 'may be held responsible' for the accident;
• inquiries are only concerned with the particular circumstances of an accident, not with any of the other hazards workers may continue to face;
• it may take months before the findings are released;
• any recommendations for safer mining are made in confidence to management. Workers are not consulted or informed.

Special inquiries

The Mines and Works Act allows unions to request the government mining engineer to hold special inquiries into hazardous conditions. Although he must investigate the problem, whether or not to hold an open inquiry is left to his discretion.

Eleven workers were killed and over a hundred hospitalised by three rockbursts in the Carletonville area in December 1983. At the accident inquiries no one was found responsible for the deaths. Mining continued as before although rockbursts were likely to recur and kill more workers. The lack of findings was tantamount to approving techniques and rock support methods which had been shown to be inadequate by these multiple death accidents.

NUM demanded a special inquiry at West Driefontein, one of the affected mines. The government mining engineer refused after examining the inquiry records and 'detailed reports' he had requested from the mine management and the chief mine inspector of the area. NUM requested copies of the reports, but was informed that: 'The reports referred to . . . are official documents and therefore cannot be furnished to you'. The withholding of information relating to safety frequently proves a hindrance to union attempts to improve conditions.

Going beyond inquiries

Worker responses to fatal accidents have gone beyond representation at inquiries. After Hlobane 30 000 workers nation-wide laid
down tools for half-an-hour in mourning and protest. Miners stopped work twice when two workers were killed at Rietspruit Colliery
in January 1984.

In February 1985 a third worker was crushed to death at
Rietspruit, this time by a front-end loader. Workers held a two-
hour memorial service during working hours despite an earlier
management refusal. Four shaft stewards were suspended and the
rest of the workforce struck in sympathy. Management used union
bashing tactics to break the strike: shaft stewards were arrested and
workers tear-gassed. Most workers eventually returned to work
after a management ultimatum and a show of force by mine security
guards. About 90 workers remained out and were summarily
dismissed.

Safety and job reservation on the mines

Mine safety and racial discrimination underground are interwoven.
Safety has been the pretext for job reservation in the mines since the
1890s. The Mines and Works Act enshrines job reservation. At Vaal
Reefs black miners for the first time challenged aspects of the Mines
and Works Act during April 1985. Work stoppages and a 'work to
rule' according to the regulations under the Act culminated in the
dismissal of 14 400 workers. Two issues lie at the heart of what is
developing into a multi-faceted campaign by NUM:

1. The Act reserves tasks essential to safe production for white
   miners, and some coloured miners in the Cape. They receive extensive training and high wages. NUM members claim that in
   practice black miners do these tasks without proper training or
   decent wages.
2. Management pays white miners incentive bonuses to maximise
   production. Nearly half of white miners' wages are made up of
   bonuses. But production depends wholly on the work performed by black miners, with all the hazards this entails. As supervisors, white miners are not exposed to the hazards black
   workers risk. When conditions are dangerous the Act allows

workers to withdraw only with the permission of the white miner in charge. White miners are often reluctant to grant permission because delays reduce their bonuses. In a nutshell, black miners take the risks while white miners earn their bonuses and management maximises production.

While on the face of it a black/white political question is at stake, mineworkers are tackling fundamentals of safety and of management control. Their struggle for safer work inevitably informs and confronts broader issues.

The struggle for compensation for occupational diseases

Compensation for occupational diseases is governed by the Occupational Diseases in Mines and Works Act for mineworkers and by the Workman's Compensation Act for all other workers except domestic workers.

The workman's compensation commissioner tightens up

In December 1984 doctors outside the state bodies and the Johannesburg area lost their access to a joint medical panel for diagnosing occupational disease prior to certification by the workman's compensation commissioner.[4]

Prior to 1984 the commissioner regarded the Medical Bureau for Occupational Diseases as the only authority for decisions on medical diagnosis prior to compensation. This body has an historical record of racial discrimination: it was set up early in this century for the medical examination of white miners and to this day will not allow its facilities to be used to examine black miners.

In 1984 a fairer system was instituted whereby doctors were able to obtain a diagnosis from a joint panel consisting of doctors from the Medical Bureau for Occupational Diseases and the National Centre for Occupational Health, on the basis of medical reports and chest X-rays alone.

In the same year there was in fact a sharp increase in the number of compensation claims for occupational diseases submitted via this route to the workman's compensation commissioner. This load had sprung principally from trade union activity in the health and safety field.

NUTW has screened 5 000 of its members for byssinosis, a chronic lung disease caused by exposure to cotton dust.[5] The disease was included in the schedule of compensable diseases under the Workman's Compensation Act in 1973, but between then and 1983 only one claim was ever submitted. As a result of union screening, 69 claims were submitted for compensation. Thus far only nine have been successful. The remaining cases are either undecided or awaiting appeal against the commissioner's negative decision. The first contested claim took two years to resolve through the appeal process. When the SA cotton textile industry is considered as a whole, a further 600 cases of disabling byssinosis may be anticipated in the future.

As a result of survey work and medical checks on around 2 000 exposed GWU members in the transport[6] and asbestos-cement industries, about 70 claims for asbestosis and mesothelioma were initiated during 1984. Fifteen cases of another scheduled disease, silicosis, were found in 130 foundry workers in a study commissioned by GWU in 1984. Although the risk of silicosis for foundry and other workers outside the mines has long been known, this disease has not been studied in other industries and mines in South Africa until very recently.

When the panel system was changed in December 1984, a considerable number of the above claims that were being processed were returned for resubmission directly to the commissioner. The situation then reverted to the original one. The workman's compensation commissioner now defers only to the Medical Bureau for Occupational Diseases for decisions on diagnosis in considering compensation claims. Patients within the Johannesburg area still have the possibility of being examined physically at the National Centre for Occupational Health clinic, thereby expediting their claims in the old way. For workers suffering from occupational diseases in areas remote from Johannesburg, however, the procedure becomes once again more bureaucratic and inefficient.

Difficulties for workers in obtaining compensation

Problems with compensation legislation

Compensation laws are structured in such a way as to benefit maximally the employer and the state, and to place every conceivable obstacle in the path of workers (or their families) seeking monetary relief for injury, pain and suffering, disability, lost earning capacity and death as a result of bad working conditions.[7] Civil litigation in respect of claims for damages from employers is ruled out. In its place are ridiculously low payments which must be painstakingly extracted from an administration that seems to see its main task as saving money by reducing payouts to workers from the accident fund and by assiduously invalidating claims on any conceivable ground.

It has always been difficult for workers to obtain adequate compensation for injury and illness sustained at the workplace. Typical difficulties include bureaucratic obstruction and delay, the very small amounts involved and the fact that workers are frequently fired after injury or illness. Trade unions and advice offices dealing with workman's compensation claims are well aware of the pitfalls in the path of those seeking relief after disabling injury at work.

It is possible for an employer to get away with operating an unsafe factory, because there are few standards regulating safety at work, and the factory inspectorate is not large or efficient enough to enforce these few standards anyway.

It is even more difficult to obtain compensation for occupational disease than it is for injury. Each case of occupational disease which is medically diagnosed must pass a rigorous set of criteria and examinations by extremely vigilant medical inspectorates in the compensation commissions before there is a possibility of receiving compensation. This process may be so lengthy that workers die before the claim is accepted and compensation received.[8]

In South Africa, there are no published figures for occupational disease claims submitted, accepted or rejected in terms of the Workman's Compensation Act.

But trends in most other developed countries indicate that the majority of workers suffering from occupational diseases do not submit claims. Even when claims are made only a small proportion are ever successful.[9] Members of the working class are in addition generally known to have the lowest rate of claim on social welfare benefits.[10] In South Africa, this is aggravated by racial discrimination[11] and the administrative ineptness of 'homeland' bureaucracies. Legislation covering compensation for mines and factories, first passed many years ago, remains racially discriminatory. This makes it difficult for black workers to gain compensation.

Official criteria used for the diagnosis of occupational diseases

Certification of occupational disease depends critically on the diagnostic criteria employed by the workman's compensation commissioner. These criteria are generally not publicly available to doctors examining prospective cases of occupational disease. In the past, racially discriminatory standards with no adequate scientific basis have been used in the assessment of disability on which the money value of claims depends.[12]

A specific struggle was waged by the NUTW over access to the official criteria and their adequacy in the diagnosis of byssinosis. The official criteria were only eventually revealed during a court appeal against a negative decision by the commissioner in relation to a claim for byssinosis. These diagnostic criteria, which were put forward by the Medical Bureau for Occupational Diseases as the basis for compensating byssinosis, were found to be out of date and inadequate.

Problems after the diagnosis of an occupational disease

There is a presumptive standard for the diagnosis of scheduled occupational diseases in miners under the Occupational Diseases in Mines and Work Act (ODMWA). If a diagnosis of a scheduled disease and proof of exposure can be established, it is presumed that the person has an occupational disease caused by the exposure and compensation follows.

Under the Workman's Compensation Act, things are less easy.[13] If both of these conditions are met then causation is assumed and the claim has a good chance of success, but compensation is not automatic or guaranteed. The zeal of the medical inspectorate can be seen in a recent case of mesothelioma which fulfilled the presumptive criteria for compensation. The inspectorate raised additional obstacles with the result that the worker had no financial support when he needed it most and, in fact, died months before his family received compensation.[14]

There are few scheduled diseases, especially for industry. Where an occupational disease is not scheduled, the burden of proof of causation rests with the worker/claimant. As is generally the case in law, it is easier for something to happen than it is to prove that it did happen. Occupational asthma is a case in point. In 1983 the FCWU was involved in a study among grain milling workers in Cape Town.[15] A high proportion (37%) of workers were found to have this disease, which has been compensable in Britain and other countries for several years now. A process has been set in motion to have occupational asthma placed on the schedule of the Workman's Compensation Act, but its outcome is still awaited.

Racial discrimination and compensation

Compensation legislation in South Africa is relatively advanced when compared even with many developed countries. Historically, however, the laws have applied or have been applied in practice mainly to white workers. When it reported in 1981, the Nieuwenhuizen Commission to rationalise compensation legislation viewed the present system as 'liberal' and expressed concern at potential increased costs to the compensation fund if more blacks were to apply than in the past as a result of deracialisation of the law. The point was stressed that this would have to be accompanied by a tightening up of the system.

Mine managements must by law ensure that all workers are regularly screened. But the medical and technical monitoring measures employed to detect pneumoconiosis differ for black and white mineworkers, amounting in effect to racial discrimination as evidenced in the disparity in the percentages receiving compensation. In 1983-84 almost three times as many white as black miners were certified for compensable disease (29,7% white compared with 10,2% black miners per million risk shifts worked).[16] In addition, compensation for white miners is much higher in financial terms. Even after the 1985 increases, black miners may only receive a maximum of R1 969 while white miners' benefits top at R29 517.

The number of black miners compensated for heat illness is very low when compared with reports of heat related illnesses in the gold mines by NUM shaft stewards. Figures for heat illness among white miners are disproportionately high, given the fact that they form so small a part of the underground workforce, and are markedly less exposed by virtue of their lighter physical workload.[17]

Problems of reliance on company health information

The main requirement for a successful claim is a medical diagnosis. Yet the medical profession remains ignorant of occupational diseases. There are few specialist occupational physicians in South Africa. Company doctors are best placed to detect occupational diseases and yet their yield of cases has by all accounts been very low in the past, especially for black workers.

In industries where there is exposure to asbestos, surprisingly few cases have been turned up by company medical personnel in the past. In an asbestos-cement factory, a very low rate of case-finding over decades took a sudden upswing in 1984 when GWU won recognition and had their own doctor examine workers (*Argus*, 18.01.84; *CT*, 14.01.84). Twenty-three certified cases of asbestosis were pensioned off by the company's Cape Town factory in 1984. The company's press statement reported that 35 cases were found over the past 37 years; this means that over the preceding 34 years only 12 other cases of asbestosis had been discovered. In the transport industry where asbestos is handled, company doctors have passed all workers as normal, while screening of the same workers by GWU has resulted in numbers of asbestosis cases being diagnosed and compensated.

The compensation system depends on information supplied by the employer and/or company doctor, with forms and correspondence travelling between the Workman's Compensation Commissioner and the employer. In many cases submitted by union-appointed doctors, the commissioner has not subsequently dealt with these doctors, but rather with the employer. Because of this bias towards the employer an enormous weight is placed upon the accuracy of the employer's records. Yet GWU, on gaining access to company medical and work records, has found critical errors and/or omissions which could result in rejection of claims by the commissioner.

Lack of worker representation in the compensation apparatus

The Workman's Compensation Commission is a public body and should be representative of workers as well as of employers and the state. There are no representatives of the independent trade unions on the commission. This has serious implications for the expenditure of the commissioner's fund. The large surpluses accumulated every year are returned to the employers by way of rebates, and funds are allocated to the National Occupational Safety Association (NOSA), which workers see as closely identified with management.

The inequity of this situation is also highlighted in the concern expressed by the Nieuwenhuizen Commission that deracialisation of the ODMWA, in the context of increasing unionisation, might result in massive expenditure on compensation of black workers. Not one of the members of this commission represented black workers.

Conclusion

As more of the independent unions take up the health and safety problems of their members, not only are they commissioning more professional services (legal, medical, engineering, scientific) to look into the extent of these problems, but workers are being increasingly involved in monitoring, self-surveys and record-keeping activities. In this way, the accuracy of exposure records can be assured, and the independence of medical and technical evaluations can be guaranteed.

Workers are being trained in basic health and safety principles and hazard recognition. This equips them with the necessary information to fight effectively for better health and safety on the factory floor. In this as in many other areas, during the period under review, the independent trade unions and their members have shown the importance of worker representation, worker-generated information and worker initiative in the resolution of their problems. This is particularly important in the context of the unrepresentative and undemocratic institutions in which workers work or from which they receive welfare.

Notes

1 'Machinery and Occupational Diseases Safety Act regulations', *South African Labour Bulletin*, 9(5), March 1984; Industrial Health Reasearch Group, 'MOSA handbook', *South African Labour Bulletin*, 10(3), December 1984; 'Note on the regulations under MOSA', *South African Labour Bulletin*, 10(5), April/May 1985.

2 'CCAWUSA maternity agreement', *South African Labour Bulletin*, 10(2), October/November 1984; J Daphne, 'Maternity rights: CCAWUSA shows the way', *South African Labour Bulletin* 10(5), April/May 1985.

3 Technical Advice Group, 'Accidents', *South African Labour Bulletin*, 10(3), December 1984; J Leger, 'Hlobane accident', *South African Labour Bulletin*, 9(5), March 1984.

4 'Changes in workman's compensation', *South African Labour Bulletin*, 10(4), 1985; 'Workman's compensation', *South African Labour Bulletin*, 10(8), 1985.

5 'Brown lung campaign', *South African Labour Bulletin*, 9(7), 1984.

6 J Myers, D Garisch et al, 'A respiratory epidemiological survey of stevedores intermittently exposed to asbestos in a South African port', *American Journal of Industrial Medicine*, 7(4), 1985.

7 W Hammer, 'Design defects and worker's compensation', in JS Lee and WN Rom, eds, *Legal and Ethical Dilemmas in Occupational Diseases and Health* (Anne Arbor Science, 1982).

8 D Garisch, 'Workmen's compensation — who pays the price?', *South African Labour Bulletin*, 9(7), 1984.

9 JT Hughes, jnr, 'Byssinosis compensation in North Carolina: a ten year policy review (1971-1980)', in Lee and Rom, eds, *Legal and Ethical Dilemmas*.

10 Working Group on Inequalities in Health, *Inequalities in Health* (DHSS, London, 1980).

11 *Report of the Commission of Enquiry into Compensation for Occupational Diseases in the Republic of South Africa (Nieuwenhuizen Commission)*, RP 100/1981.

12 J Myers, 'Differential ethnic standards for lung functions or one standard for all?', *South African Medical Journal*, 65, 1984.

13 *Niewenhuizen Commission*, 25.

14 Garisch, 'Who pays the price?'.

15 Industrial Health Research Group, 'Health and safety — grain workers in Cape Town', *South African Labour Bulletin*, 10(5), 1985.

16 *Report of the Compensation Commissioner for Occupational Diseases for the Year Ended 31 March 1984*, RP 57/1984.

17 *Mining Statistics*, Department of Mineral and Energy Affairs, 1982, RP 48/1984.

Trade Union Membership in South Africa

(Unions are grouped as federations where these exist. Figures quoted by unions in most cases relate to membership in February 1985, although some figures go back to December 1984. The *SA Review* is unable to vouch for their accuracy.)

Azanian Confederation of Trade Unions (AZACTU)

Seven black consciousness unions recently formed this new union federation. AZACTU's Pandelani Nefolovhodwe was unable to provide membership figures for the individual unions, although he says they have a combined membership of 75 000. They are:

African Allied Workers Union (AAWU)
General secretary: Cunningham Nqcukana.

Amalgamated Black Workers Union (ABWU)
General secretary: Jabulani Nhlapo.

Black Allied Mining and Construction Workers Union (BAMCWU)
General secretary: Pandelani Nefolovhodwe.

Black Electronics and Electrical Workers Union (BEEWU)
General secretary: Thandisizwe Mazibuko.

Black General Workers Union (BLAGWU)
General secretary: Henry Madikoto.

Hotel, Liquor, Catering and Allied Workers Union (HOTELICA)
General secretary: Hamilton Makedama.

Insurance and Assurance Workers Union of SA (IAWUSA)
General secretary: Joe Rakgoadi.

National Union of Workers of SA (NUWSA)
General secretary: Hamilton Makedama.

Council of Unions of SA (CUSA)

President: James Mndaweni
General secretary: Phiroshaw Camay
Membership: 147 100.

Broom and Brush Workers Union
General secretary: Mary Ntseke
Membership: 1 000.

Building Construction and Allied Workers Union (BCAWU)
General secretary: Aaron Nthinya
Membership: 27 264.

Food Beverage Workers Union (FBWU).
General secretary: 'Skakes' Sikhakhane
Membership: 16 124.

National Union of Wine, Spirits and Allied Workers
General secretary: Fay Mandy
Membership: 5 000.

SA Chemical Workers Union (SACWU)
General secretary: Michael Tsotetsi
Membership: 30 000.

SA Laundry, Dry Cleaning and Dyeing Workers Union
General secretary: Agnes Molefe
Membership: 4 071.

Steel, Engineering and Allied Workers Union (SEAWU)
General secretary: Jane Hlongwane
Membership: 28 927.

Transport and Allied Workers Union (TAWU)
General secretary: James Sikhosana
Membership: 23 327.

Textile Workers Union (Transvaal)
General secretary: Evelyn Selora
Membership: Union refused to supply information.

United African Motor and Allied Workers Union (UAMAWU)
General secretary: Dora Nowatha
Membership: 10 873.

Vukani Black Guards and Allied Workers Union
General secretary: No appointment
Membership: 514.

Federation of SA Trade Unions (FOSATU)

President: Chris Dlamini
General secretary: Joe Forster
Membership: 118 950.

Chemical Workers Industrial Union (CWIU)
General secretary: Rod Crompton
Membership: 13 750.

Jewellers and Goldsmiths Union
General secretary: Ted Frazer
Membership: 470.

Metal and Allied Workers Union (MAWU)
General secretary: Thembi Nabe
Membership: 34 000.

National Automobile and Allied Workers Union (NAAWU)
General secretary: Fred Sauls
Membership: 20 250.

National Union of Textile Workers (NUTW)
General secretary: John Copelyn
Membership: 15 720.

Paper Wood and Allied Workers Union (PWAWU)
General secretary: Rafiloe Ndzuta
Membership: 11 430.

Sweet, Food and Allied Workers Union (SFAWU)
General secretary: Jay Naidoo
Membership: 12 250.

Transport and General Workers Union (T&G)
General secretary: Jane Barrett
Membership: 11 080.

South African Confederation of Labour (SACOL)

President: Gert Diederiks
General secretary: Lodewyk Nicolaas Cilliers
Membership: 115 025.

White Building Workers Union of SA
General secretary: Gert Beetge
Membership: 9 000.

Mineworkers Union (MWU)
General secretary: Arrie Paulus
Membership: 24 000.

Provinsiale Huishoudelike Personeel Vereniging
General secretary: Alida Selliers
Membership: Union refused to supply figure.

Provinsiale Medewerkersvereniging
General secretary: Jack van Rensburg
Membership: 4 000.

SA Diamond Workers Union
General secretary: Robin Rich
Membership: 300.

SA Engine Drivers, Firemens and Operators Association
General secretary: Ivo Meyer
Membership: 7 100.

SA Iron, Steel and Allied Industries Union ('Yster en Staal')
General secretary: Henry Ferreira
Membership: 35 300.

SA Karweierswerknemersvereniging
General secretary: 'Koos' Botha
Membership: 507.

SA Staatsdiens- en Provinsiale Werkvereniging
General secretary: Alida Selliers
Membership: Union refused to supply figure.

SA Transport Services Employees Union
General secretary: Gert Janse van Rensburg
Membership: 11 000.

SA Railways and Harbours Salaried Staff Association
General secretary: Piet Peterson
Membership: 27 200.

Unie van Treinpersoneel en Bedryfsgrade Groep 'C'
General secretary: Johan Bernade
Membership: 7 200.

West Rand Development Board Personnel Association
General secretary: Kobus Botha
Membership: 1 200.

Trade Union Council of SA (TUCSA)

President: Robbie Botha
General secretary: Vacant
Membership: 330 000.
(Only unions with more than 14 000 members are listed).

Artisan Staff Association
General secretary: Willie van der Merwe
Membership: 24 297.

Building Society Officials Association of SA
General secretary: Corrie van Vuuren
Membership: 15 783.

Garment Workers Union of the Western Province (GWU-WP)
General secretary: Louis Petersen
Membership: 58 500.

Mine Surface Officials Association (MSOA)
General secretary: Robbie Botha
Membership: 14 629.

National Union of Clothing Workers of SA (NUCW)
General secretary: Lucy Mvubelo
Membership: 18 831.

National Union of Leatherworkers
General secretary: 'Bokkie' Fourie
Membership: 26 480.

SA Typographical Union
General secretary: Lief van Tonder
Membership: 42 713.

Textile Workers Industrial Union (TWIU)
General secretary: Norman Daniels
Membership: 20 310.

United Democratic Front-linked unions

Clothing Workers Union (CLOWU)
General secretary: Zubeida Jaffer
Membership: 500.

General and Allied Workers Union (GAWU)
General secretary: Sydney Mafumadi
Membership: 45 000-50 000.

General Workers Union of SA (GWUSA)
General secretary: Dennis Neer
Membership: Union refused to supply figure.

Municipal and General Workers Union (MGWUSA)
General secretary: Johnson Gamede
Membership: 4 000.

Motor Assemblers and Component Workers Union (MACWUSA)
General secretary: Dennis Neer
Membership: Union refused to supply figure.

National Iron, Steel, Metal and Allied Workers Union
(NISMAWU)
General secretary: Mathews Oliphant
Membership: 5 000.

National Federation of Workers (NFW)
General secretary: Mandla Cele
Membership: 25 000.

National General Workers Union (NGWU)
General secretary: Donsie Khumalo
Membership: 10 000.

National Union of Print and Allied Workers (NUPAWO)
General secretary: Thembekile Sahluko
Membership: 5 000.

Orange Vaal General Workers Union (OVGWU)
General secretary: Philip Masia
Membership: The *SA Review* could not contact the union.

(Cape-based) Retail and Allied Workers Union (RAWU)
General secretary: Alan Roberts
Membership: 3 000.

(Transvaal-based) Retail and Allied Workers Union (RAWU)
General secretary: Donsie Khumalo
Membership: 4 000.

SA Allied Workers Union (SAAWU)
General secretary: Sisa Njikelana
Membership: 100 000.

SA Domestic Workers Association (SADWA)
General secretary: Margaret Nhlapo
Membership: 10 000-11 000.

The SA Scooter Drivers Union (SADU)
General secretary: Lucky Mdlaivana
Membership: 900.

The SA Mineworkers Union (SAMWU)
Acting-general secretary: Sisa Njikelana
Membership: Union has yet to hold its first general meeting.

SA Railways and Harbours Workers Union
Acting-general secretary: Solomon Pholotho
Membership: The *SA Review* could not contact the union.

Independent unions

(Only unions with more than 10 000 members are listed.

Food and Canning Workers Union (FCWU)
General secretary: Jan Theron
Membership: 30 000.

Amalgamated Engineering Union (AEU)
General secretary: Tom Neethling
Membership: 33 000.

Cape Town Municipal Workers Union (CTMWU)
General secretary: John Ernstzen
Membership: 11 500.

Commercial, Catering and Allied Workers Union of SA
(CCAWUSA)
General secretary: Emma Mashinini
Membership: 40 000.

Engineering Industrial Workers Union (EIWU)
General secretary: Aubrey Benn
Membership: 19 000.

General Workers Union (GWU)
General secretary: David Lewis
Membership: 11 500.

Motor Industry Combined Workers Union (MICWU)
General secretary: Des East
Membership: 32 987.

National Union of Mineworkers (NUM)
General secretary: Cyril Ramaphosa
Membership: 110 000.

SA Boilermakers, Iron and Steelworkers, Shipbuilders and
Welders Society
General secretary: Ike van der Watt
Membership: 52 000.

SA Electrical Workers Association (white)
Electrical and Allied Trade Union of SA (coloured and Indian)
Electrical and Allied Workers of SA (African)
General secretary: Ben Nicholson
Total membership: 33 000.

United Mining, Metal and Allied Workers of SA (UMMAWSA)
General secretary: Sam Ntuli
Membership: 11 000.

Introduction
Gerhard Maré

Events unthinkable even in the recent past now occur routinely in South Africa, as the economic and political consequences of decades of apartheid and repression come to fruition. In response, the state and capital are promoting a range of actions, strategies, pronouncements and plans designed in the short term to reimpose stability and order, and in the long term to maintain South Africa as a stable, profitable, capitalist society.

However, the single most dramatic step, the declaration of a state of emergency, has not produced stability. Instead it has been a factor in forcing the rand down to disastrous levels. Of course, while the emergency has been presented as an exceptional tactic, this ignores the fact that there has been a state of emergency operative in a part of South Africa (the Transkei) for all but a brief period since the early 1960s. Across the country, resistance escalates and killings continue. The brutality of police action reaches white South Africa mainly through reports of court interdicts on torture in detention, and through international outrage in response to more extensive media coverage available outside this country.

Aside from direct repression, state response to mass resistance is to fumble about in search of 'gesprekleiers' to negotiate with, looking to an array of discredited community councillors, avaricious bantustan leaders and church figures. Monopoly capital, with a keener sense of long-term planning, attempts to cover all options: business leaders have opened the door for opposition politicians and even Afrikaans students and clergy to make or attempt the pilgrimage to Lusaka to find out what the ANC wants in a future

South Africa and how it perceives the path leading to that future.

Internationally, the disinvestment campaign and moves to institute sanctions against South Africa continually seem to gain momentum, despite opposition from the US administration and its aging president and from the equally conservative Thatcher government in Britain. But capitalism in South Africa is in such a bad way that those opposing disinvestment have to admit that continued investment would do no more than *alleviate* the poverty, starvation and unemployment that have become routine features of this country. More than 25 years ago, Chief Albert Luthuli called for sanctions on the grounds that they would help shorten the period of suffering, an argument that seems to have come into its own today.

Under such pressures, South African capital and the state are coming to differ increasingly openly as to the desirable pace and limits of reform and the best means of achieving long-term political stability. More and more directly and desperately, big business is criticising the state's role. But the difference is as to means, not ends. Both capital and the state agree on the need for political stability. As the president of ASSOCOM said at its annual congress in October 1985, the business community is interested not in politics, but in political stability.

The first contribution in this section, by Coleman and Webster, considers that most basic and direct of the state's tactics — detention and repression by the police and army in 1984-85. Their exhaustive account gives content to discussion of the state's response to the present national uprising — that aspect of its policy which organised business finds so counterproductive.

Cobbett, Glaser, Hindson and Swilling describe a development in policy with long-term structural aims. They argue that in place of the geography of Grand Apartheid, a system of regional economies which cut across bantustan borders is being promoted. This, they write, could mean 'abandonment of the political and territorial premises of apartheid, though not necessarily of race and ethnicity'. Regionalism may serve as the basis for a federal system which, some business and state planners believe, would enable majority rule in a unitary state to be avoided. They refer to what the press terms 'the KwaNatal option', which could serve as the pilot project for a new federal South Africa. Of course, from a different perspective this option is described as 'the seat of the counter-revolution'. The prospect of such strategies on the part of the state casts into relief the very real need for analysis of regional class configurations, histories and organisational forms — all crucial to implementing, or resisting, a federal policy.

Hudson and Sarakinsky examine the dilemmas of a petty bourgeoisie facing racial discrimination. Their article continues the argument raised by Hudson in the introduction to the section on 'Politics and Resistance' in *South African Review 2*. Hudson pointed to the possibility that 'the state's black local government strategy will lead to an entrenched and durable political division within the dominated classes' by favouring the 'specific interests of the black petty bourgeoisie'.

In the present volume, Hudson and Sarakinsky outline the forms of state discrimination against the African petty bourgeoisie until 1975, when the African Bank was launched. This marked a turning point, the beginning of gradual relaxation of racially discriminatory measures against the African petty bourgeoisie. The authors believe that the effect of these changes has been qualitative, 'rendering highly unlikely any participation by this class in a popular alliance struggling for national liberation and the destruction of apartheid'. Actions during the recent clashes in Natal townships by Africans aspiring to bourgeois status and their vehement opposition through the regional African Chamber of Commerce, Inyanda, and the Inkatha movement to the national consumer boycott, lend weight to this analysis.

Social stratification, and attempts to win over the Indian and coloured petty bourgeoisie, is a theme of the article by Pirie. He deals with the Group Areas Act and comments that 'desegregation of residential group areas has never been contemplated officially'. The state's attempts to advance the petty bourgeoisie have not so far brought about changes more than skin-deep, though desegregation of business areas appears a likely development.

Greater social stratification in the townships is one of the effects that Hendler, Mabin and Parnell also point to in their examination of changes in state housing policy. They trace the ebb and flow of state involvement, finding that many more houses are being built for Africans in the 1980s than in the 1970s. They point out too that capital has been centrally involved in the supply of housing through construction contracts and supply of materials, though the state has been the prime mover. The trend towards involvement of the private sector has also seen direct involvement of large finance and housing companies, an involvement which will in turn affect state policy, the authors predict. State housing policy must not be seen merely as an ideological smokescreen, but as something that will have real effects, they warn.

The contribution by Maré examines some aspects of the use and abuse of that old rallying cry 'democracy' in the South African context. Its starting point is the claim to widen democracy made in support of the tricameral constitution. The successful boycott of the 1984 elections for 'representatives' to the Indian and coloured parliamentary houses has indicated a clear popular rejection of this position. But because the *term* democracy has been so besmirched through its misuse by the state and individuals aspiring to cooption by the apartheid state, it becomes all the more urgent that democratic *practice* be maintained by organisations opposing the state, and that the term be given a different content.

Repression and Detentions in South Africa

Max Coleman and David Webster

The South African state has detained over 25 000 people in the three decades since its security legislation was introduced. Earlier periods and trends provide the context for a review of the pattern of state repression in the last two years culminating with the declaration of a state of emergency on 21 July 1985.

The statistical information supplied below is gleaned from a number of sources: press reports, *Hansard*, lawyers, police press releases, interviews with released detainees and, above all, from the carefully researched Detainees' Parents Support Committee (DPSC) monthly reports. Despite meticulous efforts, attempts to supply accurate figures on detentions are impeded always by the secrecy in which the security police shrouds its activities. Its officials release the names of detainees with great reluctance, and only to an interested party, such as next-of-kin or the detainee's lawyer. Thus the DPSC figures are usually lower than those of the police. Under the state of emergency, however, the number of detainees can be ascertained as police do release names of detainees.[1]

Overview of security legislation

In 1982, the government introduced the Internal Security Act (ISA) to streamline and consolidate existing security legislation. The ISA superceded, and included major aspects of, the old Internal Security Act, section 6 of the Terrorism Act, and section 22 of the General Law Amendment Act. The new legislation contained four sections providing for detention of people deemed by the security police to be a danger to state security.

The first, section 28, while not permitting interrogation, allows for indefinite preventive detention. It is used to remove activists from circulation in order to cripple organisations to which they belong or to block an initiative in which they may be participating. The second, section 29, is an updated version of section 6 of the Terrorism Act. It empowers a police officer of the rank of lieutenant-colonel or above to detain for questioning a person whom the state believes is a threat to state security, has committed an offence endangering state security, or possesses information relating to the above. The detainee may be held indefinitely, or until he has answered questions (and usually written a statement) 'to the satisfaction of the police'. Most detainees are held under this section, and extensive abuse and torture of detainees takes place. Though a review board technically examines cases of detainees held longer than six months, it has not to our knowledge been instrumental in ordering the release of detainees.

The third, section 31, empowers an attorney general to detain a person deemed to be a potential state witness. Thus an officer of the court, rather than a security policeman, can invoke security law to detain someone. The period of detention may not exceed six months, or the duration of the trial in which the detainee's evidence is required. Recent treason trials have shown a tendency to drag on for very long periods, so detainees under section 31 may be held for up to two years.

The fourth, section 50, introduces a 14-day period of preventive detention. A low-ranking police officer may detain a person deemed instrumental in an unrest situation in the belief that such a detention will defuse the problem. For further detention under this section, permission must be obtained from a magistrate. In practice, people held under this clause are frequently transferred to section 29 detention before the 14 days expire, although some are released before the expiry date.

The state of emergency is empowered by the Public Safety Act of 1953, which invokes powers considerably wider than those of the Internal Security Act. Powers of arrest and detention are extended to any member of a 'force', including the SA Police, the Railways Police, the SA Defence Force and the Prison Service, or any person nominated by them. The arresting officer can be 'any commissioned, warrant or non-commissioned officer' in a 'force'. Detainees are held for an initial 14-day period, after which permission to detain them further must be obtained from the Minister of Law and Order. Thereafter the detention is indefinite.

The Public Safety Act provides for a particularly punitive form of detention, allowing for interrogation. The conditions of detention are severe: detainees are held in isolation, reading material was initially limited to a holy book, and visits to detainees are extremely difficult to obtain. A stringent set of rules regulates detainee behaviour: contact with other detainees is forbidden, as is singing, whistling or other forms of behaviour deemed rowdy or insubordinate.

State repression in 1984

Detentions

The wave of repression during 1984 was the most severe since 1976-77. Roughly 100 detentions occurred nationally each month, a considerable increase over the previous two years (see figure 1 below).

Detentions accurately reflect the tempo and scope of democratic struggle. The DPSC, which has monitored security police activity since 1981, recorded several changes in security police strategy and tactics.

In 1981, 772 known detentions were recorded. In 1982, detentions dropped to 264, but doubled in 1983 to 453, and rose 250% in 1984 to reach 1 149. A significant change in the pattern of detentions occurred in 1983. Before then, trade unionists as a group were most severely affected. But with the launch of the UDF and its initiation of anti-tricameral parliament campaigns, growing numbers of activists engaged in political, community and civic affairs were detained. This created the space for the emerging unions to consolidate their organisational gains with somewhat less police harassment than before.

Fig 1. Detention trends: 1981-1985

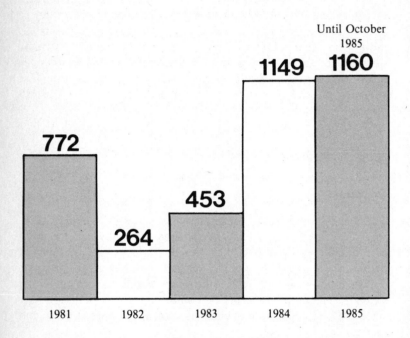

Fig 1. Detention trends: 1981-1985

The breakdown of detentions in 1984 is as follows:

Detentions by area	1984	Percentage of total	Percentage of total excluding bantustans
Transvaal	420	37	71
Natal	67	6	11
Eastern Cape	96	8	16
Western Cape	7	0,5	1
OFS	5	0,5	1
Ciskei	123	11	—
Transkei	407	35	—
Venda	1	—	—
Bophuthatswana	1	—	—
Unknown	22	2	—
	1 149	100	100

Transvaal: In 1984 the Transvaal bore the brunt of security police harassment, accounting for 37% of all detentions in South Africa (over three times the 1983 figure), and 71% excluding detentions in the bantustans. The majority of these detentions were a result of struggles concerning implementation of the new constitution. Major centres affected were:

Vaal	130	(mostly during Oct/Nov)
Soweto	106	
Johannesburg	50	
East Rand	38	
Pretoria	27	
Alexandra	21	
Northern Tvl	17	

A smaller number of detentions was registered in Eldorado Park, Lenasia, Potchefstroom, West Rand and country areas.

Natal: Natal experienced 67 detentions, double the 1983 figure, made up as follows:

Durban	37
Pietermaritzburg	17
Zululand	13

Eastern Cape: The figure of 96 detained in 1984 was one-and-a-half times the 1983 figure. Centres most affected were:

Port Elizabeth	48
Graaff-Reinet	18
Queenstown	16
East London	9
Cradock	5

Western Cape: The boycott of the coloured and Indian elections in this region was the most successful in the country, and political activity was as widespread as in other regions. Yet only seven people were detained, about 1% of the total, and all in Cape Town — a surprisingly low figure for so important an area. This highlights regional differences in security police strategy: the Eastern Cape and Transvaal have a tradition of open repression while the Western Cape police appear to rely on extensive use of the courts to harass political opposition.

Northern Cape and Orange Free State: No detentions were recorded in the Northern Cape, but Bloemfontein security police are beginning to use detention as a weapon against community protest.

Ciskei: After the wave of detentions during the bus boycott in 1983, the 1984 figure of 123 represents a considerable reduction, but security police repression in the area is still rampant.

Transkei: The second highest number of detentions occurred in the Transkei as a result of the detention of almost an entire village near Engcobo which rebelled against an unpopular local headman, and the detention and expulsion of almost all students at the University of Transkei.

Detentions by activity	Total	Percentage of total
Scholars, students, teachers	583	51
Trade unionists, workers	51	4
Community and political workers	226	20
Clergy and church workers	11	1
Journalists	7	0,5
Unspecified or unknown	271	23,5
	1 149	100

Every year the group suffering most severely from repression changes, as different spheres of struggle become prominent. In 1984, struggles over school and university education and political rights came to the fore. In particular, the Congress of South African Students (COSAS) actively mobilised students, demanding democratic student representation, better schooling, an end to corporal punishment and sexual harassment of female students, and the removal of the upward age limit for scholars. Students and teachers accounted for over half the dententions of 1984. The DPSC identified 90 COSAS members, and 13 members of the Azanian Students Movement, a black consciousness-oriented group, who were detained. The detention of almost the entire COSAS leadership demonstrated the state's clear intention to crush the organisation.

Community and political activists were the other major category of detainees. Some 226 of them were detained, 20% of the total number of detentions. Ninety-seven detainees were from youth organisations and 55 from civic or residents' associations. Most detainees were members of the UDF and its affiliates, and were harassed because of their activities in organising and mobilising communities against the new constitution, and later against black local authorities. These struggles were most notable in the Vaal Triangle, East Rand, OFS, Cradock, Grahamstown and Graaff-Reinet.

The hardest hit political groupings were:

UDF leadership	33
Azanian Peoples Organisation	23

Members of the Anti-President's Council Committee, the Release Mandela Committee, the Natal Indian Congress, and the DPSC, all UDF affiliates, accounted for another 15 detainees.

Trade unionists, with 51 detentions, represent a relatively small but extremely important target group. Their harassment brought sharp reaction internationally and from local organised commerce and industry.

Church organisations and journalists did not escape harassment, although the number detained was small.

Legislation used for detentions

DPSC records show that the detention provisions of the Internal Security Act were used as follows:

Section 28,	providing for 'preventive' detention	28 persons
Section 29,	providing for interrogative detention	280 persons
Section 31,	providing for detention on the instructions of an attorney general as a potential state witness	18 persons
Section 50,	providing for short-term preventive detention	72 persons

Security police detained 152 persons under section 50 of the Criminal Procedure Act, or under no legislation at all, for questioning for periods up to 48 hours.

Security legislation in the bantustans is similar to the Internal Security Act and was used to detain 532 persons in Transkei, Ciskei, Venda and Bophuthatswana.

Concealing detentions

Fate of detainees	1984	Percentage	
Released without charge:			
within 48 hours	179⎤	15⎤	36%
after a longer period	236⎦	21⎦	
charged and convicted	16	1	
charged and acquitted	403	35	
charged and awaiting trial	167	15	
died in detention	1	—	
still in detention	146	13	
reported escaped	1	—	
	1 149	100	

The government pays a heavy price internationally if it appears too repressive. Hence the pressure to clean up its image by detaining fewer people, or appearing to do so.

In June 1984, the Protection of Information Act was invoked to restrain the press from publicising certain detentions. Government statisticians also disowned bantustan detentions, despite the close relationship between 'homeland' and South African security forces.

From September 1983, at the time of the referendum for the new constitution, police began to use less overt methods to intimidate and harass activists. Fewer people were detained under section 29. Frequently, detainees were held under section 50 of the Criminal Procedure Act which provides for ordinary criminal investigation, so decreasing the overall numbers of security detentions. As detainees may only be held for 48 hours, they were frequently subjected to intense pressure during interrogation. Thus when Paris Malatji was shot dead during interrogation, police denied this was another death in detention as he was held under section 50 of the Criminal Procedure Act. If, after the 48 hours allowed, a detainee appeared to have more information to interest the police, further detention was empowered by security legislation.

Police began to use the informal 'call-in' card to collect information about particular campaigns, to intimidate activists, their colleagues and potential members, and to attempt to recruit informers. A note was slipped under the door of the home of an activist during the night or the day when no-one was there. The recipient was requested to present himself, with reference book, at a certain police station. There he was interrogated for a period between several hours and a day. Afterwards he was usually allowed to go, though sometimes detention followed.

'Hidden Repression', a survey of Transvaal organisations conducted by the DPSC and the Detainees' Support Committee (DESCOM), found that 222 members of the 37 organisations surveyed were subjected to call-in cards.[2] As no security legislation was used, there was no statistical record of the interrogation. However, by mid- to late-1984, as unrest escalated, all attempts to avoid the use of Section 29 were abandoned.

Use of the courts

From mid-1983 the state embarked on a new strategy, which attempted to criminalise its extra-parliamentary opponents by charging detainees with minor or even frivolous charges. In 1983, for instance, the state charged only 15% of all detainees, of whom 43% were convicted. In 1984, 62% of detainees were charged, and of the cases completed, only 1,2% were convicted.

Charged detainees could be held without bail for lengthy periods, as under the Internal Security Act an attorney general can issue a certificate refusing bail. In 1985, defence lawyers won a series of legal victories against this arbitrary power. One instance was the Pietermaritzburg treason trial involving UDF leaders. Here, Justice Milne found that the court had jurisdiction over granting bail, despite an attorney general's certificate refusing it. In response, the courts began setting bail conditions equivalent to a banning order for the accused, who were restricted to a particular area, and not allowed to participate in political activity. UDF patron Allan Boesak, charged with offences under the Internal Security Act, was initially confined to his house at night, virtually under house arrest. Subsequently his bail conditions were moderated.

This tactic successfully removed key leaders from their organisations and communities, while meeting the demand of overseas organisations for the government to 'charge or release' its political opponents.

Informal repression

Security police also began to rely on informal coercion rather than detention. DESCOM and DPSC described this development in 'Hidden Repression', from which most of the material in this section is drawn.

Informal intimidation was used to disrupt the daily working of organisations. It included raiding offices, meetings and houses, confiscation of essential documents, records and financial statements, telephone tapping and obvious surveillance of offices and individuals, who were followed on foot or by car. Opposition organisations often had difficulty hiring offices or buses for meetings, presumably because of police intimidation of the companies concerned. Organisations were frequently prevented from obtaining venues for meetings, or meetings were banned, as were funerals at which political speeches might have been made. Fake pamphlets were distributed cancelling meetings or changing venues. For example, before the UDF launch in 1983, pamphlets flooded the Transvaal advising that the UDF launch in Cape Town had been postponed and the venue moved to Sharpeville.

The security police also interfered with the ability of organisations to communicate with their memberships and constituencies. Door-to-door house visits were difficult to conduct due to harassment such as arrests and the confiscation of pamphlets. Placard demonstrations were often disrupted, and at meetings, strikes, demonstrations, and even cultural events such as the UDF People's Festival in March 1984, police made their presence obvious, for example, by openly filming participants.

Informal repression was also aimed at individual activists. They received death and bomb threats. Bricks were hurled through their windows and their houses were broken into or fired at with shotguns. Their assailants sprayed paint onto cars, slashed, over-inflated or deflated tyres, drained oil from the car sump, or removed the ignition. Dead pets, especially cats, were left on the doorsteps or tied to the door handles of activists' homes. Some attacks were believed to be perpetrated by police, others by unknown individuals who had access to unlisted telephone numbers and little-known addresses. Victims frequently blamed the police, the SADF, the 'system', pro-apartheid forces, political opponents, or Inkatha. In some cases their accusations were verified.

Torture and abuse of detainees

In September 1982, the DPSC produced a memorandum on torture in detention. Several forms of detainee abuse were noted as common practice nationwide. These included: solitary confinement, beating, slapping and kicking; enforced standing for lengthy periods; enforced physical exercise; sleep deprivation; being kept naked during interrogation; manacling in uncomfortable positions (for example wrist to ankle); suspension from poles, known as 'the helicopter'; attacks on genitals; and electric shocks. Allegations to the DPSC by released detainees indicate that these methods were still used in 1984.

An alarming new development was the introduction of closed-circuit television in the cells at John Vorster Square in Johannesburg. Police claimed this would protect detainees, and prevent them committing suicide. But released detainees attest that the 24-hour surveillance of their every movement added immeasurably to the stress of solitary confinement and detention.

The security police behaved capriciously in delivering food parcels supplied by families for detainees. Parcels were used as a reward for cooperative detainees and withheld from the recalcitrant. The parcels are psychologically important to detainees, supplying a link to the outside world and an indication that people care about them. They are also an important dietary supplement. The police argue that the parcels are a privilege, and claim that prison diet is perfectly adequate and balanced, and is worked out by a qualified dietician. This is disputed by the DPSC whose evidence shows that Protea and Diepkloof prisons in the Transvaal are particularly inadequate in this respect.

Banning of persons during 1984

At the beginning of 1984, 12 people lived under banning orders served in terms of the Internal Security Act. On 26 September, banning orders on two people were withdrawn well before the expiry date. On 31 October, a three-year banning order was served on Abel Dube immediately after his release from two-and-a-half years of detention. Thus the year closed with 11 persons restricted by banning orders.

Listing of persons during 1984

The *Government Gazette* of 29 June published the names of 200 listed people who may not be quoted. Contravention of this ban in terms of section 56(1)(p) of the Internal Security Act carries a prison sentence of up to three years.

Banning of gatherings during 1984

Section 46 of the Internal Security Act empowers the Minister of Law and Order or a magistrate to ban or impose restrictions on gatherings. On 30 March, the minister renewed the annual ban on all outdoor political meetings for a further year. He extended this ban to all indoor political gatherings in 21 magisterial districts for the period 12-30 September 1984. In August, the Ciskei introduced a general ban on all gatherings of more than 20 persons, while Venda banned all political meetings for 20 days in September during 'independence' anniversary celebrations.

Specific meetings, arranged mostly by UDF and its affiliates, were banned on specific dates by magistrates of the following districts: Johannesburg, Vereeniging, Vanderbijlpark, Sharpeville, Seshego, Port Elizabeth, Uitenhage, East London, Queenstown, Cradock, Mdantsane and Zwelitsha.

A number of funerals were restricted under section 46 of the Internal Security Act to specific dates and times. The number of mourners was limited; placards, banners, freedom songs and political orations were prohibited and any procession on foot or diversion from the shortest route disallowed. This action was taken by magistrates in Johannesburg, Boksburg, Benoni, Heidelberg, Alberton, Verulam, Port Elizabeth, Grahamstown, Uitenhage, East London and Mdantsane.

Deportations

Nine people were deported from Transkei by the Transkei security police. Eight were professors or lecturers at the University of the Transkei, and the ninth was a part-time student and journalist. Five were South African, three American and one German.

Banishment

Two people were banished by the Minister of Law and Order to a designated district according to banning powers in the Internal Security Act. Nomzamo Winnie Mandela was restricted to Brandfort in the Orange Free State and Abel Dube to Messina in the Northern Transvaal.

A second form of banishment, under jurisdiction of the Minister of Home Affairs, deprives an African person of his South African citizenship, and declares him a citizen of an 'independent homeland' and therefore an alien in South Africa under the Aliens Act. Entry into 'South Africa' without a visa is illegal and punishable by law. The two people affected were Charles Nqakula, born in Cradock, and Steve Tshwete, born in Springs, who both were confined to Ciskei.

State repression in 1985

The declaration of the state of emergency on 21 July 1985 resulted in a rapid increase of detentions and repression under the Public Safety Act. As the emergency was restricted to 36 magisterial districts, the Internal Security Act was still used to harass activists in the remaining 229 districts.

Trends in 1985 confirmed what had become evident in 1984. As the UDF emerged as the major internal political force for change and liberation, it remained the major target of state repression. Towards the end of 1984, along with the successful boycott of the coloured and Indian tricameral parliamentary elections, the number of detentions rose sharply. The government's programme of reforms could be implemented now only by coercion and not consensus. From 1985 it was clearer than before that the security police played a political role to keep the present power bloc in control.

Detentions under the Internal Security Act

During the first six months of 1985, 215 people were detained, about 36 per month on average. The Transvaal bore the brunt of these detentions, though the northern Cape, Galeshewe (Kimberley) and Huhudi (Vryburg) were also hard hit. In March, in addition to the annual ban on outdoor gatherings, the Minister of Law and Order imposed a three-month ban on any indoor meetings conducted by 29 organisations in 18 districts. By May, the Transvaal accounted for 30% of the detentions. Ciskei followed closely with 27%, and Northern Cape with 15%. Students accounted for 25% of the detentions, and political and community workers for 40%.

In June, the focus of repression switched to the Western and Eastern Cape. The March ban on indoor meetings was renewed and expanded to include 64 organisations in 30 magisterial districts. Most of these organisations were UDF affiliates, with the exception of the Azanian Peoples Organisation (AZAPO) and the Azanian Students Movement (AZASM). Six treason trials involving 52 people, 43 trials under the Internal Security Act involving 383 people, and 53 other politically-related trials involving 513 people were all pending, and 107 political trials had ended.

Despite continued state repression of extra-parliamentary opposition, popular protest, student and civic action continued unabated. By mid-1985, South Africa was in the throes of the worst economic recession since the 1930s, unemployment had risen to unprecedented heights of around 30% of the workforce, and the central government had failed to meet even the most reasonable demands concerning inferior education, rental increases and transport costs. The community councils, elected without mandates and with extremely low percentage polls, were increasingly unpopular and bore the brunt of township anger. All around the country, in large cities and small rural towns, a combination of spontaneous and directed political protest emerged. The police responded with increasing violence.

July 1985 marked a watershed in the year. The state of emergency was declared, and detentions under the Internal Security Act escalated. Forty-five people were detained under the Act, of whom about half were from the Transvaal, and overall 70% were students and political workers. By August, the pattern had crystallised. The DPSC, despite the proven reliability of its information-gathering network, was aware of only 186 detentions (an increase of over 400% on the previous month), far below the official figure of 555. Most of the additional 555 detentions were under section 50's 14-day provision.

That the DPSC was ignorant of these detentions reflects the alarming success of the security police in conducting their operations in secrecy. Police statistics and lists of detainees also do not mention the many people arrested for short periods of up to eight hours under the Public Safety Act, for example the brief arrest and questioning of 122 mourners returning by bus from a funeral in Cradock.

During September the number of detentions under the Internal Security Act was lower, with 121 detentions. The pattern of detentions and the violence used to quell township protests revealed that the state had an undeclared state of emergency in magisterial districts outside the formal state of emergency.

The state of emergency

The declaration of the state of emergency coincided with the Cradock funeral of four UDF activists, Matthew Goniwe, Fort Calata, Sparrow Mkhonto and Sicelo Mhlauli, who were brutally murdered in mysterious unsolved circumstances which amounted to political assassination. The emergency came into force at midnight on Sunday 21 July, and from that moment an unprecedented wave of detentions followed. Police raided the homes of activists and rank-and-file members of opposition organisations, mostly linked to UDF and particularly COSAS, and detained them in the early hours of Sunday. Buses carrying mourners from the Cradock funeral were intercepted and in Johannesburg 42 passengers were detained out of the 122 originally arrested.

The emergency unleashed oppression more severe than that following the Soweto 1976 uprisings and the 1960 state of emergency. In 1960, 2 154 people were detained and 18 011 arrested and charged with various offences. In the first three months of the current emergency, over 5 000 people were detained. Figures released by the Minister of Law and Order show that from the beginning of 1985, over 14 000 people were arrested on public violence charges. Between January and 31 October 1985, at least 685 people had been killed (the police acknowledge that 66% of these deaths were due to police action) and over 24 000 injured[3] since September 1984, when the violent suppression of rent protests in the Vaal Triangle triggered escalating repression. In the 10 months prior to the state of emergency, the politically-related death rate ran at 1,5 per day. After the declaration of the emergency, it rose to 3,5 per day, giving the lie to ministerial claims that the increased powers of the security forces successfully lowered the level of violence in the townships.

Several trends in detentions are apparent. The first two weeks saw mass arrests and detention of leaders and rank-and-file members of organisations. In a second phase the detentions were targeted on activists and fewer people were detained.

26 August marked the beginning of a third trend and an escalation of state repression. Allan Boesak was detained under section 29 of the Internal Security Act, Paddy Kearney of Diakonia and three End Conscription Campaign workers were held in Durban, and COSAS, the most effective, militant and mass-based UDF

affiliate, was banned. The ban on COSAS was particularly significant as up until then the state had attempted to immobilise the UDF
and its affiliates by detaining its members and leadership rather
than by banning organisations.

State of emergency detentions after three months

A regional breakdown of detentions indicates that by October the
Eastern Cape accounted for 60% of the detentions. In Port
Elizabeth 289 people were detained, 51% of the Eastern Cape total.
Uitenhage accounted for 15%. Detentions in small rural towns
amounted to 34% of the total.

The remaining 40% of detentions occurred in the Transvaal, of
which 41% were drawn from Johannesburg: mainly Soweto, Alexandra, Fordsburg and Lenasia. The East Rand was also hard hit,
amounting to 44% of the Transvaal total.

Most detainees were rank-and-file members from civic, student,
youth, women's, clergy, journalist, human rights, trade union,
political and community resource organisations, of which 86%
were affiliated to the UDF. The percentage of detainees belonging
to student groups rose to 25% of the total, and youth groups com-
prised 60%. Young people under 25 were the major victims of
police repression, making up 60% of all detainees.

In the first two months of the state of emergency, police raided
the offices of opposition organisations, many of which were
support groups for community and worker organisations, and confiscated documents. Organisations raided include the Johannesburg Democratic Action Committee; Community Resource
Information Centre; Media and Research Services; Silkscreen
Training Project; Adult Education Project; Health Information
Centre; UDF head office; South African Allied Workers Union;
General and Allied Workers Union; Joint Union Education Project; *Speak*, a community newspaper; COSAS; Soweto Youth Congress; End Conscription Campaign; and Phiri Catholic Church
youth programme. The police also raided meetings, two of which
were called to discuss the state of emergency and the detainee support work. Security police broke up the first meeting after all present were photographed and their names taken. The second was
disrupted by the removal and detention of three participants.

The DPSC was unable to discover the organisational affiliation of all detainees, but most fall into nine categories: civic, youth, student, women's, student, political, human rights, community support, and sports organisations, and trade unions.[4]

Extension of the state of emergency

The Western Cape was initially excluded from emergency regulations. Activists organised a successful schools boycott and a consumer boycott of white shops. When Carter Ebrahim, Minister of Coloured Education, closed the schools under his authority, students, teachers and parents reoccupied some of them. Security forces met with stiff resistance in some areas, notably Athlone, and perhaps in frustration, retaliated with the notorious 'Trojan Horse' ambush of Thornton Road. Police used a railway truck as a decoy for stone throwers, and then hidden marksmen in boxes on the back of the truck fired on the crowd. Three people died and many were wounded.

At midnight on Friday, 25 October 1985, State President PW Botha extended the emergency to the Western Cape, including eight magisterial districts around Cape Town, Paarl and Worcester. Over 70 UDF activists were detained under section 50 of the Internal Security Act before the extension of the emergency to prevent them going into hiding. On the same day the state president also lifted the state of emergency in six districts — five in the Eastern Cape and one in the Transvaal. However, these districts had been relatively quiet, and only a few people had been detained.

The onslaught on the UDF

UDF office bearers suffered extreme repression. Two UDF executive members, Matthew Goniwe and Victoria Mxenge, were assassinated in as yet unsolved murders. The state held 36 UDF office bearers under the Internal Security Act, and 13 under the Public Safety Act. Some were detained more than once. Seven are on trial, of whom four were refused bail by an attorney general's certificate.

Twelve of the 16 members of the UDF National Executive were detained. They were:

Curnick Ndlovu   Chairperson   Detained, S29 ISA

Popo Molefe	General Secretary	Detained, S29 ISA, awaiting trial, treason, (Delmas)
Mosiuowa Patrick Lekota	Publicity Secretary	Detained, S29 ISA, awaiting trial, treason, (Delmas)
Mcebisi Xundu	Member	Detained, S29 ISA, redetained, Transkei PSA
Edgar Ngoyi	Member	Arrested, awaiting trial, murder
Yunus Mohamed	Member	Detained, S29 ISA
Titus Mofolo	Member	Detained, S29 ISA
Oliver Mohapi	Member	Detained, S29 ISA
Steve Tshwete	Member	Detained, S29 ISA, (escaped)
Zoli Malindi	Member	Detained, S50 ISA, then PSA
Trevor Manuel	Member	Detained, S50 ISA, then PSA
Jomo Khasu	Member	Detained, S29 ISA

UDF Regional Executive Committees

Transvaal: Nine of the 18 members of the Transvaal REC were detained.

Albertina Sisulu	President	Detained, S29 ISA awaiting trial, treason, (PMB)
Ram Saloojee	Vice-President	Detained, PSA
Ismail Mohamed	Vice-President	Awaiting trial, treason, (PMB)
Paul Mashatile	General Secretary	Detained, PSA
Eddie Makue	Minute Secretary	Detained, PSA
Matthews Sathekge	Student Portfolio	Detained, S29 ISA
Amanda Kwadi	Women's Portfolio	Detained, S29 ISA
Paul Maseko	Labour Portfolio	Detained, PSA
Titus Mofolo	Treasurer	Detained, PSA

Eastern Cape: Two of the six members on the Eastern Cape REC were detained, while a third was assassinated.

Edgar Ngoyi	President	Arrested, awaiting trial, murder
Henry Fazzie	Vice-President	Detained, PSA
Matthew Goniwe	Organiser	Assassinated (murder unsolved)

Natal: Ten of the 16 members on the Natal REC were detained, while one was assassinated.

Archie Gumede	President	Detained, S28 ISA awaiting trial, treason, (PMB)
Mcebisi Xundu	Chairman	Detained, S29 ISA, then Transkei PSA
Billy Nair	Vice-Chairman	Detained, S29 ISA
Yunus Mohamed	Secretary	Detained, S29 ISA
Victoria Mxenge	Treasurer	Assassinated (murder unsolved)
Russel Mpanga	Release Mandela Committee	Detained, S29 ISA
Nosiswe Madlala	Natal Organisation of Women	Detained, S29 ISA
Paddy Kearney	Diakonia	Detained, S29 ISA
Themba Nxumalo	Unionist	Detained, S29 ISA
Ian Mkize	Joint Rent Action Committee	Detained, S29 ISA
Lechesa Tsenoli	Publicity Secretary	Detained, S29 ISA

Border: Six of the ten Border REC members were detained.

Ntombazana Botha	Assistant Treasurer	Detained twice, S29 ISA
Andrew Hendricks	Publicity Secretary	Detained, S29 ISA
Lucille Meyer	Additional Member	Detained twice, S29 ISA
Yure Mdyogolo	Additional Member	Detained, PSA
Hintsa Siwisa	Treasurer	Detained, Ciskei National Safety Act

Steve Tshwete	President	Police announced his detention under S29 ISA on 23.08.85, and denied it on 26.08.85

Western Cape: Thirteen of the fourteen Western Cape REC members were detained.

Zoli Malindi	President	Detained, S29 ISA, S50 ISA, PSA
Trevor Manuel	Secretary	Detained, S50 ISA, PSA
Wilfred Rhodes	Vice-President	Detained, S29 ISA, PSA
Christmas Tinto	Vice-President	Detained, S29 ISA, PSA
Miranda Qwanyashe	Secretary	Detained, S29 ISA
Ebrahim Rasool	Secretary	Detained, S29 ISA
Zoliswa Kota	Publicity Secretary	Detained, S29 ISA
Joe Adam	Treasurer	Detained, S29 ISA
Goolam Abubaker	Fund raiser	Detained, S29 ISA
Mildred Lesiea	Additional Member	Detained, S29 ISA Detained, S50 ISA, PSA
Mountain Qumbula	Additional Member	Detained, S29 ISA, PSA
Graeme Bloch	Additional Member	Detained, S29 ISA, S50 ISA, Charged, illegal gathering
Syd Luckett	Additional Member	Detained, S29 ISA

Nationally and regionally, state repression has affected 50 of the 80 executive members of the UDF, that is 63%. A similar pattern of extreme state repression occurs at lower levels of the UDF. It is evident that the state aims to crush the UDF by removing its leaders rather than banning the organisation and incurring international displeasure. A DPSC analysis of the affiliations of individuals and organisations supports the view that the declaration of a state of emergency was aimed primarily at the UDF. Prior to the extension of the emergency to the Western Cape, where detainees' affiliations were known, 86% of them were members of UDF-affiliated organisations.

Other organisations affected include the black consciousness groupings of AZAPO and its student wing, AZASM, and the trade union grouping CUSA (Council of Unions of SA), which together account for 6% of detentions. The remaining 8% of detainees are drawn from groups such as clergy, journalists or sporting bodies which have no direct political affiliation.

This picture changed somewhat after the extension of the emergency to the Western Cape. Here again, the majority of detainees are UDF-affiliated, but there are also numbers of those detained who belong to organisations such as the New Unity Movement, Qibla, the Cape Action League, and some National Forum-linked groups.

Deaths in detention or police custody

An accurate count of people who have died in the hands of the security police is almost impossible. It is rendered even more difficult by the police tactic of making political arrests without invoking security legislation. Thus the DPSC has introduced a new category of 'politically-linked deaths in police custody'.

According to DPSC records, 54 people had died in detention up to the end of 1983. From 1984 to October 1985 at least four died in detention and 14, held for political reasons, in police custody.

The detainees were:

Samuel Tshikudo, died 20.01.84 of 'medical neglect', age 50, held under the Venda Terrorism Act.
Mxolisi Sipele, died June 1984, in hospital while held by Transkei security police.
Ephraim Mthethwa, died 26.08.84, age 23, found hanged in cell in Durban, awaiting trial after six months detention.
Andries Raditsela, died 06.05.85, age 29, a Chemical Workers Union shop steward, of head injuries in hospital after being held under section 50 of the Internal Security Act.

Deaths in police custody are too numerous to detail individually, but some deserve special mention. Sipho Mutsi, of Odendaalsrus, aged 20, was a member of COSAS and taken in for questioning under the Criminal Procedure Act in May 1985. Police claimed he went into convulsions while sitting on a chair, but the post mortem found he died of extensive head injuries. The King William's Town police station was responsible for the death of three UDF activists over a period of five weeks, in July and August 1985. The last was Mbuyiselo Mbotya, age 35, who died of head injuries a day after he was apprehended in Ginsberg township.

Deaths, political violence and the role of the military

Another alarming trend during 1985 was the increasing number of disappearances or assassinations of political leaders and activists. With so many activists in hiding, and police concealment of detentions, a person who has disappeared is extremely difficult to trace. In most cases the family of the missing person has given him up for dead.

Some notable disappearances include that of Topsy Mdaka and Siphiwe Mtimkulu, two Port Elizabeth COSAS members who went missing in 1983. Mtimkulu was suffering from thalium poisoning which he had contracted in detention, and was suing the Minister of Law and Order for R150 000. More recent disappearances include Sipho Hashe, Champion Galela and Qaqawuli Godolozi, executive members of the Port Elizabeth Black Civic Organisation who vanished in late 1984.

In June 1985 four Eastern Cape UDF activists, Matthew Goniwe, Sparrow Mkhonto, Sicelo Mhlauli and Fort Calata, first reported as missing, were found murdered. At least 15 political activists have been assassinated in recent years. They include these four Eastern Cape UDF members, UDF Tembisa activist Brian Mazibuko; Durban civil rights lawyer and UDF treasurer Victoria Mxenge; Durban trade unionist Thabo Mokoena; Umlazi UDF supporter Mandla Mdlela and Natal AZAPO member James Ngubeni. The deaths in Natal are largely attributed to Inkatha 'armed impis'. Threats to the lives of activists and their families are commonplace, and many homes of activists have been attacked with petrol bombs and hand grenades. Assassinations have also occurred outside South Africa. In June 1984, in Lubango, Angola, Jeanette Curtis and her four-year-old daughter were killed by a parcel bomb apparently destined for her husband, Marius Schoon, an ANC member.

Deaths in the streets of townships have escalated. In the three months since the state of emergency was declared 350 people have died. The massacre of 21 mourners in Langa, Uitenhage, in 1985 is the most notorious mass killing, but similar incidents have occurred and passed unnoticed because of the smaller numbers involved.

The role of the military in suppressing unrest has escalated over the past year. A precedent was set in Sebokeng on 23 October 1984, when soldiers entered the township. Over 7 000 policemen and soldiers conducted house-to-house searches. The use of the SADF was formalised by the state of emergency, and in many areas the army superceded the police in authority. Human rights organisations, such as DPSC and Black Sash, were inundated with complaints about SADF brutality. Allegations of rape, assaults and electric shock torture were common. The organisations have affidavits alleging assault and interrogation in army camps.

The situation is exacerbated as army units have minimal training in crowd control, and tend to be armed with R1 rifles and 'sharp' ammunition, rather than the less-deadly weaponry issued to police units. With reason, township residents are incensed at the military presence in their locations, and regard it as tantamount to a state of civil war.

Notes

1 We include the national states or independent bantustans in our statistics for several reasons. First, we do not recognise their independence from South Africa; second, their security legislation is directly modelled on South Africa's with scarcely a word changed, except in the title; third, their security forces are trained, and often staffed, by South Africa; and finally the two groups of security forces are in close collusion. In short, the 'homeland' security police are South African creations, and behave in a similar way to their mentors.

2 'Hidden repression: report of results of a survey of 37 Transvaal organisations, September 1983-July 1984' (DESCOM/DPSC, Johannesburg, 1984).

3 These figures are an update provided by the SA Institute of Race Relations and *Financial Mail*, 13.09.85.

4 Organisations whose leaders or members were detained under the state of

emergency include the following categories:

i. Civic Associations
PEBCO (Port Elizabeth Black Civic Organisation)
SCA (Soweto Civic Association)
GRCA (Graaff-Reinet Civic Association)
ERAPO (East Rand People's Organisation)
Organ for Peace (Fort Beaufort)
GRACA (Grahamstown Civic Association)
DUCA (Duduza Civic Association)
Port Alfred Civic Association
Katlehong Action Committee
Tembisa Civic Association
Tsakane Civic Association
Tsakane Homeseekers

ii. Youth Organisations
SOYCO (Soweto Youth Congress)
KWAYCO (KwaThema Youth Congress)
AYCO (Alexandra Youth Congress)
PEYCO (Port Elizabeth Youth Congress)
UYCO (Uitenhage Youth Congress)
STEYCO (Steytlerville Youth Congress)
TSAYCO (Tsakane Youth Congress)
DUYO (Duduza Youth Organisation)
LYL (Lenasia Youth League)

iii. Students
COSAS (Congress of South African Students)
AZASO (Azanian Students Organisation)
NUSAS (National Union of South African Students)
Parents/Students Committee

iv. Women's Organisations
PEWO (Port Elizabeth Women's Organisation)
FEDTRAW (Federation of Transvaal Women)
WWM (Wits Womens Movement)

v. Political
TIC (Transvaal Indian Congress)

UDF (United Democratic Front)
JODAC (Johannesburg Democratic Action Committee)

vi. Trade Unions
FOSATU affiliates (Federation of South African Trade Unions)
CUSA affiliates (Council of Unions of South Africa)
SAAWU (South African Allied Workers Union)
GAWU (General and Allied Workers Union)
MACWUSA (Motor Assemblers and Component Workers Union of South Africa)
CCAWUSA (Commercial, Catering and Allied Workers Union of South Africa)

vii. Human Rights Groups
DESCOM/DPSC (Detainees Support Committee/Detainees' Parents Support Committee)
ECC (End Conscription Campaign)

viii. Community Support Organisations
MARS (Media and Research Services)
CRIC (Community Resources Information Centre)
STP (Silkscreen Training Project)
ERC (Economic Research Committee)
AEP (Adult Education Project)
HIC (Health Information Centre)

ix. Sporting Organisations
SACOS (South African Council of Sport)
EPCOS (Eastern Province Council of Sport)

South Africa's Regional Political Economy: A Critical Analysis of Reform Strategy in the 1980s

William Cobbett, Daryl Glaser,
Doug Hindson and Mark Swilling

Introduction

Since the late 1970s the apartheid state has faced a sustained and deepening crisis of legitimation.[1] This crisis has been exacerbated by the attempt, and failure, to implement the post-Soweto 'Total Strategy' reforms — reforms which left the territorial and political basis of grand apartheid intact. Since the end of the short-lived boom of 1979-82, the crisis of political legitimacy has been amplified by the slide into economic depression, and the scope for concessionary economic reforms has been drastically curtailed.

For some time, the state has been caught up with the immediate threat of escalating opposition in the townships, the symptoms of the deepening economic crisis, and spreading international hostility to apartheid. But while this has been happening, elements within the ruling groups, both inside and outside the state, have been attempting to map out a longer-term strategic offensive aimed at defusing political conflict and restructuring the economy. Faced with a shrinking material basis for concessionary economic reform and growing mobilisation behind the demand for the extension of political rights, the country's ruling groups have begun the search for political solutions to the crisis.

The schemes now being formulated take as their starting point the ultimate inevitability of political incorporation of black people into a single national state in South Africa. They aim to meet this in ways that ensure that real power remains in the hands of the ruling classes.

The move towards political reforms for black people has gone beyond the stage of discussion and planning in certain areas of policy. Already an important pillar of the emerging strategy has gained expression in local government measures passed in 1985.[2] However, much of what is planned has so far only appeared in general policy statements. It is also evident that important facets of the strategy are still in the stage of formulation or are deliberately being held back for the moment. The fluidity of political conditions in South Africa is such that state strategy is the subject matter of open debate and contestation, and is unusually susceptible to official reconsideration and reformulation. Nevertheless we believe it is possible to identify the major contours of an emerging strategy which has been pursued with increasing determination by reformers within the commanding heights of the state since late in 1984.

This offensive is significant in that it goes well beyond the policy package associated with the Wiehahn and Riekert Commission reports, the Koornhof Bills, the new constitution, and the confederation of ethnic states — it goes beyond the 'Total Strategy' formulated by PW Botha in the late 1970s.[3] In contrast to these policies, it abandons the political and territorial premises of apartheid, though not necessarily those of race or ethnicity, and envisages the eventual reincorporation of the bantustans into a single national South African state.

The manner in which this will occur is by no means clear or decided. However, this process of political reintegration of the bantustans is intended ultimately to result in the reorganisation of the territorial basis of South Africa's economic and political system. Central to the reform strategy is the conception that the present provinces and bantustans will be superseded by metropolitan and regionally-based administrative structures through a process of merging, absorption and cross-cutting of present geographical boundaries. It is this geographic outcome of the intended reform strategy that has led us to describe the complex of evolving measures as the state's regional strategy.

The aim of this article is to describe, anticipate and critically analyse the outlines of the emerging regional strategy. Its three major components are new controls on labour movement and settlement, regional development policies (notably industrial decentralisation), and local and second tier government reforms and corresponding constitutional changes. We examine each of these three components and their interconnections.

These changes are a ruling-class response to escalating township struggles, the determined resistance of squatter communities to removal, the dogged efforts of unions to unite migrants and locals, and mass rejection of the new constitution. They have also been shaped by the operation of glacial forces which have produced a concentration of industry and population in and around South Africa's metropolitan industrial and commercial centres. The development of metropolitan-centred and wider regional sub-economies over a decade and more, we argue, has eroded the primary division between the 'white' and bantustan areas on which apartheid was constructed; and has eroded the dualistic spatial framework on which South Africa's political economy was based.

A central issue taken up in the paper is the debate over the possible construction of a federal system in South Africa. We examine major alternative conceptions of the basis of federalism — geographic and ethnic — and show how they correspond to or contradict other plans to divide South Africa into metropolitan and wider planning and administrative regions.

The paper ends with an assessment and critical analysis of the regional strategy.

Industrial decentralisation and influx control policies

Labour movement and settlement controls

The basic aim of the urbanisation strategy set out by the Riekert Commission report in 1979 was to resolve the township crisis by giving recognition to the permanence of urban Africans and to secure their economic welfare by making urban jobs even more inaccessible to the relatively impoverished rural workforce.

The commission drew a sharp distinction between insiders — 'settled urban Africans' with residence rights under section 10 of the Urban Areas Act — and outsiders — Africans domiciled in the bantustans with temporary employment contracts in the white cities. While insiders were to be allowed to move freely within the urban areas subject to the availability of housing and employment, far stricter controls were to be applied to outsiders wishing to enter these areas. The new system of influx control was to be exercised by fortified labour bureaux called assembly centres.[4]

What distinguished this policy from traditional apartheid was official acknowledgement of the right of a (narrowly defined) group of African city residents to remain in white South Africa. This right did not, however, include access to the political realm. Urban Africans would only be allowed to exercise national political rights within their designated bantustans.

Thus the recommendations set out in the Riekert report were framed within the basic political and geographical premises of traditional apartheid: that the majority of Africans could be contained within the bantustans and that even those who resided in white South Africa could be treated as citizens of independent, or potentially independent, black states.

In the six years since the publication of the Riekert Commission report and acceptance of its recommendations by the government there have been repeated attempts to implement this policy through drafting new legislation and reorganising the administrative machinery of labour control. All attempts thus far have failed to give effect to the basic Riekert strategy of dividing the African population into insiders and outsiders and implementing the legislation necessary to maintain this division.[5]

The breakdown of the Riekert approach was due to struggles waged against it by squatters resisting removal; by international pressure groups; and also by big capitalists (for example through the propaganda exercises of the Urban Foundation). The organisational efforts of the union movement, which served to unite long-distance migrants, commuters and urban dwellers, contributed to the erosion of 'insider/outsider' divisions rooted in the 'white' South Africa/bantustan divide.

Traditional labour movement controls in South Africa were designed to regulate the flow of African workers from rural to urban, and from bantustan to 'white' areas. However, the de facto incorporation of parts of bantustans into the suburban peripheries of various metropolitan areas such as Durban and Pretoria over the last 10-15 years, and rapid and relatively unrestrained migration within bantustans from the rural areas to these metropolitan peripheries within bantustans is an important structural factor underlying recent policy changes.

The crucial consequence of these structural changes is the massive increase in the size of the cross-border commuter labour force and the relative decline in long-distance labour migration.[6] Despite their formal legal status, commuter populations have become effectively indistinguishable from urban insiders, even though they are located on the peripheries of the metropoles. Recent legislation has recognised this by allowing commuters to retain section 10 rights. What these processes amount to is the occupational and residential stabilisation of the African working class in and around the metropolitan areas — the formation of what we call new regional proletariats in South Africa.

The recognition of regional labour markets and the possibility of creating these was considered in the White Paper on the Creation of Employment Opportunities (1984). It approved of the policy, which

> . . . pays particular attention to the need for creating more employment opportunities and places greater emphasis on *dealing with labour matters in a regional context* [our emphasis].[7]

Similarly the Department of Constitutional Development and Planning (DCDP) has expressed the view that labour supply areas should be identified with specific regions.[8] This clearly cuts right across the Riekert conception in which rights of labour mobility were to be restricted to urban insiders within 'white' South Africa.

The distance of Port Elizabeth, the East Rand and, most importantly, Cape Town from bantustans has rendered cross-border commuting non-viable in these areas (the Bronkhorstspruit township called Ekangala which is sited in KwaNdebele is changing this picture in the case of the East Rand). Even in these cases the state has proved incapable of preventing the permanent urbanisation of people who previously would have been prevented from entering these areas except as long distance migrants. State attacks on squatters have given rise to explosive situations — in particular at Crossroads. The resultant struggles received considerable international coverage and forced the state to accept the permanence of large informally settled African populations in Soweto-by-the-Sea and Crossroads; to build new townships in 'white' South Africa (as at Khayelitsha); and to grant leasehold rights to established Western Cape African townships such as Nyanga and Guguletu. This shift of policy is expressed in the recent scrapping of the 'coloured labour preference' policy in the Western Cape, which reserved jobs in this area for coloured workers.

Organised industry's recently intensified campaign against influx control involves, in part, a concern to defuse the types of conflicts that have beset Crossroads. Capital also recognises that, in one form or another, 'urbanisation' is taking place in spite of influx control,[9] and this makes the political costs of the system appear even higher. Nor are the costs to capital only political: at a time of recession and inflation the administrative costs, the rigidities that influx control introduces into the labour market, and its impact on urban wages have appeared excessive.

No doubt some businessmen hope that the exposure of organised labour to competition from a regional surplus population will put pressure on urban wage rates and thus erode the gains made by the independent trade union movement in the years immediately following the Riekert report. Certainly capital has called for greater play of market forces, involving a wider, more flexible definition of 'urban' and 'urbanisation' policy in an effort to counter the advance of militant unionism.[10]

The fundamental flaw of the urbanisation strategy set out by the Riekert Commission of 1979 was that it failed to address the twin issues of the urbanisation of the bantustans and African rural impoverishment inside and outside the bantustans. The success of its strategy of strengthening influx controls and segregating urban African 'insiders' from 'outsiders' hinged above all on securing the economic viability and independence of the bantustans as well as the legitimacy of their political systems. In fact the six years since the Riekert report appeared have witnessed a mounting crisis of bantustan legitimacy. This has occurred through the exposure of desperate rural poverty, a flight from the countryside to the urban bantustan areas and into the peripheries of the white-controlled cities, increased reliance of Africans resident in the bantustans on incomes earned in the white-controlled economy through migration and commuting, and heavy dependence of the bantustan states on the South African treasury.

The failure of the Riekert strategy has led both the state and capital to reconsider and reformulate urbanisation policy within a framework which rejects the premises and objectives of traditional apartheid, and to replace it with a concept of 'planned urbanisation'. In essence the emerging policy of planned urbanisation involves a widening of the official definition of 'settled urban' Africans to embrace sections of the de facto urban African population in and around the cities. This new definition of the metropolitan areas is expressed in the recent Regional Services Council (RSC) Act which provides for the inclusion of African townships within bantustan areas abutting metropolitan areas into the administrative ambit of these new local government structures.

This last provision is a decisive break with the notion of the bantustans constituting independent economic and political units which underpinned the Riekert strategy. The new definition of a metropolitan area includes urban and (potentially) quasi-urban settlements within parts of the bantustans — those within commuting distance of the industrial and commercial centres of the country. These areas are now being seen as falling within the sphere of the Regional Services Councils.

In another move which corresponds to the shift in policy some metropolitan administration boards have, for over two years, given 'administrative' section 10 rights to workers resident in commuter areas if they previously held such rights in the prescribed urban area concerned. More recently legislation has been passed which enables Africans to retain section 10 rights after they have been moved from a prescribed area into a bantustan.[11] In this way the meaning of 'local' labour has changed.

The state's current urban policy which acknowledges the inevitability of African urbanisation, but seeks to control it, has been called 'planned urbanisation'. This policy does envisage the incorporation of some previously excluded sections of the African urban population into the administrative and financial ambit of the new metropolitan regions. But its aim is far from allowing unregulated rural-urban migration and settlement. Rather it aims to limit the growth of established townships in the core metropolitan areas and encourage homeless township families as well as some squatter families to move to new residential areas, called deconcentration areas, which are being established on the peripheries of the metropoles. These residential areas are to be linked to deconcentrated industrial and commercial centres which are intended to provide employment opportunities for the local residents.

There are undoubtedly limits to the ability of the metropolitan centres to generate employment and revenue to cater for growing numbers of African workers and their families leaving the countryside for the squatter settlements on their peripheries. Thus, inevitably, new forms and mechanisms of exclusion are being adopted to complement and make possible those of incorporation of the urban population already discussed.

Central among these mechanisms are the Regional Services Councils which are being developed as powerful administrative and fiscal centres. The proposed employment and turnover taxes which are intended to generate revenue for the Regional Services Councils are clearly designed to increase the cost and reduce the incentive to employ African workers in the established metropolitan centres and encourage their employment in deconcentration areas and development points. If successful, these fiscal measures could gradually replace the overtly racist and repressive direct influx and pass controls presently exercised by the labour bureaux.

Incorporation of new sections of the urban African population under the jurisdiction of these councils necessitates at the same time the exclusion of others. Thus while some sections of the urban population will be targeted as beneficiaries of redistributive expenditures within the RSCs, others undoubtedly will be excluded. Thus a crucial unresolved issue is the formulation of criteria of inclusion and exclusion.

At the minimum, sections of the population resident in the rural areas within the bantustans will undoubtedly be deemed to have no claim on the revenues generated and controlled by the RSCs. If these people are to be prevented from migrating to the urban areas and thereby increasing urban unemployment, measures must be designed to control movement within the bantustans between their urban and rural districts. In some areas where the tribal labour bureaux have collapsed, the Development Boards are already operating mobile recruitment and registration units which selectively allocate employment and exclude some rural workers from urban employment.[12] Recent work done in the south-central areas of Bophuthatswana has exposed an apparently systematic attempt to harass non-Tswana people in squatter areas who commute to employment in Pretoria or the industrial areas of Brits-Rosslyn.[13] These examples point to the types of ethnically-based physical movement and settlement controls that may be expected from the new dispensation.

The evolving system of movement and settlement controls is linked to an emerging housing and employment strategy. The Riekert Commission insisted that the right to move from one urban area to another should be qualified by availability of approved housing and employment in the area to which a person wished to move, and restricted this right to Africans with existing permanent urban residence rights under section 10 of the Urban Areas Act. These principles are being modified to meet the aims of planned urbanisation. While approved housing and employment remain necessary qualifications for movement and settlement, the standard of housing and employment deemed acceptable is being reduced.

Housing controls within established metropolitan townships have been relaxed to some degree and provision for some new sites made, largely for commercial housing construction and sale. Most expansion is, however, planned in the new deconcentration areas. Some of these areas, such as Soshanguve near Pretoria, may be incorporated into the bantustans, while others, such as Khayelitsha near Cape Town and Soweto-by-the-Sea near Port Elizabeth, are now likely to remain outside the bantustans.

The employment-linked movement and settlement controls advocated by the Riekert Commission are similarly to be modified in order to allow for the accommodation of larger numbers of Africans in and around the metropolitan areas. The essence of this strategy is to deregulate economic activities in the urban areas and thereby foster the growth of 'informal sector' employment. This will entail the removal of health and safety regulations and exemptions from wage determinations in designated industrial areas.

The concept of 'planned urbanisation' thus seeks to replace bantustan policy with measures designed to regulate population movement and settlement within newly defined spatial units which are centred on the metropolitan areas and embrace neighbouring bantustans or parts of bantustans deemed to fall within their labour supply catchment areas. The objective of this policy is to link such residential areas to industrial deconcentration points not subject to the stringent wage and health regulations and high tax structure of the core metropolitan areas and to promote the growth of employment and income through the fostering of informal sector activities.

Industrial decentralisation

Industrial decentralisation policy has sought for decades to lend economic and political credibility to the bantustans, and was as such predicated on the geographical division between 'white' South Africa and bantustans. When, in 1975, the physical planning branches of the state divided South Africa into 44 planning regions deemed to be geographically and economically 'functional', they were still forced to take as a starting point the continued centrality of bantustan development and 'homeland' policy.

In 1981, however, Prime Minister Botha unveiled a regional development plan premised on a division of South Africa into eight development regions — the boundaries of which cut across bantustan boundaries, as part of what the Buthelezi Commission termed the 'soft-borders' approach. This entailed the planning of economic development within coherent regions free of the constraints imposed by political borders. Its corollary was the creation of the 'multi-lateral' decision-making structure to coordinate development between South Africa and the Transkei-Bophuthatswana-Venda-Ciskei (TBVC) states; the Development Bank of Southern Africa; and the establishment of Regional Development Advisory Committees (RDACs) to identify planning priorities within regions.

The eight regions are more than mere abstractions superimposed on the map of South Africa. Rather, they correspond to changes in the geographical patterns of capital location and labour settlement that have been developing since the late 1960s. These changes are, in part, the unintended result of previous decentralisation policies which, more from practical necessity than philosophical conviction, promoted suburban industrial development in places such as Hammarsdale, Brits and Rosslyn. They are also the legacy of the classical apartheid policy of limiting African urban settlement in 'white' South Africa, and promoting growth of towns behind bantustan boundaries.

Industrial development in South Africa's metropolitan centres has been seen as evidence for the validity of spatially dualistic theories. In the radical literature bantustans are believed to be the product of a process of underdevelopment, upon which the expansion of capitalist centres of industrial activity was based. Generalisations of this kind take as their starting point the notion that bantustans occupy a uniform position within a national division of labour. In reality the bantustans are highly differentiated entities — if in fact they can be regarded, economically, as constituting coherent entities at all.[14]

In our view, the expansion of the metropolitan space-economy since the late 1960s has entailed two facets: on the one hand an urbanisation process that has enmeshed and integrated growing sections of the bantustan populations into the metropolitan industrial working classes; and on the other the dispersal (in part through state inducement) to the metropolitan peripheries (on both sides of the 'borders') of productive activities that are closely tied to the central metropolitan economy through specialisation, the industrial division of labour and monopolistic relationships of ownership and control. It is this fundamental economic dynamic that we call integrative dispersal. This concept allows us to grasp the role that bantustans, metropolitan expansion, urban concentration, and regional economies play in a new emerging division of industry and labour.[15]

The new industrial decentralisation policy takes cognisance of these changes in two ways:

1. It seeks to ensure that the growth of metropolitan regions is not unnecessarily limited, and attaches considerable importance to deconcentration points. ' . . . [It] will largely be necessary to rely on a process of *deconcentration* through which the benefits of agglomeration in the metropolitan areas will be spread over a wider area without aggravating pressure on the metropoles'.[16] In encouraging these trends, the state is acknowledging and attempting to build upon previous patterns of capital-dispersal.
2. It is now encouraging the dispersal of capital to the high-incentive industrial development points (selected outlying areas with the potential for further growth) rather than primarily to remote industrial points in bantustan hinterlands (five to eight points, according to Croeser). This policy bases itself on the notion of 'balancing growth poles', which designates certain towns with proven growth potential as 'growth points'. Their expansion and development is encouraged in order to draw investment away from the traditional highly industrialised metropolitan centres. The designation of certain major towns as growth points themselves (Bloemfontein, East London, Port Elizabeth) is intended to facilitate this process.

The new official emphasis on deconcentration is one of several measures designed to encourage private sector participation in the regional development programme. Certain capitals have responded to the upgraded decentralisation incentives, but sections of organised industry continue to view the state's decentralisation programme as an artificial attempt to redistribute resources between regions, rather than allowing the regions to compete freely against each other. Free inter-regional competition could, in the view of the Federated Chamber of Industries (FCI), ' . . . lead to the revitalisation of the South African economy',[17] whereas induced dispersal is viewed as imposing intolerable costs on industries based in the metropolitan heartlands, namely, the PWV area, Durban-Pinetown, Port Elizabeth-Uitenhage and Cape Town. Industrialists have recently expressed opposition to the indirect fiscal controls which the state now intends using to encourage industrial dispersal and to strengthen the tax base of the Regional Services Councils, shortly to be installed (*FM*, 15.03.85).

State planners intended the new approach to regional development to provide the basis for the future political and economic map of South Africa, whether defined in federal or confederal terms. As the Buthelezi Commission remarked, ' . . . through its new approach to regional development the government is taking the economic route to power sharing rather than the political one, which is unacceptable to its constituency'.[18]

While the planning bodies associated with the development regions, like the RDACs, may not themselves evolve into administrative units, they are seen as a testing ground for 'cooperative decision-making' and future constitutional arrangements. Clearly, there is no inevitability that the precise boundaries drawn up in the 1982 regional development policy will ultimately become the geographical boundaries of a second tier of government. What is apparent, however, is that the bantustans/provinces can no longer constitute the basis of a second tier of government and therefore new intermediate regional governmental units need to be established.

Constitutional restructuring

Apartheid's racially exclusive democracy was predicated on a system that reproduced cheap and differentiated labour power.[19] We have argued that this system has broken down and is being replaced by the formation of regional proletariats and sub-economies. The combined effect of this process and the crisis of political legitimation generated by the mounting national struggles for non-racial democracy created the conditions for the ruling classes to rethink the question of African political representation.

During the course of extensive debates key reformist groups have begun to perceive the metropolitan and development regions as providing the most appropriate geographic foundations for the construction of new local and regional authorities evolving towards a possible federal system. What follows is an examination of the institutional forms that the state introduced in 1984-85, followed by a discussion of the debate over how these structures can be built into a post-apartheid federal system.

During the last half of 1984 and 1985 the state restructured the third and second tiers of government to conform with the procedure laid down in the 1983 President's Council (PC) reports. This 'consociational' structure was originally designed to underpin the tri-cameral parliamentary system, and hence excluded Africans. But sustained nation-wide resistance to the constitution and popular revolts in the townships during 1984 forced the state to incorporate Africans into the RSCs (the upper level of the third tier of government) in November 1984, and to restructure those departments which control African affairs at the first tier level. This abandonment of the PC's consociational/confederal vision[20] has put federalism on the agenda for a wide range of reformists.[21] These include English-speaking liberals, bantustan leaders, influential Afrikaner verligte academics, ideologues and politicians, organised industry and commerce, and the coloured and Indian parliamentary parties.

The third tier

The third tier is composed of local authorities which deal with 'own affairs' for each racial group, and the RSCs which cater for 'general affairs' at metropolitan level.[22]

RSC representatives will not be elected, but nominated by all the local authorities in a given metropolitan region, including the black ones. Each local authority will have one representative for every 10% (or part thereof) of RSC-provided services that it consumes. None will be allowed more than 50% of the votes on the RSC, and a two-thirds majority is required for a decision. Thus those authorities which use the most services (that is, the white ones where industry is located) will have the greatest say.[23]

The RSCs will become the most powerful bodies involved in the provision of public goods at the local level. The most important local authority functions will be transferred to them. Although RSCs are based on local authorities as defined by the Group Areas Act, they are in fact a form of local government that will govern across group area boundaries. In any case, group areas will probably be substantially modified once the new Demarcation Board replaces the old Group Areas Board. The declining importance of traditional boundaries is evident in the proposed establishment of 'grey' Central Business Districts (CBDs) as well as in proposals to place industrial areas under the jurisdiction of black local authorities (*Star*, 05.06.85) and to place some 'homeland' areas under the jurisdiction of the RSCs.

RSCs are designed to be self-financing to facilitate the withdrawal of the central state from the provision of public goods and services. To this end, a new tax system incorporated into the RSC Bill is designed to raise R1,3-billion in the four main metropolitan areas. There will be two taxes: a regional establishment levy which is a tax on turnover that may not be added onto prices in the same way as GST; and the regional services levy which is a tax on wages, salaries, and returns from profits that may not be deducted from employees' pay packets.

The new tax system elicited a howl of protest from organised commerce and industry. The Association of Chambers of Commerce (Assocom), the FCI, and the SA Property Owners Association criticised the system as 'totally unworkable' (*BD*, 09.05.85). They argued that the new tax will increase the number of bankruptcies, exacerbate unemployment and fuel inflation, and have tried to stall the Act in order to allow the Margo Commission on taxation to review it.[24]

Despite these strong objections, the state is determined to find a way to resolve the urban crisis and meet the demands of its moderate African allies. Minister of Cooperation and Development Gerrit Viljoen admitted in May 1985 that it had been a mistake to establish black local authorities without providing them with a viable revenue base (*FW*, 19-22.05.85). The RSCs, which were first mooted in certain inner-state circles in 1981,[25] are designed to over-come this weakness by accomplishing (at least in theory), three ob-jectives:

1. Substantial redistribution of resources from white to black areas. Instead of increasing rent and service charges to finance urban renewal, oppressed communities will in fact be paying for it in-directly because the new taxes will increase consumer prices.
2. Facilitate the withdrawal of the central state from the provision of public services and deflect national political demands down to the local level.
3. The tax on turnover and labour costs is intended to encourage decentralisation of economic activity from the metropolitan areas.

The redistributive and legitimising role of the RSCs is unlikely to succeed in the near future for three reasons:

1. The third tier is in ruins in the African townships. In 1983, 34 black local authorities were introduced and by the end of 1984 there were meant to be 104. By April 1985 there were only three still func-tioning (*RDM*, 16.04.85) as a result of mass resistance. Although this is unlikely to prevent redistribution, it will substantially under-mine the legitimacy of the RSCs.
2. The RSCs are extremely undemocratic, with the balance of power weighted in favour of big business and the petty bourgeoisie because voting capacity depends on 'user strength'. The democratic principle of proportional representation is totally absent, leaving the large impoverished communities politically powerless.
3. The economic crisis currently facing the state, and the debates between monetarists and redistributionists, will continue to con-strain supply of public services and hence the management of capitalist urban reproduction.

The second tier

In May 1985 the state announced that provincial councils would be scrapped. They will be replaced by strong executive and administrative committees appointed by the state president. Contrary to the recommendations of both the majority and minority reports of the PC in 1983, and the Council for the Coordination of Local Government Affairs (released in April 1984), the new second tier authorities will have extensive legislative and executive powers. They will deal only with 'general affairs'.

The scope of jurisdiction of these authorities has not been outlined explicitly, but there is little doubt that they will be based on the eight development regions. Already a substantial planning infrastructure exists on this level, including the RDACs, Development Advisory Committees, the Regional Liaison Committees for those regions that include independent bantustans, the planning branch of the DCDP, and the Development Boards.

Most provincial council functions will be transferred to the first and third tiers, and the second tier will in the near future take charge of local government, regional development, labour movement controls, and transport.

There has not been an official statement on whether Africans will be included on the second tier. Minister of Constitutional Development Chris Heunis has hinted, however, that African interests will be accommodated (*Star*, 11.05.85), and a top official in the Department of Constitutional and Development Planning has said that representatives of the non-independent states will be included. More significantly, the FCI's demand that the second tier be given substantial powers to coordinate regional development strategies across bantustan boundaries within a federal framework has been granted.[26]

The Natal-KwaZulu region is the most advanced as far as the politics of the second tier in an emerging federal order is concerned. Reformers of all persuasions, including elements in the National Party (NP) and the state, have suggested in recent months that the Buthelezi Commission and the Lombard Report[27] be used as a framework for consolidating Natal and KwaZulu into a single regional unit (*Star*, 07.05.85; 05.05.85; 10.03.85; *FM*, 03.03.85; *RDM*, 16.04.85; *BD*, 21.05.85). In May the cabinet considered a plan to implement this. It would involve consolidating KwaZulu into an area stretching from KwaMashu outside Durban to the Mozambique border which would contain 'white' towns like Empangeni, Eshowe and Richards Bay. Natal would then stretch from the north of Durban, and include the south coast and East Griqualand. In keeping with the Buthelezi Commission, the two parts would be governed by a central federal authority. In June the first step was taken when the New Republican Party and NP representatives in the Natal Provincial Council began to formulate a framework for establishing a statutory body to deal with 'general affairs' for Natal-KwaZulu as a whole (*Star*, 06.06.85).

The Buthelezi Commission called for a federal legislative authority for all races in Natal-KwaZulu to be elected on a one man, one vote basis with proportional representation. The multiracial executive should be co-chaired by the provincial administrator and KwaZulu Chief Minister Gatsha Buthelezi. Other recommendations were: a minority veto for 10% of legislature; that legislation should be tested by the courts; a Bill of Rights; and minimum group representation. Although these proposals were rejected by Finance Minister Owen Horwood in 1982, in May Cooperation and Development Minister Viljoen announced in parliament that the Buthelezi Commission was in line with President PW Botha's policy that the only alternative to the complicated task of further consolidating KwaZulu was to recognise that Natal and KwaZulu are economically and hence politically inter-dependent (*Star*, 06.06.85). This announcement was followed by a meeting between PW Botha and Buthelezi which the press interpreted as another step towards the implementation of a regional federal solution for Natal-KwaZulu (*ST*, 19.05.85).

Although the new second tier system centralises power in the hands of the DCDP, this is designed to facilitate the transition to multiracial regional authorities that cut across bantustan boundaries in the long run. The politicised nature of the old provincial councils (with the Transvaal moving increasingly to the right), would have prevented a technocratic top-down transition to multiracial regional authorities in the manner envisaged by the Buthelezi Commission and Lombard report. The fact that they have extensive powers suggests that the regions will be able to develop according to regionally specific economic, political and ideological conditions and the way in which these are used by local economic and political elites.

The first tier

There is a new consensus that 'no real progress in stabilising and normalising relations between people within South Africa or between South Africa and other countries can be made unless legal racial discrimination is removed in the political institutions of this country'. The future 'legitimacy of the Republic of South Africa both internally and externally depends on this issue'.[28] Stoffel van der Merwe, National Party MP and ideologue, wrote in a pamphlet which PW Botha approved that 'Now, in 1985, we have reached a stage where it [the national convention] can be postponed no longer'.[29]

The state has not yet presented a coherent outline of what a future first tier will look like. Instead, the special cabinet committee formed in February 1983 to investigate the 'urban black problem' established a multi-party negotiating forum in January 1985. This was to discuss with 'black leaders' ways to include Africans in higher levels of decision making. Commonly referred to as a 'mini-national convention', the forum generated a spate of declarations of intent, as various ruling group interests tried to force the state to give it a clear federalist agenda. However, much to Buthelezi's chagrin, the state has refused to issue a declaration of intent, on the grounds that negotiations should remain open-ended. Instead, the state has introduced a range of reforms used by officials to demonstrate the state's good intentions. These include the repeal of the sex laws, the removal of the ban on multiracial political parties, the announced moratorium on removals, easing of influx control, moves to deracialise CBDs, and promises to incorporate blacks into higher forms of decision making.

Stoffel van Der Merwe's NP pamphlet maps out a corporate federal structure for the central state that would involve establishing a Black Assembly to deal with African 'own affairs' for 'non-homeland' Africans. This would then link up to a supra-parliamentary coordinating organ made up of representatives from the Black Assembly, the tri-cameral parliament, and independent bantustan states. In this way the dual 'own affairs'-'general affairs' structure would be replicated on all three tiers, leaving the NP's white power base intact — a model that PW Botha calls 'cooperative coexistence'. This has been interpreted by some observers as the first step towards a geographic federation (*Star*, 19.05.85).

The regional or geographic federal alternative proposed by the PFP, the Labour Party, Inkatha and big business is critical of the racial federal model because it concentrates power in the central state. They call for the transfer of substantial power to democratically-elected regional and local federal authorities, with KwaZulu/Natal as the first laboratory for a future geographic federation. This implies that the future form of the central state should be designed only after the lower tiers have been established.

In the meantime, powerful reformers in the state have substantially modified key central state institutions. The recent cabinet reshuffle saw a significant shift of institutional power. The state under 'grand apartheid' controlled every aspect of African life in 'white' South Africa through a separate department (Native Affairs through to the present Department of Cooperation and Development — DCD) and by way of the 'homeland' states in 'black' South Africa.

The DCD is now virtually defunct. The following functions have been transferred to other departments over the last year: African education to the Department of Education and Training, labour bureaux to the Department of Manpower, commissioners' courts to the Department of Justice, relations with 'homelands' to the Department of Foreign Affairs. In the cabinet reshuffle, responsibility for black local government *and* the Development Boards was transferred to the DCDP. This leaves the DCD in charge of trust land and development aid for the 'non-independent' bantustans. The DCDP now controls the following: all local authorities and RSCs through the multiracial Council for the Coordination of Local Government Affairs (CCLGA); the second tier which includes the new regional committees, RDACs, Regional Liaison Committees, and significantly the Development Boards;[30] liaison with the bantustans through the multi-lateral coordinating bodies; 'homeland' consolidation; and group areas.

This Bonapartist concentration of power in the DCDP clears the way for a process of reconstruction that may have far-reaching implications for the federalist momentum. The fact that it works closely with capital in the RDACs, with the bantustans in the multilateral structures, and with moderate urban Africans in the CCLGA and Development Boards, means that it will be directly exposed to the combined demand of these interests for a more coherent geographic federation to ease South Africa out of the present interregnum.

The federalism debate

After 1979, reformers inside the state began to recognise that the Verwoerdian vision of parcelling South Africa up into independent ethnic states was unrealisable.[31] Those institutional pillars of apartheid, the bantustans, could not achieve either economic autonomy or political legitimacy. Their reintegration into a common economic planning and political framework was increasingly seen as inevitable, notwithstanding the granting of 'independence' to Venda in 1979 and Ciskei in 1981.

The concept of federalism has a long history in the English-speaking reformist community.[32] The Progressive Party advocated a federal formula as far back as 1962, following the recommendations of its internal Molteno Commission. The United Party adopted a federal programme in 1972, and its successor, the New Republic Party, has advocated a 'federal-confederal' option for South Africa.[33] Both parties view African urbanisation as inevitable, and accept the corollary that sections of the African population must eventually be politically accommodated within central state political institutions.

Set up by the KwaZulu legislative assembly, the 1982 Buthelezi Commission received strong support from English-speaking liberals in Natal. It argued for a single geographically-based federal administration for Natal and KwaZulu.[34] The report hinted that a national federal system, in which Natal and KwaZulu together made up one of a number of regional units, provided a long-term solution to South Africa's problem of national political representation.[35]

Before the 1985 parliamentary session, the government was publicly committed to establishing a confederal system which required bantustan leaders to accept independence and then enter into an 'international' agreement linking them to South Africa. Some bantustan leaders — for example Sebe of the Ciskei and Mphephu of Venda — supported the government's ethnic confederal blueprint, and resisted the idea of geographical federation in which bantustans would lose their 'independence'.[36]

Other bantustans refused independence (KwaZulu, Lebowa, Kangwane, Gazankulu and Qwaqwa), and two 'independent' bantustans (Transkei and Bophuthatswana) openly rejected Pretoria's schemes for confederation. In July 1983, the leaders of these bantustans, excluding Bophuthatswana, issued a declaration of intent in which they stated that, in the event of their opting for a constitutional arrangement, they would structure it on a regional non-racial and non-ethnic basis.[37]

There is considerable ferment among Afrikaner verligte reformers, both within and outside the National Party (*FM*, 23.11.84; 14.06.85). Van der Merwe's pamphlet acknowledges that grand apartheid has met with insuperable problems and enumerates several new possibilities:

> The national states might obtain powers over some of the areas outside their borders; local authorities might be given considerably wider powers; local authorities might be linked together in authoritative structures encompassing larger areas; new bodies comparable to the white provincial councils might be established; a national assembly of black people outside the national states might be brought into being; some of these bodies might be involved in decision-making at the highest level in conjunction with the South African parliament and the governments of the national and possibly even the independent states.[38]

Two key features are present here: a search for means of incorporating Africans within central state institutions, and retention of race or ethnic identity as the basis for political representation. This may lead to what has been termed corporate federalism (or federal/confederalism), where membership of racial or ethnic group, rather than territorial location, defines the composition of the federating units.

Another model has been proposed in reports sponsored by organised industry and commerce (notably ASSOCOM and the Sugar Association).[39] They call for a federation based on geographically rather than racially or ethnically defined units. ASSOCOM's report rejects corporate federalism on the grounds that it will be seen to be racist and calls instead for a geographic federation which can protect minority group rights while simultaneously creating a single national state.

Federalism is seen by the ruling groups as resolving the problem of incorporating Africans politically, while retaining and strengthening a capitalist system. Both conceptions of federalism, corporate and geographic, have in common two basic features: the view that 'economic freedom and the private enterprise ethic — as well as the norms with which they are associated — are best entrenched in a future political system embodying the principles of federalism or confederalism';[40] and the belief that federalism is preferable to both apartheid and a majoritarian unitary state, because it allows for the creation of a new nation-state which grants political rights to all its subjects while 'protecting minorities'.

In fact, concern for group rights masks more fundamental fears. Firstly, that a state dominated by a black majority could begin building socialism, or at least impose a welfare state system that entails 'confiscatory taxation',[41] fiscal indiscipline, high minimum wages, and nationalisation. (The latter is certainly implied in the Freedom Charter). Secondly, the too-rapid advancement of an inexperienced black elite into senior positions in the civil service, government and business could lead to managerial inefficiency and administrative 'chaos'.[42] The third fear is that ethnic conflicts under majority rule (including violence directed at whites) could lead to economic and political breakdown.

Proponents of federalism argue that the only way to prevent a black majoritarian state imposing socialism or a welfare state from above is to establish relatively autonomous local and regional political entities. These would hold sovereign power over limited coercive apparatuses and economic policies, fragmenting a national majority regionally.

Federalism also lends itself to a system of institutional checks and balances both regionally and within the central state. These include structures like an independent federal reserve bank, separate legislative houses, a separate legislature, executive and judiciary. Further, entrenched constitutional provisions could protect freedom of contract, the status of the currency, minority veto rights, the right to property, and so on. A federal system would thus limit any one group's access to political power.

A central government operating according to these principles might for example have to:

• accept unpopular monetary measures imposed by the (ostensibly apolitical) federal reserve bank; or
• secure acceptance of legislation from two legislative houses; or
• accept limits on its power to impose its policies on particular regions; or
• allow the constitutionality of its policies to be tested by an in-

dependent judiciary.

This is what Lombard and Du Pisanie call 'polycentrism'. Such 'division of sovereignty'[43] is a prescription for minimal or limited government, which leaves the state incapable of affecting radical changes. Reformers in the ruling groups hope a federal system would place the central state above political conflict, making it difficult to mobilise nation-wide forces around demands with national scope. A federal state would by default leave intact the foundations of the economy and relations of production, and expose only marginal or localised elements of the economic system to modification.

The meaning of 'group rights' and the theory of ethnic pluralism thus becomes apparent. The apartheid legacy of 'ethnicity' is now being used by many reformers as a rationale for a federal system which could provide the basis for a reconstituted capitalist political economy. Ethnicity need not necessarily be legally entrenched, because apartheid has ensured that racial and ethnic groups are already geographically separate.

The call for some kind of federal solution is rapidly becoming the cornerstone of consensus among those favouring a reformist solution in South Africa.

A critical analysis of regional federalism

This paper has not attempted to provide a holistic analysis of the current period of crisis and restructuring in South Africa. Such an analysis would have required an examination of a number of developments that we have left out of our account, or have only superficially touched upon: the economic stagnation of the 1970s and 1980s; the current recession; the resurgence of various forms of oppositional politics; the 1984-85 township rebellion culminating in the state of emergency; and numerous other factors that have combined to make the present conjuncture extremely fluid and unpredictable.

We have argued that a consensus has emerged within the reformist elite about the need to implement changes that go well beyond the 'Total Strategy' initiatives of the late 1970s and early 1980s. In part this further metamorphosis of the reform process is the outcome of increasingly intense conflict between the regime and its opponents — in particular its failure to establish legitimacy for the new black local authorities and the tri-cameral parliament and, more recently, its inability to curb the wave of popular demonstrations, boycotts, strikes and other civil disturbances that began early in 1984.

It was these events which forced the government to include Africans in the RSCs, to reexamine the question of African political participation in the central state, and to consider substantial modifications to its influx control policies.

However we also argue that the necessity for and tendency of state restructuring in these areas can only be fully understood in relation to changes in South Africa's spatial reproductive economy. By this we mean the development of new patterns of capital and labour location, in particular the dispersal of capital from metropolitan heartlands to metropolitan peripheries and other regions; the enmeshing of certain bantustan labour supply areas into the process of metropolitan urbanisation; and the crystallisation of regional economies and regional proletariats. These processes, which have drained of meaning the conventional dichotomies of bantustan/white South Africa and urban/rural, have informed thinking about the RSC concept as well as debates around second tier regional structures in a future federation. They have also directly shaped the regional development strategies. Finally, they have influenced aspects of the emerging policy of 'planned urbanisation'.

We have shown, briefly, how the devolution of power, the partial 'deracialisation' of administration and the proposed federalist system are being developed as an alternative to 'majoritarianism' and all that the ruling groups fear would accompany majority rule: bureaucratic breakdown, social disruption, intercommunal conflict, welfare statism, socialism.

The more immediate purpose of these initiatives is to help the state reimpose 'law and order', secure a degree of popular quiescence and regain control of the pace and direction of political developments. The 'reforms' are consciously designed to arrest, rather than promote, rapid and fundamental change. They are therefore unlikely to satisfy crucial popular demands.

The reform initiatives will face popular pressure for rational economic planning to reduce unemployment and inflation and for improved provision of basic services. The restructuring process involves a curious combination of 'free market' and 'redistributive' policies. On the one hand, the central state, confronted by a fiscal crisis and committed to a monetarist economic programme, is cutting back its role in the provision of welfare services (as for example in the case of bread and transport subsidies). At the same time, the state is confronted by a political crisis in the urban areas, and recognises that it has to improve the quality of life of black townships in order to restore stability there. Its solution is to force the RSCs to subsidise expenditures in the townships through their payroll and turnover levies.

The logic seems to be threefold. First of all, such a programme (theoretically) allows the central state to insulate itself from competition over the allocation of resources, thereby localising these conflicts. Secondly, devolution of fiscal responsibility forces capitalists to choose between subsiding metropolitan services or relocating their investments to decentralisation growth points. In other words, businessmen cannot have it both ways: if they insist upon the desirability of urbanisation they must be willing to pay for it.

And finally, since the total resources available for redistribution remain limited, especially in a period of economic stagnation, it is impossible for the state to satisfy every locality's claims on social resources. Given that this is so, it makes sense for the central state to allow local and metropolitan governments to rely on their own fiscal resources, however unequal these may be. The likely result is increased inequality between metropolitan regions. To offset this (and its potentially explosive political consequences in areas like the Eastern Cape) the state is relying on persuading capital to relocate to less developed regions in response to incentives offered there. These incentives form part of a decentralisation programme that is itself expensive, at least in the short to medium term.

Whether these various objectives — central state withdrawal, metropolitan upliftment and regional development — can be accomplished simultaneously, especially in a period of low economic growth, remains very doubtful. Consider the dilemma facing the metropolitan authorities. Since the RSCs would enjoy a minimum of financial support from the central state, the only way they could hope to deliver adequate services to the black urban areas would be by raising metropolitan taxes and levies beyond the levels presently envisaged. If they raise taxes beyond a certain point, they could provoke either a capital flight to regions offering better incentives or else an investment slowdown that would further reduce economic growth in the economy as a whole.

If they choose to spend beyond their means the RSCs could generate a series of local fiscal crises, forcing the central state to bail out troubled councils in an ad hoc way. The state's overall borrowing requirements would have to expand (whether it is the central state or the metropolitan authority that does the borrowing), and this in turn could swell the national debt, create inflationary difficulties or force interest rates to rise. The alternative would be to cut back on the provision of services.

If the RSCs cannot provide goods on a scale that meets the increasingly insistent demands of poor and working people in the urban areas, they could be forced into a game of 'divide and rule', playing some recipients of social goods off against others. With considerably more goods available for distribution in black townships than in the past, metropolitan authorities could, in some cases, play such a game quite effectively. They — and the central state — would thus acquire new resources of social control.

Faced by increasingly sophisticated techniques of cooption, popular organisations will have to rethink their own tactical and strategic responses. Under these circumstances it will be more important than ever to reiterate the demand for democratically-determined social welfare priorities, and for services that address the needs of the poorest regions and social strata within regions. These demands will have to be backed up by an increasingly articulate call for strategies to promote economic recovery in ways that are not detrimental to the interests of the working class.

The reforms cannot satisfy popular demands for democratic participation in the reform process. Political restructuring is proceeding in a top-down, managerial way, with at best a small circle of influential reformers and black collaborators being drawn into decision making. The public language of ruling group reformers is framed in the imagery of the free market economy, technocratic neutrality, local democracy, consensus and consultation. Its private agenda — where such an agenda exists — is shrouded in deliberate secrecy. Public deception is central to the timing and delivery of reforms; it is seen as crucial to defusing opposition from both the right and the left. If it should fail to contain popular opposition effectively, the state is more ready than ever to resort to repression.

It seeks reform, but as a precondition for that it demands tight control.

Reformers will maintain constant vigilance against all political initiatives not amenable to state manipulation. They are determined to force others to conform to their own plans. This requires that they negotiate only from a 'position of strength' — which means ensuring the weakness of community organisations, trade unions and political groupings seeking fundamental change through grass roots struggle. Deception and repression are thus the constant companions of 'reform'.

Reformers in the state cannot satisfy popular demands for democratic political representation. While accompanied by talk about the 'devolution' of power, the reorganisation of the state system involves a combination of centralising and decentralising tendencies. Crucial functions — for example, security, the formulation of the reform programme, foreign policy — are being concentrated in executive organs insulated from electoral pressures and public scrutiny. These organs include the office of the president, top officials in a few key departments (like Constitutional Development and Planning), and the State Security Council. These are the commanding heights of the authoritarian-reformist state that the Botha leadership has set in place.

At the same time, second and third tier structures will be given genuine powers, but mainly (it seems at this stage) of an administrative kind. For example, while the RSCs are likely to command considerable resources, their sole function will be the management of certain kinds of 'hard' services at the metropolitan level. At the same time an attempt is deliberately being made to remove the RSCs from the field of political contestation, to present them instead in a neutral, technical visage. They will also be predicated on indirect, rather than direct, representation and on the over-representation of wealthier municipalities. Devolution of power along these lines does not involve real democratisation.

The final demand that the 'reforms' cannot satisfy is the demand for national democratic rights — for the effective transfer of sovereignty to the representatives of the majority of South Africans. The emerging federal framework is intended to prevent national democratic forces from mobilising against the central state and, should they come to control that state, it is designed to prevent them from effectively using it to bring about radical social and economic changes.

The ideological rationale for anti-majoritarian federalism lies in the argument that minority rights need to be protected from 'majority domination'. And, indeed, one can readily concede that minorities should have 'rights' — rights to freedom of speech, press, association, religion, petition, to practice their own culture, to equal political rights, to safeguard their material well-being. But minorities do not have the 'right' to entrench their political and economic privileges at the expense of the majority.

In South Africa the right of the majority to rule — whatever form that rule may take — remains non-negotiable. This is the basic right demanded in the Freedom Charter and other popular manifestos, and is implicit in the programme of the workers' movement.

Conclusion

The fate of the 'reform' process is extremely uncertain. Whether or not it gains any substance will depend on the outcome of struggles within the ruling party and in reformist circles; it will also depend on struggles between reformists and their opponents both on the right and in the popular movements; finally, it will depend on the state of the economy. Yet it would be wrong to dismiss the restructuring process as simply cosmetic. It could prove real enough to reshape, in important ways, the terrain upon which struggles over fundamental change are being played out.

The 'reforms' could have a considerable impact on, for example, the resources available for the cooption of sections of the black population. They could also affect the international saleability of South Africa's constitutional order. These are but two of the many areas in which their influence could be felt.

How far the restructuring process 'succeeds' will depend on how seriously it is taken by its opponents. To dismiss the 'reforms' in advance as illusory or unworkable, or to suppress discussion of their content and direction, would automatically enhance their effectiveness as weapons in the hands of the ruling groups.

The claim that the 'reforms' are cosmetic is likely to carry less analytical and moral force as time goes by. A much more powerful criticism would be one that exposes the real motives behind the 'reforms', decodes the discourses and shows, concretely, why — and where — they are unlikely to satisfy key popular demands. We have commenced, but by no means completed this task.

We should not however assume that the entire 'reform' process is so pervaded with repression and authoritarianism, or that it so uniformly expresses the will of the ruling class and the imperatives of class domination, or that it is so immutable, that some of its elements are not open to transformation into something more democratic and into something capable of advancing certain popular objectives.

The 'reforms' are complex and varied; some offer more spaces and opportunities than others. We need to seriously examine these spaces and opportunities, both to assess their importance to short- and medium-term strategy, and in order to determine what elements, if any, can be built upon in the struggle for a radically different order.[44]

If we accept that the process of building democratic structures must begin in the here and now, and that certain progressive reforms are possible prior to the achievement of full democratic rights, then we must ask whether, and to what extent, the reform process is generating resources and openings that can be utilised as a part of a 'politics of transformation'.[45] Can some of the emerging structures be utilised by organisations seeking to institutionalise genuinely democratic practices? Can they be used to secure material concessions that in turn could help to bolster the credibility, and power, of those organisations?

It may be wrong to adopt a principled but purely rejectionist response, in advance, to everything that the restructuring process delivers; what is needed instead is the capacity to buttress rejection with rigorous critical analysis, and to modify rejection, where necessary, with a careful assessment of new strategic opportunities.

Notes

1 See, for example, J Saul and S Gelb, *The Crisis in South Africa. Class Defence, Class Revolution* (Monthly Review Press, 1981); G Moss, 'Total Strategy', *Work in Progress*, 11, 1980; D O'Meara, 'Muldergate and the politics of Afrikaner nationalism', *Work in Progress*, 22, 1982; R Davies and D O'Meara, 'The state of analysis of the Southern

African region: issues raised by South African strategy', *Review of African Political Economy*, 29, 1984; D Glaser, 'The state, the market and the crisis', *Work in Progress*, 34, 1984.

2 See the Regional Services Councils Act, passed June 1985.

3 *Commission of Inquiry into Legislation Affecting the Utilization of Manpower*, RP 32/1979 (Riekert Commission); and *Commission of Enquiry into Labour Legislation*, RP 47/1979 (Wiehahn Commission).

4 D Hindson, 'The role of the labour bureaux in South Africa: a critique of the Riekert Commission Report', in (ed) D Hindson, *Working Papers in Southern African Studies Volume 3* (Johannesburg, 1983).

5 D Hindson and M Lacey, 'Influx control and labour allocation: policy and practice since the Riekert Commission', in *South African Review One* (Johannesburg, 1983).

6 See BENBO, *Statistical Survey of Black Development* (1982), Part 1, Tables 24 and 26.

7 White Paper on *A Strategy for the Creation of Employment Opportunities in the Republic of South Africa*, 11(2.32) (1984).

8 Department of Constitutional Development and Planning — submission to the Regional Development Advisory Council (NRDAC), 02.08.84, 6(c).

9 G Relly, 'Influx control and economic growth', in (eds) L Schlemmer and H Giliomee, *Up Against the Fences* (Cape Town, 1985).

10 Relly, 'Influx control'; M Swilling and J McCarthy, 'Transport and political resistance: bus boycotts in 1983', *South African Review Two* (Johannesburg, 1984).

11 S Bekker and R Humphries, *From Control to Confusion: The Changing Role of the Administration Boards in South Africa, 1971-1983* (Pietermaritzburg, 1984).

12 S Greenberg and H Giliomee, 'Labour bureaucracies and the African reserves', *South African Labour Bulletin*', 8(4), 1983.

13 J Keenan, unpublished mimeo, Sociology seminar, University of Witwatersrand, 1985.

14 This point was made by J de Villiers Graaff in 'Homeland function and dependency; a case study of reformist potential', paper presented to the Development Society of Southern Africa, University of the OFS, 1984.

15 The transformation of South Africa's spatial economy cannot be understood by those who remain trapped within two key assumptions that, until recently, pervaded the literature on apartheid: firstly, the assumption that South Africa can be understood as a spatially dualistic society, differentiated into two coherent but radically different entities

called bantustans and 'white' South Africa; and secondly, that these spatial entities correspond exhaustively to distinct, even if inter-connected, forms of social reproduction.

16 Summary of Report of the Study Group on Industrial Development Strategy (Kleu Report) (1983), 21, 10.8.

17 G Maasdorp, 'Coordinated regional development: hope for the Good Hope proposals?' in Schlemmer and Giliomee, *Up Against the Fences*.

18 ' . . . and what about the Black People?', National Party pamphlet, (1985), 9.

19. D Kaplan. 'The South African state: the origins of a racially exclusive democracy , *The Insurgent Sociologist*, X(2), Fall 1980.

20 NP pamphlet, ' . . . and what about the Black People?'.

21 See J Lombard in *Sunday Times*, 03.03.85; and M Forsyth, *Federalism and the future of South Africa* (South African Institute of International Affairs, Johannesburg, 1984).

22 The RSC Bill went through its second reading in early 1984, after which it was referred to a parliamentary select committee where its controver-sial tax system and racial composition was reviewed. It was passed by parliament in June 1985.

23 At this stage the provincial administrator will appoint the chairperson, decide on the number of representatives and can make rulings on deci-sions that are not supported by a two-thirds majority.

24 The Margo Commission into the tax system in South Africa has not yet reported.

25 Interview with G Croeser, Deputy-Director of Finance.

26 See FCI Memo, 'Regional development in South and Southern Africa', submitted to the meeting of the National Regional Development Ad-visory Council (NRDAC), 02.08.84.

27 J Lombard, *Alternatives to the Consolidation of KwaZulu (Natal)* (University of Pretoria, 1980).

28 ASSOCOM Memorandum, *Removal of Discrimination Against Blacks in the Political Economy of the Republic of South Africa* (emphasis in the original).

29 See NP pamphlet, ' . . . and what about the Black People?', 9.

30 There is evidence that these boards are to be phased out. See *Star*, 06.06.85.

31 NP pamphlet, ' . . . and what about the Black People?'

32 The possibility of uniting South Africa on a federal or confederal basis was first raised in a serious way by Lord Carnarvon's confederation scheme in the 1870s, and was raised again by the proposal of Milner's

Kindergarten that South Africa be united on the basis of federation rather than union.

33 B Hackland, 'The economic and political context of the growth of the PFP in South Africa, 1959-78', *Journal of Southern African Studies*, October, 1980. On the NRP, see *Star*, 09.03.85.

34 Buthelezi Commission, *The Requirements for Stability and Development in KwaZulu and Natal*, Vol 11, 4.2.1, 76.

35 Buthelezi Commission, Vol 11, 5.4, 111-115 and 6.6.2, 126.

36 The term is borrowed from Fleur de Villiers, *Sunday Times*, 23.05.80.

37 South African Institute of Race Relations, *Survey of Race Relations in South Africa* (Johannesburg, 1983), 316.

38 NP pamphlet, ' . . . and what about the Black People?', 13.

39 ASSOCOM Memorandum, *Removal of Discrimination*,; and Lombard, *Alternatives to Consolidation*.

40 ASSOCOM Memorandum, *Removal of Discrimination*, 2.

41 ASSOCOM Memorandum, *Removal of Discrimination*, 24.

42 NP pamphlet, ' . . . and what about the Black People?'.

43 ASSOCOM Memorandum, *Removal of Discrimination*.

44 G Adler 'The state, reform and participation', paper presented to the Contemporary Studies Seminar, Sociology Department, University of the Witwatersrand, 31.07.85.

45 A Erwin, 'On unions and politics', paper presented to ASSA Conference, University of Cape Town, July 1985.

Class Interests and Politics: The Case of the Urban African Bourgeoisie

Peter Hudson and Mike Sarakinsky

At its sixth congress in 1928, the COMINTERN directed the Communist Party of South Africa to switch its focus from directly anti-capitalist class struggle and to concentrate on the struggle for national liberation and the creation of an 'independent native republic'[1] as a stage towards the overthrow of capitalism in South Africa. Ever since, the possibility of an alliance of all oppressed black classes has been at the centre of political debate within resistance organisations on the South African left.

Although it has been modified and refined over the years — for example by the introduction of the concept 'national democracy' in the 1950s and 1960s[2] — the central argument of proponents of such an alliance has changed little since the late 1920s. They claim that South Africa is best understood as a colonial society, albeit of a 'special-internal-colonial type'.[3] In South Africa, as is held to be the case in all colonial societies, the central political antagonism is said to exist not between classes, but between colonised and colonising nations. Consequently the different classes comprising the oppressed nation are said to have convergent interests.

It is argued for example that obstacles placed by the colonising state in the path of the development of the indigenous national bourgeoisie led it to join the other colonially dominated classes in the struggle for national liberation. In the case of South Africa, which is considered specific in that the colonising (white) nation occupies the same territory as the colonised group, this type of analysis proposes that the class interests of the indigenous national bourgeoisie led it into alliance with the other oppressed (black) classes in a common struggle to destroy apartheid.

Acceptance of the primacy of colonial-national domination in

South Africa leads Nolutshungu, for example, to argue that white capital and the state are only prepared to contribute towards the development of a black bourgeoisie to the extent that this will make possible more effective control of this class.[4]

> . . . [I]t is important to emphasise that the point of the argument is not quantitative but qualitative. It is not that very little is being spent on black *embourgeoisement* (the sums could, conceivably, be substantially increased), or that this class is small relative to white capital. The crucial issues are autonomy and the politics of accumulation: the relations that are being forged, the interests that have priority, and the political reasoning which prevails, are more consistent with . . . containment rather than transformation, *encadrement* rather than *embourgeoisement*.[5]

In this approach, colonial domination within South Africa sets extremely narrow limits to the possible modification of relations between the state and social classes. Short of the total destruction of apartheid and full national liberation, such relations are not considered susceptible of any real modification.

It is correct to insist, as do the protagonists of this approach, that neither the political identity of a group nor the political alliances it forms can be immediately deduced from its class identity. Class interests and demands are always shaped by the specific conditions obtaining at a given moment in a society. These cannot be overlooked when explaining the specific strategies pursued by agents in order to realise these interests. Such strategies cannot be 'read off' from a group's class identity.[6]

The question that needs to be addressed, however, is whether the colonial model can provide an adequate explanation of the place of the black bourgeoisie in South African society today, and more particularly of the urban African bourgeoisie on which the following analysis focuses. Can this model elucidate the current relationships between the urban African bourgeoisie, white capital and the state? Is it able to elucidate the way class and national relations are developing in South Africa today, or has it lost much of whatever descriptive accuracy and explanatory utility it may once have had?

Until the late 1970s, African entrepreneurs were subject to a complex network of legal restrictions controlling among other things the location, size and types of business they could undertake in urban areas. Since 1975, however, these restrictions have been progressively lifted, to such an extent that it does not seem an exaggeration to suggest that a qualitative change is taking place in the position of the urban African bourgeoisie. This change, in our view, renders highly unlikely any durable participation by this class in a popular alliance struggling for national liberation and the destruction of apartheid.

The formation of NAFCOC

In 1955, the African Chamber of Commerce (ACOC) was formed from amongst the members of the Orlando Traders Association founded in 1945. In 1963 ACOC changed its name to Johannesburg African Chamber of Commerce (JACOC), and again in 1964 to National African Chamber of Commerce (NACOC). In 1969 NACOC became the National African Federated Chamber of Commerce (NAFCOC).[7]

African entrepreneurs have always faced a range of legal and extra-legal restrictions on their operations in the urban areas, and have continuously made representations to the state for reforms. In 1963, soon after Sharpeville and the 1960 state of emergency, JACOC was granted an historic first meeting with the Deputy Minister of Bantu Administration and Development (BAD). Some issues raised by JACOC were: the right to operate businesses in urban areas; state aid for these businesses from the Bantu Investment Corporation (BIC) which had been set up in 1959 to assist bantustan entrepreneurs; and clarification of the legal restrictions facing them. The last request was the only one granted.[8]

NAFCOC continued to press for reforms with no success until 1975. Its demands over the years included: removal of restrictions on African business expansion; changes in the structure and operation of the BIC; exemption of African entrepreneurs from influx control; issuing firearms to African entrepreneurs; that representatives of local African Chambers of Commerce should sit on licensing boards; that African entrepreneurs should be allowed to own land and property for business premises in urban areas; removal of white trading rights in and around the African residential areas; amendments to the tax laws affecting Africans; legislation making NAFCOC membership compulsory for all African entrepreneurs; recognition of and consultation with NAFCOC by the state; opening white business areas to African entrepreneurs, who should be allowed to operate more than one business and lease more than one trading site; that the range of goods African traders could sell be increased beyond 'daily necessities'; and that African companies or partnerships be allowed.[9] Only in 1975 was the legal trend to increase restrictions on African entrepreneurs reversed, and many of NAFCOC's demands began to be met.

The legal history

The major Act restricting African entrepreneurs in the urban areas is the Native (Urban Areas) Act of 1945. It stated that only 'lawful residents' in the urban areas (in terms of section 10) were allowed to trade there, and then only with the approval of the local authority and the Minister of BAD. Trading permits would only be issued if the township superintendent was satisfied that, inter alia:

• a site in the appropriate ethnic area of the township was available;
• the applicant was a fit and proper person to reside in the area;
• the applicant was free of infectious diseases;
• the applicant would erect whatever premises were needed (he could therefore own the premises, but not the land);
• the applicant was 21 years old or more;
• the site would only be occupied by the applicant and dependents.

In 1959, the status of Africans in the urban areas as 'temporary sojourners' was reinforced when the Minister of BAD stressed that African entrepreneurs should be persuaded to transfer their assets to the bantustans.[10] The BIC was set up to promote this process.

Further restrictions on African entrepreneurs were introduced in 1963. They included: Africans were only allowed one business undertaking; only daily essentials for Africans could be sold; companies and partnerships were prohibited, as were African financial institutions, industries and wholesale concerns; and Africans were no longer permitted to erect and/or own business premises. This last was the responsibility of the local authority.[11]

Again in 1968, further restrictions were imposed on African

entrepreneurs. These included:

• Bantu Affairs Administration Boards were now allocated trading sites and could specify the type of trade undertaken;
• the Administration Board had to approve all alterations to existing buildings;
• the trader could not dispose of trading rights without Administration Board permission;
• only lawfully resident Africans could be employed;
• the trader could not be absent from the business for longer than three months, and a manager or supervisor could not be appointed;
• profits could not be shared with anyone other than the trader's dependents;
• traders had to keep financial records;[12]
• trading licences had to be renewed annually;[13] and
• African traders had to show proof of 'homeland' citizenship when applying for trading licences and sites in the urban areas.

In 1969, the state tried to fragment NAFCOC by forcing it to reorganise along ethnic, regional lines. NAFCOC rejected this demand in principle but implemented it in a diluted form to appease the state. This the state found unacceptable, and it rejected all NAFCOC's numerous subsequent memoranda listing grievances and demands until 1975.[14]

In May 1975, after a meeting between the prime minister, the Department of BAD and bantustan leaders, certain reforms affecting African traders were announced. Procedures for renewal of African trading licences were to be brought more in line with those for whites, Africans would be allowed to trade in a wider range of commodities, and to run more than one business on the same premises. Partnerships were legalised, ownership of businesses in the bantustans no longer meant that enterprises in the urban areas had to be forfeited, and 30-year leaseholds were reintroduced.[15] The new regulations came into affect in May 1976.[16] These reforms marked the turning point in state policy regarding African entrepreneurs.

In November 1975 NAFCOC launched the African Bank, a project first suggested to it in 1964.[17] Africans had always had problems raising capital. The BIC only lent money to 'homeland' entrepreneurs and the lack of freehold title meant that Africans had no security to offer white banks in return for loans. Most importantly, the restrictions on African businesses meant that they could not generate sufficient capital themselves for expansion. The establishment of the African Bank is therefore a crucial landmark in the evolution of the African capitalist class.

The state allowed the African Bank to sidestep a number of legal restrictions. It was permitted to open its head office in the centre of Johannesburg, which was officially irregular because African enterprises were otherwise only allowed in African areas. The bank was an illegal African financial institution, as well as an illegal African-owned and controlled public company in partnership with white capital. Most shareholders were Africans with other business interests, though legally Africans could only have interests in one business. Several whites were employed in managerial positions, despite the fact that Africans were legally only allowed to employ other Africans with section 10 qualifications, and were not allowed to employ managers. Restrictions on the size of African business premises (350 square metres) were ignored, as was the fact that 'banking' was not one of the professions Africans were legally allowed to enter.[18]

Upon the African Bank's registration with the Registrar of Financial Institutions, its paid-up capital was specified at R1-m and no white bank could become a majority equity holder. Consequently, the share capital was divided as follows: 50% to the general public but restricted to Africans, 20% to 'homeland' governments, and 30% to white-controlled banks (Volkskas, Trust Bank, Nedbank, Barclays Bank and Standard Bank).[19]

The importance of the establishment of the African Bank cannot be overestimated. At last a financial institution with considerable resources, closely linked to NAFCOC, was created specifically to meet the financial requirements of African enterprises. Moreover it was sanctioned by the state, and white capital was integrally involved in its establishment and operation.

Its opening gave new impetus to NAFCOC, whose president, Sam Motsuenyane, defined its major tasks in the years to come as: ' . . . the promotion of sound working relationships between NAFCOC and both the central and homeland governments, to the end that a favourable climate for black business can be created'.[20]

The township uprisings of June 1976 gave a new boost to the state's reformist initiatives vis-a-vis the African bourgeoisie. In

August 1976 NAFCOC was again given an interview with a senior government official, Deputy Minister of BAD Willem Cruywagen. It was the first meeting between the state and NAFCOC since 1963, and gave NAFCOC 'new hope'.

NAFCOC was recognised to the point that an annual meeting with the deputy minister was agreed upon. Further, administration boards were in future to consult with NAFCOC's local and regional branches on all matters concerning African business. Other reforms announced after this meeting were that Africans would no longer have to produce 'homeland' citizenship certificates when applying for trading licences and sites in the urban areas; the range of commodities African traders could sell was increased; and the possibility of Africans establishing small industries in the urban areas was to be investigated.[21]

NAFCOC's cause began to be taken up by white capital, in particular by the Federated Chamber of Industries (FCI), the Afrikaanse Handelsinstituut (AHI) and the Association of Chambers of Commerce (ASSOCOM). They called for removal of restrictions on African businesses, and specifically suggested that small African industrial and manufacturing plants be established and promoted.[22]

This pressure resulted in a number of new reforms announced in November 1977. They gave effect to the promises made by the deputy minister of BAD a year earlier, and reiterated concessions made in the course of the year. New regulations included: African entrepreneurs could operate more than one business, provided all were on the same site; the number of trades and professions Africans could engage in was expanded from 26 to 66; although African traders could still only employ other Africans with section 10 qualifications, they no longer needed written permission from the local authorities to do so; the stipulation that a trader risked losing his trading licence if absent for longer than three months fell away, as did medical requirements for obtaining a licence; insolvency no longer automatically led to the cancellation of a trading licence.[23]

A month later, in December 1977, further concessions were announced. African traders were now allowed to enter all trades and professions since the schedule of 66 previously approved ones was repealed. Many of the arbitrary powers of the administration boards over African business were withdrawn, and trading licences could now be obtained from local licensing boards, which were branches of the Department of Inland Revenue. This brought licensing requirements for Africans into line with those for whites.[24]

In July 1977, community councils were introduced to administer African townships in place of the Urban Bantu Councils (UBCs). Among their various tasks were allocation and administration of the letting of dwellings, buildings and other structures, and the allocation and administration of sites for churches, schools and trading purposes.[25]

In 1976 NAFCOC had decided to seek representation on the highly discredited UBCs[26], and it was no surprise that it opted for participation in the new councils despite widespread rejection of them by most other Africans.[27] The councils were seen by African entrepreneurs as vehicles to advance their interests through control of the allocation of trading sites. They believed moreover that as councillors they would gain access to the higher echelons of the state, in particular to departments and ministers in positions to advance their cause. In particular, for African entrepreneurs membership of the councils consolidated an official legitimacy which they had only recently begun to enjoy.[28]

Despite the new developments, African traders still faced many obstacles. When, in August 1978, NAFCOC finally met the Minister of Plural Relations (formerly BAD), Dr Connie Mulder, its representatives raised the following points:

• Capitalisation of African businesses was still a major problem because of the difficulty in raising loans. In this regard property and land ownership by freehold in the urban areas were crucial for Africans.
• Permission to establish African-owned industries in the urban areas was presented as an urgent demand.

Once again the meeting resulted in promised concessions: the minister suggested increased and regular contact between NAFCOC and himself; he was prepared to allow service industries (such as panelbeating, welding and building) to be owned and operated by Africans in the urban areas; he promised to investigate the issue of firearms to African entrepreneurs; he again suggested increased consultations with NAFCOC by administration boards; he mentioned a commission of inquiry which was expected to recommend changes to the taxation system benefiting African entrepreneurs; he referred to the proposed introduction of 99-year leaseholds; he had no objection to NAFCOC establishing a development corporation to assist African entrepreneurs with capital loans; and he asked NAFCOC's opinion on the movement of white capital into African areas.[29]

Later in 1978, 99-year leaseholds were introduced for Africans in the urban areas[30], and in 1979 the new Minister for Plural Relations, Dr Piet Koornhof, announced further lifting of restrictions to allow service industries to operate freely in African areas.[31] In May 1979 Koornhof addressed the NAFCOC annual conference, thereby underlining the growing contact betwęen the state and NAFCOC.

NAFCOC was increasingly gaining a hearing in state structures. In 1978 it was invited to submit a memorandum to the Bantu Affairs Commission stating remaining grievances, and later in the same year was requested to submit a memorandum to the cabinet committee which was reviewing the position of urban Africans. NAFCOC's demands included removal of restrictions on the size of African business premises, as well as those on the sharing of profits with non-dependents, and that traders should not be limited to one trading site, nor prevented from employing non-Africans. New demands were that Africans be allowed to trade in white Central Business Districts (CBDs); that trading rights cease to be restricted to Africans with section 10 qualifications and that all restrictions on manufacturing and industrial enterprise be removed.[32]

The Urban Foundation

In the aftermath of the June 1976 uprising, white capital began calling for political reforms which would deracialise the capitalist economy and thereby prevent political grievances from becoming a threat to the economic system itself. In particular the removal of restrictions on African entrepreneurs and the creation of a politically stable African middle class were seen as priorities.[33] The Urban Foundation (UF) was established by a group of large white business corporations to improve 'the quality of life' of urban Africans by practical projects such as township upgrading, and to promote the 'free enterprise system' through the support of entrepreneurship amongst Africans.[34] Sam Motsuenyane, NAFCOC

president, was a member of the UF, which after some hesitation
provided NAFCOC with a loan towards the establishment of Black
Chain Supermarkets.[35]

The Riekert Commission

The release of the Riekert Commission Report and the state's acceptance of most of its recommendations in its White Paper are
generally considered the starting point of the current restructuring
initiatives.

As regards African entrepreneurs the Commission recommended
that:

1. Allocation of trading sites to wholly-owned African businesses,
   whether individuals, partnerships or companies, should be
   vested in community councils or advisory boards, and not be
   dependent on other criteria such as place of birth, residence or
   employment.
2. Community councils should make recommendations on the admission of non-African traders to the townships, and on the
   creation of delimited free trade zones in the townships.
3. Zones open to trade by all races should be created in white
   CBDs.
4. Conditions for issuing trading licences in African areas should
   be the same as in other group areas.
5. African traders should be allowed to obtain more than one
   trading site in townships.
6. Provisions requiring that African traders personally run their
   businesses should be dropped.[36]

The recommendation that trading sites be allocated by community councils was already in line with state policy, while removal of
criteria restricting access to trading sites was accepted as in need of
attention. It was pointed out, though, that since 1978 Africans with
permanent residence rights in terms of section 10 1(a) or (b) were
allowed to trade in African areas other than those prescribed in
their residence qualifications.

The state again accepted that community councils should make
recommendations on admission of non-African traders and on

creation of free trade zones, but added that community councils should consult with NAFCOC on these issues. Point 3 (above) was also accepted, and the intention to amend the Group Areas Act of 1966 accordingly was stated. Points 4, 5 and 6 (above) were already in line with state policy.[37]

Despite the state's acceptance of the Riekert recommendations, legislation implementing them was slow in coming. Amendments to the Group Areas Act were only made in mid-1985.

The Small Business Development Corporation (SBDC)

At the Carlton Conference in 1979, PW Botha, then prime minister, called for a new 'development strategy'. This included the involvement of the private sector in small business; rationalisation of all existing development programmes; involvement of all population groups; and promotion of commercial development and service industries in African urban areas.

At the conference, Anton Rupert of the Rembrandt Group called for the creation of a small business development corporation. The Panel for Economic Cooperation and Strategy investigated the proposal, and as a result the SBDC was founded in November 1980 and registered as a public company in 1981.

The SBDC was set up as a joint state-private sector undertaking because of ' . . . increasing awareness in recent years that a new approach was needed to encourage small business entrepreneurship amongst all population groups'.[38] Its function is to provide all population groups with loans and/or share capital, facilities such as buildings and industrial parks at reasonable rentals, training, advisory and after-care services, and underwriting of bank credit facilities.[39]

Upon registration the SBDC's authorised share capital was R150-m. The state and the private sector were each to hold equal shares. Relevant assets of existing state development corporations were transferred to it, namely certain assets of the Industrial Development Corporation (IDC), the net assets of the Development and Finance Corporation (DFC), and the net assets of the Indian Industrial Development Corporation (IIDC). Private sector shareholders have a controlling majority on the board of directors, of which Motsuenyane of NAFCOC is a member.[40] According to a SBDC official, most of its loans are to African entrepreneurs.[41]

Investigation into the Group Areas Act

The Strydom Commission of Inquiry into the Group Areas Act was established in 1983, after requests for amendments to the Group Areas Act (GAA) by NAFCOC, AHI, the South African Institute of Race Relations, the Johannesburg CBD Association, ASSOCOM, FCI and a number of white local authorities.[42]

The commission reported that the Act embodied 'legal coercion' which 'conflicts with [the] free market system'[43] and that therefore 'separation in trade' should be phased out by 'easy stages' through introduction of 'free trading areas' on application by local authorities.[44]

The President's Council report

Throughout 1984 white capital and state investigation bodies called for deregulation and stimulation of the informal sector, and for the removal of restrictions on small businesses in general and African businesses in particular in order to promote the free enterprise system.[45]

In 1984 the President's Council Committee for Economic Affairs presented its report on 'measures that restrict the functioning of a free market orientated system in South Africa'. The committee's brief was to investigate factors which 'hamper the participation of members of the . . . lesser developed population groups' in the 'market economy'.[46]

The committee argued that ' . . . evolutionary constitutional reform must be accompanied by more and better opportunities for meaningful participation in the economy by the lesser developed population groups as entrepreneurs and employers in order to en- sure acceptance of the system and to achieve sustained peaceful development. *They must therefore experience the advantages of the market system if they are to accept it*'.[47] Consequently the commit- tee wished to record 'that the removal of restrictions inhibiting the entrepreneurial initiative of the less developed groups (regardless of whether they are caused by socio-economic factors or legal restric- tions) together with a more flexible attitude towards the informal sector and a coordinated implementation of a purposeful small business development programme, would all be prerequisites for the eventual full development of trade and service facilities' [among the 'lesser developed groups'].[48]

The report provides an extremely detailed discussion of 'legal' measures which need to be amended or repealed, as well as 'socio-economic factors' which need to be redressed, particularly with regard to the 'lesser developed groups' in order to promote a 'free market system' in South Africa.[49]

Since then the Minister of Economic Advisory Services, Eli Louw, has announced that the government has accepted the principle of deregulating the small business sector as official policy.[50] PW Botha has reiterated this intention and announced that further funds will be channelled to the SBDC.[51]

The Group Areas Amendment Act of 1984

In July 1984 the Group Areas Amendment Act was passed, allowing introduction of 'free trade zones' in the white CBDs. Such areas would be proclaimed by the Department of Community Development after applications by white local authorities had been investigated and approved by the Group Areas Board, and would be open to trade by all population groups, who may own land and/or building premises for trading purposes in these areas in terms of the Act.[52]

Freehold title for Africans

Breaking dramatically with previous policy, the state president in his 1985 opening address to parliament raised the possibility of introducing freehold ownership rights for Africans in urban areas. Lack of freehold has been one of the major obstacles in the way of the development of the African bourgeoisie as a social class, and has always figured very prominently among the grievances of African entrepreneurs. In response to numerous representations, the state president said, 'I sympathise with these representations and understand the significance that property rights have for people . . . . The government is therefore prepared to negotiate with political leaders of the communities involved on the granting of property rights in the areas concerned in the RSA and in the self-

governing national states'.[53] Seven months later he announced that
the government had 'already accepted the principle of ownership
rights for blacks in the urban areas outside the national states'.[54]

Although it might still be an exaggeration to suggest that the urban African bourgeoisie is on the brink of 'taking off into self-
sustaining growth'[55] it does seem that its position vis-a-vis the state
and white capital has, since 1975, undergone a very significant
change. Through NAFCOC it has developed institutionalised
means of consultation with both the state and white capital, both of
which have of late given it considerable support. Moreover, its
principal demands have either been acceded to, or (as for example
in the case of freehold title in urban areas) are about to be granted.
What may in 1980 have seemed to Southall an 'extremely tentative . . . cautious, even timid',[56] policy of relaxing constraints
upon African entrepreneurs is, under the pressure of events and of
a changing balance of political power, becoming progressively
bolder and more purposeful.[57]

Increasingly it appears that the apartheid state is capable of absorbing the demands of the urban African bourgeoisie, and that it
is possible for this class to grow in both size and power within the
parameters of apartheid. This means that it is chimerical to continue proposing, and hoping to see established, an alliance of all
'nationally oppressed' classes which has as its aim the overthrow of
apartheid.

Notes

1 On this period see HJ Simons and R Simons, *Class and Colour in South
   Africa* (Harmondsworth, 1969).
2 See P Hudson, 'Once more on the Freedom Charter: national
   democracy and socialism', *Africa Perspective*, 27 (forthcoming), for a
   discussion of the concept 'national democracy'.
3 See, for example, South African Communist Party, *The Road to South
   African Freedom — Programme of the South African Communist Party* (1963); J Slovo, 'South Africa: no middle road' in B Davidson (ed),
   Southern Africa: The New Politics of Revolution (Harmondsworth,
   1976); Anon, 'Colonialism of a special kind', *Africa Perspective*, 23,
   December 1983.
4 See S Nolutshungu, *Changing South Africa: Political Considerations*

(Manchester, 1982), chapter 3.

5 Nolutshungu, *Changing South Africa*, 90-91.

6 See E Laclau and C Mouffe, *Hegemony and Socialist Strategy —
   Towards a Radical Democratic Politics* (London, 1985), for an extensive analysis and critique of 'class reductionism' in Marxist theory.

7 SMS Keeble, 'The expansion of black business into the South African
   economy with specific reference to the National Federated Chamber of
   Commerce in the 1970s', MA thesis, University of the Witwatersrand,
   1981, 3, 22, 27, 30.

8 Keeble, 'The expansion of black business', 25-27.

9 Keeble, 'The expansion of black business', 111-119; 'Black business —
   restrictions and frustrations', *African Business and Chamber of Commerce Review* (hereafter *African Business*), 3(9), May 1975, 26-27.

10 South African Institute of Race Relations, *Survey of Race Relations*,
    1958-9, 249.

11 Circular Minute No A12/1 — A8/1 1963, from the Dept of BAD to
    local authorities.

12 Government Notices R1036 and R1267 1968, *Government Gazettes*
    2096, 14.06.68, and 2134, 26.07.68.

13 This was introduced in 1969: Keeble 'The expansion of black business,
    58.

14 Keeble, 'The expansion of black business', 27.

15 *Hansard*, 01.05.75, col 5233-4; 'New deal for urban traders', *African
    Business*, 3(9), May 1975, 9.

16 Government Notice R764, *Government Gazette*, 5108, May 1976.

17 Keeble, 'The expansion of black business', 252-3; *African Business*, 4
    (1), January 1976, 27.

18 Keeble, 'The expansion of black business', 263.

19 Keeble, 'The expansion of black business', 258.

20 'Presidential policy statement', *African Business*, 4 (6), June 1976, 11.

21 'Minister gives urban businessmen new hope', *African Business*, 4 (9),
    September 1976, 6.

22 See, for example: 'White business call for radical change', *African
    Business*, 4 (10), October 1976, 6-8, 23; L McCrystal, 'The growth im-
    perative', *African Business*, 4(11), November 1976, 15-17; Dr HJJ
    Reynders, executive director FCI (later to be in charge of the National
    Manpower Commission), 'Prospects for industrial development by
    blacks in urban and homeland areas', paper delivered at NAFCOC An-
    nual Conference and published in *African Business*, 5 (6), June 1977,
    41-44.

23 Government Notice R2292, *Government Gazette* 5795, November 1977.
24 Government Notice R2488, *Government Gazette* 5820, December 1977.
25 Community Councils Act, 125 of 1977.
26 *African Business*, 4 (11), November 1976, 11.
27 See for example *African Business*, 5 (12), December 1977, 7; 10 (10), October 1978, 17; and Keeble, 'The expansion of black business', 344-350.
28 Keeble, 'The expansion of black business'.
29 'Mulder promises reforms and more consultation', *African Business*, 6 (9), September 1978, 10-11; Keeble, 'The expansion of black business', 330-333.
30 Bantu (Urban Areas) Amendment Act, 97 of 1978.
31 *Hansard*, 08.02.79, col 303-5. Since then a considerable number of such concerns have been established with the assistance of the SBDC and the Urban Foundation in industrial parks and have moreover been supported by both the state and white capital through the granting of numerous contracts. *African Business*, 5 (12), December 1977, 12; 6 (12), December 1978, 11, 13; *RDM*, 06.09.83; 04.11.83; 12.03.84; 19.04.84; *Star*, 12.10.83.
32 Keeble 'The expansion of black business', 331-337; 'Black manufacturers want fair deal from government, *African Business*, 6 (12), 1978, 5.
33 See note 22 above.
34 'Catalyst for change' *African Business*, 5 (8), August 1977, 14.
35 Keeble, 'The expansion of black business', 372. In 1978 *Die Transvaler* convened a thinktank ('dinkskrum') of Afrikaans capital which made an unsuccessful attempt to establish relations with African capital via NAFCOC.
36 *The Report of the Commission of Inquiry into Legislation Affecting the Utilisation of Manpower*, 1979.
37 White Paper on the *Riekert Report*.
38 SBDC Annual Report, 1982, 5.
39 SBDC Annual Report, 1982, 3.
40 SBDC Annual Report, 1982, 2, 6.
41 Mike Smuts, general manager for development, SBDC, in response to a question at a public lecture, University of the Witwatersrand, 24 July 1985.
42 *Report of the Technical Committee of Inquiry into the Group Areas Act of 1966, The Reservation of Separate Amenities Act of 1953 and Related Legislation*, 1983.

43 *Report of the Technical Committee*, 21.

44 *Report of the Techinical Committee*, 22, 66.

45 See for example National Manpower Commission Report, 'An investigation of the small business sector in the Republic of South Africa with special reference to factors inhibiting the growth of the informal sector', 1984; Mike Rosholt, 'Reforms for black business urged', *RDM*, 26.06.84; 'Project free enterprise', UNISA South Africa School of Business Leadership and Human Sciences Research Council, 1984; 'Bosses call for action to prevent repeat of the North's free enterprise breakdown: black mistrust jolts business', *ST*, 08.07.84; 'Free enterprise system isn't welcome among South African blacks', *RDM Business Day*, 31.10.84.

46 Report of the Committee for Economic Affairs of the President's Council, 'Measures which restrict the functioning of a free market orientated system in South Africa', 1984.

47 'Measures which restrict the functioning of a free market', 2-3, emphasis in the original.

48 'Measures which restrict the functioning of a free market', 125, parentheses in the original.

49 'Measures which restrict the functioning of a free market', 95-119, 166-174.

50 'New policy for small business welcomed', *Star*, 02.08.85.

51 Transcript of the address by State President Botha at the opening of the Natal National Party Congress, 15 August 1985.

52 *Hansard*, 27.06.84, col 9960-10 007; 28.06.84, col 10 097-10 120; 02.07.84, col 10 324-10 352.

53 *Hansard*, 25.01.85, col 13.

54 Transcript of address by State President Botha, 29.

55 R Southall, 'African capitalism in contemporary South Africa', *Journal of Southern African Studies*, 7 (1), 1980, 70.

56 Southall, 'African capitalism', 49, 64.

57 See, for example, the recently announced blueprint drawn up by the SBDC which stresses the crucial role to be played by African entrepreneurs in the South African economy of the future and suggests specific strategies to promote the growth and interests of this class. A sum of R500-million has been pledged by the state and white capital towards its implementation (*Star*, 19.08.85).

'More of a Blush than a Rash': Changes in Urban Race Zoning

Gordon Pirie

The adoption of the Group Areas Act by a narrow parliamentary majority in 1950 launched urban South Africa on a course of territorial racial segregation which, although not new, involved unprecedented levels of central state intervention. The Act sought largely to control and direct ownership, occupation and transfer of land (including residential, commercial, professional and industrial premises) so that zones of coloured, Indian and white settlement and activity would emerge within urban areas. The policy of rigid race zoning was intended to minimise friction between the races and thereby avoid social conflict.

Segregation of urban Africans had already been provided for by the 1923 Native (Urban Areas) Act. Africans were only affected indirectly by Group Areas Act provisions, as when they were displaced to make way for new townships for other race groups.

After 30 years of application, the Group Areas Act has reshaped the South African urban landscape quite dramatically. Upwards of half a million people, 120 000 families and 2 700 traders have been moved from their original homes and business sites to new ones in roughly 1 700 group areas. This massive programme of relocation and dislocation, of reorganisation and disorganisation, was undertaken at enormous financial cost to the state, which bore the expenses of administration, survey, land acquisition, demolition, removals, compensation and new construction.

The policy caused great suspicion, anguish and resentment, particularly among coloureds and Indians, who were disproportionately affected. Visible social distress, deputations and protests made locally by opposition political parties and others, as well as international derision and several adverse court judgements, all failed to halt or substantially modify the aims or workings of the policy.[1] Minor concessions involved granting exemptions in respect of trade rather than housing. For example, exemptions were awarded to hard-pressed entrepreneurs for occupation of premises in areas not proclaimed for use by any other race group.

Whereas a determined and committed apartheid government was deaf to external criticism, reservations and objections voiced by its own appointed commissioners were more successful in urging reappraisal of the group areas scheme, and relaxation of certain of its provisions.

In 1976 the Theron Commission reported on the grievances, bitterness and inequitable trading opportunities which the Act had produced.[2] With government assurances that more extensive use would be made of exempted trading areas, restrictions were then removed from occupation and ownership of land and property in industrial zones outside designated group areas. Then in 1978 government announced that it was calling a halt to the removal of some 3 000 traders scheduled to be resited.

During the following year the Riekert Commission reported, criticising group areas schemes for not being cost effective, for favouring white immigrants over long-settled coloureds and Indians, for inconveniencing the general public, and for their incompatibility with free enterprise in that they impaired competition, consumer sovereignty and maximisation of welfare.

Although the commission shrank from unqualified opening of trading areas, it recommended desegregation of selected areas or premises in Central Business Districts (CBDs). Government response to Riekert was generally favourable. However, it was made clear that opening trading areas would only be permitted if it did not lead to residential mixing,[3] and if it did not lead to underutilisation of the 1 200 or so business areas erected by the Department of Community Development for displaced coloured and Indian merchants.

Beginning with the observations and recommendations of Theron and Riekert, in the late 1970s government became increasingly amenable to revision of group areas legislation. This was the case at least in respect of commercial, professional and industrial activity; desegregation of residential group areas has never been contemplated officially.[4]

After the Prime Minister's 1981 reference to the need to open trading areas, a committee of the President's Council recommended the following year that trader exemptions be given more easily. These changing ideas were symptomatic of a new spirit of racial accommodation and cooperation, and were in line with gathering concern in government circles to promote small business enterprise and to forge a more extensive middle class among people other than whites.

Material conditions which impelled change included economic decline in CBDs as a result of the flight of white capital to the suburbs, and enterprising evasion of the law by racially disqualified businessmen. This last consideration made commercial race zoning only token in some places. Information available on pertinent minority shareholding and nominee arrangements indicates that in the medium-sized conservative Transvaal town of Rustenburg in 1983, 40 Indian businesses were conducted in the names of whites, and 50 Indians had a 49% share in property.[5]

Under these circumstances, government launched an enquiry into group areas and related legislation. Reporting in 1983, the so-called Strydom Committee endorsed Riekert's proposal to deproclaim CBD group areas for commercial and professional occupation and ownership. A parliamentary select committee subsequently resolved that these recommendations be put into effect. It went on, however, to suggest that in addition to requests from a local authority, any individual or group, or government itself, could initiate requests for opening a CBD. Next, it was decided that areas eligible for proclamation as open trading places need not be confined to CBDs. The proposals were taken to parliament midway through 1984. This was the last Westminster-style parliament in which whites alone could control race zoning.

The debate in the House of Assembly on the Group Areas Amendment Bill (B113-84) was lengthy and acrimonious.[6] The Minister of Community Development approached the Bill in a matter-of-fact fashion, and it was left to Nationalist Party backbenchers to defend the policy change. Turning his back on the sanctity of past group areas provisions, one government speaker, while acknowledging that group areas were 'a very sensitive matter in South African politics', offered that 'the Act is not a principle that must apply for all time, like a sacred cow' (*Hansard*, 27.06.84, col 9978). Another toned down the significance of the proposed amendment by stating that it represented merely the implementation of 'a policy undertaking given five years ago by the government' and that it was 'no threat whatsoever to the survival of the whites' (*Hansard*, 27.06.84, col 9995).

The official opposition, the PFP, supported the Bill despite its disapproval of the Group Areas Act and its conviction that better and more extensive concessions should have been made. Government was encouraged in its piecemeal reforms, although one PFP member impugned the Bill as a 'laughable', 'superficial' and 'totally inadequate' amendment which rectified only 'one or two minor injustices' (*Hansard*, 27.06.84, col 10001).

Vocal but numerically insignificant opposition to erosion of group areas came from the right-wing Conservative Party, which attempted the ultimate parliamentary censure by proposing that the Bill be read again in six months' time. CP members accused the government of pandering to commercial 'fatcats' who were adversely affected by CBD ailments, legalising a *de facto* illegal situation of nominee holdings, granting the state president meddlesome and dictatorial powers, opening the door to unavoidable subsequent residential desegregation, crowding out white people, and taking over PFP policy (*Hansard*, 27.06.84, cols 9970, 9971, 9972, 9974, 10097).

Apart from unedifying polemics, it emerged from parliamentary and public discussion that not all business areas in towns and cities would be opened automatically after promulgation of the approved amendment. Whereas this would be the case for all existing exempted areas,[7] opening of other places would be subject to official, government or departmental investigation. Additionally, 'openness' was shown to be relative and not absolute. Whereas coloureds and Indians may occupy as well as own property in open areas, other blacks may only exercise non-transferable rights. This particular limitation on openness arises out of the requirement that desegregation complement, not conflict with, any other settlement laws. This means, for example, that local edicts in Northern Natal and the Orange Free State preclude desegregation of business zones, and that Africans cannot own premises because of nationwide limitations on their proprietary rights (*Star*, 19.02.85).[8]

The procedure adopted for definition and declaration of open trading areas defers only partly to the discretion of local authorities. Far from his being called on to intervene only in cases

where the wishes of a local authority and its residents are in conflict, proclamation involves approval by the state president in consultation with the appropriate provincial administrator. This may
take place only after the Group Areas Board has received written
representation on advertised changes, and after it has heard
evidence in public.[9]

This cumbersome and time-consuming procedure is an inheritance of the general group areas policy. Its retention con-
tradicts the avowed aim of administrative devolution. At the same
time as it keeps government ultimately accountable for opening
business areas, it also gives government no direct powers to insist
on their being opened. In addition, the review procedure may be expected substantially to slow the pace at which trading areas may be
opened. As it is, promulgation of the Group Areas Amendment
Act (No 101 of 1984) was delayed until May 1985 (*Government
Gazette*, vol 239 (9759) proclamation No 91) so that all exemptions
under the old Act could be finalised first. This meant that the opening of a total of 26 already exempted areas was delayed so that
finality could be reached on another four areas which were still
under investigation prior to qualifying automatically for the status
of an open area.

In many South African towns and cities, business and professional interests as well as local authorities are likely to support
moves to end segregation. In some cases there will be pressure to
open more than just CBDs. For example, in both Port Elizabeth
and East London the local Indian Management Committee has
called for the entire city to be declared a free trade zone. (*DD*,
27.02.85; *EPH*, 26.02.85). In other cases, local authorities may be
adamant about refusing desegregation or restricting it to select
areas.[10]

Befitting its standing as the premier urban centre, Johannesburg
led moves to CBD desegregation, white consent having been given
in 1984 by the city council, and white approval by the Transvaal
Chamber of Industries and the Afrikaanse Handelsinstituut. Impatient at and frustrated by bureaucratic red tape and unwillingness
to regularise what already existed, the Johannesburg Chamber of
Commerce and the local CBD Association took matters into their
own hands as early as September 1984. When it became apparent
that promulgation of desegregation provisions was going to take a
long time, the two organisations petitioned the state president to

allow the country's only black-owned and managed registered commercial bank to occupy premises in central Johannesburg under temporary permit.[11] Arguing that there was 'no need to wait for the opinions of other cities and towns, which may make their own representations when they so wish', the petition also made the point that 'the existing proclamation of most of the CBD as a "white" area constitutes unjust discrimination not only against shopkeepers but also against business and professional people and members of the public who are not white' (*FM*, 25.01.85).

The adoption in 1983 of a new constitution for South Africa, the beginnings of a tricameral parliamentary system in 1985, the repeal of the Mixed Marriages Act in the same year, and continued investigations by the Strydom Committee into the Group Areas and the Reservation of Separate Amenities Acts, are all considerations which bore and continue to bear on territorial racial zoning. Scrapping inter-racial marriage restrictions has implications especially for residential zoning and property titles and inheritance. Desegregation of public facilities such as restaurants, clubs, cinemas, parks and public transport will complement desegregation of premises, and may also force further relaxation. The new South African constitution has as an explicit national goal the promotion of private initiative and effective competition, something which will make territorial segregation in the business and professional arena increasingly irresistible.

Finally, in the new parliament, in which residential segregation is a 'general affair', coloureds and Indians now have the opportunity to propose, advise on, block and be party to legislative amendments. In debate, coloureds and Indians are now in a position to extract from a cabinet minister the admission that the Group Areas Act has been applied unfairly in many cases (eg *Hansard*, House of Delegates, 06.02.85, col 477). At the first sitting of the Houses of Representatives and Delegates, debate on no-vote private members' motions suggested that neither House would be satisfied with anything less than the total abolition of group areas legislation (*Hansard*, House of Delegates, 06.02.85, cols 438-478; *Hansard*, House of Representatives, 11.02.85, cols 339-383). Government assent to such a far-reaching step is, as President Botha has indicated, quite unlikely: 'I am not prepared to undertake anything more in connection with the Act' (*Hansard*, House of Delegates, 23.04.85).

Removal of CBD restrictions does not remove all concern about trader discrimination. It has been pointed out that the Group Areas amendment might have detrimental effects on traders operating under nominee arrangements. The authorities may now actively search out and eliminate such operations (which the Strydom Committee labelled 'evil') as take place outside open trading zones: 'a very real fear is that some local authorities will . . . find this Amendment a convenient law with which to identify a small block within the CBD as open, and then clamp down on those who fall outside this block' (*RDM*, 28.02.85).

This observation broaches the crucial matter of the unequal way in which desegregation will affect previously disqualified entrepreneurs and professionals. Certain differences are due to the accident of location: individuals in different towns will face different desegregation arrangements at different times, and within any one town, the same may occur within CBDs or as between CBDs and outlying business areas.

Other differences will arise out of distortions previously brought about in the urban economy by group areas provisions and by loopholes in these. Though detailed evidence is not available, it may be surmised that traders who already have substantial interests in central areas (for example through minority shareholdings or nominee businesses) have advantages over those who operated outside central business areas. Prospective 'outside' proprietors and tenants are now effectively penalised by inflated land, property and rent charges in CBDs. They are also disadvantaged by past limitations on clientele sales (and thereby on capital accumulation) by virtue of having been located away from the most vigorous commercial areas where shoppers, especially workers, congregate.[12]

To some onlookers, the Group Areas Amendment Act introduces only procedural changes and contains no compulsory measures which will make any difference to African, coloured or Indian business people and professionals (*Hansard*, 27.06.84, col 9998). Although lawyers, doctors and entrepreneurs need no longer endure the humiliation of asking to work in places of their choice at the risk of being refused, there is no compulsion for any business district to be opened, and desegregation proclamations may be rescinded 'so there will still be control' (*Hansard*, 28.06.84, col 10110). A policy of desegregated but confined business areas will also continue to impose artifical capacity restrictions on expansion of existing enterprises, and on the launching of new ones — over and above the usual limitations of land use zoning. For the present, group areas reform seems set to bring a blush rather than a rash to the complexion of South Africa's urban areas.

Notes

1 South Africa's group areas have attracted widespread comment. For recent reviews, see JA van S D'Oliveira, 'Group areas and community development', in WA Joubert (ed) *The Law of South Africa*, vol 10 (Durban, 1980), 327-418; GH Pirie, 'Race zoning in South Africa: board, court, parliament, public', *Political Geography Quarterly*, 3, 1983, 207-221.

2 A glaring instance of unequal opportunity arises in relation to increasing CBD patronage by Africans, coloureds and Indians who 'are allowed to spend money but . . . not allowed to earn it' (*Hansard*, 27.06.84, col 9997).

3 If caretakers are disqualified by reason of their racial class from living on the premises which they own or supervise, it would be necessary for them to acquire exemption permits (*Hansard*, 02.06.84, col 9979).

4 'It would encroach too much on vested interests and hence cause too much friction' (*Hansard*, 27.06.84, col 9995).

5 *Report of the Technical Committee of Enquiry into the Group Areas Act, 1966, the Reservation of Separate Amenities Act, 1953, and related legislation* (South Africa, 1983).

6 *Hansard*, 27.06.84, cols 9960-10007; 28.06.84, cols 10097-10120; 02.07.84, cols 10324-10352.

7 The House of Assembly was informed that there were 30 such exempted areas. Elsewhere (*Star*, 19.02.85) there were said to be 44. A PFP member declared the '32 exempted areas' a 'pathethic number . . . particularly when one considers the quality of what has been created . . . the Government's record with regard to open trading areas is deplorable' (*Hansard*, 27.06.84, col 9997).

8 As from 1985, Africans who qualified for 99-year leases were entitled to freehold (*SStar*, 21.04.85), but presumably only in respect of residential property.

9 'Who needs a bunch of bureaucrats to "identify" and "investigate" the screamingly obvious?' (editorial, *RDM*, 23.02.85).

10 In Pretoria, where opening of 'public' parks is a contentious issue, a

city councillor declared that opening the CBD would be 'an attack on Afrikaner culture and would make ghettos of the city centre' (*Star*, 01.03.85).

11 On four previous occasions Afribank had been refused permission to locate in central ('white') Pietersburg (*FM*, 25.01.85).

12 It has also been argued, however, that business proprietors previously excluded from CBDs have unfairly benefited from low rentals in government-constructed premises. *Report of the Technical Committee of Enquiry*.

Rethinking Housing Questions in South Africa

Paul Hendler, Alan Mabin and Sue Parnell

In the midst of the growing hopelessness of the housing situation in the country, there has recently been some debate over the role of housing in South Africa's political economy. For example, at the Carnegie Conference in Cape Town in April 1984, all participants in the housing working group identified the existence of a critical housing shortage. But there was no consensus on its causes or solutions. There was disagreement over the state's new housing policy, which stresses self-help and homeownership as solutions to the problem. The explanations for these shifts in housing policy vary. One popular argument maintains that the state has abdicated its role as chief landlord to diffuse political action. Whether or not such a scenario was behind policy, the state is seen as being responsible for the inadequate provision of shelter in South Africa, and it is the state which is called upon to supply these wants, whether the demand is made by community organisers or by trade unionists. The state moreover continues to be the target of a politics generated in part by the continuing shortage or even complete absence of affordable housing and building materials.

Another area of debate concerns a long-standing issue: how is the housing question to be approached, particularly in apartheid South Africa? Is it to be understood primarily in terms of the necessity for state and capital to ensure the reproduction of labour-power? Or is housing to be seen first and foremost as a means of control over the black population, linked ever more closely to influx control and urban segregation?

To unravel these various facets of housing in South Africa, at least three advances are necessary. In the first place, recent analyses of the housing situation — such as those of Bloch, the Labour

Research Committee, Maré, McCarthy and Smit, Ratcliffe or Wilkinson[1] — lack empirical detail. The urgent need for more empirical research further requires a more historically-informed analysis. For this reason, our review of ways and means of rethinking the housing question embarks first on a brief examination of the history of state involvement in housing, of segregation, and of shortage. From there, we move on to a second neglected question: housing as a form of capital accumulation. Thus, we consider the role of the building industry and private interests more generally in both the production and distribution of housing. Finally, the relation of the housing question to other political concerns in South African society is briefly considered.

Uneven development of state housing supply

The state's recent withdrawal from the arena of housing supply and management draws attention to the enormity of its previous involvement. Over the past century the direct intervention of the state has characterised the evolving urban environment. But in the past two or three years, and particularly since the announcement of the 'great sale' of state-owned houses, attention has focused more on the impact of the privatisation of housing. These discussions tend to assume that the state has relinquished its involvement in housing. Clearly, this is not the case. Nor is the state's movement away from direct housing provision without precedents.

In the period before 1920, 'state' housing had its origins in the 'low-income' housing programmes of some municipalities. In Cape Town, for example, the municipality initiated schemes for its employees, while a few 'needy groups' were supplied with accommodation from municipal funds. Attempts to extend these projects and to raise government funding were thwarted by the First World War. Despite a growing awareness of the potential problems of some city areas, there was no central state housing policy or action. Housing for the poor remained the voluntary responsibility of local authorities and housing supply varied between regions. It was not until the scare of the 1918 influenza epidemic that this situation changed. Following a commission of enquiry, the Housing Act was passed in 1920. It provided for low interest rates on state loans for the construction of assisted housing. Under the Act, local authorities became responsible for initiating, constructing and managing the housing schemes. Grants were to be made for specific racial groups. Thus, even before more specifically racist legislation, working-class people were residentially segregated by the state through its control of housing funds.

A decline in the provision of state-funded housing ensued in the late 1920s. The introduction of the Slums Act in 1934, and later the Asiatic Land Tenure Acts, not only caused intense personal distress, but deepened an already critical housing crisis. As with the earlier legislation, responsibility for implementing the state's new housing policies in the 1930s fell to the local authorities. Thus it was municipalities which declared slum areas, and, in part, funded rehousing programmes. Local authorities also faced the needs of a growing urban population. To cope with this demand, interest rates for housing loans from the central state to local bodies were reduced. New housing schemes were built on a larger scale than previously. The appearance of Coronationville, Orlando and Jan Hofmeyr in Johannesburg occurred at this time. Strict racial segregation in public housing was also reinforced by these developments: slum residents from areas such as Doornfontein were separated into coloured, African and white schemes. However, by the late 1930s a lack of funds had resulted in the dropping of sub-economic schemes, and the introduction of homeownership. A decline in construction was matched by declining vacancy rates in public housing schemes. But with renewed and massive urbanisation after 1939, shortages and waiting lists became the norm. The flurry of building which marked the years immediately after the passage of the Slums Act was not repeated until after the war.

The resurgence of state housing provision came about for a number of reasons. Squatter movements and other political factors were involved. In 1949 it was reported that

> alarmed by the recent growth in unemployment among building workers, and aware of the possible political consequences to itself, the Government has made a new offer to local authorities to induce them to embark again on housing projects they had been told they must abandon for lack of funds (*Star*, 09.09.49).

Interest rates were again lowered, site and service schemes introduced, and a boom in public construction took place. The

boom, however, was curtailed by the introduction of the Group
Areas Act. Uncertainty generated by the unknown future racial
status of areas of land handicapped council construction plans.
There were delays in the allocation of land, particularly for
coloured and Indian group areas. Demolitions reduced the supply
of housing while the demand increased, partly due to the removal
of people from areas proclaimed for other 'groups'. Local
authorities faced major difficulties in providing anything approaching adequate housing.

The emerging conflict between central and local authorities
resulted in the creation of the Bantu Resettlement Board (with all
the powers of a local authority) to carry out removals where a
municipality would not cooperate — as in the Sophiatown case.
Any costs incurred could be charged to the relevant municipality.
The fiscal burden imposed on municipalities was, in part, relieved
by the introduction of brewing monopolies to finance 'native
revenue accounts'. The enormity of the housing crisis could not,
however, be addressed on such financing alone. Large-scale borrowing by the state from the private sector — at intermediate
interest rates, but with guaranteed repayment — provided the
resources to construct large areas of housing, particularly in
African townships on the Witwatersrand. Such construction activity
continued into the 1960s, but slowed as a funding crisis again
gathered in 1964 and 1965. In addition, state resources were increasingly engaged in the erection of bantustan townships like Ga-
Rankuwa and Mdantsane. Between 1960 and 1970, 77 410 units
were built in the bantustans, at a total cost of R63,4-million.

In the early 1970s the newly-formed Bantu Affairs administration boards finally wrested African housing from the municipal
sphere. The boards largely stopped such construction of new housing as still continued in the prescribed urban area (ie non-
bantustan) townships, and in some cases diverted their own funds
to the construction of commuter or even 'migrant family' towns in
the bantustans (such as Phuthaditjaba or Lebowakgomo). Within
all these townships access to alternative accommodation (squatting,
subletting or privately constructed houses) was severely curtailed.
The overall result of the processes described has been the
emergence of the state as the major or in many cases the sole
landlord. This is true even in bantustan towns where, despite
the thrust of the past two-and-a-half decades to encourage home-

ownership, those living in formal housing units in urban areas such as Umtata, Mafikeng, Umlazi or Mabopane are often state tenants.

Public housing has not been restricted to African townships, of course. State intervention is perhaps most clearly reflected in row upon row of 51/6 and 51/9 'matchboxes' in the African townships, but it does not end with them. As regards coloureds, Indians and whites, state involvement in the housing process has taken a variety of forms. Much of this housing has been 'assisted', or the state has provided economic and sub-economic units for people of low income. Many people, particularly Indians and coloureds, have ended up in state-provided housing either because of clearances under the Slums Act in the 1930s and 1940s, or because of evictions under the group areas legislation of the 1950s. While the majority of those moved have been working-class people, these removals also resulted in the presence of a large middle class in some state housing schemes. A further form of state involvement began with housing programmes for returning soldiers after the Second World War. Such state sponsored schemes were based on the notion of homeownership. Along with estates funded from the same sources as coloured and Indian housing (that is, by municipal borrowing from the National Housing Fund) these schemes help explain the fact that, for example, 10% of housing occupied by whites in Johannesburg was initially state-motivated.

The predominance of the state as initiator, supplier, allocator and controller of housing in South Africa became singularly obvious in recent decades. This predominance affects specific groups and areas differently. The responses of tenants and those who lack housing altogether at a time of great unemployment and housing shortage is likely to be very specific, even if there is a shared sense of the state as the responsible party. It is these variations which require far more penetrating historical and empirical research if they are to be understood, let alone overcome — whether from a political viewpoint or from the standpoint of housing supply.

Housing and the private sector

One important aspect of housing concerns the involvement of the private sector. But this involvement has largely remained invisible, at least in the academic and political literature on the subject.

Capital accumulation has always taken place in the housing sector of the economy. Furthermore, there have always been possibilities for capital accumulation in relation to *state* housing provision. The lenders of construction capital during the 1950s made profits when their funds financed the building of Soweto and other townships. Recent analyses often ignore the *production process* of township housing, and pay little attention to the fact that much state housing has not been produced by the state or its own agencies. Many houses have been produced by capitalist concerns and sold to the state. Where state agencies have themselves built housing — for example, the Cape Town City Council's Building and Production Unit — the building materials which they have used have mostly been purchased from capitalist suppliers.

Historically, accumulation in the African residential building industry has been drastically limited by the high cost of buildings relative to the low level of wages. Monthly instalments on a bond for what is arguably the cheapest serviced unit (ie the notorious 51/9 and 51/6 'matchbox' houses) are well above the average income of most African workers. Most African houses have therefore been built from state funds while the provision of services has been subsidised by employers. In white residential building, and to a lesser extent with coloured and Indian housing, relatively higher wages have allowed greater possibilities for accumulation.

In terms of the amended Housing Acts of 1957 and 1966, all proposed public housing projects in the country have to be approved by the National Housing Commission. Money for the building projects was loaned to local authorities and later to the administration boards from the National Housing Fund. The interest charged on such loans at present is between 3,5% and 9,25% — which is much lower than the current 19% or more at the building societies. These loans were only made if the proposed projects were consistent with overall state policy. As mentioned above, during the late 1960s and the early 1970s state policy drastically limited the building of African houses. But changes in government housing policy from the late 1970s created further possibilities for accumulation. The most significant of these recent changes is the introduction of home ownership under 99-year leasehold, the sale of state housing at special discount rates, and the lifting of restrictions on the operations of private development companies in the townships. Recently the state has announced its intention of reintroducing much wider freehold tenure.

Current research on the Witwatersrand by one of the authors reveals that African residential buildings are once again becoming a significant field of capital accumulation. In 1985 private development company and state investments in this field are expected to reach R172,2-m, representing a 40% increase since 1981. Between 1975 and 1983, total investment in African houses as a percentage of total investment in all houses increased by 195%. Since 1980 accumulation in the areas associated with residential structures (ie township infrastructure and the provision of trading services) has also shown a remarkable growth. By 1984, R424-m had been invested in the electrification and upgrading of African townships on the Witwatersrand and it is expected that by 1990 an additional R440-m will have been spent.

The accumulation of capital in the African housing market has taken place within the limitations of central government policy — and has also been shaped by local government functions. Historically the various local agents of the central government had the power to organise and administer the entire business of building and allocating houses. They farmed out sections of this work to private subcontractors. Today the roles of local government and private capital have changed somewhat. The various local agents of the central government now still have the power to allocate sites to building firms, to accept tenders, to enter into contracts for building and to deliver state-funded houses to the residents. What has changed is the overall management of these schemes — be they state funded or private initiatives. They are now more often than not undertaken exclusively by private development companies, acting as the main contractors.

The creation of a living environment requires more than the simple construction of a house, and state involvement in housing hence includes the provision of services. The supply of services, however rudimentary, involves the mobilisation of huge amounts of capital. This expenditure has always been in part a responsibility of local authorities. At present the development boards supply bulk and link infrastructure. Private capital provides site infrastructure — equivalent to half the cost of an average matchbox house (R12 000 for a house, R6 000 for a site). Recently the state has proposed a new tier of metropolitan based authorities — the so-called regional services councils — to facilitate the provision of bulk infrastructure to black areas. All local authorities are supposed to have representation on these regional councils, though voting strength will be weighted in favour of wealthier bodies. The importance of this situation for the state's new housing policy must be acknowledged. Even if residents provide their own accommodation on serviced sites, the local (or regional?) state is still in a position of control. It determines the location of sites and the quality of services. At present, the future of both local and regional government is uncertain; yet the impact of its restructuring has already been considerable.

Trends in the delivery of housing

Between 1970 and 1980 the administration boards possessed a monopoly over local authority housing functions in African townships. After the Riekert Commission some of these powers have devolved to a new third tier of government. A conflict of interest appears to have arisen between the boards and the black local authorities which were inaugurated in 1983. The former were established to administer the townships, in the tradition of Verwoerdian apartheid, as areas of temporary sojournership for Africans. The boards tend to be staffed by a bureaucracy decidedly paternalistic towards those whom it perceives as its wards. The new town and village councils, on the other hand, reflect a *leitmotiv* of the 'reformists' in the Botha administration — the cooption of Africans with permanent urban residential rights in support of capitalism. The councils have the support of the 'reformists' for a greater devolution of administrative power. These bodies lack any meaningful electoral support — indeed, in certain parts of the country violent popular resistance has led to the demise of many of them. On the Witwatersrand, however, they have developed to the point where they now have the power to allocate township land for building purposes.

In addition to state allocation, development companies play a significant role in the distribution of houses on the private market. Operating as marketing organisations, they organise the subcontracts for the installation of site infrastructure and the erection of the superstructure. They also liaise with building societies, securing bond finance where required, and with employers on behalf of prospective homeowners. The majority of the 60 000 African breadwinners on the Witwatersrand who qualify financially as potential homeowners are state employees, and as such are aided through government housing subsidies. Generally, building societies are the principal providers of loans to township residents to cover the cost of construction. By 1982, 1 324 bonds under the 99-year leasehold system were registered with various building societies. This figure has probably increased with the stronger push towards home-ownership.

Business activity in the African housing market on the Witwatersrand has broadened the base of accumulation in this area. Amongst the top companies involved, Gough Cooper was expected to increase its turnover by 429% during 1985, Schachat Homes by 132%, Econo Homes by 108% and the African Development and Construction Company by 6,9%. A host of small African building contractors are also accumulating capital in this area. Included in this group are H and T Construction, Sefatse Contractors (both of Vosloorus), A Masondo (of Katlehong), Siyasana, Tembisa Construction Company and Fritz Construction Company.

The additions and alterations market and the self-help schemes suggest themselves as important areas for accumulation, though perhaps less significant than conventional house building. At present the two self-help projects on the Witwatersrand — one at Katlehong and the other at Naledi — incorporate a total investment of R19,1-m. Between 1981 and 1983, 3 600 plans for additions and alterations were approved in Soweto alone, representing a total sum of R35-m.

According to the National Association of Home Builders its members are showing increasing interest in the African market to counter the shrinking building and property markets (*ST*, 05.05.85). This view appears to be borne out by the activities of the Schachat and Goldstein groups, both of which seem to have found a ready alternative in the African townships. By 1984 Gough Cooper Homes was contributing 18,2% towards the overall turnover of the Goldstein group and a massive 57,4% towards pre-tax profit. As a subsidiary company of Schachat Holdings, Schachat Homes expects to be contributing 20% towards overall group turnover by the end of 1986.

Further analysis reveals that access to large capital resources is a characteristic of companies which dominate this field. Several of the top development companies which account for 69% of annual capital turnover in this market belong to groups which have access to enormous sums of capital. Through its joint owners (the West German-based multinational Siemens, and General Electric Power Distributors) the consortium organising the electrification of Soweto has access to literally billions of dollars in assets (*FM*, 24.05.85).

Access to large capital resources and the use of sophisticated marketing techniques do not by themselves guarantee success in the African residential building industry. Companies also seem to require political influence at both local and central government level. For example, appropriate connections may help to secure building land which is at the disposal of black local authorities. However, even wielding influence over local councils does not ensure the continuation and expansion of business activities. Construction firms may also have to overcome strong obstacles posed by some development board personnel. One way to address these difficulties may be through influence at central government level.

The explosive political situation in the African townships poses a singularly large threat to the continuation of business activities. Accordingly, some of the companies involved in the housing sector have committed themselves to actively changing central government policy. Prompted by strong business interests, the Urban Councils Association (UCASA) sent a memo to the Special Cabinet Committee on Black Constitutional Development, making extensive demands for the restructuring of the political status quo, within the confines of the 'free enterprise system'. Reform of existing legislation and the establishment of the Small Business Development Corporation has allowed the emergence of small African-owned concerns in the building construction and materials field.

In 1983 the housing shortage was estimated to be 160 000 units. Over the last five years an average of only 5 476 houses have been built annually on the Witwatersrand. At this rate it would take 30 years to wipe out the existing backlog — and much longer if one took into account increases due to population growth. Public statements to the contrary notwithstanding, private business is probably unable to overcome this massive African housing backlog.

Nevertheless, despite the serious backlog, progressively more residences are being delivered in the townships than during the early 1970s. In 1970, 3 703, in 1971, 1 089 and in 1972 only 954 houses were built for Africans. In contrast 2 649 African residential buildings were built on the Witwatersrand during 1981, 2 102 during 1982, 2 881 during 1983, and 5 919 during 1984. By the end of 1985 it is estimated that a further 6 129 will have been built. These houses vary. The cheapest are built by self help while the more expensive are delivered by conventional private sector and government means.

The future of the housing question

Recent analyses of the housing question contain several misrepresentations. One of these is to see the state's African housing policy as a mere ideological smokescreen without any basis in reality. State housing policy cannot simply be relegated to the status of myth. Recent changes in policy have not only led to increased expenditure on housing and the provision of services and township infrastructure — they also dovetail with other aspects of the restructuring process, affecting new social stratifications in the African townships. One emerging stratum is the small sector in the building construction and related industries. Another is the fledgling real estate sector. Homeowners and tenants form further strata. The state's attempt to devolve more administrative power to the third tier of government (ie the local councils) cannot be dismissed. On the Witwatersrand, at least, these bodies deliver residential stands, a significant aspect of the delivery of housing. The book on the black local authorities and their bureaucracies is not yet closed, cut off though they are from popular support. Another area that is often ignored is the significant number of businesses involved in African housing. Our research suggests that these firms have some effect on state housing policy.

Differing political views of the relation between national politics and the housing question appear to explain the different approaches to which we have referred in this article. In one view, the housing issue allows for mobilisation of communities for purposes of achieving national political goals. On the other hand, there have been attempts to treat housing as a major political issue in its own right. In this case, the goal is to improve the allocation of housing in the short term.

There is another reason for analysing the housing question to which little attention has been directed in the limited South African literature. Housing is, after all, the largest single use value which people consume in most societies. It also demands large applications of resources. In the longer term, the allocation of resources to housing in South Africa will have to undergo radical changes. It seems to us to be necessary to develop an understanding which will serve to aid in these changes. For these reasons, fluctuating processes of building and allocating housing need to be investigated. A full and rigorous treatment of these issues awaits another occasion. This review will have succeeded in its aim if it contributes, however modestly, towards such studies.

Notes

1 See, for example,

R Bloch, 'The State in the Townships: State, Popular Struggle and Urban Crisis in South Africa 1970-1980', a dissertation submitted to the Faculty of Arts of the University of the Witwatersrand in partial fulfilment of the requirements for the degree of Bachelor of Arts with Honours in Development Studies, 1982;

Debate on Housing, Development Studies Group/Southern African Service, Information Publication 4 (University of the Witwatersrand, Johannesburg, 1980);

Labour Research Committee, *Ruling the Townships: Housing, Services, Influx Control and Local Government*, (Johannesburg, 1983);

JJ McCarthy, and DP Smit, *South African City: Theory in Analysis and Planning* (Johannesburg, 1984);

P Wilkinson, 'A place to live: the resolution of the African housing crisis in Johannesburg 1944 to 1954', African Studies Institute Seminar paper, University of the Witwatersrand, July, 1981.

In contrast, see

P Hendler, 'Capital accumulation and the allocation of residential buildings in the African townships of the Witwatersrand, 1980-85', African Studies Institute Seminar paper, University of the Witwatersrand, September, 1985.

The New Constitution: Extending Democracy or Decentralising Control?

Gerhard Maré

> . . . the task of constitutional reform assigned to the President's Council has as its goal the broadening of participation in the political system and the expanding of accountability. Our task, in a nutshell, is to produce a democratic constitution.
> — Denis Worrall, chairperson of the constitutional committee of the President's Council, 1981.

During World War 2, the state's propaganda onslaught in the US has been described as showing

> a strange tendency to resort to abstraction and emotive appeals to 'democracy', the 'American way of life' etc, all of which worked to produce a powerful but rather vague consciousness of forces threatening to destroy American values.[1]

The use of democracy as a rallying cry — everybody must be in favour of it, and any defence and extension of democracy must be lauded — is not new. A constant feature of the South African state's selling of the new constitution has been the insistence that it involves an 'extension of democracy' (one even detects the admission that the previous system had not been democratic). Vague appeals to democracy are made, portraying it as a fragile value under threat from the forces of extra-parliamentary and violent change in the country, aided by Soviet imperialism and its Cuban surrogates.

In an SABC 'Comment' programme dealing with the by-elections for the House of Assembly in May 1985, the presenter said that there was a 'faction in black politics that opposes democratic reform because it conflicts with its own programme for establishing its authoritarian dispensation through violent change'. He then developed a theme that is becoming one of the most common strands in the state's ideology, namely that this onslaught on democracy needs to be countered by a stable SA, achieved through 'the unyielding enforcement of measures to restore and maintain law and order . . . . Only then can the goals established through consensus-advancing democracy in a system upholding the principles of group security and individual freedom and opportunity be achieved'.

It has been argued that 'bourgeois democracy is not completed through a single act of extending the franchise but is rather a long-run historical process'.[2] In SA however, there has been a steady erosion of democracy from a base that already made a mockery of the term. Before examining the 'extension' that is said to be taking place at present, it is necessary to sketch briefly that background.

Disenfranchisement

South African parliamentary history records a process of excluding sections of the population from central political authority (except when the vote was extended to white women in 1930). Before Union in 1910, the Boer Republics and the British colonies all had voting systems that were qualified in some way, with the common effect of excluding Africans and other black people from any or from equal participation.

In Natal, for example, where the 'Charter of Natal' (1856) apparently had no colour bar, an Act of 1865 effectively disenfranchised Africans since, while supposedly granting them the vote, it introduced several qualifications. The applicant had to have been exempted from 'Native Law' (in other words 'detribalised') for seven years; had to have lived in Natal for 12 years; had to have a letter of recommendation signed by three qualified whites and endorsed by a magistrate; and even then was only granted the vote at the discretion of the governor. No wonder that in 1903, after 39 years of this franchise, only three Africans in Natal were allowed to vote. (By 1909 the number had doubled to six.) In the Free State Republic all burghers could vote, but to be a burgher you had to be white and had to meet certain residence and property qualifications.

With Union, the principle of exclusion of black people was entrenched in the constitution, and over the next 73 years whatever limited and increasingly indirect voice the majority of South Africans had in the central authority was whittled away.[3] Africans who still qualified for the vote were removed from a common roll in 1936, and in 1959 even indirect representation was abolished. (At that stage, it affected only 17 500 registered African voters.) Abolition of common rolls for Indians took place in 1946 and for coloured people in 1951.

Subordinate political structures

At the same time, separate and subordinate political structures were being established for the African population, along the lines of racial and ethnic divisions. For example, in 1951 the Bantu Authorities Act was passed, and in 1959 the Promotion of Bantu Self-Government Act. The latter Act recognised eight 'national units', geographically based on the 'recognised heartlands of the Bantu areas', and administratively based on a 'tribal authority' system that even before the 1951 Act bore little resemblance to any precapitalist ('traditional') authority structure.

While the bantustan structures were certainly in every way subordinate to the central state, the unfolding of the 'homeland' policy was presented by government as in line with the granting of independence to colonial states in Africa during this period. From 1956 to 1959, five states in Africa had become independent, while in 1960 17 states achieved this status.

Prime Minister Hendrik Verwoerd said that 'we cannot govern without taking into account the tendencies in the world and in Africa'. 'Positive cultural nationalism' was to take the place of African nationalism, 'the monster which may still destroy all the best things in Africa', according to Bantu Administration Minister MC de Wet Nel in 1959.[4]

The bantustans were not established, however, primarily in response to international pressure: of greater significance were internal factors like the urbanisation of the African population. An attempt was being made to deflect African and black political demands for a democratic say in government, to disorganise an increasingly self-conscious African working class, and to provide internationally acceptable justification for the racially exclusive system of rule in South Africa. The state's attempted solution was to redefine the antagonism of class and racial relationships into a non-antagonistic mould, into 'simple differences', into cultural pluralism and ethnic nationalism.

Limits of democracy for whites

'Democracy' within the central state structures was being reserved for whites only, while 'own' systems of government were being created for other races (bantustans for Africans; a Coloured Persons Representative Council, activated in 1969; and a SA Indian Council in 1968). But even for whites there have been limitations on democratic participation, because of the Westminster system of 'single-member constituencies . . . a system which exaggerates the representation and influence of majority parties'.[5]

If, for example, a proportional system had applied in the 1981 general election, the National Party (NP) would have had 95 (rather than 131) representatives, the Progressive Federal Party (PFP) 31 (rather than 26), the New Republic Party (NRP) 13 (instead of 8) and the Herstigte Nasionale Party (HNP) 25 (instead of 0).

Another problem with the electoral system for whites has been the 'loading' and 'unloading' of seats. This practice has effectively meant an increased representation of rural areas at the expense of urban areas[6] as rural seats tended to represent smaller numbers of constituents than urban seats.

For government, this was advantageous while the dominant theme of NP mobilisation was Afrikaner ethnicity, making possible wide support for the party from workers, small-scale farmers and the rural petty bourgeoisie. As O'Meara put it: 'In the Transvaal, an ideology of the Afrikaner *volk* was articulated', anti-imperialist and anti-monopolies. In the Cape, however, NP strength had always been with the 'wealthier capitalist farmers and a small group of financial capitalists'.[7] The more clearly articulated capitalist interests of the Cape could not dominate in political mobilisation as that region's share in representation in parliament had steadily declined from 51 seats in 1910-15 (out of a total of 121 seats) to 54 seats in 1970 (out of 166). The share of the Transvaal voters had increased from 36 to 73 seats in the same period.

Erosions of democracy

Since the National Party came to power in 1948, there have been some drastic changes in the economic structure and political alignments in the country. I will examine two moments in that period before the 'extension of democracy' in the 1980s.

Removal of coloured voters

The 1953 white elections were fought immediately after the removal of coloured voters from the common roll through the Separate Representation of Voters Act of 1951. This Act unleashed a five-year battle as the NP did not, in 1951, have the necessary two-thirds majority in both houses of parliament to change the constitution. Both the appeal court and the senate were enlarged and loaded in the process. During this crude and cynical manipulation of the limited democratic rights of whites in order to deprive coloured people of the even more limited rights they had, the NP issued an election pamphlet entitled 'Democracy in Danger'. It argued for the 'sovereignty of Parliament' and took an anti-imperialist stance, arguing that the entrenched clauses (which called for a two-thirds majority) were the 'product of British pressure'. It concluded:

> Save the Will of the People
>   Save Democracy
> The National Government Represents the People.[8]

The 'dictatorship' option

The 1970s presented a very different picture from the apparent self-confidence of the 1950s elections. The 1960s had been a period of economic growth and political repression. The 1970s saw the reemergence of militant working class organisation and the beginning of an economic crisis of major proportions.[9] Part of the state's response to this general crisis was a backpedalling on its commitment to 'democracy', even for whites. The attack was led by the most undemocratic of capitalist state apparatuses — the military.[10] In an interview in 1977 (*ST*, 13.03.77) General Magnus Malan, then chief of the SA Defence Force, said one of the 'snags' with the total strategy approach was the 'conflicting requirements of a total strategy and a democratic system of government'. A former political science professor at Rhodes University, John Seiler, said that he had been told that the military had suggested to Defence Minister PW Botha that a military takeover might be necessary to initiate change in the inertia that characterised BJ Vorster's last two years as prime minister (*Star*, 07.05.80).

The 1977 constitutional proposals envisaged such a concentration of power into the hands of the executive state president that 'dictatorship' and 'one-party state' tags were frequently used of Vorster himself. Headlines like 'No danger of dictatorship, says Vorster' and 'Treurnicht tipped as president in possible one-party state' frequently appeared in the commercial press.

In 1979-80, there was open speculation that PW Botha, then prime minister, was to become an 'enlightened dictator'. (Allister Sparks in *RDM*, 14.06.80; Tertius Myburgh in *ST*, 17.02.80; Harvey Tyson in *Star*, 13.10.79). Most of this speculation hinged on the existence of the State Security Council and the way in which the Botha regime was removing decision-making from the visible parliamentary terrain. But there was a change from the sensationalism and fearfulness that surrounded reporting of the Vorster 'dictatorship option'. Dictatorship, suspension of democracy, and such terms were now being linked to the need for reform and the power needed by Botha's 'agents of change' to act against the 'democratic wishes of the Party's own supporters' (*ST*, 02.12.79). Harry Schwartz of the PFP called for support for the 'moves towards real change' that Botha was said to be making (*DN*, 29.11.79). Spokespeople for monopoly capital, such as Anglo American's Gavin Relly, were openly advocating support for Botha, while certain academics were optimistic about the new decade. Herman Giliomee wrote that 'the 1980s hold the hope of a new and somewhat more just South Africa' (*ST*, 24.02.80).

1980 saw total strategist Magnus Malan brought into the cabinet as minister of defence. Now he was being hailed by political correspondents in the English-language press as having 'a reputation for political enlightenment' and a 'mischievous sense of humour' (Ivor Wilkens in *ST*, 31.08.80). 'Victory at all costs' was Malan's message in his first policy speech.

Later in 1980, two further voices were added to the debate on dictatorship/reform. They were those of Willie Breytenbach (then research chief with the SA Foundation) and Stoffel van der Merwe of the Rand Afrikaans University (now NP MP) (see for example *SE*, 03.08.80). Breytenbach argued that 'entrenched white democracy' was the main impediment to change in South Africa. Van der Merwe wrote that reform increases radicalism and elicits a violent response from radicals. This apparent paradox, so the argument went, was because reform was seen to reflect a weakness within the state. The solution was to clamp down very strongly, to show the might of the state and reestablish the climate of 'law and order' within which reform could continue.

A year after Van der Merwe's and Breytenbach's contributions, the arch-conservative US academic, Professor Samuel Huntington, turned up at the Rand Afrikaans University to deliver the same message in much greater detail:

> Centralisation of power may also be necessary for the government to maintain the control over violence that is essential to carry through major reforms. No reform occurs without violence . . . the reformer must be ready to welcome and use violence when it serves his purpose.[11]

Minister of Constitutional Planning, Chris Heunis, opened the conference at which Huntington spoke, the theme of which was 'Stability and Reform'.

The profound manner in which Huntington's address to the Political Science Association of South Africa prescribed or reflected state strategy is clear in the light of subsequent events and in the way in which one of the ideological arms of the state, the SABC, has taken up the refrain of violence/reform in its interpretation of events for the white population. To give only two examples from the 'Comment' programme (13.05.85 and 29.03.85):

> There is a clear relationship between current reform initiatives in South Africa, the widespread unrest in black urban areas and the police action to enforce law and order in those areas . . . . In the present disordered situation, effective law enforcement action provides an essential substructure of security. But it is on the comprehensive reform programme that is built upon the substructure that the country's prospects

for peace, progress and development, in a free and demcoratic society, depend.

and

It is an essential condition for successful reform that law and order must be maintained; the one will not be achieved unless there is a determination to enforce the other. Hence the President's announcement that he had given instructions for appropriate steps to be taken to restore and maintain law and order. It is no coincidence that in a period of historically unprecedented reform in SA the country should be subjected to outbreaks of violent unrest.

Growth of conservative opposition forces

In the 1981 elections, the NP lost a considerable number of voters, if not a significant number of seats, to the HNP and PFP. In 1982 the NP split, with Andries Treurnicht forming the Conservative Party (CP) and claiming the true tradition of the NP policy of apartheid. Botha no longer needed increased political power to act against the wishes of his own party members. But now he was faced with a clearly-defined ultra-conservative force. The formation of the CP probably did more than anything else to ensure the overwhelming majority Botha achieved in the 1983 white referendum on the new constitution. With the help of the English-language press, he could now argue that he was left only with the 'good guys', the reformers.

The NP split confirmed a loss of support for the party that had been in progress since the mid-1970s, and showed that the voters who were leaving the NP were moving to the far right of organised white politics.[12] Increasingly the NP, as the governing party, was reflecting more directly the interests of the dominant monopoly sector of capital. The outward manifestations were there in 1979 when the Mine Workers' Union failed through strike action to deflect the state and the mine owners from what was perceived to be an assault on the privileges of white workers.[13] It was reaffirmed by the well-publicised displays of 'toenadering' at the Carlton and Good Hope Conferences, and has over the years been given substance in the 'coming corporatism' which is discussed below.

Ditching old allies

The present economic crisis has aggravated the position of many whites, but particularly of white workers, civil servants and the petty bourgeoisie generally.[14] Unemployment among all workers has grown tremendously and whites are no longer excluded. National servicemen are being warned not to expect jobs as easily as in the past. The Afrikaans-language press has devoted considerable space to the plight of unemployed and retrenched white people. Living standards have declined sharply. The agricultural sector, another traditional sector of support for the state, has also come under fire, specifically the maize producers of the northern provinces, who suffered a surprising defeat in 1985 at the hands of those they believed to be their political representatives.

NAMPO, the producers' representative body, had recommended a 23% increase in the price of maize to the Maize Board, which put the request forward to the state. It was turned down, whereupon NAMPO members on the Maize Board resigned. A suspension of deliveries by some farmers in protest failed, as sufficient maize had been stockpiled to allow the state to ride it out.

Professor AW Stadler (*SE*, 10.03.85) argued that there has been a change in the NP's 'populist' style and in the alliance of Afrikaner business, agriculture and workers since the 1960s. The party was losing support:

> These thoughts may have passed through the minds of government leaders and party managers as they set about reorganising the state structure during the late 1970s. For certainly, one of the effects of the new constitution will be to insulate government decision-making from 'popular' pressures and diminish institutional bases for political groups which mobilise support via party-electoral politics. The constitution is also likely to institutionalise and entrench the bias towards the representation of big business and technocrats in policy-making and government.

The interests that have of necessity been harmed by the state's policies favouring big capital (some farming interests; white workers; civil servants who had to forgo bonuses; and the many small businesses going insolvent each month) can no longer be counted on to be democratic in the right way, ie to vote for the

National Party.

In this climate, the *Vaderland* editorialised in 1985 on the need to restore the balance between the strength of an urban and a rural vote by equalising the number of voters in the two types of constituency. This suggestion probably counts on a defection from PFP and NRP supporters that would more than compensate for the loss of disaffected Afrikaners. The 1983 constitution makes the same provision as the Union constitution did for a delimitation commission to allocate voters to constituencies on a regular basis.

Not that the present holders of power need ultimately concern themselves with electoral politics if there should be the possibility of losing power through the ballot box. The extensive and non-accountable powers of the state president, the provisions for government in the event of a deadlock in the consensus system, and the willingness to abolish democratic rights, all point the way to the most likely option for a threatened NP and its allies in future.

Consolidating new political allies

These future allies are apparently to be drawn from other groups brought into parliament through the 'plural democracy' advocated by Botha and Heunis. This would further decrease the importance of a large majority among white voters. Commentators have remarked on the particularly close relationship between the majority parties in the three chambers. The new constitution appears to be serving admirably to bring like-minded elites together, above the hurly-burly of democratic, mass and accountable politics. On a symbolic level, this was illustrated in June 1985 by the Homburg-topped figures of Allan Hendrickse and Amichand Rajbansi addressing and saluting 'their' ethnic components of the similarly accoutred Minister le Grange's SA Police.

The NP's tricameral parliament has, in effect, brought together individuals who are then touted as 'political leaders of significant segments of a plural society'. This is a rather idiosyncratic version of what is in any case an undemocratic system, namely consociationalism.[15]

When PW Botha talks of 'full participation in the decision-making process', he is at present referring to participation in the tricameral system based on the acceptance of ethnic or racial identity, rather than what is usually understood by bourgeois democracy, namely the participation of individuals. Increasingly government, or reform-supporting ideologues, are pressing for an extension of consociationalism (rather than democracy) to be able to bring in other ethnic groups (such as the Inkatha movement) or groups defined by other criteria. (See the proposals of the Buthelezi Commission which have received much comment and are still likely to be taken seriously by state reformers.) It appears that the proposed second (provincial) and third tier (regional services councils) government will try to accomplish just this.

Consolidating economic allies

Political representation has been further changed through a process of increasing corporatism that complements the political process of consociationalism. Corporatism here refers to the measures taken by the state to bring economic interests, whether of the bourgeoisie or of the working class, into the orbit of state institutions that deal with functional issues, such as having a national wage policy set by representatives of capital, labour and the state; or involving capital in policy formulation in the arms industry. Prinsloo has linked growing corporatism in South Africa with changes in accumulation strategies notably towards export-promotion, increasing mechanisation, and monopolisation, and writes that 'such an accumulation strategy involves the rejection of the former accumulation strategy which principally favoured small firms, the white working class and state employees',[16] exactly those interests being peripheralised politically.

Capital and the state have been involved in open communication at Carlton and Good Hope, in commissions (notably De Lange on education and Wiehahn on labour reform) and in institutions (like the National Manpower Commission). The recently reconstituted Economic Advisory Council offers a clear example of the structures of corporatism with more than half the 42 members coming from the private sector. Party political representation can no longer cope with economic and social demands from the dominant monopoly sector on the state, and demands on monopoly capital by the state. Prinsloo points out that consociationalism and corporatism both have the effect of bringing about a 'decline of the party political and parliamentary form of representation' and of 'increasing the independence of the executive branch of the state'.[17]

Decentralising state control

This trend of removing party representation will be given a further boost with the establishment of second and third tier government in South Africa. The provincial councils, and with them the reality of NRP authority in Natal, and the threat of CP/HNP control in the OFS and Transvaal, are being abolished. Instead this level will be administered (for 'general affairs') by a government-appointed council.

At the third level, regional services councils (RSCs) are being established. As with the provincial level, this restructuring involves not a decentralisation and widening of political participation and election of representatives, but decentralisation of administration and functional interest representation. The chairpersons of the RSCs are to be appointed by the second level administrators, who will also identify 'regional functions' which will then fall under the RSCs and not under local authorities. It appears that the provincial administrators will have the same powers to overrule and take over the functions of the RSCs as the state president has in relation to central authority. It is at these two levels that Africans will probably first be brought into the juggernaut that is the new constitution.

Challenges to the state in the 1980s

For all South Africans, not only whites, this amounts to a further reduction of political accountability and public scrutiny of government. The political process that coloured people were finally excluded from in the 1950s is not the same as the political process they have been offered in the 1980s.

Another key issue affecting democracy in the central authority in the 1980s is the enormous growth of extra-parliamentary political and economic organisations. It is here than an alternative democratic practice is being created, devaluing the claims of 'extended democracy' in the tricameral parliament and through other reform measures.

This devaluation has occurred on the one hand through the overwhelming success of the boycott movement against the 1984 elections. Parliamentary representation of 'groups' under consociationalism can only have legitimacy if representatives have significant group followings. On the other hand, alternative participatory and accountable structures, such as those within the independent trade unions, have been created.

It is the threat posed by alternative democratic structures and practices that has made the concept of democracy such a central issue in the state's propaganda onslaught against extraparliamentary organisations. 'Mob lawlessness', 'savagery', 'those who would destroy all prospects for democracy' are the terms used to describe such organisations. This onslaught will no doubt intensify in the future.

Conclusions

Even through this brief overview it can be seen that 'democracy' has had a rough ride in South Africa. The patterns of representation according to race, set before the twentieth century, were carried into the stage of industrial capitalism.

A Human Sciences Research Council report on inter-group relations points out that with the overlap of race and class, racial exclusion and discrimination have exacerbated class antagonisms (SABC discussion, 03.07.85). It is extremely unlikely that the state will be able to do anything at this stage to remedy the situation. If it cannot even represent the interests of white workers adequately against capital, it seems absurd to suggest it will be involved in any meaningful redistribution towards the black working class. The economic crisis makes this totally impossible in the foreseeable future. This is not to deny the limited degree of redistribution that will no doubt arise out of the 'own affairs' budgets of the coloured and Indian chambers in the new parliament.

With the accumulation crisis in the 1970s and 1980s, capital and the state can no longer afford full participation by the white working class and other non-dominant white class interests.

These changes ironically are opening the way for white extraparliamentary politics. Signs are present in the activities of the far-right Afrikaner Weerstandbeweging (AWB) and such displays as the thousand tractor parade through the streets of Pietermaritzburg by disaffected farmers during February 1985. Assassinations of black and white opponents of apartheid, both within and outside South Africa, are on the increase and there are alarming reports of the possible existence of a 'death squad' at least in the Eastern Cape. Extra-parliamentary need not mean extra-state.

The state is caught in a cleft stick. On the one hand, the economic realities of contemporary South Africa make a widening of democracy and a more just allocation of resources an impossibility. On the other hand, political unrest and the civil war that is raging increase demands by capital for political options to be opened up. Incorporation into any structure that arises out of the present system of rule has, however, been thoroughly discredited.

The establishment of democracy outside parliamentary structures serves as a permanent reminder of the lack of democracy within state structures. It probably represents the greatest challenge to the state's attempts at controlled incorporation of as many 'leaders' and organisations of the oppressed as possible. It was not as a Christian, but as a politician, that PW Botha went to the Zionist Christian Church meeting at Moria during April 1985. The message that the Afrikaans-language press drew from the meeting was that a number of such 'gespreksforums' (dialogue forums) have to be created with credible leaders. The involvement of leaders in government, and certainly not the 'extension of democratic rights', is the name of the consociational game.

Notes

1 AP Foulkes, *Literature and Propaganda* (London, 1984), 84.
2 Allan Hunt, 'Marx — the missing dimension: the rise of representative democracy', in Betty Matthews (ed) *Marx — A Hundred Years On* (London, 1983), 89.
3 See the discussion in LJ Boulle, *South Africa and the Consociational Option: A Constitutional Analysis* (Cape Town, 1984), 78-99.
4 See T Dunbar Moodie, *The Rise of Afrikanerdom* (Berkeley, 1975), 265.
5 Boulle, *South Africa*, 77.
6 Kenneth A Heard, *General Elections in South Africa 1943-1970* (Lon-

don, 1974), 9.

7 Dan O'Meara, ' "Muldergate" and the politics of Afrikaner nationalism', *Work In Progress*, 22, 1982, 7.

8 Heard, *General Elections*, 54-55.

9 See O'Meara, ' "Muldergate" ', 2-3; Stephen Gelb and Duncan Innes, 'Economic crisis in SA: monetarism's double bind', *Work In Progress*, 36, 1985; and John Saul and Stephen Gelb, 'The crisis in South Africa: class defence, class revolution', *Monthly Review*, 33(3), 1981.

10 For a fuller discussion of total strategy, see Glenn Moss, 'Total strategy', *Work In Progress*, 11, 1980.

11 Samuel Huntington, 'Reform and stability in a modernising multiethnic society', *Politikon*, 8(2), 1981.

12 See, for example, Craig Charney, 'Towards rupture or statis? An analysis of the 1981 South African general election', in DC Hindson (ed), *Working Papers in Southern African Studies, Volume 3* (Johannesburg, 1983); and Craig Charney, 'Restructuring white politics: the transformation of the National Party' in SA Research Service (ed), *South African Review One* (Johannesburg, 1983).

13 Carole Cooper, 'The mineworkers strike', *South African Labour Bulletin*, 5(3), 1979.

14 See Karen Jochelson, 'Unions and right-wing politics', *Work In Progress*, 37, 1985.

15 Roger Southall, 'Consociationalism in South Africa: the Buthelezi Commission and beyond', *Journal of Modern African Studies*, 21(1), 1983, 79.

16 MW Prinsloo, 'Political restructuring, capital accumulation and the "coming corporatism" in South Africa: some theoretical considerations', *Politikon*, 11(1), 1984, 33.

17 Prinsloo, 'Political restructuring', 35.

Introduction

Susan Brown

Opposition politics and the economy have combined to provide the central thrust behind the dramatic changes in South Africa's social parameters during 1984-85. The policies of this country's major opposition movements have hardened, as the scope of opportunity perceived by them has altered radically. Fuelling their gathering momentum is the rising tide of popular resistance, fed by anger at endlessly spurious 'reform' promises which are inseparable from the crudest repression by police and army in the townships. This combines with unabated inflation and unemployment (about a quarter of the economically active African population) to provide not just impetus but inevitability to popular mobilisation.

The ANC, despite the severe setback of the South African-Mozambique Nkomati Accord of March 1984, thus had strong grounds for the optimism displayed at its Kabwe conference in June 1985. In his paper tracing the movement's development during the 18 months prior to the conference, Tom Lodge counterposes the police version of events to that of the ANC and its officials.

On the one hand, he concludes, the logistical difficulties of armed struggle have increased in the face of the Accord and the co-operation — enforced to a greater or lesser degree — of neighbouring countries like Botswana and Swaziland with South Africa. On the other hand, while the ANC's organisational growth internally might well be outpaced by mass acceptance of the movement's symbols, Lodge argues that in the present climate 'one of the achievements of the ANC's "armed propaganda" is that [it] can influence to an extent the course of popular political assertions without having to manipulate or organise them'.

Thus, according to Lodge, it is not surprising that the Kabwe conference, the first of its kind since 1969, produced fresh commitment to popular insurrection, reaffirmation of leadership, and demonstration of high morale generated by hope of attainment of the organisation's goal of revolutionary change.

Jo-Anne Collinge's analysis of the UDF, and particularly of the state's intensifying campaign against it, is constrained by the *sub judice* rule imposed by two major treason trials pending when she wrote her account. Nonetheless, Collinge provides an account of the UDF's undertakings during 1984, from the Million Signature Campaign and the campaign against the constitution to its affiliates' participation in the November 1984 stayaway. She describes its policies and relationships towards students, on sport, with AZAPO and Inkatha. A striking theme is the intensification of state action against the UDF, which builds to a climax with the declaration of the emergency in mid-1985. She concludes: 'The state, as yet unwilling to ban the UDF itself, is using detention to cripple the organisation and trials to criminalise it'.

The National Forum antedates the UDF as an alliance. Initially conceived as a vehicle to resolve ideological conflict, it has in fact become identified with the ramifications and developments of the black consciousness position. Na-iem Dollie's article provides an account of the changing policies and positions adopted and debated by the NF on issues such as class, race and ethnicity and the question of land ownership. Relations with other organisations, from trade unions to the UDF to Inkatha, are also discussed, and Dollie hints at the beginnings of cooperation in some regions with UDF-linked organisations and individuals.

Nicholas Haysom's account of the Langa shootings of March 1985 and of the Kannemeyer Commission of Enquiry into the event provides a sobering reminder of the context in which opposition activists work. The violence — indeed, an attitude close to war psychosis — on the part of police especially in Eastern Cape townships, has played no small part in fanning the flames of resistance. Haysom's evaluation of the findings of the Kannemeyer Commission suggests that Justice Kannemeyer's preconceptions as to the correct role and behaviour of the police blinded him to the flaws in the police version of events. The power of the police, which is the power of life and death in South Africa's townships, is subject to no effective checks, given such presumptions.

The last two articles in this section deal with the economic developments that underlie the political and social dynamics of 1984-85. Duncan Innes provides a succinct analysis of the way in which the state's economic policies, undertaken in imitation of the Reagan and Thatcher austerity measures which had indeed contained inflation rates, proved inappropriate and disastrous in the South African context.

The South African authorities believed that driving the economy into recession, producing an effective devaluation of the rand against other currencies and a favourable balance on the current account of the balance of payments, would clear the way for a healthy, inflation-free recovery in due course. This failed to reckon with the greater vulnerability of this economy relative to those of the capitalist West, the lack of a South African welfare state system to cushion the impact of unemployment, and the lack of political legitimacy of the current regime.

The consequent unrest, coupled with government vacillation and indecision on reform, undermined the rand still further, and led to the attempt by international creditors to cut off, or at least reduce, credit to an increasingly obvious bad risk. Monetarist policies have been disastrous in political and human terms, have damaged South Africa's economic base and left the economy facing bleak prospects.

Karl von Holdt's contribution examines in more detail the structural components of the South African economy and its place in the international order; he is equally critical of the monetarist strategy and points to the inextricable interlinkages of economic and political policy. Lower wages, lower mass consumption and higher unemployment constitute offensives against the working class, he believes, making the recession an arena for intensified class conflict. For Von Holdt, it is unlikely that any state initiatives on the economic front will be able to resolve the structural constraints binding the economy and dividing society.

'Mayihlome! — Let Us Go To War!': From Nkomati to Kabwe, The African National Congress, January 1984 - June 1985

Tom Lodge

Two conflicting perceptions influence public discussion of the African National Congress's development since the Nkomati Accord denied its guerillas transit through Mozambique. In April 1984 the president of the African National Congress (ANC), Oliver Tambo, contended that despite the agreement, ANC activity would 'reach its highest peak in the next few months'.[1] Five months later Tambo claimed that Nkomati had not seriously affected the ANC because its guerilla organisation had an established presence within South Africa. According to Tambo, the struggle was 'going ahead . . . perhaps more vigorously than before'.[2] Tambo's claim was in conformity with other statements by ANC spokesmen. Two weeks earlier in Maputo Joe Slovo maintained that the 'ANC's military strategy had been premised on the fact that it could not demand or expect from neighbouring states the kind of rearbase facilities other liberation movements in Africa had enjoyed . . . [it] never expected what FRELIMO had in Tanzania'.[3] Not only was the ANC capable of sustaining its current level of activity, but moreover it was 'poised to intensify the armed liberation struggle in South Africa and deliver the final blows on the criminal system of apartheid'.[4] 'We have got the capacity', asserted a senior ANC member interviewed in *Sechaba*, 'to intensify the armed struggle in

South Africa'. The problems created by the Accord were not fundamental ones. 'The strategy for change does not require a rethink from us'.[5] Indeed, in the context of the late 1984 upsurge of township violence, there were unprecedented opportunities for furthering the implementation of that strategy:

> We believe a very rare combination of revolutionary factors is maturing before our very eyes. If the liberation movement seizes this important moment and builds upon it the prospect of people's power is within our sight.[6]

Police statements, though, were from their own point of view no less sanguine. The ANC, South African Police (SAP) spokesmen insisted, did not have 'an established infrastructure' to facilitate guerilla operations in the country. The movement remained dependent on logistical links across South African borders. Post-Nkomati difficulties had resulted in lowering of morale, a spate of defections, and recruitment difficulties. In 1984 a record number of ANC combatants had been killed or captured by the police, and a slackening in the tempo of armed insurgency pointed to arms supply and manpower problems (*ST*, 15.12.84; *RDM*, 23.06.84). In this view, the exuberant tone of public pronouncements by ANC leaders is merely a rhetorical facade concealing considerable demoralisation and strategic disagreement.

This survey will attempt to demonstrate which view is the more justified: the public optimism of the ANC or the dismissive view accorded to it by its police adversaries. A discussion of the most obvious manifestation of its presence within South Africa, the armed insurgency of Umkhonto we Sizwe, will precede examination of developments affecting the external section of the organisation. The period reviewed will be from the beginning of 1984 to the end of June 1985. The starting point has been chosen to maintain a continuity of narrative with contributions to earlier volumes of the *South African Review*, otherwise the date of the signing of the Nkomati Accord, 16 March 1984, would have been a more logical point from which to begin. The end of June roughly coincided with the conclusion of the first major internal conference that the ANC has convened since 1969. The period closes, then, with an important event in the ANC's history, the implications of which will be assessed in the concluding part of this article.

Guerilla activity

At first sight, South Africa's armed diplomacy would not appear to have seriously hampered the ANC's ability to wage urban guerilla warfare. According to the University of Pretoria's Institute for Strategic Studies, 44 attacks occurred in 1984 which could be attributed to the ANC, while the first six months of 1985 witnessed a rise in the frequency of attacks with 40 incidents recorded by 19 June. My own statistics, drawn from press reports, are of a comparable order: a total of 38 incidents for 1984, of which 32 happened after the signing of the Nkomati Accord, and 41 in the first six months of 1985.[7] Most of the 1984 guerilla activity took place between the beginning of April and the end of August, and was located principally in Durban (12 attacks) and Johannesburg (12 attacks). Between September and the close of 1984 only nine attacks were recorded, mainly of a fairly minor variety (railway lines, water pipelines, and electrical sub-stations).[8] The SAP contends that much of the 1984 sabotage was the work of a group of 50 guerillas sent into the country just after the signing of the Accord, and that the decreasing momentum of insurgency towards the end of the year could be the consequence of the capture or killing of guerillas as well as of the time it took for the ANC to construct its logistical lines across Botswana (*ST*, 15.12.84). Apparently confirming police claims were several skirmishes between ANC guerillas and both South African and Bophuthatswanan security forces between September 1984 and February 1985.[9] The geographical focus of the guerilla offensive has remained on the whole unchanged, with Johannesburg and Durban still the most affected centres.[10]

In contrast to the early insurgency, most targets selected by guerillas were in the main business districts or in the industrial areas of the towns concerned.[11] Only a small proportion of targets chosen by saboteurs were situated in black townships. This, together with a growing tendency for guerillas to launch attacks during working and commuting hours, signifies a shift in strategy: increasingly guerilla activity is intended to have an impact on all sections of the community, as opposed to being mainly directed at establishing a following for the ANC in the townships. The range of targets was significantly extended to include the offices and headquarters of private employers. In 1985 the ANC claimed responsibility for three attacks made on the premises of companies involved in labour

disputes.[12] ANC representatives have on several occasions threatened attacks on facilities owned by multinational corporations
operating inside South Africa.[13] The most popular targets, though,
remain those associated with the security forces or with the institutions of apartheid: guerillas bombed military administrative
offices, government departments, police stations, and court
buildings on several occasions.[14] Most sabotage was accomplished
through the use of limpet mines, though in Durban two car bombs
exploded during commuting times. The second of these was, according to the ANC, intended for a military convoy which habitually
passed through an industrial estate. It was detonated prematurely
and killed five civilian passers-by. In a public statement Oliver
Tambo angrily reprimanded the men responsible for not taking
adequate precautions to avoid harming civilians.[15] The ANC denied
responsibility for a bomb placed outside a crowded Durban
restaurant and also issued a disclaimer for two grenades hurled into
the homes of two coloured members of parliament (*Star*, 21.06.85;
13.06.85). During the period the ANC continued to abjure attacks
specifically mounted to inflict civilian casualties, though its
guerillas seemed less and less concerned to safeguard civilian lives.

It does appear that lines of supply and communication which
traverse South Africa's frontiers are still important in upholding
the ANC's military activities. The pause in the sabotage between
September and February would seem to corroborate this as would
an admission by Tambo reported in the *International Herald
Tribune* in January 1985 that 'we have had to be very careful over
the past three months . . . Nkomati . . . affected our communi-
cations systems . . . [we] have got to be economic with our
manpower' (17.01.85). A Zimbabwean newspaper quoted Tambo
ascribing the let-up in guerilla actions to 'arrangements . . . being
made, organisation . . . taking place'.[16] One important task was
obviously the transport of arms through Botswana: in January
1985 the Botswana Defence Force discovered a large quantity of
weaponry in Gaborone, and the SAP claims to have unearthed
several recently established arms caches in the Western Transvaal
and the Free State (*Cit*, 24.05.85; *Star*, 28.01.85; *FM*, 28.06.85).
But it would be wrong to conclude from this that the South African
authorities can effectively prevent the ANC from operating inside
the Republic by recreating the *cordon sanitaire* previously afford-
ed by the British and Portuguese colonial administrations.

For however successful the South African government is in intimidating its neighbours into signing defence and non-aggression
agreements, infiltration of small numbers of guerillas is likely to
continue. The Swazi authorities, who collaborate closely with the
South Africans in restricting ANC activity, have been unable entirely to halt Umkhonto infiltration across their border.[17] The scale
of armed activity undertaken by Umkhonto at the moment could
be the work of a very small group; indeed the police assert that the
number of guerillas operating inside the country at any one time
does not exceed 30 (*Star*, 21.06.85). The chiefly ideological and
demonstrative functions of the present level of insurgency do not
require a large army. The raid on Gaborone earlier this year may
intimidate the Botswana government into cooperating more intimately with the South Africans, but this would not eliminate the
possibility of small groups of guerillas moving swiftly through its
territory. If the much better equipped South African security
forces cannot prevent the traffic of guerillas across their own
borders, what can be expected from the meagre resources of
poorer, less intensively administered neighbouring countries? In
any case, ANC strategical conceptions have in the last few years
shifted away from the conventional guerilla scenario which would
assign a predominant role to the specialised military force which
Umkhonto constitutes.[18] Well before the Nkomati Accord there
were signs that ANC strategists were considering ways of heighten-
ing the level of local participation in the insurgency, of broadening
the social base of the armed struggle. A debate conducted in the
columns of *African Communist* in 1983 suggested methods
through which this could be accomplished: the creation of 'temporary training bases' offering courses of a weekend's duration,
and the building of an army of 'part-time' guerillas as the first
stage in the preparation of a warfare of popular insurrection.[19] In
1985 the ANC appealed for the formation of small bands of armed
youth who, equipped with home-made weaponry, should put
themselves in the vanguard of popular township struggles.[20] Most
of the sabotage undertaken by Umkhonto does not necessitate a
great deal of technical expertise — limpet mines are not complicated devices[21] — and therefore guerilla offensives would not
have to depend in the future upon a steady stream of graduates
from the ANC's training camps entering the country. The SAP
claims that efforts to localise the guerilla force are already under

way and that this is manifest in the grenade assaults on the homes of policemen, black local councillors, and coloured parliamentary politicians.[22] In the case of the latter, the responsibility was claimed by a hitherto unheard-of body, the Western Cape Suicide Squad. The police have suggested that such groups receive their weaponry and training from the ANC, but operate independently from Umkhonto units so that the ANC can publicly disassociate itself from the more controversial of their activities.[23] No evidence has been produced yet to substantiate such an hypothesis, but the attacks themselves, whether the work of the ANC, truly autonomous organisations, or *agents provocateurs*,[24] do indicate the existence of a constituency quite ready to respond to the ANC's insurrectionary exhortations.

It is difficult to assess how prepared the ANC is to mobilise and enlist such a following. The ANC has declared 1985 to be the 'Year of the Cadre', in acknowledgement of the need to step up the work of constructing an internal organisation.[25] A *Rand Daily Mail* correspondent citing 'sources close to the movement' reported that there was a 'strong feeling [that] the ANC . . . has neglected the situation . . . inside the country' (10.09.84). All the trial evidence of the last few years would appear to support the contention that the establishment of permanent internal organisational structures has lagged behind military activity.[26] It may be significant that guerillas have not been very active in the areas affected by the recent township unrest: there have been no attacks attributed to the ANC in the southern Vaal, none in the Eastern Cape, and only a few on the East Rand. Of course, it may be the case that guerilla activity is partly intended to divert police attention away from those areas where really vital ANC organisational initiatives are under way. One should not, though, overstate the importance of the creation of elaborate organisational networks. One of the achievements of the ANC's 'armed propaganda' is that the ANC can influence to an extent the course of popular political assertions without having to manipulate or organise them. Communal support for the ANC is evident at every public gathering in the townships: the anthems sung by the crowds, the poetic and dramatic homage paid to the guerillas by youthful orators, and the green, black, and golden flags all bear witness to this. Most recently, at a political funeral in Cradock, the appearance of a banner of the South African Communist Party (SACP), was greeted with joyful applause (*ST*, 21.07.85). It is true that when the ANC publicly invoked a communal rebellion to render the townships ungovernable,[27] it was in reality responding to a course of events already in motion, but nevertheless, it is possible that in recent months some of the township insurrectionists have been consciously inspired by the ANC's appeal. Today a revolutionary movement of considerable proportions exists in the black townships of South Africa, and the ability of ANC cadres to exercise a commanding influence over it can only be a matter of time.

Relations with the region

In the Southern African regional context this has been a difficult phase for the ANC, requiring all the diplomatic skills at its disposal to maintain a semblance of cordial relations with some of the Frontline States. Though discussions between the South African government and Mozambique had been in progress since mid-December 1984, with three separate meetings between then and the ceremonial signing of the non-agression pact at Nkomati on 16 March, the implications of the agreement came as a surprise to the ANC.[28] Western financial pressure on the Mozambicans, as well as famines in Tete and Inhambane and the spoilation resulting from MNR activity forced the Mozambique government to undertake to prevent ANC guerillas from using its territory for transit or bases.[29] Henceforth the ANC would be allowed only to maintain a small diplomatic mission in Maputo. The agreement itself could have been anticipated; as early as January *The Star* reported that the ANC had been compelled to remove some of its facilities from southern Mozambique (11.01.84). But it does seem that the ANC leadership was kept completely in the dark as to what they could reasonably expect as the eventual outcome of the earlier meetings. Oliver Tambo met Samora Machel in January, when many of the essentials of the pact had been decided, but the Mozambican president told him nothing.[30] ANC officials in Maputo were at a particular disadvantage as few of them could speak Portuguese.[31] Ruth First's assassination in 1983 lost to the movement one of the few people it had with the necessary degree of sympathetic insight into Mozambican politics to understand the pressures affecting FRELIMO politicians.[32] Even more startling to the ANC than the

Accord itself 'was the fanfare and publicity and later the clamp-down on our people in Mozambique'.[33] In April 1984 the Mozam-bican army raided all ANC houses in Maputo, detaining several people, and confiscating the hand weapons originally provided by FRELIMO for the self-protection of their guests. Oliver Tambo was refused a transit visa, nearly two hundred ANC members had to leave the country, and finally, probably more wounding than anything else, Mozambican officials began justifying their new relationship with South Africa by placing the ANC's struggle in a different conceptual category from their own anti-colonial revolu-tion:

> The difference in South Africa is that the ANC is carrying on a fight for civic rights and not an armed struggle for national liberation, because South Africa is a sovereign republic recognised by the United Nations . . . (*Star*, 09.02.84).

Since Nkomati, critical pan-African reactions, fence-mending ef-forts by the ANC starting with a delegation headed by Thabo Mbeki, and the continuing progress of the MNR, despite South African pledges to discontinue support for it, have helped to modify Mozambican enthusiasm for the Accord. Nevertheless, the FRELIMO leaders remain critical of the ANC's emphasis on arm-struggle, counselling instead a flexible strategy which would include among its components the exploitation of any opportunities which emerged for dialogue with South African government represen-tatives, strengthening links with Western governments (and, con-versely, playing down the ANC's relationship with the SACP and with European communist administrations), and deepening the ANC's involvement in popular forms of mass action — civil disobedience and strikes.[34] 'Effective political action inside South Africa could exploit the contradictions appearing in the apartheid edifice', Mozambican officials apparently informed Joe Slovo, one of the key strategists on the ANC's military committee. Slovo was also told that the ANC's sabotage campaign had brought it 'no nearer to taking power physically' (*SStar*, 17.02.85). The ANC's military efforts have been perceived with similar scepticism by the Zambians. President Kaunda probably influenced Sam Nujoma to declare in April 1984 that an independent Namibia would be in no position to provide for the needs of ANC guerillas (*Star*, 18.04.85;

RDM, 02.06.84).

At least in Mozambique the ANC has not had to contend with active complicity between the country's administration and the South African security forces. In Swaziland a secret agreement concluded with South Africa in 1982 commits the Swazis to helping to combat the ANC. They have proved as good as their word. For example, in June 1984, an ANC member was held after fighting between ANC men and Swazi soldiers. The police confiscated completed petition forms from the United Democratic Front million signature campaign. Some names on the forms were underlined, and the police claimed that their prisoner was on his way to Maputo to deliver the lists to ANC offices there. On the assumption that the ANC intended to use these lists for recruiting purposes, the Swazis handed them over to the SAP (*Cit*, 21.06.84). Other events have also served to deepen the rift between the ANC and the Swazi government. Fighting between Swazi forces and Umkhonto groups broke out on several occasions in the course of 1984, and over 100 ANC men were deported.[35] The ANC was said to be involved in the killing of a deputy police commissioner.[36] During 1984 ANC insurgents raided two police stations, in Mbabane and Bhunya, and succeeded in releasing seven of their comrades.[37] In October 1984 the Swazis deported to South Africa Babalezi Bulonga, a former SRC president of the University of Swaziland and a man rumoured to have ANC connections.[38] According to the Swazis and the SAP, ANC guerillas still enter South Africa from Swazi territory: on 18 June 1985 roadblocks were put up in northern Swaziland in an attempt to thwart ANC infiltrators from Mozambique (*Star*, 19.06.85).

The ANC's initial response to these events was conciliatory: two senior members of the hierarchy, Jacob Zuma and Moses Mabhida, visited Mbabane in April 1984 and had talks with the police commissioner and the Ministers of Justice and the Interior. They brought with them apologies for the violence in which ANC people were implicated, and arranged for a forthcoming visit by Oliver Tambo (*Sow*, 03.05.84). Tambo's visa difficulties with the Mozambicans forced the cancellation of this visit. This led to a breakdown in official communication between the ANC and the Swazis, and in May 1984 the ANC was reported to have asked President Kaunda to act as an intermediary.[39] But the mutual antipathy which exists is probably too great to be resolved by tactful diplomacy. For in Swaziland the ANC is confronted with an administration of a very different character to that of Mozambique. While the FRELIMO leadership had to be coerced into limiting its support for the ANC, the Swazis evidently did not need much persuasion. To a fundamentally conservative ruling order the ANC constitutes a domestic political threat. Moreover, with their links with South African business, the present rulers of Swaziland are not especially predisposed to favour a revolutionary transformation of South African society.[40] Not suprisingly, recent ANC statements which mention Swaziland have an undertone of bitterness quite unusual in the formal courtesy which normally characterises the ANC's public references to independent black African governments.

As we have seen, since the Nkomati and Swazi agreements, Botswana has acquired an enhanced strategic significance for the ANC. Two ANC delegations visited Gaborone in February and March 1985, the second headed by Oliver Tambo. On both occasions the main subject of discussions between the ANC visitors and the Botswana officials was the activity of ANC members in Botswana, some of whom were in prison for arms offences (*SStar*, 17.02.85). In March, the Botswana government prepared a list of South African refugees whom it recommended should leave the country for their own safety. The list was presented to the visiting ANC delegation with the assurance that it did not constitute an ultimatum, nobody was going to be forced to leave.[41] Botswana apprehensions were vindicated on 14 June 1985 when South African soldiers attacked ten buildings in Gaborone which they claimed were used by the ANC. They killed 12 people, including two domestic workers and a six year old child. Of the other nine, the SAP asserted that eight were ANC members and that the premises destroyed in the attacks were used to train guerillas, plan sabotage, and administer the passage of arms through Botswana. It claimed that several of those who had been killed had been involved in running crash courses in the use of hand grenades. It identified one of the victims of the raid, 71-year-old Dick Mtsweni, as 'finance and logistics chief' for the ANC in Gaborone. The security police stated that the main purpose of the raid was to obtain intelligence. The raiders brought back with them account books, bank statements and telephone bills which the police suggest demonstrate that ANC facilities in Gaborone were providing a crucial communication link between the ANC command structure and its 'western front' inside South Africa. Amongst the other trophies of the raid was a computer with its software, ostensibly the property of the Solidarity News Service, which the South African authorities argue was a front for an ANC intelligence-gathering operation.[42] If these claims can be accepted, the savage episode would appear to represent an important setback for the ANC, but to date there has been no independent assessment of the police evidence, nor have there been any arrests or trials linked to the raid. It is, though, a little unlikely that the ANC would situate strategically vital facilities in a place as vulnerable as Gaborone. This would be especially surprising in the light of previous well-publicised SAP successes in penetrating the security of the ANC's Gaborone organisation. Of course, the main function of the attack may have been quite unrelated to the significance of the targets; it could have been directed principally at intimidating the Botswana authorities into allowing their Defence Force to come to some kind of informal arrangement with the South Africans.[43] Botswana is unlikely to concede a public agreement, but it can be expected that the ANC will in future find it more difficult for its guerillas to cross the country.

Though the Frontline States represent increasingly difficult terrain for the ANC, the fresh obstacles here have been to an extent offset by developments affecting South Africa. First, a succession of township revolts since September 1984 directed against the newly implemented local councils have seriously challenged the power of the authorities to effectively govern black communities. The revolts can partly be explained by socio-economic factors: recession, high rates of youth unemployment, and inflation; but they are also the result of an intense degree of communal politicisation which has been in progress since the late 1970s. The ANC's 'armed propaganda' has certainly played an important part in this, and the revolt of the townships greatly expands potential scope for ANC guerilla and political operations.

Secondly, apparently endemic political violence in South Africa has stimulated the international campaign for economic sanctions as well as enhancing the ANC's status in Western Europe and North America. The scale of the internal challenge to the South African authorities and their growing degree of international isolation have probably been the main elements in influencing the ANC leadership to believe that, in the words of a National Executive statement of April 1985, 'The future is within our grasp'.[44]

Contributing to this optimism has been the growing sentiment among white South Africans in favour of official government contact with the ANC. An Afrikaans Sunday newspaper ran a series of articles based on an interview conducted by the deputy editor with ANC officials in Lusaka.[45] An HSRC poll found 43% of its white respondents in support of talks with the ANC (*RDM*, 22.12.84). The Students' Representative Councils at Rand Afrikaans University and at Stellenbosch voted in favour of unconditional talks (*Star*, 03.05.85). All this took place against a background of rumours that government and ANC representatives had already met (*SStar*, 06.01.85). The ANC vigorously denied that anything of this kind had even been contemplated. Nevertheless, during a visit to the United States, Oliver Tambo professed himself willing to meet leaders of the South African government (*Star*, 25.04.85), though this was later qualified by several conditions. Any talks should have as their mutually agreed goal a united, democratic, and non-racial South Africa. The ANC would have to have a popular mandate to enter such negotiations (*CP*, 28.04.85). The fact, though, that the ANC is prepared to consider the eventuality of negotiations represents a significant conciliatory shift in its public posture. This is probably a reflection of new recognition of the possibilities of attracting official and public support in Western countries. It may also be motivated by the need to retain the goodwill of those Frontline states which are inclined towards dialogue (*SStar*, 03.02.85). An ANC pamphlet despatched from Harare which had as its theme the future reconciliation of white and black South Africans and their building together of a new society may also have been prompted by a wish to placate Frontline concern (*RDM*, 29.12.84).

The implications of the Nkomati Accord, and the fresh opportunities presented by the upsurge of civil strife inside South Africa and international reactions to it were two considerations which helped to determine the decision to hold the Kabwe Consultative Conference. Another may have been internal disunity. For the first time in some years there have been reports of divisions within the leadership and serious rank and file discontent. The ANC National Executive was reported to be divided over the emphasis which should be devoted to armed struggle and on the subject of negotiations, with the principal division allegedly developing between the right and left sections of the leadership (*SStar*, 06.01.85.) The former was said to be in the ascendant, with SACP members losing influence (*RDM*, 10.09.84). Two camp mutinies were believed to have broken out, one in Tanzania and one in Angola. The Tanzanian mutiny, described by a French publication, arose from the discontent of Umkhonto cadres deported from Mozambique, impatient for action, and critical of what they perceived to be the caution of their leaders (*Star*, 18.03.85). The Angolan dissent, as described by SAP spokesmen, was in reaction to poor food, austere living conditions, and unpopular military operations against UNITA (*RDM*, 23.04.85). It is difficult to evaluate such reports. It is possible that they may be overdramatised representations of real disaffection. Oliver Tambo, in a speech to ANC students in May 1984, denied that splits existed within the ANC but conceded that:

> There are people who are dissatisfied from time to time about one thing or another. Sometimes the dissatisfaction is justified. Sometimes the dissatisfaction arises because someone has been careless. So, we are not perfect.[46]

As shall be evident, the decisions of the Kabwe conference do seem to reflect a preoccupation with internal disciplinary matters which can be interpreted as a response to rank and file criticisms. But the executive elections and the strategic resolutions of the conference would seem to confirm that whatever ideological and strategic disagreements exist within the hierarchy, the factionalist impression created by SAP statements and journalistic speculation is misleading.[47]

The Kabwe conference

It is too early for a definitive analysis of the Kabwe conference. Too few details are publicly available, and so any interpretation of its decisions has to be tentative. The groundwork for the conference was extensive. ANC units were instructed in mid-1984 to consider the appropriate strategies to develop in the light of the Nkomati Accord (*RDM*, 10.09.84). ANC groups from both the internal and external structures of the organisation submitted position papers to the committee responsible for determining the contents of the conference agenda.[48] Oliver Tambo and the majority of the National Executive apparently were hoping for an open and unrestricted debate.[49] Before the conference it was already clear what the main issues of substance were going to be: military strategy, the question of soft targets, the role of workers, and the shortcomings of underground organisation.[50] The conference itself, held between the two historically significant dates of 16 and 26 June in the small town of Kabwe in Zambia, was reportedly marked by an atmosphere of unity, bellicosity, and self-confidence (in notable contrast with the prevalent tone of the previous consultative conference in 1969).[51] Eleven major decisions emerged from the proceedings.[52] These can be divided into three groups: military, organisational, and political.

Decisions affecting military policy included a resolution authorising Umkhonto to strike in future at 'soft' or civilian targets, a decision to intensify 'people's war', and the election of a War Council. Lower-echelon sentiment for dropping the restraints limiting guerilla activity which could cause civilian casualties has been strong for some years. The connotations of this decision are as yet unclear. Tambo in interviews given in the months before the conference predicted that a change in ANC policy on soft targets was likeiy, but nevertheless insisted that ANC attacks would not be 'specifically directed at civilians'. But certain civilians do now fall into the category of what the ANC considers to be 'legitimate targets': prominent government supporters, border area farmers, anti-union company officials, civil defence workers, and, of course, state witnesses and police informers (*CP*, 30.06.85). The resolution in favour of 'people's war' is a significant step which has been openly propounded over the last two years.[53] In essence, it will involve a redirection of effort away from attacks on major economic and strategic installations (attacks which require considerable pre-planning and technical expertise), and a concentration on forms of military activity which directly undermine the government's administrative capacity and which allow for mass participation. Such a campaign will inevitably bring more frequent confrontations with the security forces and will depend to a much greater degree on popular support.[54] Previous statements by ANC leaders demonstrated a feeling that Umkhonto's sabotage campaign had serious political limitations:

Our people should not be mere spectators in the intensifying political and military struggle against the enemy. Every form of support should be given to our cadres as they confront the enemy in the cities, towns and villages of our country. The doors of the houses of our people should be open to our cadres. Everybody should realise that he has got a role to play to ensure the success of our military operations. To ensure that every cadre, as he throws a grenade in the house of a policeman, into the barracks of the fascist army, that the cadre must be able to get away, must be able to survive in order to be able to fight tomorrow. The task of fighting the enemy cannot just be relegated to the ANC and MK, but should be the task of all patriots of our country . . . [55]

In this context a surprising omission from the publicly available resolutions was a stated recognition of the need to build up internal political organisation to facilitate this kind of public support for guerilla operations. Tambo before the conference acknowledged that he felt that ANC organisational structures within South Africa were inadequate.[56]

It is possible to interpret in this fresh commitment to popular insurrection a pragmatic perception of the difficulties consequent upon expanding the relatively 'high-tech' sabotage activity to a point at which it could present serious obstacles to the functioning of the economy.[57] Here there may have been an element of self-criticism: as Oliver Tambo conceded in May 1984, 'In fact, we have tended to think that Umkhonto we Sizwe will do it all and Mozambique will help us do it'.[58] It could also be the case that 'people's war' is a response to the Mozambican counsel that the ANC should give priority to forms of action which could involve large numbers of civilians.[59] It may be significant that the ANC in April 1985 produced a statement which called for a revolutionary leap in which Umkhonto action would be only one element in a struggle which would also include 'long-lasting' work stoppages, the establishment of alternative local authorities, the formation of youth crime prevention units, and the mutiny and resignation of black councillors, policemen and soldiers.[60] But as well as the perception of the constraints recently affecting ANC operations, a quite different set of considerations could have affected the redirection of strategy. The exultation stemming from the township revolt and the ANC's mounting domestic and international status may have engendered a feeling that a really decisive revolutionary challenge and the South African state's capitulation were no longer distant possibilities to be attained through a very protracted struggle. If this is the perspective of the ANC command, then it would make sense to limit the economic damage inflicted by guerilla warfare (as well as continuing to exercise a degree of humane restraint with regard to harming civilians).

There were four main organisational decisions. All ANC members are in future to undergo military training.[61] A code of conduct has been adopted governing the sexual and social relationships of all ANC personnel, as well as their consumption of alcohol. Both these measures can be understood as responses to the disciplinary problems and the discontent which have been manifest in the training camps. The National Executive has been expanded from 22 to 30 members. This has enabled the leadership to retain virtually the whole pre-Kabwe executive but has allowed the election to the new executive of younger African and non-African members. At the Morogoro conference, rank-and-file membership of the external section of the ANC was opened up to Indians, coloureds and white ANC sympathisers, but the ANC National Executive remained racially exclusive. The Kabwe conference has removed this last vestige of 1950s 'multiracialism' so that, in the words of Oliver Tambo, the organisation could 'reflect in [its] structures the kind of South Africa we say we envisage'.[62] The move has, of course, brought the ANC into line with the predominant trend in the current evolution of internal black political organisations.

The four political resolutions rejected any dialogue with South African government representatives unless the total dismantling of apartheid was a common objective, reaffirmed ANC support for disinvestment and economic sanctions,[63] committed the ANC to making efforts to work with the rival Pan-Africanist Congress, and called for trade union unity as a preliminary to a sustained campaign of industrial action to bring the government to its knees. None of these represent a significant alteration in ANC official policy. If, as some sources before the conference intimated,[64] there was a significant force within the movement pressing for a more privileged role to be allocated to the working class in both ideological and strategic terms, then it would appear that the leadership has succeeded in fending off such a challenge. Certainly nothing in the conference decisions could imply a 'workerist' advance on policy adopted in 1969 at Morogoro.[65] The resolve to try and bring about a rapprochement with the PAC is a new departure, but does echo recent ANC statements deploring the internecine conflict between 'progressive democrat' and black consciousness groups within South Africa. Taken as a whole, the political decisions seem to represent a rejection of the strategic options recommended by the more cautious of the ANC's Frontline allies.

Finally, the Executive elections can also be seen as a reaffirmation of leadership and a confirmation of the earlier ideological balance in the organisation's hierarchy. The eleven new members of the executive include three men and one woman drawn from the 1950s generation of political activists who join ten other veterans of that period who were reelected. The four comprise Joe Slovo, an important figure on the ANC's military committee, a former Johannesburg lawyer, and a leading Communist Party member since the 1940s; Mac Maharaj, imprisoned on Robben Island in 1964 for his role in the first Umkhonto campaign, and a member of the political and military committees of the ANC; Reg September, once a leader of the South African Coloured People's Organisation, ANC representative in London and later Madagascar; and Ruth Mompati, a woman with strong nationalist convictions who worked during the 1950s as a clerk in Oliver Tambo's legal partnership. The younger new members are in their late thirties and forties. They are evenly balanced between those with a mostly military background and people who have served as diplomats, researchers, and administrators. Among them are two men, James Stuart and Pallo Jordan, who have worked especially closely with Oliver Tambo. The others include the editor of *Sechaba*, Francis Meli, who holds a doctorate from the University of Leipzig,[66] and Anthony Mongale, former ANC representative in East Berlin. Meli is believed to be a marxist, but the philosophical inclinations of the other younger men are not known. Two former members of the Executive failed to gain reelection. These were John Motsabi and Andrew Masondo. Masondo's removal from the Executive may have been due to the discontent in the training camps. Before the conference his official posts were national political commissar and head of security. As such he was responsible for internal disciplinary matters. Emerging unaltered from the elections is the fairly equal division of influence between non-communists and

SACP adherents, the predominance of men of Tambo's generation, and the absence of anyone with recent experience of internal
conditions in South Africa.[67]

Conclusion

This survey began with an exposition of two analyses of the ANC's
recent development, one an external view, hostile and disparaging,
and the other a partisan perspective, confident and hopeful. Both
contain elements of truth. As the SAP version suggests, the ANC
has had to contend with formidable adversities in the last 18
months. The evidence does suggest that the progress of its internal
organisation within the country has tended to be outpaced by the
rising momentum of popular struggle.[68] But the ANC's exhilara-
tion is also reasonable: to compensate for the logistical obstacles of
the post-Nkomati period has been the appearance of very promis-
ing conditions for mobilising and inspiring a mass movement.
Moreover, the shifts in ANC policies have been logical responses to
fresh circumstances. The decisions of the Kabwe conference
indicate that, contrary to police perceptions, morale within the
organisation has never been higher. The times are changing, and
for many South Africans, the possibility of revolutionary change
has ceased to be a chimerical article of faith and has become instead
a goal attainable within the span of their lives.

Notes

1 *Africa Report* (New York), May-June 1984, 28.
2 *The Guardian* (London), 06.09.84.
3 *The Guardian* (London), 29.08.84.
4 Oliver Tambo, quoted on Radio Freedom, Addis Ababa, 1930 GMT,
   09.07.84.
5 Chris Hani and Mac Maharaj, 'A people's army fighting a people's
   war', *Sechaba*, November 1984, 28-29.
6 *Zimbabwe Herald*, 27.05.85.
7 See also figures cited by the Minister of Law and Order, *House of
   Assembly Debates*, 09.04.85, 994-995. ISS figures reported in *Star*,
   21.06.85.

8 This is according to ISS statistics. I have found press reports for only six of these and have surmised the nature of the others by comparing my own data with that provided by the Minister which gives details of targets, but no dates.

9 *Sunday Times* (London), 10.02.85.

10 The geographical distribution of attacks between 1 January 1984 and 30 June 1985 is as follows:
East Rand 6, East Transvaal 1, Ermelo 1, Johannesburg 20, Pretoria 4, Roodepoort 1, West Transvaal 8

Durban 20, North Natal 3, Pietermaritzburg 2

Bloemfontein 2, Kroonstad 1, Welkom 1

Cape Town 4, Umtata 3

Unknown 1

11 The attacks can be classified in four categories:
Central businesses and industrial districts 37
White suburban areas 3
Rural 10
Black townships 13.

12 These were the AECI offices, Johannesburg (*Star*, 26.06.85); Anglo American Gold and Uranium Division, Johannesburg (*Star*, 04.05.85); and the Anglo Vaal building, Johannesburg (*Star*, 04.05.85).

13 *Zimbabwe Herald*, 29.03.85, and *The Observer* (London), 31.03.85.

14 My figures provide the following breakdown: government offices and foreign missions (10); petrol depots (2); power installations (5); railway lines, signal boxes and trucks (6); police stations (2); SAP personnel and state witnesses (12); private property (1); business premises (4); others (7).

15 *The Guardian*, 11.08.84.

16 *Sunday Mail* (Harare), 20.01.85.

17 See for example the report of ANC infiltration into Swaziland in mid-June 1985 in *Star*, 19.06.85.

18 At one time selected Umkhonto recruits were instructed in the use of heavy field artillery weapons, implying a vision of the transition in the future to conventional warfare. *Star*, 19.10.79.

19 See Comrade Mzala, 'Has the time come for the army of the masses?', *African Communist*, 89, 1982; Khumalo Migwe, 'Further contribution on arming the masses', *African Communist*, 89, 1982; Thanduxolo

Nokwanda, 'The dangers of militarism', *African Communist*, 91, 1982.

20 *Zimbabwe Herald*, 27.05.85.

21 For a description of the mines used by the ANC, see *Star*, 26.06.84.

22 For examples of such attacks, see *The Guardian*, 22.02.85, and *Star*, 12.06.85.

23 See interview with Craig Williamson, *Financial Mail*, 28.06.85.

24 Especially controversial in this context were the abortive grenade attacks in which six local political activists were killed by their own weapons on 26 June 1985 in KwaThema, Duduza and Tsakane. For different explanations of the incident, see 'Booby trap mix-up may have killed 7', *Star*, 27.06.85; 'Major shift in ANC home policy', *City Press*, 30.06.85; and 'Booby trap clues to grenade blast deaths', *Weekly Mail*, 19.07.85.

25 *Sechaba*, January 1985, and *Sunday Mail*, 20.01.85.

26 See Tom Lodge, 'The African National Congress in South Africa, 1976-1983; guerilla war and armed propaganda', *Journal of Contemporary African Studies*, 3(1-2), October 1983 - April 1984.

27 *Zimbabwe Herald*, 27.05.85.

28 For details of the initial impact the agreement made on the ANC, see Joseph Hanlon, *Mozambique: the revolution under fire* (London, 1984), 261 and Jonathan Steele, 'Mozambique's pact with Apartheid', *The Guardian*, 22.05.84.

29 Hanlon, *Mozambique*, 252-262.

30 Steele, 'Mozambique's pact'.

31 Hanlon, *Mozambique*, 261.

32 Hanlon, *Mozambique*; see also Glenn Frankel, 'In exile, militant battles South Africa', *International Herald Tribune*, 16.07.85.

33 Editorial, *Sechaba*, May 1984.

34 *The Guardian*, 16.07.84; *Sunday Star*, 03.02.85; *Africa Confidential*, 22.05.85, 2.

35 *The Guardian*, 04.01.85.

36 *The Guardian*, 29.12.84.

37 *The Guardian*, 04.01.85.

38 *The Guardian*, 04.01.85.

39 *The Guardian*, 25.05.84.

40 See John Daniel, 'A comparative analysis of Lesotho's and Swaziland's relations with South Africa, (ed) SARS, *South African Review Two* (Johannesburg, 1984), 236-237.

41 *Botswana Guardian*, 24.05.85.

42 See Williamson interview, *Financial Mail*, 28.06.85; 'ANC terror

hideouts destroyed, *Paratus*, July 1985, 18-22; and 'Eight activists among the dead', *Star*, 21.06.85.

43 According to PW Botha a meeting between him and Dr Gaotitiwe Chiepe resulted in the agreement that 'the security forces of the two countries would once again attempt to come to an understanding on practical arrangements on how to combat the growing danger' (the activities of the ANC in Botswana — TL). *Star*, 21.06.85.

44 NEC of the ANC, 'ANC call to the nation: the future is within our grasp', Lusaka, 25.04.85.

45 Piet Muller, 'Steun aan UDF is vir eie gavin, sê ANC', *Beeld*, 12.12.84.

46 Oliver Tambo, 'We are a force', *Sechaba*, October 1984.

47 ANC sources concede that ideological differences exist in the organisation but contend that these bring about a productive dialectic rather than debilitating conflict.

48 The preparations for the conference are described by Howard Barrell in 'Planning for people's war', *New Statesman*, 25.01.85; and 'ANC prepares for consultative conference', *Work In Progress*, 35, February 1985, 4-8.

49 Barrell, 'Planning for people's war', and 'ANC prepares for consultative conference'.

50 Barrell, 'Planning for people's war', and 'ANC prepares for consultative conference'.

51 For a revealing glimpse into the mood of the 1969 Morogoro conference, see Joe Slovo, 'The life and times of JB Marks', *African Communist*, 95, 1983, 89.

52 'South Africa — Causus belli', *Africa Confidential*, 03.07.85.

53 For the clearest statement to date on the concept of people's war, see Hani and Maharaj, 'A people's army'.

54 For ANC strategic thinking in this direction, see 'Presidential statement: the dream of total liberation is in sight', *Sechaba*, March 1984; *Africa Confidential*, 22.05.85; and 'The time for popular insurrection is ripe', *Zimbabwe Herald*, 27.05.85.

55 Hani and Maharaj, 'A people's army'.

56 *New Statesman*, 25.01.85.

57 As Joe Slovo points out, 'We're not going to destroy the enemy with sabotage blows even if we managed to double or triple the scale of attacks'. *Guardian Weekly* (London), 10.02.85.

58 Tambo, 'We are a force'.

59 *Africa Confidential*, 22.05.85, 2.

60 *Africa Confidential*, 22.05.85, 2.

61 *Africa Confidential*, 03.07.85, 1.
62 *New Statesman*, 25.01.85.
63 *Africa Confidential*, 03.07.85.
64 For example Howard Barrell in *New Statesman*, 25.01.85.
65 At Morogoro the working class was accorded with the status of con-stituting 'a distinct and reinforcing layer of our liberation and socialism'. See 'Strategy and tactics of the South African revolution', in (ed) A La Guma, *Apartheid* (London, 1972), 203.
66 Francis Meli's doctorate was awarded for an historical dissertation he completed during the 1960s on the African policies of the Communist International.
67 Though it is possible that younger more recent exiles may be rising to positions of importance in the structures which are directly subordinate to the NEC. Thozamile Botha, trade unionist and community leader in Port Elizabeth in the late 1970s and early 1980s, is now a member of the external South African Congress of Trade Unions executive.
68 It is noticeable, for instance, that much of the unrest has been concen-trated in areas comparatively unaffected by ANC sabotage in 1984 and 1985, the East Rand and Eastern Cape.

The United Democratic Front

Jo-Anne Collinge

Within a year of its national launch in August 1983, the United Democratic Front (UDF) posed a fundamental challenge to the legitimacy of the National Party 'reform' plan. It orchestrated election boycotts which left no doubt that the new tricameral parliament meant rule by white South Africa, in alliance with a very small percentage of the minorities the government hoped to coopt. At the same time, from mid-1984 increasing numbers of UDF affiliates began to participate in direct mass action. This arose in part from the 1983 electoral rejection of the revamped black local authorities. This challenged not only the legitimacy of these institutions but their very existence.

Popular protest in townships across the Transvaal, Free State, Northern Cape and Eastern Province was often followed by violent confrontations between security forces and residents, with considerable loss of civilian life. Increasingly the township-based police force became a target for physical attack.

In a third phase of struggle in mid-1985, key UDF affiliates in the Eastern Cape attempted to drive a wedge into the white ruling group by means of a consumer boycott. This was designed to induce commercial interests to pressurise the government to institute reform and to give in to numerous demands such as removal of SADF troops from townships and lifting the state of emergency. The solidly sustained Eastern Province boycotts began to be emulated in the Transvaal, Western Cape and Northern Free State by August 1985.

The government clearly saw the UDF as a controlling force in the countrywide popular resistance. By the Front's second birthday (when it described itself as a loose alliance of almost 600 community organisations and trade unions of varying sizes), a wide range of security provisions had been used against it, decimating its leadership. These included 'preventive' detention of key figures, treason charges against 38 national leaders and Vaal area activists, blanket bans on meetings, sweeping detentions of regional leaders and second-rank national leaders for interrogation, use of emergency measures to incarcerate hundreds of rank-and-file UDF supporters, and the banning of a key affiliate, the Congress of South African Students (COSAS).

During the same period the UDF also faced more sinister reprisals from unidentified organisations, such as petrol bombing of Front and affiliate leaders' homes, abductions and political assassinations — as in the case of Cradock leaders Matthew Goniwe, Sparrow Mkhonto, Fort Calata and Sicelo Mhlauli, as well as Durban lawyer Victoria Mxenge and the mysterious disappearance of Sipho Hashe, Champion Galela and Qaqawula Godolozi.

The two treason trials which involve a total of 38 accused, predominantly UDF leaders, make it difficult to examine the debate about the nature and extent of the Front's challenge to the apartheid system. It is alleged in one trial that the UDF has been used by the African National Congress to promote its aims, and in the other that the UDF itself aimed to overthrow or endanger the state by violence or the threat of violence.

The wide ambit of allegations in these ongoing trials means that many questions about the UDF are best left for private consideration. Such issues include the relative roles of spontaneous action and organised resistance in wrecking local government systems in township after township. The related question of the ideological potency of the Front — its ability to inspire specific action by propounding certain general principles — is also closely linked to the points at issue in court. Given these constraints, what follows is a largely descriptive account of events within the UDF from early 1984 to mid-1985.

Campaigns and issues

The Million Signature Campaign

The first half of this period was dominated by two major cam-

paigns — the Million Signature Campaign and the boycott of the
August elections for the tricameral parliament. The declaration
which signatories to the Million Signature Campaign were asked to
endorse summarised the principles on which the Front was founded: commitment to unity in opposing apartheid and to the creation
of a non-racial democratic South Africa; opposition to the
Koornhof laws on 'black administration' and to the new constitution. As Howard Barrell wrote in the previous *South African
Review*, the purpose of the campaign was twofold: 'The major
aims were political education and a strengthening of the Front, but
the UDF also recognised the propaganda value locally and internationally of such a register of opposition.'[1]

The secretarial report to the National General Council (NGC)
meeting of the UDF in April 1985 suggests that the campaign's successes are to be found mainly in organisation-building. Although
hundreds of thousands signed the declaration, the one million mark
was never reached — and neither, it seems, was the envisaged propaganda value of the campaign attained.[2] The UDF ascribed this
partly to harassment of activists collecting the signatures. Some
signature forms were confiscated by police in Mankweng near
Pietersburg and Pretoria, and right-wing elements reportedly
assaulted activists and stole signature forms in places as far apart as
the Cape Peninsula, Johannesburg and Grahamstown. Some months
later, in June 1984, Minister of Law and Order Louis le Grange
alleged that Million Signature Campaign forms had been confiscated by Swazi police from members of the African National
Congress. Spokesmen for the Front dismissed suggestions that it
had supplied lists as a recruiting aid to the ANC, and pointed to the
stolen forms. The ANC also issued a statement denying receipt of
the forms.

These initial government suggestions of UDF-ANC links were a
mild prelude to a barrage of allegations. Nationalist attacks on the
UDF reached new heights as the 1984 August elections for the
coloured House of Representatives and Indian House of Delegates
drew near. The UDF's election boycott campaign culminated in
simultaneous mass rallies countrywide on 19 August. They were
convened to mark the first anniversary of the national launch of the
Front, but in effect demonstrated a huge non-racial groundswell
against the 'reform' package. Feeling that state action against the
UDF was imminent was reflected by speakers at this occasion.

Transvaal vice-president Frank Chikane told a Johannesburg audience of over 3 000 that if the government harmed the UDF, 'the people will realise they [the ruling group] do not want peaceful change in South Africa' (*Star*, 20.08.84). Front patron Allan Boesak warned a Cape crowd of about 6 000 to prepare for greater oppression of apartheid's opponents (*RDM*, 20.08.84).

Within two days, security police were in the homes of leading UDF men in the Transvaal and Natal, taking them into 'preventive detention' in terms of section 28 of the Internal Security Act. Among those taken were one of the three national presidents of the UDF, Archie Gumede; the presidents of the Transvaal and Natal Indian Congresses, Essop Jassat and George Sewpersadh; and UDF publicity secretary 'Terror' Lekota. The Front's general secretary Popo Molefe went into hiding but was detained in October, almost immediately after he resumed his duties.

The campaign against the constitution

The detentions did not stem the momentum of the campaign against the new constitution,which was after all the *raison d'etre* of the Front. The grounds for opposing the 'reform' parliament had been spelled out in the UDF's first newsletter a year before the polls. 'The President's Council and the new parliament are a government plan to try to divide us,' the newsletter argued. 'The government wants to fool us that coloureds and Indians will share in apartheid's power and privileges. But they only want to use the masses of our coloured and Indian people. There will be four whites to every two coloureds and one Indian in the racist parliament. So apartheid will stay' (*UDF News*, August 1984).

At the end of 1983 there was strong feeling within the Front that it should bring pressure on the government to hold referenda within the coloured and Indian communities, along the lines of the referendum for whites in November 1983. Those who held this position argued that the UDF would not simply be asking its supporters to abstain from electoral participation, but would engage the state more directly in demanding that people be enabled to register rejection of the constitution by less ambiguous action than a stayaway. The countervailing argument was that the boycott had the potential to unite people, while a referendum could be divisive because it would be ethnically implemented — and the wider public might see this as more than a tactical concession to ethnicism. Eventually a compromise was reached: the UDF itself refrained from calling for ethnic referenda, but set its affiliates free to do so should they feel local conditions dictated such action.

In the event, no affiliate launched a real campaign for referenda. In Natal and the Transvaal, the campaign to boycott Indian and coloured elections was spearheaded by UDF affiliates — the Natal Indian Congress, the Committee of Concern, the Transvaal Indian Congress and the Transvaal Anti-President's Council Committee — always with visible backing, on platforms and in demonstrations, from UDF central structures. In the Cape, local and regional UDF committees, together with the Cape Housing Action Committee and the Muslim Judicial Council, were at the forefront of the campaign. The strategy of UDF organisations was to rally an independent base of support for a boycott of elections designed to destroy the legitimacy of the 'reform' package. The Front's validity as an all-race, all-class national movement was virtually staked on this campaign against cooption of racial minorities.

Leafletting, door-to-door campaigning and, above all, successful public meetings were the main methods employed in the campaign. Political commentators were impressed by its vigour. Just before the poll for the House of Delegates, Gary van Staden of *The Star* wrote: 'In the space of just 21 days the TIC addressed 19 meetings across the length and breadth of the Transvaal and spoke to about 10 000 people. None of the participating parties has reached anything like that number of potential voters' (*Star*, 24.08.84). Immediately after the poll for the House of Representatives, Brian Pottinger of the *Sunday Times* wrote: 'The Labour Party's efforts in the early 1970s pale in comparison to the mobilisation and organisation undertaken by the UDF and its affiliates' (*Sunday Times*, 26.08.84).

The overall rallying cry during the campaign was defence of non-racial democracy. Coloured and Indian people were urged to resist cooption into the ruling group to become 'junior partners' in the maintenance of apartheid. African members of the UDF joined vociferously in campaign rallies urging potential voters not to betray South Africa's voiceless minority. The mechanics of the constitution, its financial implications, and the prospect of coloured and Indian youth having to serve in the Defence Force were additional angles of appeal frequently employed from platforms and in pamphlets. The detention of leading members of the Front and the Indian Congresses on the eve of the House of Representatives election was used by the Front to argue the justness of its own cause and the anti-democratic character of the 'reform' scenario.

The official percentage polls for the elections were 30% for the House of Representatives and 20% for the House of Delegates. The UDF, however, calculated the percentage of those who voted as a proportion of the total Indian and coloured population over the age of 18, as recorded in the 1980 census. The adjusted figures showed that only 17,5% of coloured people, and 15,5% of Indians, had voted.

The consulate siege

The issue of detention without trial was brought into international focus between September and December 1984 by the Durban Consulate sit-in by six Natal leaders of the UDF and NIC, including UDF president Archie Gumede. The Six took refuge in the British consulate in Durban to avoid being served with detention orders in terms of section 28 of the Internal Security Act. The sit-in demonstrated the lukewarm support victims of South Africa's security laws could expect from the Thatcher government, but it nonetheless opened a rift between Pretoria and Downing Street. Because the British, however grudgingly, accommodated the Six, the Botha government was provoked into refusing to return the 'Coventry Four' to stand trial in Britain for illicit arms deals.

Township unrest

Just five days after the election for the House of Delegates the Vaal rent protest turned into a bloody confrontation between unarmed residents and police. In just under a week, the death toll rose to 66 according to ministers of religion in the area, although the police count of fatalities was in the region of 30.

High school pupils' protests in support of the right to democratic representation, an end to corporal punishment and age restrictions on scholars, as well as a range of issues specific to each area, claimed lives in the East Rand, Pretoria, the Free State and Eastern Cape by mid-1984. After the Vaal uprising, conflict became endemic in the townships of these regions, with each round of government-inflicted deaths and detentions giving rise to a fresh wave of protest and subsequent violence.

The UDF had affiliates in areas such as the Vaal, the East Rand and the larger Eastern Cape towns. In many smaller towns, engagement with the authorities on specific issues preceded the formation of community organisations which in many cases eventually affiliated to the Front, as for instance in Tumahole (Parys), Leandra, Huhudi (Vryburg) and Thabong (Welkom).

From September 1984 the UDF's activities began to take the form of reaction to the repression of township resistance and support for local struggles. The precise role of the UDF in forming local organisations or in steering existing organisations into direct action against apartheid structures is a question presently before the courts.

Solidarity with students

The UDF itself has not undertaken direct action in relation to education. But it urged all affiliates to rally behind the Education Charter Campaign of the Azanian Students Organisation (AZASO), the Congress of South African Students (COSAS), the National Union of South African Students (NUSAS) and the National Education Union of South Africa (NEUSA). The task of the UDF was to situate the education struggle within the overall strategy of challenging apartheid, according to the latest secretarial report to the NGC.

A resolution taken at the NGC meeting in April 1985 called on affiliates to set up structures to ensure adult participation in educational issues, and to encourage formation of progressive teachers' organisations.

The November 1984 stayaway

In an unprecedented show of unity the UDF and its affiliates joined a full range of progressive trade unions, including the Federation of South African Trade Unions, the Council of Unions of South Africa and various 'community' unions, in launching a two-day work stayaway on 5-6 November. The action was initiated by COSAS, and was orchestrated by a coordinating committee of union and community representatives, the Transvaal Regional Stayaway Committee.

Widely successful in the Pretoria-Witwatersrand-Vereeniging area and in scattered towns beyond this region, the November stayaway was judged by observers to be the most widely and solidly supported action of its kind in 35 years (*RDM*, 08.11.84; *Star*, 20.11.84; *Star*, 21.11.84).

The demands made by workers who withheld their labour for the two days were mainly political (the resignation of community councillors, the withdrawal of police and troops from townships, the release of political prisoners and detainees, the recognition of pupils' democratic rights) and economic (a halt to rent and bus fare rises, GST and 'unfair' taxes). The reason for UDF involvement was made plain by Frank Chikane, who described the action as a determined attempt to get the attention of those in power. 'The underlying demand is that the government should listen to the voice of the people and get rid of apartheid' (*Star*, 06.11.84).

The stayaway was followed by the detention of a range of people in terms of section 29 of the Internal Security Act, and five key organisers were charged with subversion. The case has not been heard as four of the five accused have estreated bail and disappeared, and charges against the fifth have been conditionally withdrawn.

Black Christmas 1984

The UDF backed a call made initially by certain unions for Christmas to be observed as a time of mourning for those killed, maimed or detained as a result of township resistance. It called on people to refrain from extravagant spending, to stay away from large festive occasions and in their family circles to observe silences in memory of the victims. The Black Christmas was not a simple consumer boycott, UDF spokesmen stressed. Appeals were made to churchmen to mention victims in their Christmas services. Meetings were planned to launch the time of mourning on 16 December. Those in Soweto and Kagiso were disrupted by bans, but in Tembisa thousands turned out to support the call for mourning.

The All Blacks' tour

In April 1985 the general council of the Front resolved 'to cooperate with and support the South African Council on Sport and all other organisations inside and outside the country in mobilising mass resistance against rebel tours and in particular the New Zealand rugby tour'.[3] Publicity secretary 'Terror' Lekota told a press conference that the UDF would take demonstrations to the airports and playing fields, though it could foresee from events such as the Uitenhage shootings that protesters would face violence (*Star*, 09.04.85). The government's response was designed to create the impression that the UDF had threatened the All Blacks with violence, and the anti-tour stance immediately made headlines.

The UDF's position on the tour had all but faded from public debate when the New Zealand court application that prevented the visit was made. The UDF, through the Reverend Arnold Stofile who was sent to New Zealand as a guest of Halt All Racist Tours, gave evidence in support of the court application to prevent the tour. Asked by the court if the tour would be a threat to lives, Stofile reportedly replied: 'Our people are always brutalised in these situations — and I ask that the people of New Zealand spare us the agony of seeing our people brutalised (*Star*, 24.07.85).

Foreign investment

Since its launch the UDF has taken a position in favour of disinvestment. This was reiterated at the last general council meeting when the Front asserted in a resolution: 'We believe that foreign investments do not benefit the oppressed and exploited people of South Africa but bolster the apartheid government.'[4] United States imperialism, and particularly the political and military interventions of the Reagan administration 'aimed at subverting progressive states and movements', received special attention at the meeting.

The question of disinvestment was not publicly addressed by the UDF until June 1985, when a statement was issued following talks of the national working committee on the matter. The statement came amid heated public debate following moves in the United States Congress to curtail future investment. The UDF condemned foreign investment while refraining (for legal reasons) from advocating disinvestment. This statement, issued by acting publicity secretary Murphy Morobe, described foreign investment as complicity in apartheid, and a vicious exploitation of both the mineral resources and labour power of South Africa (*Star*, 13.06.85).

The UDF highlighted the fact that the Pretoria government and 'its apologists and imperialist friends have been straining at the leash, trying to show how blacks will suffer when foreign capital is withdrawn' but none of the liberation movements had opposed disinvestment. It added that no popular leaders had attempted to propagate support for foreign investment. The UDF demanded the right for people freely — and without fear of prosecution — to discuss the disinvestment issue. 'Until then the assumption must be that the majority of our people support the disinvestment call.'

In early April 1985 a demonstration against foreign investment was mounted at the Citibank premises in Johannesburg. Five UDF and trade union representatives later met managers of the United States-owned bank to debate the issue in the presence of the media.

Structures and policy

The UDF was arguably the first internal anti-apartheid movement in decades to assemble a leadership of national stature. It drew on widely-respected veterans of the 1950s and 1960s such as Archie Gumede and Albertina Sisulu. It elevated established community leaders like Frank Chikane, Cheryl Carolus, Cassim Saloojee and Matthew Goniwe to greater prominence. Also involved were a number of men released from Robben Island or from long-term banning orders, including Murphy Morobe, Steve Tshwete and, most notably, 'Terror' Lekota. Its roadshow-style mobilisation until September 1984 featured inter-regional exchange of speakers and extensive local and foreign media coverage. All contributed to the establishment of a high-profile national leadership.

However, the Front remained a loose structure. Its regional committees — which vary in structure according to local needs — have a key organising function. But affiliates cede autonomy to the UDF only in matters concerning the challenge to the new constitution and the Koornhof laws. The UDF has deliberately avoided taking policy on 'ideological' issues so as to be able to unite a broad spectrum of opponents to the new-style apartheid. It hoped initially

that black consciousness organisations and the entire range of progressive trade unions would associate themselves with the UDF. Of
these constituencies only CUSA and the 'community' unions,
which helped conceive the Front, joined.

The strength of affiliates which subscribe to the Freedom
Charter grew substantially in 1984-85. COSAS established branches in remote townships and evidenced unprecedented support in
large urban areas of the Cape and Transvaal. In scores of
townships, mostly on the platteland, a typical pattern was
establishment of a trinity of community organisations — a civic
group, a women's group and a youth organisation. Youth groups
often consciously style themselves 'congresses', indicating their
Charterist base, and many women's groups are also founded on the
Charter.

Despite the growth of Charterist influence within the Front, the
UDF itself has refrained from committing the total alliance to this
position. However, the statement by acting publicity secretary
Murphy Morobe, issued as a challenge to President PW Botha
before his August 1985 'Rubicon' speech, was couched largely in
terms of political and economic demands made in the Freedom
Charter.

Until mid-1985 the UDF was equivocal on the question of a national convention to negotiate a new political settlement. While
Lekota expressed general support for the principle, the Front as a
whole had not taken a formal decision on the move, Cassim Saloojee said (*RDM*, 29.06.84; *FM*, 31.08.84). 'We are realistic enough
to say a national convention cannot simply be called. There would
have to be the building up of democratic opposition in this country
to the point where we can make this a realistic demand.' Other
preconditions such as the release of jailed political leaders and the
safe return of exiles would have to be met, he added.

When the Progressive Federal Party called for a Convention
Alliance at its 1985 Natal congress a month after the declaration of
the state of emergency, the UDF sharply rejected the move on the
grounds that the essential preconditions had not in any way been
met (*Sow*, 03.09.85).

Relations with other organisations

The UDF and the ANC

The UDF was accused of being an ANC front even before its formation, in smear pamphlets distributed in all major cities two days before the national launch in August 1983. They dubbed the Front 'the old white-dominated SACP-ANC Alliance dressed up in a new guise' (*Star*, 19.08.83). Immediately after the launch, as the patrons and presidents of the Front became known (including such names as Nelson Mandela, Walter and Albertina Sisulu, Helen Joseph and Ahmed Kathrada), *The Citizen* was moved to comment obliquely: 'The UDF looks like an organisation which is being used by the same forces (of the 1950s) in a new guise, plus the latest left-wingers, radical and church leaders' (*Cit*, 23.08.83). *The Star* commented: 'To include among its patrons a committed supporter of the underground Communist Party (Dennis Goldberg) who is serving life imprisonment for his role in plotting revolution is to invite questions about the motivations of the UDF' (*Star*, 23.08.83).

The UDF itself did not address the question of ANC ties until December 1983, when publicity secretary Lekota released a statement reacting to the ANC's expression of support for the Front at the Commonwealth Conference. 'While we welcome the support of the ANC just as we welcome the support of any organisation of those opposed to the constitution and the Koornhof Bills, there are no links between the UDF and the ANC. Nor can there be any links under the present circumstances', Lekota said (*Cit*, 05.12.83).

In early 1984 there were occasional references in the press to the UDF-ANC question. *Die Vaderland* insisted: 'It is the skin of Esau but the voice of Jacob. The voice of the UDF but the spirit and principles of the Congress Alliance' (*Vaderland*, 06.04.84). Inkatha began to suggest that the UDF was working hand in hand with the ANC (*Star*, 06.05.84; 25.05.84). In June, Minister le Grange said that UDF Million Signature campaign forms had been found in the hands of the ANC in Swaziland — a claim which both the UDF and the ANC disputed.

On at least four occasions after this Le Grange made strongly-worded attacks on the UDF, linking it with the ANC and SACP. On the first occasion, the eve of the House of Representatives election, he declared: 'It is a known fact that there are organisations and people planning to thwart free and democratic elections and they are enthusiastically backed by the SACP and ANC Alliance which openly seeks the overthrow of the democratic system in South Africa.' Le Grange did not mention the UDF by name. But within hours of the Minister's threat to act to prevent disruption of elections many UDF leaders had been detained and this was seen as confirmation that his reference had indeed been to the UDF (*RDM*, 21.08.84). On 6 October the Minister made his meaning more plain: 'The UDF is pursuing the same revolutionary goals as the banned ANC and is actively promoting a climate of revolution.' Le Grange said that the UDF was responsible for up to 80% of deaths in incidents of political violence (*Star*, 06.10.84).

On 27 February 1985, after 16 UDF leaders had been charged with treason and furthering the aims of the ANC, the Minister (in apparent disregard of sub judice rules) told students at the Rand Afrikaans University that the UDF shared the aims and objectives of the ANC and SACP, and that it aimed to make the country ungovernable (*Star*, 27.02.84). He repeated this speech some weeks later to a meeting of businessmen. In April President PW Botha, speaking in parliament, made similar allegations against the UDF. He added:

> While it is accepted that real grievances exist which create unrest among black people, the aim of the UDF and most of its structures is not peaceful socio-economic and political change. Their end is the destruction of our system of government and civilised values. The immediate aim of the UDF is to mobilise the masses and incite them towards confrontation with the authorities. They hope in this way to create a spiral of increasing violence which will culminate in revolution (*Cit*, 20.04.85).

'Terror' Lekota addressed some of the early allegations about links or similarities with the ANC in an article written for the *Rand Daily Mail*. 'The UDF was formed in the 1980s of a South Africa that was marked by more than 70 years of organised African resistance to colonialism under the leadership of the ANC. Consequently all the things which parliamentary and extra-parliamentary opposition groups are saying today against apartheid, oppression and exploitation have been said before by the ANC and quite often with more eloquence,' he said. Lekota pointed out that in its 48 years of legal existence there was no tactic or campaign the ANC had failed to try out in efforts to persuade the government to meet black demands. He also observed that the fact that both the UDF and the ANC were non-racial was not particularly significant. 'It is as if to say only members of the ANC can see beyond the superficiality of skin colour' (*RDM*, 29.06.84).

UDF treasurer Cassim Saloojee told the *Financial Mail*: 'When we talk of Mandela as one of our true leaders we are talking of the role he played in the development of liberation organisations. It must be understood that many of those incarcerated (in the early 1960s) were leaders of the Congress and other democratic movements at a time when these were functioning legally and openly. Their contribution cannot be ignored. They articulated the aspirations of our people in a way which no other organisation did. Hence we recognise them as genuine leaders.' The Front itself, he argued, represented the 'resurgence of an open legal democratic movement in opposition to basic injustices' (*FM*, 31.08.84).

The UDF's leaders continually warned that action against the Front would be construed by the masses as closing down the last avenue of peaceful change. They also reiterated that there was no link between the SACP and the ANC, and that the UDF did not envisage overthrowing the state by violence.

The UDF addressed the question of its role in relation to mass protest action of late 1984 and early 1985 at its Easter conference. The secretarial report to the general council took a critical view of the UDF's organising ability, saying that it had failed to keep pace with popular resistance and that mass action had consequently lacked discipline.[5] Lekota added that the UDF intended to engage increasingly in mass action: 'We remain entirely committed to the non-violent approach. [But] the struggle must be placed in the hands of the people. We are not here to struggle on behalf of the people but with them' (*Star*, 09.04.85).

The substance to these contradictory claims by the state on one hand, and the UDF on the other, will be for the supreme courts of Natal and the Transvaal to determine as the two major treason trials proceed.

The UDF and AZAPO

Violence has plagued the relations between the UDF and the

Azanian People's Organisation (AZAPO). In its early months of existence the Front held talks with AZAPO with the hope that the latter would affiliate. It did not, but on occasion the organisations shared platforms — at Turfloop in October 1983, in a Johannesburg protest against Inkatha's killing of students at Ngoye University a month later and, more recently, at the 1985 June 16 commemoration in Soweto. AZAPO consistently and promptly refuted its supposed authorship of smear pamphlets against the UDF. And in the build-up to the tricameral parliamentary elections, AZAPO supporters joined what were essentially UDF protest actions (for instance the Lenasia picket) without friction.

Conflict between the two movements began at student level, with violent outbursts in Pietersburg and on the East Rand in late 1984 and early 1985. Initial reports presented the UDF's student affiliates as the assailants — claims which were sharply denied by the Front, which said its violence had been defensive or retaliatory. In January 1985, the visit to South Africa by United States senator Edward Kennedy almost led to clashes between AZAPO and the broader public, including some UDF supporters, when a small group of AZAPO demonstrators wrecked a meeting of thousands at Regina Mundi in Soweto.

By May and June 1985 in the Eastern Cape continual attacks and counter-attacks took place between UDF and AZAPO supporters, with serious injury and destruction to property on both sides. The national leadership of both groups made pleas for peace but the clashes continued in Port Elizabeth.

The apparent inability of national and local leaders to contain the conflict gave rise to the popular explanation that 'third force' provocateurs were responsible. Certainly, inflammatory pamphlets purportedly put out by the UDF and AZAPO were fakes and were vehemently disowned by both organisations — a fact that the SABC persistently ignored while citing them as evidence of 'black-on-black' conflict.

Violence against Eastern Cape leaders came to a head with the assassination of Matthew Goniwe and his three Cradock colleagues outside Port Elizabeth at the end of June. While police suggested that AZAPO was responsible (*Star*, 07.07.85), the UDF insisted that pro-apartheid or 'system' death squads were to blame — a view which it voiced so loudly and pointedly that Deputy Minister of Foreign Affairs Louis Nel issued a statement that his government 'took the strongest possible exception to callous insinuations' about the deaths (*Star*, 05.07.85). With the Goniwe killings, apparent AZAPO-UDF clashes ceased entirely in the Eastern Cape, and reported incidents of friction stop short at that point. But the disappearance of three leaders of the Port Elizabeth Black Civic Organisation (a UDF affiliate) — Sipho Hashe, Champion Galela and Qaqawula Godolozi — remained unsolved.

The UDF and Inkatha

The strife between UDF and Inkatha is nearly as old as the Front itself. It began in November 1983, when opposition by UDF supporters at Ngoye University to an Inkatha rally on campus led to demonstrations and teargassing, followed by invasion of the hostel by Inkatha impis. They killed four students and injured scores more. One Inkatha youth also died. At a memorial meeting for the victims, UDF speakers in Johannesburg condemned Inkatha's Chief Gatsha Buthelezi as an oppressor and dictator, and described Inkatha as a divisive tribal force. Following the Ngoye attack, Buthelezi issued a challenge to the UDF to meet him. But within days of the invitation, Inkatha acted against UDF supporters at a meeting at Mpumulanga (where Front supporters required police escort to leave their meeting for a place of safety). Inkatha also allegedly intimidated a national conference of the Association of Black Reformed Churches of South Africa (ABRESCA) to the extent that it abandoned its venue in KwaZulu and fled in the dead of night to Durban. Leading UDF men were among the clerics present. Under these circumstances the question of talks was firmly ruled out by the UDF.

In May 1984 UDF president Archie Gumede, addressing a meeting near Hammarsdale, was attacked by men whom he claimed were Inkatha members and was dragged unconscious from the hall. In August 1984 two Inkatha members were killed in Lamontville when they allegedly attempted to disrupt the funeral of a local leader in the township, which had long resisted incorporation into KwaZulu. The killing of UDF Natal region leader Victoria Mxenge by persons unknown, and the subsequent attack on UDF supporters attending a memorial service for her, heightened animosity between Inkatha and the UDF.

The explosion of conflict in the Durban area in August 1985, during which more than 75 lives were lost in a single week, was clearly a three-way clash involving the security forces, Inkatha, and UDF supporters.

Relations with the international community

The UDF has consistently addressed itself to the international community, through diplomatic representatives in South Africa, by sending key members abroad to meet directly with foreign office staff and members of government of European countries, and by contact with opposition and extra-parliamentary pressure groups. International contact reached its peak during the Durban Consulate saga of September to December 1984, but it had started well before then and continued into 1985. In May 1984 the Swedish labour movement newspaper, *Artbetet*, awarded the UDF its 'Let Live' human rights prize, affording the Front wide exposure in Northern Europe and meetings with Scandinavian ministers of state.

There has been substantial contact with the United Nations, especially its anti-apartheid structures. The 1985 UDF secretarial report claimed that virtually all foreign anti-apartheid forces had rallied to the support of the Front and that such organisations had played a vital role in moving governments to take a position against Pretoria. 'Those governments which have stood up against South Africa have done so largely because of the strength of the anti-apartheid movements in those countries,' the report claimed. It went on to explain:

> Our comrades must realise that there is a difference between the administration of certain countries and the progressive forces therein. Reagan supports apartheid by way of constructive engagement, but it does not follow that all American people are behind constructive engagement. The activities of the Free South Africa Movement and the anti-apartheid congressional lobby headed by Edward Kennedy clearly demonstrate this point.[6]

While lauding Senator Kennedy's efforts the UDF decided against meeting him during his January 1985 visit — a decision taken in the light of his scheduled talks with Buthelezi.

The extent of UDF contact with foreign politicians appears to be determined by the degree of sympathy shown for the anti-apartheid cause rather than an attempt to take a place in the international pecking order. The Front has attempted particularly to reach out to the socialist parties within the European Economic Community, whether they are in government or in opposition. The effect of international lobbying, the secretarial report said, was the deepening isolation of South Africa to the point that even the Reagan administration found it 'extremely difficult to support the South African regime openly.'[7]

With the build-up to the Natal treason trial of 16 national UDF figures, enormous international attention and criticism focused on their continued incarceration under security laws, and on their subjection to a charge as grave as treason. Forty United States senators of both parties petitioned the Botha government, 125 British MPs registered their protest, and the United Nations debated the question.

Nonetheless, by mid-1985, the devastating security measures taken against the UDF had forced it to function virtually underground, despite the fact that it was still entirely legal. At the end of August, according to the Detainees' Parents Support Committee, 45 out of 80 members of the national and regional executive committees of the Front were in detention, awaiting trial, or had been assassinated. 'The majority of the remaining UDF executive members have been forced into hiding, through threat of detention or, in some cases, due to threat against themselves or their families. The state, as yet unwilling or unable to ban the UDF itself, is using detention to cripple the organisation and trials to criminalise it'.[8]

Notes

1 H Barrell, 'The United Democratic Front and National Forum: their emergence, composition and trends', (ed) SA Research Service, *South African Review 2* (Johannesburg, 1984), 18.
2 UDF Secretarial Report, 1985.
3 Resolution of NGC, April 1985.
4 Resolutions of NGC, April 1985.
5 Secretarial Report, 1985.
6 Secretarial Report, 1985.

7 Secretarial Report, 1985.
8 Detainees' Parents Support Committee, August 1985 Report.

The National Forum

Na-iem Dollie

In a document entitled 'Let Us Build the United Front', circulated nationally in 1981 and early 1982, a united front of people's organisations was mooted:

> The time has come to combine our forces in a united front that represents the vast majority of the black workers and of the radical black middle class.[1]

For at least a year afterwards, this idea was current among activist and caucus groups and intellectuals representing views across the left political spectrum.

In time, and after discussions were held between some of these groups, the February 1983 congress of the Azanian People's Organisation (AZAPO) saw a call for a national united front to oppose the new constitutional deal and the Koornhof Bills.

The AZAPO leadership took the first steps to establish a National Forum Committee (NFC) to coordinate plans for a national forum which was scheduled for the weekend of 11-12 June 1983. The National Forum (NF) was conceived as a 'non-partisan, non-party-political national effort'.[2] It was intended to become a vehicle through which ideological differences could be resolved in a comradely manner, and aimed to mobilise and consolidate the liberatory efforts of the oppressed against the constitutional proposals.

The NFC included church notables like Desmond Tutu and Manas Buthelezi, unionists Phiroshaw Camay of the Council of Unions of SA (CUSA) and Emma Mashinini of the Commercial, Catering and Allied Workers Union of SA (CCAWUSA), political and civic figures like Saths Cooper, Kehla Mthembu, Neville

Alexander, Joe Variava, and SA Council on Sport (SACOS) activists Frank van der Horst and Colin Clarke. Allan Boesak, head of the World Alliance of Reformed Chruches, agreed to serve on the committee but failed to turn up for the first forum.

About 800 delegates and observers from some 200 organisations gathered in Hammanskraal for the first forum. Prominent among the organisations represented was AZAPO, at the time the only legal national political organisation of the oppressed. It was composed of a number of branches with black student, middle- and working-class membership across the country. Delegates and observers from the Cape Action League (CAL), a front of civic, sports, student, youth and cultural organisations in the Western Cape with a multi-class membership, also played a significant role. CUSA was represented, and the SA Allied Workers Union (SAAWU) and the Congress of SA Students (COSAS) sent observers.

Papers delivered spanned a range of topics, from 'the role of the church in the liberation struggle', to issues related to nation-building and the search for national unity.[3] The forum broke into four commissions of about 250 people each to discuss respectively the basis for principled unity, the impending anti-new deal campaign, the land question and a framework for a set of minimum demands. Then the forum convened again to deliberate on a 'Manifesto of the Azanian People'. This manifesto was unanimously approved at the end of the two-day conference and was referred back to constituent organisations for further discussion.

A bitterly contested issue concerned white participation in NF meetings. A CAL member, Neville Alexander, put one position:

> There are many people among the whites who are committed to the ideal of liberation and who are prepared to make sacrifices. They must be allowed to play a part in the struggle, but the leadership of the struggle must remain with the black working class.[4]

Opposing this thesis, an undiluted nationalist position advanced at the first forum held that the handful of whites committed to the struggle should organise in their own communities.

The link between the national and class struggle was another question raised in general debate. Letsatsi Mosala from the Black

Allied Mining and Construction Workers Union (BAMCWU), argued:

> In South Africa there is national oppression, but there is also economic oppression. The two cannot be separated. They go hand in hand (*CT*, 21.06.83).

The second meeting of the NF was an internal summit on the Nkomati Accord. It was held at the Edendale Lay Ecumenical Centre in Pietermaritzburg on the weekend of 20-22 April 1984. An input paper entitled 'Let's fight against the organ-grinder'[5] was delivered by Alexander. It attempted to situate South Africa in a 'geostrategic perspective'. The official NF view of the Nkomati Accord was much less conciliatory than the views advanced in the input paper, reporting that it interpreted Nkomati as revealing Mozambican leaders as 'tools of imperialism'.[6] The NF saw the Nkomati saga as part of the 'intensification of the imperialist assault . . . aimed at stemming the tide of the total liberation of the people of South Africa'.[7]

It was agreed that the liberation movement would have to focus more on internal mobilisation and organisation. It was emphasised that:

> . . . the policy of building up internal bases through political organisation and mobilisation remains valid and relevant regardless of what detailed changes are made by the forces concerned in the tactics of armed struggle.[8]

The summit considered that calls for abandonment of the armed struggle were futile and opportunistic. A decision on strategic questions of this kind had to be made by the guerillas whose position at that stage indicated amendment, not abandonment, of the struggle they had waged up to then.

The third meeting of the NF, the second national forum, was held at the Patidar Hall in Lenasia on 21 July 1984. It formally adopted the Azanian Manifesto with some minor changes, and concentrated on developing a practical plan of action for the anti-election campaign.

Significantly, at this stage, the Azanian Students Movement (AZASM) was consolidating itself nationally, and beginning to intervene more directly in the affairs of the NF. An organisation called Action Youth, an 'initiative by working, unemployed and student youth residing in Soweto, Eldorado Park, Riverlea, Bosmont and Fordsburg',[9] also began to participate.

The NF's fourth meeting was held at the Kismet Cinema in Athlone, Cape Town, on 16 December 1984. About 1 300 people attended the one-day workshop. One hundred and twenty-five people registered as delegates. An input paper entitled 'After the August Elections'[10] was delivered by Alexander.

Lively debate developed, despite the poor acoustics of the rather rundown venue and communication problems arising from the size of the commissions (about 250 people) into which those present divided. One point made was that the NF could claim much of the credit for the anti-election campaign, though the efforts of NF-oriented structures were largely ignored by the media.

An 'Isolate the Traitors' campaign for 1985 was discussed at the workshop. It was intended to focus on institutions which had become part of the state's incorporationist strategy directed at the black middle class. The campaign was to aim at making such institutions unworkable or to expose them as being unrepresentative.

The committee of notables, formed by AZAPO in 1983 during the build-up to the first forum, was finally done away with. In its place was elected a three-member steering committee composed of a national convener, co-convener and a secretary (Saths Cooper, Mandla Nkosi and Lusiba Ntloko respectively).

Issues raised in and around the NF

Zac Yacoob of the Natal Indian Congress, in his speech at the relaunch of the Transvaal Indian Congress (TIC) on 1 May 1983, touched on one of the longest-standing debates of the South African liberation struggle. On the resolution of the 'national question', he said:

> Our task is to heighten the positive features of each national group and to weld these together so that there arises out of this process of organisation a single national consciousness (*CT*, 26.06.83).

Neville Alexander opposed this thesis in his paper to the first

National Forum, concluding that ' "Ethnic" or "national" group approaches are the thin end of the wedge for separatist movements and civil wars . . . . '[11]

For a section of the NF including CAL, BAMCWU and Action Youth, a socialist solution to the national question in South Africa can be effected by setting in motion structures of national unification under the command of the black working class. It remains unclear what such structures would be, though presumably black working-class interests would dominate or be advanced through them. Initiatives to link urban and rural struggles through the creation of trade unions and other organisations of farm workers are regarded as especially significant.

Some of these 'elements of the theory of the nation'[12] are challenged by other left-wing groupings (such as the Western Cape Youth League and a new organisation in the Western Cape called Workers' Front) which though committed to the NF project are not necessarily fully supportive of the NF: while its main positions are acceptable, proposed structures and some alliances, especially with black consciousness groupings, are viewed with suspicion. One argument advanced from such quarters is that the national question was resolved in 1910, with the formation of South Africa as a bourgeois nation state. Consequently, to advance the idea of building a nation amounts to surrendering a fundamental premise of socialist internationalism, and could result in back-pedalling to a vaguely-defined 'petty-bourgeois nationalism'.

A host of other questions continue to be debated at NF meetings. Some, for example, concern which social class will control the central state apparatus in a free Azania, and the relationship between a national liberation struggle and a struggle for socialism.

The question of land ownership is another. A tendency within the NF asserts that the main objective of the liberation struggle is the reconquest of the land by the black people of Azania. This is a position superficially more militant than the equivalent demand in the Freedom Charter.[13] The official NF view not only stresses repossession of land, but also addresses questions of class ownership of the means of production, distribution and exchange.

Left disunity and sectarianism

Media representations of the political movement for radical change tend to suggest that it is divided between adherents of Black Consciousness (BC) and the Freedom Charter ('Charterists'). Superficially it might be reasonable to conclude that, because there are adherents of the Freedom Charter and of the NF's Azanian Manifesto in the UDF and NF respectively, these forums embody conflicting social forces with conflicting political objectives.

Posing the problem of disunity in this way adds grist to the sectarian mill which has disfigured the mass movement for so many years. A more constructive alternative is found in the attempt to analyse the UDF and the NF in terms of their respective class and social composition, the class interests that dominate them and the processes they have set in motion to realise their objectives.

One view holds that the NF was set up to challenge the supposed hegemony of the UDF in the mass movement. In rebuttal, NF adherents point out that the NF has never been, nor is it at present, an organisation as such, even though some individuals and organisational representatives have suggested that it transform itself into a national liberation front. And, they add, the NF convened in June 1983 with an explicit appeal to all known progressive organisations of the oppressed and exploited to attend, while the UDF was launched as a national organisation in August 1983.[14]

In the years since the first NF conference in June 1983, much water has flowed under political bridges. The field of extra-parliamentary opposition politics saw the launch of the UDF in August 1983, the successful boycott of the Indian and coloured elections to the tricameral parliament, the Transvaal regional stayaway in November 1984, endemic unrest in townships across the country accompanied by a rise in the number and influence of civic-level organisations, and the reawakening of the New Unity Movement (NUM) in April 1985. Alongside these developments, and relatively independent of them, a realignment of forces was taking place in the independent trade union movement.

The momentum of the NF and UDF since their foundation has created space for sectarianism. Many young people have been ideologically colonised, battered by debates, contradictions and conflicts that may span 40 years or more of political experience. Many of these debates have little if any relevance to the contemporary political experience of a new generation of cadres. Despite the ideological differences that keep people apart and in separate organisations, there is an urgent need to begin to work together. This, it is suggested, can be effectively achieved at the level of mass struggles.

The different organisations engaged in black protest politics reflect a range of political and ideological persuasions. At issue are differing perspectives on the nature of the South African liberation struggle, questions concerning class alliances to be forged to conduct such a struggle, and attitudes to traditional political movements like the Pan Africanist Congress (PAC) of Azania, the South African Communist Party (SACP), the Non-European Unity Movement (NEUM) and the African National Congress (ANC).

To many activists in NUM, UDF and NF, it is time for reassessment of the debates and issues raised over the past two years and the bitter struggles that marred the possibility of left-wing cohesion in the past year.

National Forum relations with other organisations

In response to a question on the differences between the New Unity Movement, the NF, and the Cape Action League, the president of NUM, Richard Dudley, commented:

> We probably have more points of agreement with CAL, which has supported non-collaboration to the hilt. One of our major difficulties with the NF was the way it was first constituted . . . . Our other difficulty with them is that although they are anti-racist, discussions in the NF have been Black Consciousness-oriented. We are not at one with the prevailing ideology of the NF, but it is a matter of time and growth.[15]

For NUM, a 'minimum programme is an open-ended one' and its political strategy is based on a self-defined 'policy of non-collaboration'.[16] NUM considers agreement on ideas and practices based on non-collaboration, and acceptance of a minimum programme, essential before it will enter into alliances with other tendencies and movements. Despite recognising the need to enter the field of alliance politics, NUM leadership seems guarded in its approach to participation in the NF. Especially objectionable to

some quarters in NUM is the assumed ideological and organisational predominance within the NF of AZAPO, which they claim is
a latter-day embodiment of a 'reactionary tendency'.[17]

The situation is rather more complex when it comes to relations
between UDF-affiliated organisations and NF-oriented structures.

For some organisations in the NF, the UDF has been since its inception a 'national convention' option. This has been argued in
both CAL and AZAPO publications. As a result, the argument
goes, the multi-class element of the UDF is the single most important feature in its operation. This, aided by an alleged 'petty-
bourgeois leadership', could result in strategies to facilitate extension of bourgeois democratic rights to black South Africans. Not
that the NF would have problems with this. The problem lies in the
NF's belief that the particular class alliance making up the UDF is
weighted in favour of negotiation with the present regime.[18] The
UDF's perceived commitment to a 'struggle for civil rights' rather
than to participation in a full-scale 'civil war' is a bone of contention.

Other groups in the NF agree that the UDF is a 'popular front',
and have criticisms similar to those mentioned above. But there is a
growing recognition that NF-oriented structures need to work
closely with the people's organisations in the UDF.

Despite polemics between the leaderships of the UDF and the
NF, the fact that there are organisations within both forums sharing similar if not identical socialist visions has become clearer over
the past year. There has been cooperation, however short-lived,
between some of them, mostly on a non-public level at this stage.
Already some cross-fertilisation has occurred. It remains unclear
just how extensive this has been or can become. The socialist left
will have to find points of cooperation in actual political struggle, if
not on their own account, then on behalf of the ordinary working
people they claim to be fighting for. More than anything else,
working-class struggles may create conditions for convergence.

In recent years the independent union movement has emerged as
a crucial — some claim pivotal — force in the liberation struggle.
The present NF leadership and some activists committed to NF
positions consider active mutual support between unions and the
political movement a vital condition for building a mass-based
political movement.

Some people in and around the NF are convinced that these

unions should play a dominant role in the NF, were they to participate. They could not only shape the form and content of the NF project, but also assert a significant union presence inside activist and other mass-based organisations.

Unions inclined towards the NF, like BAMCWU, an AZAPO project with considerable influence in the seven-member BC-oriented Azanian Confederation of Trade Unions (AZACTU), have tended to support socialist perspectives at NF meetings.

Where potential political programmes are concerned, there is certainly correspondence beween the socialist positions developed in the Azanian Manifesto, and unions' concern for the primacy of black working-class interests in the movement for national liberation.

However, to date there has been little coordination between unions involved in the NF and those involved in the new federation. Perhaps the gulfs dividing both union and political movements could to a certain extent be bridged in the process of inter-union cooperation and coordination.

Decisions about the nature and forms of interventions by unions in the political arena are on the agenda for the coming period, since it seems certain that their constituencies will exert increasing pressure on leadership to participate more overtly in political struggle.

Future prospects

At the last NF meeting in December 1984, the question of organisation was raised in an input paper, which stressed that:

> We have not reached a point where we can say that the differences that keep us [of the NF] in separate organisations have disappeared.[19]

These differences revolve around ideology, class positions and class interests. Since some in the NF see AZAPO as constituting the principal organisation in a national movement, there would be problems in transforming the NF from a forum into a unitary organisation. Such a transformation might mean that AZAPO would have to collapse its organisational apparatus to become part of a broader body within a general NF orientation. Alternatively, were the NF to transform into an organisation, it could opt to constitute itself along federal lines, with constituent organisations retaining their independence. Either way, there seems to be general agreement that both options are premature at present.

A view with considerable weight within the NF is that the Azanian Manifesto could become the kernel of a socialist political programme. The Manifesto is considered one of the most important achievements of the NF initiative so far. But a note of caution must be sounded about this set of transitional demands: for the Manifesto to become the property of ordinary working people, or for it to remain a condensation of demands thrown up in the struggles of the 1970s and 1980s, activists and militants who committed themselves to its positions would have to pay diligent attention to democratic practices and procedures. A struggle for socialist democracy is on the cards.

Its relationship with the independent trade union movement will be a crucial factor in determining the NF's future. If it is to move beyond being a 'people's parliament' in which the issues of the day are debated, NF adherents will have to pay diligent attention to serious criticisms levelled by some unionists. One such criticism reflects doubts as to how far the socialist rhetoric of the NF leadership has permeated to the membership of its affiliated organisations.

Political organisation of the working class would seem to be next on the NF's agenda. If this is the case, a reassessment of strategy and tactics may well be long overdue.

Notes

1 Reprinted in *CAL Documents* under the title 'An early view on United Fronts', December 1984.
2 Discussion with a member of the first NF Committee.
3 Speeches and resolutions in a booklet entitled *National Forum*, published by the NFC in 1983.
4 *National Forum*, 1983.
5 Reprinted in *Free Azania*, 1 (7), and in *National Forum Committee*, July 1984.
6 See *National Forum Committee*, July 1984.

7 N Dollie, 'The National Forum: seeking socialism', *Work In Progress*, 35, February 1985, 25.

8 *Free Azania*, 1 (7), 25.

9 See *Arise! Vukani*, 1 (2), magazine of Action Youth.

10 Reprinted in *Free Azania* 1 (8), under 'Political perspectives'.

11 See N Alexander, 'Nation and ethnicity' in *National Forum*.

12 See No Sizwe, *One Azania One Nation* (Zed Press, London, 1979).

13 The demand in the 1955 Freedom Charter reads as follows: 'the land shall be shared among those who work it'. The official AZAPO position on the land question reads as follows in its constitution: ' . . . To work towards the unity of the oppressed, for the just distribution of land, wealth and power to all the people of Azania'. See its consitution, section 2 (6).

14 See Dollie, 'The National Forum', 26.

15 Interview conducted by Estelle Randall with Richard Dudley, printed in the *Cape Herald*, 11.05.85.

16 Interview conducted by the author with Richard Dudley on 29.04.85.

17 See, for example, *Black Consciousness: A Reactionary Tendency*, published by the Teachers' League of SA (TLSA), January 1982.

18 See *Solidarity*, 1, newsletter of the Cape Action League, and *Cape Action League News*, 1983.

19 See 'Political perspectives, *Free Azania*, 1 (8).

Acknowledgements

Many people contributed to the construction of this article. The most valuable contributions were those from militants and activists who kept the idea of a National Forum alive. Many have indicated that they prefer to remain anonymous, and some would not share my conclusions. To them especially I would like to express gratitude for sharing their visions with me.

I would also like to thank: RO Dudley, for agreeing to an interview and spending time with me; Neville Alexander, whose insights and rigour helped to make this article more readable, and whose political work and style remain sources of inspiration; Jean Pease and Willie Hofmeyer who read all drafts and helped me formulate my ideas; Saths Cooper who helped clarify the sequence of events in the NF's formative months and who pointed out some inaccuracies; and Mandla Seleoane for spending time with me.

The Langa Shootings and the Kannemeyer Commission of Enquiry

Nicholas Haysom

On 21 March 1985 police confronted a crowd proceeding from Langa, a black township bordering Uitenhage, to a funeral in Kwanobuhle, a neighbouring township. The police opened fire, killing 20 people and injuring a further 23. Two days later, amid a mounting international furore, the South African state president appointed a commission of enquiry. It was chaired by Mr Justice Donald Kannemeyer of the Eastern Cape Supreme Court.

In the report of the commission's findings, Mr Justice Kannemeyer stated he could not and would not review the pattern of township protests and police reaction which formed the background to the tragic events in Langa. It was therefore surprising to read in the commission's report that he considered such background information an important part of the evidence. As the black community was led to believe that they were not entitled to lead evidence on this subject and thus did not do so, Kannemeyer relied solely on police evidence.

Presumably the chairman had initially feared the commission record would be burdened by a lengthy catalogue of grievances if he allowed background information to be led. He was probably right: there are many real grievances which explain township residents' protests during 1984 and 1985. But by foreclosing on the possibility of examining conditions in the townships and gaining insight into the attitudes and aspirations of their black residents, Mr Justice Kannemeyer also excluded evidence on the vital question of police reaction to township protest and general conditions in the townships. There is an intimate connection between escalating township violence and police conduct there.

In Langa, as well as other townships, increasing township protest appears to result from a combination of several factors: high unemployment, the rising cost of living and deterioration of township residents' living standards; the absence of basic services and amenities in townships bordering white areas where facilities such as electricity, tarred roads and recreational facilities are abundant and evident; imposition of rental and other service charge increases by community councils or development boards; the imposition of government-created municipal councils on township residents; and an inadequate and authoritarian education system which has produced an important group of youthful militants. This last added school boycotts to the other protests which had become regular occurrences by the end of 1984. Myriad organisations — many affiliated to the United Democratic Front — had sprung up to resist increases in bus fares and rents, to pressure the authorities to provide better schooling and housing, to protest against the new constitution, and particularly against the new community councils.

As protest became more intense in late 1984 and early 1985, it was met by greater police repression. Protest led to reaction, reaction to resistance, and resistance to intensified counter-action. In an attempt to contain the protest and resistance, which included attacks on the persons and property of black policemen, police took to indiscriminate violence and arrests, especially of black youths, in the Uitenhage townships. In one instance, three members of the Black Sash, alerted by a concerned parent, arrived at the Uitenhage police station and entered an interrogation room where they witnessed a policeman whipping a 15-year-old youth, Norman Kona. Residents also complained that police were trigger-happy, and fired teargas canisters indiscriminately into houses.

Uitenhage residents' claims about police conduct echoed similar allegations in the Vaal area. The South African Catholic Bishops' Conference released a *Report on Police Conduct During Township Protests* in November 1984 detailing allegations which suggested 'that the police appeared to believe that they were at war'. An April 1985 Black Sash report on *Police Conduct In The Eastern Cape* enumerated similar allegations about police practices, claiming these were widespread in the region.

None of this information was seriously considered by the commission. Instead, it considered exclusively the evidence of police witnesses detailing the not-inconsiderable damage to property and incidents of violence in the Uitenhage area in the months prior to 21 March.

This presented a truncated picture. Without sufficient background the commission was unable to understand the black community's contention that police had acted provocatively and had decided to teach township residents a lesson. This makes sense only in the context of the rising tensions between township residents and police at the time.

The commission of enquiry commenced on 27 March 1985. Although evidence was led on a number of aspects, the commission concerned itself with two central questions. The first was whether the police were properly prepared and equipped to deal with the situation on 21 March. The second concerned the nature of the march itself and police reaction to it — that is whether the police were justified in opening fire on the crowd of mourners.

Police administration and equipment

Findings about police preparation and equipment could only be drawn from evidence given by the police themselves. Under cross-examination, it soon became apparent that the police were not properly equipped on the day of the funeral. Their armoured riot control vehicles, called Casspirs, were not equipped with ordinary riot control equipment. The police had no loudspeakers to address a gathering, to give orders or warnings. They were not equipped with teargas, rubber bullets or birdshot, but exclusively with lethal firearms, namely shotguns with SSG cartridges and R1 rifles. The SSG cartridge carries a heavy-calibre shot which will penetrate a metal plate at 30 metres, and has a spread of about one metre per 30 metres. A single discharge of an SSG cartridge will injure a number of people, and in a crowd situation it will maim, kill and injure indiscriminately.

Police evidence on this issue was that the Port Elizabeth regional division had received a telex from police headquarters in Pretoria instructing officers that because of the increasing incidence of petrol bomb attacks, police were to 'eliminate' persons in possession of petrol or acid bombs. At a meeting about one week before the shootings, Lieutenant-Colonel Frederick Pretorius, district commandant of the Uitenhage area, instructed his men on the seriousness of the situation. Precisely what was said was disputed among the police themselves. Pretorius claimed in evidence that strict instructions were issued that armoured cars were to be equipped with proper means of riot control. However, as a result of the meeting, Major Gert Kuhn, the officer in charge of the Uitenhage police station, issued an order that Casspirs on patrol in the townships were not to be issued with birdshot, teargas or rubber bullets. The commission recalled Pretorius to explain why Kuhn had acted and testified as he did, if Pretorius had been truthful in his evidence. Kuhn had, in fact, referred to Pretorius's evidence as a 'blatant lie'. Pretorius explained that there must have been 'a misunderstanding'. The lameness of this explanation was underlined by further evidence that even Port Elizabeth-based units were similarly ill-equipped.

At various stages of the enquiry police tried to justify this lack of equipment. They said 'conventional' non-lethal forms of crowd control were ineffective in the face of 'aggressive' crowds. But as the chairman of the commission pointed out, the newspapers made daily reference to the large crowds dispersed with teargas or other non-lethal methods. It should be noted that the implication of this policy is that the most cautious and humanitarian policeman if called upon to confront or control a crowd would have had no equipment with which to address or disperse it, and if called upon to forcibly direct a crowd could do so only by committing a slaughter.

The commission's chairman correctly found that police attempts to minimise the effectiveness of teargas as a means of crowd control were unpersuasive. He went on to state that had proper equipment been available the gathering might well have been dispersed with little or no harm to the persons involved.

The chairman was most condemnatory as regards police attempts to prevent funerals. 'Had the holding of the funerals not unnecessarily been prohibited on doubtful grounds there can be little doubt that the procession could have passed through Uitenhage without incident along the normal route from Langa to Kwanobuhle which happens to pass through part of the town.' He continued:

It would seem that Cptn Goosen used Section 46 of the Act for a devious purpose. Having obtained a prohibition against holding the

funerals on inter alia a Sunday, because a funeral held on a Sunday
would be likely to endager the public peace, he proceeded to obtain an
order that the funeral could only be held on a Sunday because if held on
a weekday work would be boycotted leading to disruption of industry
which is not a ground for a Section 46 order (*Kannemeyer Report*, 166).

These commission findings are significant but inescapable. The
chairman stated that 'one can only conclude that this was the result
of a policy deliberately adopted', but he failed to make a finding as
to exactly who was responsible for this policy. He stated: 'at what
level this decision was taken, and who was responsible cannot be
determined from the evidence heard by the Commission'. (165)

Yet the chairman had an onus to call for this evidence if he
believed that further information was required to ascertain why so
many people were killed on the march. His report reveals a passive
conception of his role in calling for evidence, yet when making
findings as to what occurred and when police evidence was unsatisfactory, he allowed an active intervention of his own beliefs in
guessing what happened.

The police version

The police version of the massacre was that the funeral had been
banned late the previous day. On the day of the funeral a Casspir
came across a crowd of people assembled at the local bus terminus.
Despite police advice that funerals were prohibited the crowd continued to assemble. According to the police the crowd was
aggressive and rowdy, and singing freedom songs. People were
armed with sticks, metal pipes, knives and stones. The crowd began
marching forward along Maduna Road. Many others joined and it
quickly swelled to about 4 000.

Police alleged that people were chanting a slogan in Xhosa that
they were going to town in order to 'kill the whites'. The officer in
charge of the Casspir radioed for assistance. A Casspir commanded
by a Lieutenant John Fouche arrived from the Uitenhage side of
town. The two Casspirs formed a V across the road.

Fouche held up his hand and instructed a Xhosa-speaking
member of his staff to order the crowd to stop. The police claim
that when the crowd was about five to ten paces from the Casspir,

the leader produced a petrol bomb. Fouche said that he fired a warning shot at the same time and after one stone had been thrown he gave the order to fire. At that stage a full stone attack began. Several police witnesses claim that stones 'rained' down upon them. Police stated that there was a short volley killing 20 persons and injuring at least 23. Fouche claimed he immediately ordered a ceasefire when he saw the crowd disperse. The injured and the dead lay in the road.

Police claim they opened fire because they were instructed to do so by their commanding officer, Fouche. He in turn gave the order because he believed that the crowd intended attacking the white town of Uitenhage. After the crowd failed to obey his order to stop, he feared it would attack his men.

The community version

According to people in the community, a small group of Langa residents gathered at the bus terminal awaiting taxis and buses to take them to the funeral. Many did not personally know the deceased but it is township practice to attend funerals of persons killed by the police because they are regarded as martyrs.

A Casspir arrived at Maduna Square and ordered people waiting for transport to disperse. The Casspir then attempted to scatter the crowd by driving through it. At this stage and later when the crowd was marching, policemen on the Casspirs taunted the crowd with sinister comments such as 'we are going to show you today'; 'now we have got you'; 'where are the stones, throw them'. This evidence seems to have been accepted by the chairman of the commission.

When the transport to Kwanobuhle failed to arrive, a Rastafarian persuaded the crowd to walk. Community witnesses stated that the march was orderly and people were unarmed. People marched on the left hand side of the road in columns six abreast, and persons coming from side streets joined the procession.

The Casspir from Maduna Square proceeded to the front of the crowd as an escort. Another Casspir brought up the rear. After a while the Casspir in front drove ahead and parked at the top of a crest where it was joined by a third Casspir. The two vehicles in front of the procession formed a V blocking the road. The Casspir at the rear pulled off the road and parked next to a billboard behind the crowd.

When the crowd was approximately 50 metres from the Casspirs, a boy on a bicycle entered Maduna Road in front of the crowd. The boy, 15-year-old Moses Bucwa, was on his way to work at a poultry farm. He had not gone to work earlier because he knew of the stayaway and did not want to risk the wrath of any township residents. On his way to work he saw the procession and decided to ride in front so as to seem part of it.

As the crowd approached the Casspirs one of the policemen held up his hand. Bucwa, who was then very close to the Casspirs, tried to turn to pass them. Without warning a volley of shots came from the Casspir. Most witnesses testified the boy was the first to fall.

Community witnesses admitted the crowd sang freedom songs including one song called 'What have you done black man?' and one known as the 'Guerilla song'. They denied singing a song threatening to march on Uitenhage. They knew of no such song. Most witnesses conceded that the crowd only slowed down but did not stop when the policeman held up his hand. Many believed the police would allow them to pass by and no-one expected the police to open fire. The crowd was unarmed and some of the people in it were carrying sun umbrellas.

People fled when the shooting started. Many then gathered on the crest opposite the police and watched events. They testified that ambulances only arrived after about 25 minutes. Ambulance attendants testified that they were kept waiting outside the township for up to 20 minutes before a police escort took them to the scene.

Witnesses stated that many policemen made extremely distasteful and derogatory remarks while the injured were lying on the ground. Witness Gabriel Mathebeli said a policeman, whom he identified as Billy Ruiters, saw a person who had been shot jerking convulsively on the ground. Ruiters said in Afrikaans, 'he has got what he wanted, he is doing breakdancing' (137). Numerous witnesses claimed police picked up stones lying on the side of the road and placed them among the bodies. The community contended that the police were attempting to exaggerate the extent to which the crowd was armed.

The commission looks at the evidence

The commission's treatment of evidence relating to the exact nature of the march is extremely unsatisfactory. The chairman approached each issue separately and failed to make connections between his own findings and the overall acceptability of the police and community versions. This ad hoc approach enabled him to accept the police version except where it was patently a lie, in which cases he accepted certain significant aspects of the community version.

Legal representatives for families of victims shot on 21 March concentrated on three aspects of the police version which were patently false. These three related to the extent to which the crowd was armed; the so-called stone attack; and the existence of the boy on the bicycle.

Stone throwing

Police photographs of the incident first became available during evidence-in-chief of one of the first police witnesses. It was immediately apparent that there was not a single stone on the tarmac near the Casspirs. It became impossible to accept that the police were stoned by the crowd. Had such an attack occurred, the stones would have struck the police and the police vehicles and littered the ground immediately in front of the vehicles. It was also improbable that an unarmed funeral procession would throw stones while police were shooting at them.

Police attempts to explain this ranged from the bizarre to the absurd. A Sergeant Benjamin Rudman seriously contended that every single stone had richocheted 30 paces. A Sergeant Gerhard Stumke claimed that God miraculously intervened to prevent stones hitting him. The commission rejected the police story of the stone attack. But it then proceeded — with no foundation besides the discredited evidence — to assume that some stones must have been thrown. The chairman's explanation as to why he rejected the community version that no stones were thrown, despite the fact that it accorded more with the probabilities of the situation, is thin. Judge Kannemeyer stated: 'One also reads and hears of such evidence almost daily. Stones are weapons which are almost invariably at hand in the townships and are naturally used as missiles in most riot situations' (114). He also said that Warrant Officer Jacobus Penz's evidence — that a bare-breasted woman emerged from the crowd to hurl the first stone — was too bizarre to have been fabricated. This indicates that the chairman's imagination or personal opinion was substituted for the credible version of events put forward by the community.

Was the crowd armed?

From police evidence it was clear that the crowd was not heavily armed. The inventory of items collected by police after the shootings contained one bag of stones, three bags of shoes, hats and clothing, one umbrella, one piece of wood, one bicycle, and one iron rod. The commission rejected police attempts to explain why people should retain weapons while dropping clothing. One of the policemen who gave evidence at the chairman's request, stated that he did not see any weapons and that had weapons been carried, he would have seen them.

The chairman also found as a fact that the composition of the crowd indicated that it was not on its way to attack Uitenhage but was indeed proceeding to a funeral.

The boy on the bicycle

All police witnesses denied the existence of a boy on a bicycle. They agreed that if he had ridden in front of the crowd they definitely would have seen him.

The description of the boy on the bicycle first appeared in affidavits compiled by the Progressive Federal Party the day after the incident. The police contended that the story of the boy was entirely fabricated.

During the hearing the families' legal team also made bail applications on behalf of community members. One such request was made by Mrs Bucwa, mother of the bicycle boy. The boy was immediately bailed out and subsequently led as a surprise witness. Bucwa had not seen the bicycle since the shooting. In his evidence he clearly identified the bicycle as his own and could account for the various markings on it. Even police counsel conceded the bicycle belonged to the boy but submitted lamely that perhaps his brother was riding it. Bucwa, however, had hospital records to prove he had been shot in the head. Accordingly the chairman had no option but to accept the existence of the boy on the bicycle.

The conspiracy to fabricate evidence

If the existence of 'the boy on the bicycle' was proved, each and every police eye-witness must have lied. If Bucwa was riding in front of the crowd, it could not have been as close and as threatening as police witnesses alleged.

The families contended that the evidence of falsehoods in police testimony were not the same as the minor contradictions in the testimonies of community witnesses. These could be expected when disparate individuals attempted to recall a particularly dramatic event where many of them were in mortal danger. The police, however, had systematically fabricated evidence relating to the boy on the bicycle, as well as about the stone attack and the nature of the weapons carried by the crowd.

Since all police witnesses told exactly the same lie it can only be inferred that there was a conspiracy to put a false version before the commission. If this was the case the chairman should not have accepted any part of the police version where it was contradicted by aspects of the community version. Family submissions in this regard were strengthened by the profusion of clearly inaccurate and misleading statements issued by the Minister of Law and Order immediately after the event.

The chairman was evidently reluctant to accept that the police fabricated evidence. When faced with consistent and undamaged eye-witness evidence that policemen placed stones among the bodies of those fallen in the shooting, he stated that had the police wished to provide a proper justification for the shootings they would have placed the stones closer to the Casspirs to illustrate that they had been attacked. This placed the legal representatives for the families in a Catch-22 situation. Had the police been smarter about their cover-up, it would have been difficult to challenge. On the other hand, an apparently panic-stricken and clumsy attempt to cover up was accepted because the chairman credited the police with greater ingenuity than it showed.

But let us go back to the scene in the horrible moments after the shooting had stopped. About 70 people lay on the road, either dead or screaming in pain. It is not improbable that the first concern of the police was to show that the crowd was dangerous and thus to justify the shootings.

The chairman was prepared to accept Penz's evidence because it was so bizarre it could not have been fabricated. But he was not prepared to accept the community's evidence because he did not believe the police could have been so stupid. The commission's chairman judged witnesses Rudman and Stumke 'impressive' (153) despite the fact that he found they lied to the commission. But he was harshest in his condemnation of the ambulance-drivers. The ambulance-drivers called by the families' lawyers appear to have had no direct interest in the matter. They gave evidence as requested, despite manoeuverings by the police to prevent them from presenting evidence unfavourable to the police.

Petrol bombs

The crucial question was whether circumstances warranted police opening fire on the crowd. Justice Kannemeyer's finding and attitude finally rested on the existence or otherwise of alleged petrol bombs. The families contended that no such petrol bombs existed. They said it was possible and plausible for the police to have found the necessary bottlenecks to construct the evidence in the horror of the minutes after the shooting.

Having rejected the theory of police conspiracy to construct evidence, the chairman had no option but to accept the existence of petrol bombs. He then proceeded to find that the policemen in the Casspirs were in real danger.

Evaluating the report

It is difficult to escape the conclusion that Judge Kannemeyer brought with him subconscious perceptions of what probably took place, his own perceptions of the likely role and behaviour of policemen, and his own beliefs about the behaviour patterns of township residents. In South Africa, a white, affluent judge perceives and experiences the police differently from township residents who see and experience a more callous and brutal side of 'law enforcement'. Anyone with a little direct experience of this side of law enforcement would have a more sceptical view of the attitudes of white policemen patrolling a black township and the integrity and humanity of law enforcement officials.

Police patrolling townships are young men given awesome power

— the power of both judges and executioners. It is notable that Mr Justice Kannemeyer did not really pay attention to more general standards which should be applied before lethal weapons are used by law enforcement officials. A concern for 'the right to life' is not central to the report. This is reflected in the almost casual way the report deals with the fact that only one of the 20 people killed was shot directly from the front. The report attempts to explain this by referring to 'reaction time'. This does not answer the question as to how armed policemen could pump bullets into the back of a fleeing crowd which included women and children.

Perhaps this question cannot be answered within the narrow confines of such a judicial commission of enquiry. The answer was similarly avoided by the enquiry into the police shooting of 69 people at Sharpeville, in chillingly similar circumstances 25 years to the day before the Langa shootings. Perhaps it lies in a broader consideration of a society racially divided and at war with itself.

Monetarism and the South African Crisis

*Duncan Innes**

The monetarist economic policies adopted by the South African government in the early 1980s were intended to combat the destructive pattern of short, unstable upswings and increasingly severe recessions which had bedevilled the economy since the early 1970s. However, during the turbulent course of 1984-85, these policies have failed disastrously. Rather than depressing inflation and gearing the economy for a sound and sustained upswing, the particularly severe austerity measures introduced towards the end of 1984 led South Africa into a debt crisis. This was exacerbated by the political conflict that arose in part as a response to the official decision to drive the economy into recession. The two disastrous drops, in the value of the rand, in November 1984 and again in August 1985, intensified constraints on economic growth and rendered futile the major object of the monetarist exercise by contributing to 1985 inflation levels as high or higher than those in 1984. South African monetarist policies have exacted a high price in political instability and, partly as a consequence, have failed to attain their economic objectives. The economic outlook in the last quarter of 1985 was bleaker than it had been a year earlier.

The measures of 1984

During 1984, South Africa's financial authorities faced a number

---

* This article is based on joint work done during the past year by Stephen Gelb and myself. However, I alone am responsible for this particular version of our arguments.

of problems. The fall in the dollar price of gold was eroding state revenues. Together with unbridled consumer spending, the falling gold price fuelled a dangerously high deficit on the current account of the balance of payments, which had reached R2,86-billion in the first quarter of 1984. This deficit was undermining investor confidence, inhibiting imports and rendering it difficult to pay for borrowing which would be needed in due course for the economy to reflate.

The monetarist response focused on inflation and the balance of payments deficit as the two primary evils to be righted in order to gear the economy for sound growth in the long term. Attention was focused on South Africa's rapidly growing state expenditure, which rose from 22% of the gross domestic product in 1981 to 29% in 1984, and which was highly inflationary. Cutting state expenditure and raising interest rates to unprecedented heights, it was argued, would cure both evils. South African interest rates were already almost double those of the United States, at a time when American interest rates were regarded as excessively high. Following the abandonment of exchange controls on foreign investors in 1983, high domestic interest rates were needed to prevent foreign investors exporting capital to take advantage of the high profits on investment available in the United States.

In August 1984, the Reserve Bank raised its discount rate steeply, with the result that the crucial prime lending rate rose to 25%. Bond rates also climbed, with Barclays' rate hitting 26%, and the rate of interest on hire purchase agreements soared to 32%. As planned, the immediate consequence was to drive the economy into recession. The high cost of credit caused consumer spending to drop sharply and inhibited company borrowing. Thus both the drop in consumer demand and the reduction in company spending placed producers under pressure to cut back on expansion plans and to contract production.

High interest rates also necessitated cuts in state and parastatal expenditure. Since the South African state is the country's largest single consumer of goods and services, these cuts affected a number of sectors. Civil engineering and heavy industrial companies saw immediate contraction of demand. Sales and development in the property sector also fell because of the prohibitive bond rates, and the construction industry was hard hit. Unemployment began to rise.

The recession takes effect

An important consequence of the August austerity measures — one that within a year was to have unforeseen and disastrous effects — was the sharp increase in South African borrowing abroad. Because interest rates in South Africa were so high, it was logical for banks, businesses and the state itself to borrow in the US and Europe, where interest rates stood at about 11%.

South Africa's debt burden, already high, rose sharply. As a percentage of the gross domestic product, foreign debt rose to 26,8% by the end of 1984, compared with 8,4% in 1980. Similarly, by the end of 1984, the country's debt was equivalent to 94% of the value of its exports, compared with 23% in 1980. Thus following the August rise in interest rates, outstanding foreign bank credit rose perilously close to equalling the country's total export income. Still worse, much of this spate of borrowing was short term, and would fall due within a year.

The surge in foreign indebtedness after August 1984 combined with the strong dollar on international currency markets to cause the rand's first dramatic drop in November 1984. The South African Reserve Bank deliberately refrained from supporting the rand, allowing it to fall to approximately $0,50. The official attitude was that a sharp drop in the value of the rand relative to the dollar would be the equivalent of a devaluation. This would make imports more expensive, but income from South Africa's predominantly mineral exports would double in rand terms, while its manufactured products would be cheaper and more competitive in foreign markets. As a consequence, the balance of payments deficit would begin to right itself.

At the same time, however, those banks, companies and state institutions which had borrowed overseas found their debt and service charges doubled. Despite this, the current account of the balance of payments began to move into surplus as consumer and industrial expenditure on imports dropped. For most of 1985, the current account of the BoP has been running at an average surplus of R400-m per month.

In time, the growing surplus enabled the Reserve Bank to begin bringing down interest rates after July 1985, mitigating the extreme recessionary effects of the August package. The prime rate, for example, fell from 25% to 18,5% in October 1985. But while a 6,5%

drop sounds impressive and has lightened some of the debt servicing costs which companies face, interest rates still remain far too
high to stimulate growth, and remain much higher than those
overseas.

On closer inspection, too, the BoP surplus did not indicate the
degree of economic health that Finance Department officials
repeatedly asserted. The improved export revenue did not reflect a
strong rise in exports, but was simply a result of the fall in the rand.
Much of the income was from mining revenues that were now
worth more in rand terms. The increased export revenue therefore
did not indicate that a strong economic foundation was being laid
for future growth.

This is disturbing, as one of the South African economy's most
serious weaknesses is the failure of its manufactured goods to compete internationally. Only substantial improvements in productivity
can achieve this over the long term, laying the basis for a sustained
economic recovery. Without such a productivity rise, economic
upswings are likely to be short-term affairs.

The surplus on the current account of the balance of payments
concealed another drawback: most of it was going to service
foreign debt. Month by month during 1985, much of the income
was spent on interest payments due on established debt, whereas
the intended purpose of the surplus was ultimately to finance new
borrowing to generate a phase of economic growth. In addition,
continued political instability, combined with the contraction of
economic demand, caused foreign-owned companies in South
Africa to remit increased dividents to their parent companies rather
than reinvesting their profits to the same extent as before. Like the
debt repayments and service charges, such remittances served to
reduce the surplus on the current account.

State expenditure and inflation

Despite a number of declarations of intent, state expenditure failed
to fall. After mid-1985, the government had some success: while
fiscal spending continues to rise, its *rate* of increase has eased
somewhat. In July 1985 government spending was 38% higher than
in July 1984, while the figure for August was merely 21% higher
than the equivalent month in 1984. Overall, after the first four

months of the 1985 financial year, fiscal spending was R850-million over budget. However, 1985 tax revenue rose sharply to a level 34% higher than in 1984. This is probably due to increased revenue from the mining sector, which has been earning record profits due to the low value of the rand.

While the falling rate of increase in government spending coupled with increased tax revenue may well ease the fiscal crisis, the fact remains that the government appears committed to continuously rising expenditure. State commitment to high expenditure on its repressive apparatuses of defence and police is inflexible, and has risen with the tide of unrest in the course of 1985. High expenditure on black education, industrial decentralisation programmes and small business development is dictated by the government's perception that these programmes are crucial to the long-term political and economic restructuring of South Africa's social relations. Similarly, 'homeland development', agricultural subsidies, and sheltered employment for a large white bureaucracy are each in its way regarded as essential for political stability.

Added to this are the cost of financing the state of emergency; the cost of escalating military adventurism beyond South Africa's borders; and the rising cost of servicing the foreign debt, given the rand's failure to recover against other currencies. Faced with these increases in expenditure, the rise in tax revenue is unlikely to resolve the fiscal problem.

Ironically, but not surprisingly, the state's record in reducing inflation — the central object of the austerity exercise — is unambiguously negative. Rising state expenditure, coupled with the monetarist commitment to reduce or withdraw subsidies on basic goods such as maize and bread, continued to put upward pressure on the inflation rate, as did the cheap rand. And just when South Africans were told that the inflation rate had peaked at 16,9% at the end of August 1985, the rand fell below $0,35. Unless the rand recovers from its current low levels (below $0,40) the inflation rate is highly unlikely to come down in the immediate future. In fact, with the recent price increases in petrol, bread and parastatal tariffs still to feed through the system, it is possible that inflation could rise further. There is an additional danger that governmental attempts to reflate the economy may well be inflationary. The 10% import surcharge already imposed is a case in point. Should there also be a substantial rise in fiscal spending the possibility of hyperinflation cannot be ruled out.

Damage to the industrial base

In the course of 1985 not only has the state's monetarist policy failed in its stated aims, but it has seriously damaged South Africa's industrial base. The government's means of 'eliminating excessive demand' have put crushing pressure on industrial and commercial capital, as well as on the labour force: African unemployment is now estimated at around 25% of the economically active population. Between August 1984 and June 1985, white, coloured and Indian unemployment doubled (from 30 000 to 60 691). For the first five months of 1985, insolvencies (at 1 123) were 105% higher than for the corresponding period in 1984, when the recession was already under way. And in the first six months of 1985, company liquidations (at 1 581) were 27% higher than for the last six months of 1984.

Nor is it just smaller concerns which have been battered by the monetarist onslaught. Virtually every major industrial and commercial company has suffered losses over the past year, arising from the drop in income following the contraction of demand, combined with doubled foreign debt obligations due to the fall in the rand. The near-collapse of the Kirsh group, which in 1985 was seventeenth in the *Financial Mail's* list of Top 100 Companies, is a case in point. Only a rescue operation by Sanlam, involving a cash injection of R190-m, could salvage the group. Even Gencor incurred huge losses in its industrial division, in which four companies alone lost over R54-m. Only Gencor's massive mining profits (up by 58% in six months) enabled the group to declare a profit. South Africa's most successful automobile manufacturer, Toyota, which declared pre-tax profits of R23-m in the second half of 1984, produced a R9-m rand loss in the first six months of 1985, mainly as a result of the fact that the new car market has collapsed by one-third since 1981 (from 300 000 units sold per year to 200 000).

Economic pressures on companies also contributed to the build-up of foreign debt. Companies were forced into ever greater borrowing to stave off collapse, but because of exorbitantly high local interest rates began borrowing more abroad. As the value of the rand fell against other currencies, so borrowers found it increasingly difficult to meet repayment obligations. The present foreign debt crisis is an outgrowth of monetarist policies.

If allowed to continue, such policies may well begin to destroy South Africa's industrial base. An important indicator of the effects of economic attrition is the physical asset-stripping forced upon cash-short companies. Operating well below capacity, some companies have resorted to selling equipment abroad. In the course of 1985 the civil engineering industry, for example, has been exporting its assets at the rate of more than R100-m worth monthly. While such asset-stripping might well serve to generate cash from unused equipment in the short term, it poses serious problems for the future. Should the economy begin to pull out of recession, producers who have sold off equipment will find replacement extremely expensive. For example, a unit of capital equipment used in the cement industry which cost R1-m in 1984, cost almost R8-m rand a year later. Such asset-stripping and gearing-down, a product of the monetarist-induced recession, means that future industrial expansion will face serious hindrances.

Impediments to social restructuring

Until the middle of 1985, business interests supported the austerity package, despite its high toll. Most business spokemen saw the recession as a period of economic restructuring that would remove the drag of high inflation, thereby preparing the economy for a more sustained upswing. The austerity measures were presented, and endured, as the economic component of a process of social restructuring. The other crucial part of this was of course a successful process of political reform. Such reform would mean that South Africa was beginning to conform to at least some of the characteristics of a capitalist democracy, thereby moving towards long-term social stability.

However, as the effects of the recession began to intensify from the beginning of 1985, unemployment rose ominously in the context of unabated inflation. Elsewhere we have argued that: 'The major priority of the state and leading business sectors is to carry through these (monetarist) restructuring policies. To do this, they have to inflict severe damage on various social groups, especially workers and the poor in general'.[1] The escalation of social unrest in the course of 1985 indicated that these 'social groups' were not prepared to take this lying down.

By the middle of 1985, it seemed that the process of restructuring was threatened by the government's inability to put forward and implement political reforms that would gain it widespread legitimacy, thereby defusing the mounting unrest. In view of South Africa's high degree of dependence on foreign trade, investment and finance, business leaders were becoming concerned about foreign perceptions of South Africa as a high-risk banana state. Such concern was fuelled by the increasingly successful and respectable disinvestment campaign, especially in the United States.

But the official view was still optimistic. In July 1985, the governor of the Reserve Bank, Gerhard de Kock, still bubbled with enthusiasm for the success of the official policy: 'Prosperity and growth for all sectors of the population could be expected next year', he said, adding that 'the country's painful austerity measures were pulling the economy back into line'.

He admitted that allowing the prime rate to rise from 14% to 25% to prevent the economy from overheating had been an unpopular move which had damaged industry, had a recessionary influence, and, through its effect on unemployment, had contributed to the current unrest, but he stated emphatically that 'it had been necessary and it had worked'. The improvements on the economic front 'would bring good times for all in 1986'.

In fact, South Africa was in an extremely vulnerable position economically. Its high degree of foreign indebtedness, and especially the extremely high proportion of short-term debt (66% of the total debt burden, compared with a more normal 44% in Western industrialised countries) rendered South Africa doubly vulnerable to the loss of international financial confidence following political instability.

Under these circumstances, the declaration of the state of emergency in July might well appear inexplicable. Perhaps it may best be explained as an attempt on the part of the state to smash its way out of the vicious circle in which it was trapped by decisive, confident action. The official view was best summed up by the director-general of finance, Chris Stals, who, in one of his less intelligent predictions, argued that the emergency would be viewed positively by those abroad.

Business interests represented by the Federated Chamber of

Industries, the Association of Chambers of Commerce, the Afrikaanse Handelsinstituut and other institutions cautiously welcomed the emergency, evidently believing that the 'reimposition of law and order' would precede the announcement of far-reaching political reforms. The joint statement by ASSOCOM and the FCI, issued shortly after the emergency was declared, emphasised that repression must be accompanied by reform: 'The business community has been greatly concerned at the escalating violence in South Africa and acknowledges the need to reestablish law and order in certain areas . . . . However, organised commerce and industry also believe that security action alone will not resolve the serious conflict in black townships. To be effective, the restoration of law and order must be backed by a package of substantial reforms, to recognise black aspirations and to redress legitimate grievances'. Evidently foreign financial interests shared this view.

This hope, on the part of investors, foreign banks and local business interests, was decisively killed by President PW Botha in his notorious mid-August 'Rubicon' speech. It became obvious that the government's commitment to major reform — the political aspect of restructuring — was half-hearted, to say the least. An end to political instability was not in sight.

The post-Rubicon crisis

In the wake of Botha's speech, the rand, which had clawed its way up to $0,50, began to fall again. Prospects for repayment, and even for servicing, the foreign debt diminished as the rand fell. Rumours began to circulate that US bankers would refuse to roll over, or extend the repayment date of, the billions of dollars of short-term debt that would fall due in the coming months. And so it proved. At the beginning of September, US banks led the move to call in much of South Africa's foreign debt, estimated at about $24-billion or some R55-billion. This was no less than a massive vote of no confidence in Botha's political policy and led to the immediate collapse of the rand, which fell to $0,35.

In the face of this financial crisis, the government was forced to act: the Minister of Finance announced a package of far-reaching financial measures. First, trade on the Johannesburg Stock Exchange was briefly suspended so as to prevent foreign investors moving capital out of the country through the sale of shares. A few days later the financial rand was reintroduced to impede repatriation of foreign capital. A four-month moratorium on SA's foreign debt repayments was declared, to allow officials to negotiate terms of repayment. Significantly, these moves represented a complete reversal of previous monetarist policies aimed at introducing a 'free market' in financial and exchange markets.

In fact, it was only in 1983, as part of the monetarist programme, that the financial rand had been abolished. Now it was back, playing its original role of hampering the flight of foreign capital from the country. Foreign investors are obliged to buy foreign currencies through the financial rand system. Since the value of the financial rand is quoted at a discount to the commercial or ordinary rand, foreign investors must pay more and therefore take a loss if they want to move capital out of the country. Conversely, because the financial rand is cheaper than the ordinary rand, foreign would-be investors are theoretically encouraged to buy in.

The foreign debt crisis, and the intransigence on reform that sparked it, spurred local business leaders onto the offensive — this time in open confrontation with the government. Organised commerce and industry began expressing anti-government views and making more strident calls for reform, even taking their case to the United Nations where they openly denounced apartheid. *Business Day* called for PW Botha's resignation, and then for the resignation of the whole government. Leading Afrikaner businessmen like Louis Luyt and Anton Rupert, who had previously not spoken out, now joined the chorus of criticism, while Gavin Relly and other business leaders flew to Lusaka to consult with the ANC. Overall, local business interests were making plain their disillusionment with the government's capacity to carry through the necessary political restructuring.

The government itself did not remain immune from these pressures. The Minister of Law and Order, Louis le Grange, indicated that the state would not further escalate physical repression, while PW Botha committed himself in principle to single citizenship and a universal franchise in South Africa. As usual, though, it was too little, too late, and government equivocation on precisely how these changes would be implemented did little to increase confidence.

On the economic front, the Minister of Finance announced a

package of measures designed to encourage economic reflation. These measures — especially the increase of fiscal spending to ease the unemployment crisis and a 10% surcharge on imports to finance it — represent a reversion to Keynesian reflationary tactics and are a further rejection of monetarism. But the government's economic turnaround has not won it many friends. Christie Kuun, vice-president of the AHI, pointed out that government steps to stimulate the economy could lead to runaway inflation and the decline of the surplus on the current account of the balance of payments. This would choke off economic revival before it activated employment to any meaningful extent. 'Political expediency', Kuun argued, 'rather than sound economic considerations, appear to have led to the announcement of these steps'.

Kuun has correctly identified one side of the double bind or vicious circle the state finds itself in. Abandoning monetarism and reflating the economy cannot produce a sustained upswing, since the fundamental restructuring of social relations which monetarist policy aimed at has not been completed. Yet if monetarist policy is continued and the economy allowed to remain in recession, political unrest will intensify, and foreign confidence in South Africa's prospects will diminish further. As unemployment rises and industry runs down, foreign investors in the country will double their efforts to withdraw and the government's political support will be further eroded, even among its own constituency.

The government finds itself pushed increasingly into a corner as the vicious circle tightens. Monetarism, after all, is not merely a technical economic theory, but, as we have argued before, it is also a broader theory aimed at achieving 'a major change in the balance of power and a restructuring of the system of production'. So far, the government has failed to achieve these broader goals in South Africa. Faced with intense local resistance, increasing overseas pressure and growing division in its ranks, the government now finds itself on the defensive, to a large extent because it failed adequately to calculate the social consequences of its monetarist programme. It is now reversing many of the policies it introduced earlier. As Kuun puts it: 'This type of action indicates a lack of positive economic strategy'.

The outlook for the economy is bleak: new foreign investment on any scale is out of the question while confidence in the country's future is low. As a result of the debt crisis, South Africa will find it very hard to borrow, both because its international credit rating is damaged, and because the cost of its existing debt is almost prohibitive. As a result, financing an upswing will be a major problem. Further, with the foreign debt crisis restricting South Africa's capacity to borrow abroad, any attempt at reflation via increased fiscal spending may well put upward pressure on domestic interest rates as local borrowing would increase. This would inevitably impede reflation.

The only glimmer of hope for the government is that the dollar price of gold will rise. This could occur in response to a substantial fall in the value of the US dollar against other currencies, an international debt crisis, a resurgence of international inflation or a major international political crisis. A rise in income from gold could bring temporary relief from some of the serious economic pressures South Africa faces and lead to an economic upswing. But on its own, such relief will be at best only temporary.

Conclusion

The South African government's fling with monetarism has, it appears, left the country's economy facing worse prospects of combined high inflation and economic stagnation than it did a year ago. And this time it faces them with a weakened industrial base, an increasingly politicised labour force and a crippled currency.

Even if the catalytic political events of the past year had not had such an extreme impact, South African monetarism was unlikely to succeed. Unlike the far larger and more complex economies of the US and capitalist West, South Africa has an open economy: its imports and exports of capital and commodities have a far greater relative impact on the total economy. Hence the massive effects of the depreciation of the rand on its industrial base, which is not as resilient as that of the US or even of Britain. The South African economy — with its low productivity, dependence on mineral exports, competitive weakness in manufactured exports, and its reliance on imports of capital goods — was far more vulnerable than its policy-makers realised.

Then, too, industrialised Western nations have a welfare system that enables them to blunt the effects of unemployment on their populations. Equally, they have a far higher degree of popular political legitimacy. While unable to avoid some of the violent consequences of monetarist recession and repression, they are able to contain them. South Africa, with its more vulnerable economy, its absence of a welfare safety net, and its oppressive racial policies, cannot.

Notes

1 Stephen Gelb and Duncan Innes, 'Economic crisis in South Africa: monetarism's double bind', *Work in Progress*, 36, April 1985, 39.

The Economy: Achilles Heel of the New Deal

Karl von Holdt

> Today I wish to call on every member of the community to exercise self-control and to refrain from living beyond his or her means . . . . (A) heavy responsibility rests on both the public and private sectors and on the general public not to make excessive demands on the country's productive resources.
> — PW Botha, *CT*, 19.09.84.

> It is a hard thing to say bankruptcies and unemployment will rise. But there is no easy way to get inflation out of the system.
> — A Hammarsma, Standard Bank economist, *FM*, 09.03.84.

> Today I am appealing for people to be paid any wage, no matter how low, that they are prepared to accept.
> — Zac de Beer, Anglo American director, *RDM*, 11.03.85.

> They are weeding out people and trying to push workers to do double jobs. The recession is really only a pain to the workers and not so much to the employers. Retrenchments have affected our organisation because in factories where we were strong we are no longer strong, so it becomes a matter of keeping going.
> — MAWU organiser.[1]

> We want work! We want work!
> — Unemployed workers, Atlantis.[2]

A deep recession is currently gripping South Africa. Despite PW Botha's appeal to the general public, the recession means very different things to different classes in South Africa. At the heart of these differences lies a struggle over wealth and social resources.

This review seeks to analyse causes of the current recession, a result of the profound economic crisis which has been maturing over the last decade. The crisis springs from several factors. South African industry is stagnating — and consequently profits are falling — for lack of sufficient markets. Closely related to this is the balance of payments (BoP) problem. World demand and world prices for South Africa's traditional exports are declining, while every phase of economic growth stimulates massive import increases. The result is a BoP deficit (importing more than is exported) and increasing foreign debt. A further cause of crisis is the large portion of national wealth required to maintain the apartheid state. Rampant inflation, the low value of the rand, BoP and budget deficits, are all manifestations of the crisis.

The recession is not simply an ordinary slump in the capitalist business cycle. It combines cyclical factors with more profound and serious structural contradictions and can only be overcome by restructuring capitalist production. Present ruling-class strategy attempts this restructuring in two ways: by attacking the working class and so lowering the price of labour; and by rationalising production and so making South African manufactured goods more competitive on the international market. As the crisis bites deeper, struggles over the distribution of the nation's wealth are becoming more and more acute.

Structural crisis

Manufacturing in search of a market

The South African manufacturing industry developed essentially as an import-replacement industry, providing goods which had previously been imported for the local market.

Since 1925 local manufacturing has been protected against cheaper imports by various tariffs. However, continued growth and profits for a domestic industry require continuing growth in domestic demand. This did exist while mining and agriculture export earning increased both company and individual spending power, and while the white consumer market expanded —

particularly during the sustained economic boom of the 1960s. Of course, the impoverished black masses were not seen as a serious market for the goods their labour produced.

By the 1970s the white consumer market was clearly becoming saturated. New strategies were necessary to prevent the manufacturing industry from stagnating. In 1972 the government's Reynders Commission to investigate strategies for manufacturing industry growth reported that import replacement no longer held much potential for growth. At that stage, major imports were capital goods (machinery, transport, equipment etc), and heavy intermediate goods which required production on a huge scale to be economically viable. The South African market was simply too small for production on such a scale. Rather, the manufacturing industry would have to develop a large export manufacturing sector in consumer and intermediate goods.

This has not happened. South African industry is not internationally competitive because its products are too expensive. But industry, oriented to supplying a small domestic market, has remained relatively small-scale and has not utilised the most advanced technology.

South African capitalists complain too about another factor they claim makes their products uncompetitive. Anglo American's chief economic consultant said recently that 'the wages of a black textile worker in Johannesburg in 1982 were a third more than the corresponding earnings in Hong Kong, two-thirds more than in Rio de Janeiro and almost three times those in Seoul, Singapore, Manila and Bangkok'.[3] Whether this is true or not is difficult to ascertain. But what it signifies is that there is a growing perception among certain capitalists that wages in South Africa are too high.

Despite the Reynders Commission recommendations, and despite industry's evident inability to compete effectively, the South African government has failed to formulate a coherent strategy to develop an export industry. Avoiding the issue, in the late 1970s and early 1980s capitalists placed their faith in the emergence of a black consumer market. However, low wages and high prices prevent this market developing. Also, lower export earnings in the 1980s have shrunk the domestic market even further. The necessity to develop an export industry has therefore become an insistent theme in speeches and editorials of business leaders, government officials and economists. Manufactured exports would, they argue, compensate for the fall-off in traditional exports, improve the BoP and bring economic growth and jobs to the ailing economy. (See, for example, 'Short lived upswing?' *FM*, 21.06.85).

Of course, these conditions — saturated domestic market, decreasing production, the turn to exports — do not mean that capitalism has satisfied even the basic needs of all South Africans. Low wages and unemployment have placed many people in a position where they have no money. Capital is therefore forced to search for markets beyond the country's borders.

Imports and exports

The source of many of South Africa's economic problems is its relation to the world economy. An important aspect is the composition of imports and exports. South Africa's position in world trade and division of labour is weak. It has been further weakened by changes in the world economy.

South Africa exports primary goods (eg coal, iron, wool) and intermediate goods (mostly worked-up primary goods such as steel) and imports capital goods (machinery and transport equipment). The imbalance between imports and exports is increasing rather than decreasing, the total value of imports being roughly double the total value of exports, excluding gold. Similar situations have driven other third world countries like Brazil into massive debt. Fortunately South Africa has gold which is roughly equal in value to all other exports combined and has, until recently, been sufficient to keep the balance of payments in surplus.

The South African economy therefore depends on:

1. The world market for primary and intermediate commodities such as coal, iron, steel, platinum and copper and to a lesser extent agricultural goods;
2. The world price of gold;
3. High imports of capital goods necessary for economic growth.

The world market for South Africa's primary commodity exports — particularly coal, iron, and other minerals — has shrunk because of an international economic crisis. The 'smokestack' industries — steel, heavy engineering, chemicals — of the industrialised world, for so long the engine of the world economy, have been hit by falling demand, idle capital and bankruptcy.

This is unlikely to change with economic recovery. The crisis has forced a restructuring of the world economy. New growth industries are high-tech electronic and computer industries in the United States and Asia. This has serious implications for primary product exports which South Africa has traditionally relied on. For example ISCOR's Sishen-Saldanah iron exporting project now exports iron at a loss, because of depressed world demand and prices.

The dollar price of gold is critically important to South Africa's economy. In periods of international instability or recession the gold price generally rises when the price of key currencies, especially the dollar, is falling, and when inflation is high. For South Africa a high gold price means increased foreign exchange and mining profits which in turn fuel a business boom such as the one in 1980-1981. Since then the United States economy has recovered, the dollar has soared, and the gold price has sunk during 1983 and 1984.

Clearly South Africa cannot continue to rely on gold mining wealth. In mid-1985 the gold price rose slightly as South Africa's political instability led to international fears that production may be halted. However, variations in the gold price are determined by factors beyond South Africa's control. It will probably never approach its earlier peaks and South Africa must find other means to pay for its massive imports and to fuel economic growth.

Because the economy requires expensive capital goods imports to expand, each business boom has a built-in weakness: demand increases and production rises; capitalists invest in more plant to expand capacity and increase productivity; capital goods imports increase and push BoP into deficit and recession threatens. The 1980-81 boom illustrates this process: the sharp increase in imports in 1980 and 1981; the balance of payments deficit in 1981; and imports in 1982 no longer increasing as the economy slid into recession.

The dilemma is how to earn the foreign exchange to pay for imports necessary for growth. Many capitalists believe the answer is the same as for the stagnation of the manufacturing sector: develop manufacturing exports.

State overspending

The state too is mired down in financial crisis. Its expenditure has risen rapidly (at a rate of 18,5% per annum since 1980). In 1981-2 state expenditure was 22% of GDP; in 1984-5, 29%. Although total revenue has also increased as government has scraped the barrel for more tax, it has not done so at the same rate. The result: ever-increasing government debt, fuelling the fires of inflation.

Huge amounts of government expenditure go to the bloated bureaucracy of apartheid, to the military, and as funds for corrupt and spendthrift 'homeland' regimes. Pressure on government to spend comes from several quarters: civil servants (for higher salaries and more jobs); other white groups whose political support is important to the government, such as farmers (for increased subsidies); from the general white population; from black allies such as 'homeland' regimes; from coloured and Indian collaborators with their new bureaucracies. Also costly are necessary material concessions to defuse popular mobilisation.

Demands on state coffers increase, but its funding sources are shrinking since the crisis-ridden economy is unable to produce wealth. The March 1984 budget, presented by former Finance Minister Owen Horwood, failed to deal with these problems. His estimated expenditure of R25,4-billion was exceeded by R1,8-billion. This was partly a result of the drought, which necessitated big extensions of credit to farmers. During 1984, the government had to borrow R6-billion. Debt repayment on previous borrowings amounted to R4-billion.

The rapid slide into high expenditure, high tax and high debt-budgeting alarmed and angered capitalists. High taxes eroded profits and salaries and debt fuelled inflation. They demanded that government cut expenditure. They argued that tight monetary policy (applied in the course of 1984) pushed the burden of recession onto the private sector. The Reserve Bank also advised government to reduce spending by privatisation, terminating certain services and retrenching government employees.

The events of 1984

The balance of payments crisis

The short mini-boom of mid-1983 and early 1984 saw increased imports. These, combined with the low and falling world price of gold and low volume of traditional exports, precipitated a balance of payments crisis. The BoP current account showed an annualised deficit[4] of R2,5-billion in the last quarter of 1983 and R2,8-billion in the first quarter of 1984. Although it was less in the second quarter — R1,5-billion — the situation was still critical. South Africa had to borrow money abroad to pay for imports, which meant future growth would be undermined by the necessity to pay back loans.

The boom and inflation

Although the mini-boom was triggered by a rise in the gold price, it was sustained by a large increase in government and consumer spending. Between March 1983 and March 1984 the central government wage and salary bill increased by 30%. Bank credit expanded and gross domestic expenditure increased by 10%. Production rose to meet this demand and the retrenchments, bankruptcies and unemployment of 1982 slowed down. But the money being spent was largely borrowed money — borrowed by consumers or borrowed by government — rather than money earned from exports. Advancing credit to create new money, without creating new wealth, devalues money and prices rise. Credit is also expensive money because interest must be paid, so prices rise further. By July 1984, the inflation rate was 12% rising to over 16% by mid-1985.[5]

The prospect of ever-rising inflation alarmed the ruling class. In the view of the Standard Bank economist, Andre Hammersma, 'Inflation must be fought. In the long run, when spending has been controlled, the economy will be healthier. But once we decide to live with inflation, we will become a banana republic' (*FM*, 09.11.84). Inflation raises the prices of South African exports, making them uncompetitive in international markets. High inflation creates an unstable price environment, investment decisions become risky, and this in turn makes foreign investors wary.

Finally, the desperate poverty caused by ever-rising prices creates the conditions for strikes, 'unrest' and 'political instability', undermining what is called 'business confidence'.

The fall of the rand

A BoP deficit means the country is spending more than it is earning and is therefore going into debt. This lowers the worth of its currency. Inflation means the rand is worth less in the domestic economy — which is then reflected in its relation to other currencies. The rand also weakened in relation to the soaring price of the dollar. Because gold is so vital to the South African economy, the price of the rand in foreign exchange markets falls when gold falls.

The rand price fell steadily from 1983 onwards. In mid-1984, the Reserve Bank, rather than trying to maintain the price of the rand or soften its fall, allowed it to plummet sharply. This fall sent several shock waves through South Africa. Politically it contributed to a public consciousness of 'economic crisis' and so paved the way for the harsh monetary policies to follow.[6]

The drop in the rand sharply increased import prices and decreased those of exports. The government hoped this would discourage imports, encourage exports, and reverse the BoP deficit. The falling rand thus *reflected* the fact that South Africa was 'living beyond its means', and at the same time *acted* to alter the situation.[7]

But there was a price to pay for the falling rand: because imports are more expensive, they tend to push up production costs which in turn increases prices throughout the economy. This inevitably boosts the already high inflation rate — and again reduces exports' competitiveness. So, through the mechanism of the falling rand, the BoP crisis translated into a potential inflation crisis.

Monetary policy

In August 1984 the government took action. It announced an 'austerity package' in the realm of monetary policy. This package had two immediate aims: to change the BoP deficit into a surplus, and to reduce inflation. It was designed to do this by forcing the economy into recession through higher interest rates and tighter hire purchase restrictions. Interest rates on all forms of credit rose to unprecedented levels making it extremely difficult for private consumers and companies to borrow money.

Demand dropped and production was cut back. Thousands of workers were retrenched. Unemployed workers had nothing to spend, which further reduced demand. Companies with high borrowings were squeezed for cash to pay the new interest rates. Many were forced to the wall. Because of lower profits — and often losses — management baulked at increasing wages, which meant people again had less to spend. Many companies halted expansion plans.

Gross domestic expenditure declined at an annual rate of 5,5% in the second half of 1984. As the general level of production decreased, imports dropped sharply. By the last quarter of the year the BoP current account was showing a small surplus. The annualised surplus in the first quarter of 1985 was a massive R4-billion. As a result of tighter monetary policy and the BoP surplus the rand ceased falling and appreciated slightly in the first half of 1985.

Despite the reduction in credit and spending inflation is still rising — estimates for 1985 vary between 15% and 20%. The low rand has caused a massive increase in import prices. The 50% increase in the price of petrol was only the most dramatic of these. However, economists believe that if the present policies are continued, inflation should start declining towards the beginning of 1986.

But the Reserve Bank (which implements monetary policy), economists and capitalists argued that monetary policy alone would not suffice. They believed a disciplined fiscal policy to cut government spending was essential.

Fiscal policy

Doubtless, the brief of the new Minister of Finance, Barend du Plessis, is to effect a reduction in government spending. In March 1985, just before presenting his first budget, he announced that government employee bonuses would be reduced by a third (saving R500-million) and that 50% of staff vacancies would not be filled. Teachers, railway, post office and other state workers — politically important to the National Party — responded with an outcry. The *Cape Times* reported repeated angry shouts of 'strike, strike' at a 'rowdy' meeting of railway workers in Pretoria. President of the Artisans Staff Association, Jimmy Zurich, told the meeting: 'We have kept the railways running in spite of a 43 000 staff reduction in the past two years. And this is the thanks we get — the cut in our bonuses is the biggest blow since our salaries were reduced in 1922' (*CT*, 05.03.85).

Du Plessis' 1985 budget went some way to satisfying demands for a tougher fiscal policy to complement harsh monetary policy. Budgeted expenditure shows an increase of 11,4% over the previous year's actual expenditure — less than the rate of inflation and therefore a decrease in real terms. Revenue is to be increased through extra taxes: GST up from 10% to 12%; an added tax surcharge for individuals; extra taxation on gold and other mines and on banks and insurance companies; increased duties on imported luxury goods (to help the BoP). These taxes will reduce consumer demand. The reduction of government expenditure will also reduce demand in the economy and push it further into recession.

Reduced expenditure and increased taxes mean that the budget deficit is fairly small; and the government will not resort to bank credit or foreign loans — both of which are inflationary — to finance it. Many capitalists and economists approved of the budget, although it will deepen the recession in South Africa and so further impoverish workers and unemployed.

Recession

'It is a hard thing to say that unemployment and bankruptcies will rise', says Standard Bank economist Andre Hammersma. But bankruptcies and unemployment are not simply side effects of an onslaught on inflation: they are the means by which the capitalist economy overcomes certain internal barriers to further profit-making and accumulation.

During a recession smaller and less efficient companies are 'cleaned out' of the economy (through bankruptcy) and the working class is weakened (through unemployment). So the recession creates conditions for renewed profit-making in the next boom.

Currently the economy needs more than 'cleaning out' and 'renewal' to profit in the next boom. This boom may not come at all — so deep is the structural crisis of South African capitalism. Government and business circles believe the economy must be restructured to generate a different kind of boom — based on manufactured goods exports, rather than primary goods and gold exports. The poverty of government policy is revealed in that it appears to be relying on the recession alone to accomplish this. The severity of the recession corresponds to the immensity of the task facing it. In the absence of any other long-term planning the recession may actually disable the economy rather than rejuvenate it. Capitalists are divided on this issue but many hope, along with the government, that the recession can go some way to making South African industry more competitive by rationalising production and lowering the price of labour.

Rationalising production

In November 1984 the *Financial Mail* reported a 30% drop in furniture sales since 1983. In the last two weeks of August eight furniture manufacturers went bankrupt, and by September, 20 others had followed and more were expected. 'The crunch has yet to come', said Furniture Manufacturers Association director, W Smith. At the same time, AFCOL, the biggest manufacturer which accounts for almost half the industry's turnover, had retrenched 5% of its staff, and was 'trimming expenses and exploring the export market' (*FM*, 09.11.84).

Consumer demand for TVs and domestic appliances had also dried up. Companies in this sector have responded by merging. In December, Tek and Defy merged to form the country's largest domestic appliance group. A statement from the new company read: 'The merger is designed to bring about rationalisation advantages for both Tek and Defy in a market which has seen demand decline sharply . . . enhancing the ability to compete more effectively with imports'. 'Rationalisation' meant possibly closing a factory in Brakpan and probable retrenchments (*CT*, 07.12.84).

Two Cape Town steel factories, Consanis and Cape Steel, both engaged in heavy engineering and structural steel, were competing for the same markets. Murray and Roberts, owners of Cape Steel, bought the ailing Consanis and restructured production: Cape Steel is now responsible for structural steel and Consanis for heavy engineering. It seems retrenchments at both factories (about 100 at Consanis), accompanied this process.[8]

These examples demonstrate a general process throughout the economy. Recession sends weak companies to the wall (at an estimated rate of 14 or 15 per day). Alternatively, they are swallowed up by larger companies characterised by higher productivity and an ability to increase productivity further (through more machinery, the benefits of large-scale production and ready access to finance).

Thus the economy emerges from a recession with a higher general level of productivity and profitability. In the words of Johan van Zyl, executive director of the Federated Chambers of Industries, 'The rule of the day is the survival of the fittest. Manufacturers are concentrating on managing the recession and coming out leaner and fitter' (*FM*, 09.11.84).

Many capitalists believe that this process will provide the base to develop a more competitive export industry able to produce cheaper products. Others believe that so sweeping and savage a purging of capital's ranks through monetary policy is no substitute for carefully planned strategy to develop specific exports. 'We are undermining the productive base to such an extent that the entrepreneurial elite is being massacred', said Barclays Bank economist, Cees Bruggemans (*FM*, 10.05.85).

Effects on the working class

If the 'entrepreneurial elite' is being massacred, words fail to describe the situation of the working class. In most cases retrenchments are integral to rationalisation. Waves of retrenchments and closures have hit almost every industrial sector. In the metal industry alone, 84 000 workers were retrenched between 1982 and 1984. Between October and December 1984, 43 000 jobs were lost in manufacturing, mining, construction, electricity and transport (*CT*, 06.04.85). Each week new batches of workers become unemployed.

Management frequently uses retrenchment to weed out old, sick and militant workers. In the words of a MAWU organiser, 'I think that many factories are trying to get rid of union members, they want to kill the strength of the workers on the shop floor'.[9] The remaining workers, under threat of unemployment, are forced to work harder, faster and longer. Management often retrenches more workers than necessary so remaining workers have to work harder than before. As an employer said, 'To utilise people better, if you take away five here, maybe you can do better with three'.[10] Proportionately fewer supervisors are retrenched than production workers

— so that the screws of 'labour discipline' can be tightened further.

Management is clearly aware of this shifting balance of forces: 'Retrenchments had a positive effect on company/worker relations, they are now a little more worried about their jobs, and productivity has improved a lot because they know that can happen to them as well'.[11]

The attack on inflation, the call for 'discipline', 'sacrifice' and 'tightening of belts' veils a concerted effort to increase productivity and restore profitability. This effort includes lowering working-class standards of living and undermining its organisation so that it cannot resist. In the 'New Deal' era a ruling-class offensive through fiscal and monetary policy is more appropriate than direct political repression although the level of mass resistance to the policy of impoverishment has driven the ruling class to use force.

These policies are entirely in keeping with the attempt to make South African capitalism internationally competitive. Anglo American director, Zac de Beer, has argued that the manufacturing sector would have to provide export earnings on a huge scale, but that prospect would depend on costs and productivity. 'In the final resort', he said, 'international markets depend on price as well as quality. In this context too many South Africans have expectations of unrealistically high living standards and working conditions. In other words thrift and hard work remain the cardinal economic virtues' (*CT*, 30.08.84). De Beer also said 'I am pleading for people to be allowed to work for any wage, no matter how low, that they are prepared to accept . . . . We must discard entirely the concept of enforced minimum wages'. De Beer acknowledged that he had campaigned for higher minimum wages in the past, but said changed economic circumstances made it necessary to reduce cost, otherwise new jobs could not be created and South Africa would become a 'banana republic' (*CT*, 28.02.85).

Prospects

The ferocity of the current recession corresponds to the depth of the structural crisis facing the South African economy. Government fiscal and monetary policies are a response to the objective crisis facing the economy but they are not the root cause of the recession. The government has few options: to maintain government and private expenditure through lower interest rates and easier credit would mean deepening the BoP crisis, rampant inflation, crushing foreign debt, and a falling rand. Several third world countries like Brazil have chosen this path. The results have not been much better for the Brazilian masses than present conditions are for South Africans.

The strategy chosen by the ruling class in South Africa means greater suffering for workers, the unemployed and the rest of the oppressed majority (as well as for many sectors of the white working and middle classes). The burden of recession is not simply being shifted onto their shoulders. Rather, the recession is the arena for intensified class conflict. Intensified conflict is inevitable, because for the ruling class, the economic crisis can only be overcome through a radical cheapening of the price of labour power.

The working class is impoverished through strict hire purchase, higher GST, lower wages and mass unemployment. This impoverishment is regarded as necessary to the success of a manufacturing export strategy, so wealth is used in producing consumption goods for other countries while consumption within South Africa decreases. Such a strategy for economic recovery can never be in the interests of the working class, even if it is successful in its own terms.

But success is not that certain. For one thing, neither the state nor capital seem to have devised a coherent plan for developing an export sector. During this period of crisis and heightened competition in the world economy more than concentrated capital and a weakened working class is needed.

What is South Africa going to sell, and where? Other newly-industrialised countries, such as South Korea and Taiwan, have managed to carve out massive export markets — but that was through a sophisticated planning effort, and at a different phase of world capitalist development. The chances of pulling it off today are not good.

Even if success is achieved it would probably be based on massive importation of the most sophisticated and expensive capital goods. This could easily fling the BoP into deficit and set off a new crisis, including towering foreign debt (such as has happened to many of the newly industrialised countries). Disinvestment campaigns may also take their toll, since high technology imports — being very visible — are likely to be early casualties. Also, foreign suppliers and businesses have been reluctant to provide the most up-to-date technology to South African companies or subsidiaries. It has not suited their global strategy for South Africa to compete on the international market.

State economic strategy does not rest simply on creating the conditions for competitive exports: one aspect of the crisis is massive state expenditure, and government is sharpening its knife for substantial cutbacks. If the state is to succeed in cutting expenditure it must reduce wages and jobs in the state bureaucracy. Doubtless, the Nationalist government will encounter strong resistance (as it has already) to any such moves from its own political base in the white electorate.

Cutting expenditure also means choosing where the knife will fall. Defence or police budgets are not being cut but services such as health care, housing, food and transport subsidies are being pared down. These cutbacks shift costs onto the oppressed and combine with capital's attacks to further depress their living conditions. This opens up a fundamental contradiction in current state strategy.

The government's *political* strategy is at least partially one of reform and cooptation; while its *economic* strategy is to decrease the share of social wealth distributed to the working class and the masses in general. Yet if the 'New Deal' is to overcome its credibility problem it must make at least some difference to the material conditions under which people live and work. The expanded bureaucracies of the tricameral parliament require vast increases in government expenditure. So it is difficult to say where the government could find funds to improve living conditions when the economy itself is in decline.

However, ruling-class economic strategy is not to improve material conditions, but to worsen them. For the oppressed people and their organisations, economic and political issues are more and more inextricably linked. During 1984, their response to rulers' strategies was to transform their struggles against rent increases, low wages, unemployment and inferior schooling into a series of political attacks on the 'New Deal', on community councils, and on forces of repression.

Predictions are dangerous, but it is difficult not to see political reform disintegrating as the requirements of capital dictate an ever-harsher economic offensive against the working class. One outcome might be defeat of the workers and a new phase of capitalist profit-making. Another might be deepening stagnation and stalemate between opposing forces. A third might be opened by the growing realisation that there are no solutions within a capitalist framework and that hope lies in the struggle for an economy that is geared towards the satisfaction of human needs rather than the highest possible profits for a small crew of capitalists.

Notes

1 Quoted in I Obery, 'Recession and retrenchment in the East Rand metal industry, 1982', *South African Labour Bulletin*, 10(1), August-September 1984, 69.

2 Quoted in M Golding, 'Unemployed workers on the West Coast', *South African Labour Bulletin*, 10(4), January-February 1985, 40.

3 A Dickman, 'Economic institutions and economic reality', Senate special lectures, University of Witwatersrand, 1984, 13.

4 The annualised deficit for a particular quarter is the estimated annual deficit calculated from the deficit of that quarter and taking into account seasonal variations in trade from quarter to quarter.

5 It is necessary to make the point that the *conditions* for inflation within capitalism are created by the emergence of monopoly capitalism. The South Africa economy is highly monopolised by world standards; and where there are few sellers it is easy for them to reach agreement — either formally or informally — not to engage in competitive price-cutting, and to raise prices in concert. For a very useful discussion of this, see H Magdoff and P Sweezy, *The Deepening Crisis of US Capitalism* (Monthly Review Press, 1981), esp 127-136.

6 See D Innes and S Gelb, 'Economic crisis in South Africa: monetarism's double bind', *Work In Progress*, 36, April 1985, 37.

7 There were other spin-offs for the government: the markedly lower price of the rand against the dollar meant that, although the dollar price of gold was low, those dollars would convert to a large number of rands. Thus the profits, in rands, of the gold mines would be maintained — and so would the tax on those profits, which is a key component of state revenue (in 1980-81 tax on goldmines amounted to R2 795billion, or 21% of total revenue. In 1982-83, it was R1 320-billion or 8% — reflecting the falling price of gold.

8 Author's communication with D Lewis of the General Workers Union.

9 Quoted in Obery, 'Recession and retrenchment', 70.
10 Quoted in Obery, 'Recession and retrenchment', 55.
11 Quoted in Obery, 'Recession and retrenchment', 63.

Introduction

Glenn Moss

Destabilisation in Southern Africa, creation and maintenance of 'puppet' regimes, and a merciless commitment to anti-democratic social engineering continue as essential themes in South Africa's regional strategies. These policies have effects in the peripheries and rural areas of South Africa, as well as in neighbouring states often subject to the dictates of the regional power.

This section of the *South African Review* examines the operation of these policies in a number of areas: in Mozambique and Namibia, where social relations are partially structured by South African intervention; in regional development plans aimed at restructuring the relationships between geographical areas; in the bantustans; and in that major manifestation of apartheid's social engineering, population removal.

Jeremy Grest opens the section with a careful analysis of Mozambique's first decade of independence. He argues that grave internal economic problems, coupled to the spread of the war with the South African-backed MNR, propelled FRELIMO's leadership towards the Nkomati Accord. Despite South African contravention of Nkomati, Mozambique is unlikely to repudiate the agreement, as important FRELIMO leaders have too much political capital invested in it.

Grest concludes that socialism is on the defensive in Mozambique at present. The alternative civilisation which FRELIMO set out to build remains an elusive goal, endangered both by circumstances inside Mozambique and by external attacks from, and relations with, South Africa.

Max du Preez joins Grest in arguing that progressive politics has fallen on hard times. In a review of Namibian developments, he notes that Africa's last colony seems no closer to an independence acceptable to the majority of its inhabitants. SWAPO's military initiative is in crisis, weakened by repeated SADF raids into Angola, by the ruthless tactics of Koevoet, the notorious special police unit, and by the fact that almost a third of SWAPO guerillas are deployed with Angolan forces, needed to contain South Africa's surrogate in the area, UNITA.

In addition, argues Du Preez, SWAPO has lost political ground in the territory, its previously-organised base affected by apathy, harassment and repression.

The attempted creation and maintenance of 'puppet' regimes is not limited to South Africa's relations with its neighbours. In the bantustans, similar processes of corruption and anti-democratic practice continue. In a case study of a local authority in Bophuthatswana, Jeremy Keenan shows how corruption has a controlling role in the hierarchy of bantustan government and control. The microcosm he examines lays bare relations between the Bophuthatswanan government, the administration of apartheid, and local government.

And while the legacy of apartheid plays out its logic in anti-democratic and repressive bantustan governments, the central state remains committed to a massive programme of social engineering. Alan Hirsch explores the structures and programmes of the newly-formed Development Bank of Southern Africa, which is likely to play an important role in the direction of economic and political developments in the region, especially in rural and currently-peripheralised areas. The bank may fulfil a pivotal role in the Regional Development Programme, which divides South Africa into eight regions, cutting across bantustan boundaries. This plan could be the economic basis for a 'federal', 'confederal' or 'consociational' political initiative. But while the bank is part of the state's 'reform' initiative, it is also a logical conclusion of the apartheid system, in which 'independent' bantustans operate as 'autonomous states'. Whatever the contradictions in its role, the bank is likely to be an important actor in attempts to create an economic basis for the various federal political options currently being debated in government and other circles.

As in the past, the most brutal examples of government social engineering are seen in forced removals. Laurine Platzky points out that forced removals have not stopped, despite the government's early-1985 claim that removals would be suspended. Six of the eight categories of communities threatened by removal are still in danger. This affects over two million people. Even where the process has been suspended, government brings the full weight of its anti-democratic structures to bear against communities, attempting to create the appearance of 'voluntary' or 'negotiated' relocation.

Progressive forces have won some victories in the uneven battle against South African regional policy. But this section of the *Review* reveals the apartheid state in its nakedness, using its instruments of coercion to impose a minority will on the region.

Mozambique:
A Decade of Independence

Jeremy Grest

It is ten years since the people of Mozambique gained their national independence under the leadership of FRELIMO in June 1975. This decade has probably been as crucially formative of Mozambican society as any other in recent history, including the 1890s when the colonial system was formally installed, and the 1960s when the war of liberation began.

The first five years after independence saw FRELIMO working to consolidate its political power and to halt the rapid economic collapse brought on by the flight of capital and of skilled technical and managerial personnel from the country. The second period coincides roughly with increasing optimism at the independence of Zimbabwe and prospects of regional economic cooperation and recovery, based on the creation of the Southern African Development Coordinating Conference (SADCC). This optimism proved shortlived in the face of the effects of a spreading war with the MNR, drought and grave economic problems.

The combined effect of these crises served to propel FRELIMO's leadership in the direction of the Nkomati Accord with South Africa in 1984. This article concludes with an examination of the present situation in Mozambique, and adds some comments on possible future developments.

Political power and social reconstruction, 1975-1980

From liberation movement to government: the capture of state power

FRELIMO came to power in Mozambique in 1975 as a broad front or alliance of nationally oppressed classes committed to the overthrow of Portuguese colonialism and the socialist transformation of Mozambique.

Portuguese colonialism was highly regressive in its exploitation of Mozambique's peoples. Because of Portugal's weakness as an imperialist power, from an early period the south of Mozambique was firmly integrated into a migrant labour system linked to the South African gold mines. The central area was dominated by a plantation-style economy which subjected the peasantry to seasonal periods of forced labour. In the north, peasants were obliged to market their surplus through Portuguese trading monopolies, which profited from a system of unequal exchange underpinned by the colonial state.

Colonialism's major legacy to Mozambican society was outward-orientated development which generated poverty, ignorance and ill-health on a large scale. Its effect on class formation was to create a peasantry extensively involved in labour migration and not generally characterised by wide internal differentiation, although in the final stages of colonial rule it was state policy to encourage the growth of an indigenous middle peasantry. The working class was small and unorganised; no unions except for state-controlled syndicates were tolerated. The indigenous petty bourgeoisie was small, with extremely limited access to an education system designed to foster support for the regime.

The colonial state was both archaic and extremely repressive. Its combined effects on all strata of the Mozambican people created preconditions for the formation in 1962 of the alliance which initiated the armed struggle. FRELIMO's support base developed among the peasantry in the course of the war fought in the north, during which it created alternative structures of political power and economic organisation in the 'liberated zones'. The dominant political line which emerged, with its anti-imperialist and socialist orientation, was the product of intense internal struggles over the strategy and tactics of mobilising a guerilla war.

The colonial structure inherited by FRELIMO in 1975 provided extremely adverse material conditions for any projected transition to socialism. Further, the nature of FRELIMO, and the fluidity of Mozambican class structure in the wake of the revolution meant that both the organisation itself, and the state apparatus it came to control, became arenas of struggle for leadership by the various class forces it represented.

FRELIMO enjoyed widespread popular support in Mozambique in the period after the Lisbon coup, but it faced the problem of establishing an effective political presence in areas beyond its immediate control, particularly the major urban areas in the south. In the aftermath of the coup, a number of political parties sprang up to challenge FRELIMO's predominance and claim a stake in any negotiations for independence from Portugal. A right-wing settler-led coup attempt in September 1974 was defeated, but the resulting violence created a climate of uncertainty and panic among white settlers, many of whom fled the country.

Soon after independence most settler-owned farms, factories, shops and other properties were abandoned, often with accompanying sabotage. Large numbers of Portuguese technical, professional and skilled workers left Mozambique. The result was a rapid drop in production levels, loss of export earnings and collapse of the rural distribution network. Food supplies to the cities became an immediate problem.

FRELIMO's response to these multiple crises was to reassert its political primacy and forcibly crush its opposition, many of whom were arrested and sent to reeducation camps. At the same time it began creating structures of popular power — the Dynamising Groups — as a means of mobilising mass support countrywide. These groups succeeded in harnessing popular enthusiasm generated by the collapse of the colonial regime, and secured for FRELIMO a firmer control over the political process. FRELIMO's strategy won it widespread legitimacy and support, and in addition transferred from the liberated zones some of its key ideas on popular organisation and initiative as a method of solving problems.

Social reconstruction

FRELIMO took counter-measures to prevent the slide of the economy into collapse by nationalising abandoned or mismanaged enterprises and those considered to be of strategic importance. There was confusion and struggle at the factory-floor level over the reorganisation of production relations. New notions of worker participation mixed uneasily with more traditional ideas of managerial prerogative. Dynamising Groups were set up in all production units with a view to asserting some order in an increasingly disorganised environment. Production Councils, which came to have a more specifically technical function, were introduced later on. The working class in the cities was not organised, and FRELIMO attempted through these measures to create a stronger working alliance with it.

Many nationalisations were defensive, but some, such as those involving the health service, education, land, housing, the legal profession and funeral parlours, were undertaken with a clear view to beginning the restructuring of social relations and marked real gains for the working population. The nationalisation of the wholesale and retail trade and the creation of state-controlled people's shops was a response to the collapse of the distributive network in rural areas, but it overextended the state and ultimately created more problems than it solved.

Because FRELIMO attached particular weight to gaining and maintaining support in the cities, important agricultural policy decisions were hastily taken early on, and generated intense debate within the party as problems developed. Abandoned settler farms which had supplied the cities were restocked with expensive imported agricultural machinery to replace what had been sabotaged or driven over the border, and large-scale mechanised production on state farms was attempted. After a series of grave technical problems were encountered, FRELIMO decided to give greater emphasis to the creation of peasant farmer cooperatives as a means of socialising agricultural production.

At the village level, FRELIMO embarked on a policy of creating communal villages and concentrating provision of rural services. It was aided in this by floods in the southern provinces in 1976 when displaced people were regrouped as part of FRELIMO's relief work. In the north, FRELIMO used the strategic hamlets created by the Portuguese during the war to further collectivise peasant agriculture. In some areas, like Nampula, peasants took the initiative in creating cooperatives themselves, as a means of increasing output. In the south, unemployment became a major problem as South African mines cut back drastically on the numbers of Mozambicans recruited. In general, the peasant agricultural sector was neglected by FRELIMO in the early period, and the breakdown of the rural distribution network severely hampered efforts to increase peasant production. The early emphasis on large-scale agricultural production further diverted resources from the peasant sector, and ultimately proved costly to FRELIMO in terms of peasant support.

Major advances in social policy were recorded. The nationalised health service was reorganised to decentralise health care in the rural areas, and preventive practices were stressed. Major immunisation programmes were successfully undertaken, and health education and child-care programmes were launched. Taken together, these policies constituted a radical departure from colonial practice.

Similar gains were made in education. The number of school entrants increased greatly in the first years of independence, and a start was made in the creation of an educational system more appropriate to the needs of an independent Mozambique. Large-scale adult literacy programmes were undertaken both to spread literacy and to raise political consciousness. In the cities, nationalisation of rented accommodation and the flight of the settlers provided many Mozambicans with access to habitable accommodation at controlled rates. However, the bureaucracy controlling housing has since become a particular focus of popular discontent because of inefficiency, corruption and nepotism.

By 1977, FRELIMO was well entrenched politically. It had survived the initial crises of the transition period, and had embarked upon a reorganisation of the colonial state apparatus. The state bureaucracy had grown as FRELIMO intervened more directly in the management of the economy. At the same time, many Mozambicans experienced substantial social mobility as they moved into positions vacated by departing settlers. There was also an influx into the party of new, skilled members who had not been directly involved in the liberation struggle.

FRELIMO's Third Congress in 1977 marked the end of the transition period. It declared itself to be a Marxist-Leninist vanguard party leading the alliance of peasants and workers on the road to socialism. The congress emphasised large-scale projects and the development of a heavy industrial base to guarantee economic independence. A process of party structuring was undertaken in order to spread its influence throughout society, and elections were held at the local, provincial and national levels for the People's Assemblies.

The decision in 1976 to close Mozambique's borders with Rhodesia, to impose sanctions and to provide active support for the liberation struggle there proved a heavy burden on an ailing economy. International compensation for revenue lost fell far short of the amount promised, and the war damage to the infrastructure was considerable, while many lives were lost. In addition the Rhodesian Central Intelligence Office created the Mozambican National Resistance (MNR) out of a nucleus of ex-colonial special troops and disaffected FRELIMO guerillas. It infiltrated small units in Manica province, an area which FRELIMO had never effectively controlled, to gather information about the Zimbabwe African National Union (ZANU) and to combat FRELIMO. The MNR presence in Manica and Sofala disrupted economic activity and led to severe hardship for the peasantry exposed to its terror tactics.

By the late 1970s certain trends were evident. Reorganisation of the state apparatus had strengthened a strongly technocratic element within FRELIMO which sought large-scale, capital-intensive, and inevitably bureaucratic solutions to Mozambique's development problems. Political control was increasingly centralised, and tension between the voluntarist or populist line of 'putting trust in the people', and the technocratic thrust with its emphasis on control at all levels, emerged clearly within FRELIMO's policies. This tension was evident in most key areas of policy, and reflected struggles within both FRELIMO and the state apparatus between various class forces and tendencies unleashed by the revolution.

War on all fronts, 1980-1984

FRELIMO's 'offensives'

FRELIMO had high expectations of the 1980s as a decade of rapid development. The difficult transition period was over, its political authority was unchallenged, and production levels had stabilised with the economic recovery in 1978 and 1979. There was general optimism brought about by the end of the war in Zimbabwe and the creation of the SADCC regional economic alliance in 1979. The Ten Year Plan drawn up at the end of the 1970s envisaged an annual growth in GNP of 17%, massive increases in exports, and rapid increase in local import substitution. The plan emphasised large-scale capital-intensive projects, funded by major infusions of foreign capital. The 1980s would see Mozambique's 'Great Leap Forward' out of underdevelopment into socialism.

Against this background, the Organisational and Political Offensive was launched in 1980. It stressed rooting out inefficiency, indiscipline, laziness and corruption, and it emphasised hierarchy, discipline and productivity. At the same time the state executed a strategic withdrawal from a range of small businesses in which it had intervened, and invited black Mozambicans who had gone abroad to start businesses during the colonial period to return with their capital and skills.

Heralded by some commentators as a swing towards capitalism, these moves marked important shifts in the balance of class forces. The stress on hierarchy signalled the growing influence within FRELIMO and the state apparatus of the technocratic stratum whose skills were desperately needed after the Portuguese exodus. FRELIMO's principles of democratic participation and control, developed in the liberation struggle, were discounted during this phase as power became concentrated in technocrats' hands.

Moves back to privatisation increased the influence of commercial capital, which had survived state-imposed restrictions immediately after independence largely by resorting to illegal and speculative activities. An increasing proportion of trade was conducted through the black market where vast profits could be made. These profits were then reinvested in agriculture or fishing both as cover and as further means of illegal trading.

Technocratic and commercial interests developed a complex and contradictory relationship which reflected a transformed and reconstructed version of the former colonial ruling alliance between commercial capital and the bureaucratic class. The state's increased intervention in the economy meant a closer working relationship between them, and neither saw its interests as lying in worker and peasant control of the new state.

However, the economic recovery did not last, and the early 1980s saw a rapidly developing foreign exchange crisis leading to cuts in imported raw materials and spare parts, and a drop in overall production. This, coupled with the shortfall in projected investment levels, effectively aborted the Ten Year Plan.

FRELIMO's failure to develop an appropriate agricultural policy also began to be seriously felt in the 1980s. State farms which had been given priority in 1977 continued to run at an enormous loss. The cooperative movement stagnated through insufficient state support. The peasant family sector, crucially dependent on the market for both sale of its surplus and access to the means of production and basic consumer goods, entered a crisis with the collapse of trading networks and the failure of the state to give the sector support. Lack of basic goods led to a dramatic drop in peasant surplus production, affecting both export crops like cashew nuts and food crops like maize, cassava and beans. Under these circumstances, the black market grew very rapidly, to the point where the state lost control over the networks of trade.

The Legality Campaign launched in 1981 was a symptom of increasing abuse of power by members of the security and defence state apparatus. It aimed at curbing the growing incidence of wrongful arrests, brutality and corruption which threatened to undermine FRELIMO's popular support. Security and defence apparatuses had been rapidly expanded in the post-independence period, weakening FRELIMO's political control over them. They were also said to have been infiltrated by 'the enemy', and an appeal was made to the people to report abuses and thus dislodge offenders from the state apparatus.

SADCC and destabilisation

The creation of the SADCC economic alliance in 1979 by the Frontline States to reduce members' dependence on South Africa and promote economic cooperation between Southern African states placed Mozambique in a key position. Transport and telecommunications were given priority and the headquarters of the regional commission, the Southern African Transport and Telecommunications Coordinating Committee (SATTCC), was located in Maputo. It was envisaged that Zimbabwe's independence would mark the real start of a process of progressively redirecting Southern Africa's trade routes through Zimbabwe and Mozambique, thereby reducing the vulnerability of the region to South Africa's plans for a constellation of states which it would dominate.

Following ZANU's election victory in Zimbabwe, the South African Defence Force took over the MNR operation which had been run from Salisbury and relocated it in the Transvaal. The MNR's main base in the Gorongosa mountains was captured and its units dispersed in a combined operation by Zimbabwe and Mozambique in 1980. It seemed for a while that the MNR would not recover from the blow. However, under South African control the MNR was reorganised, rearmed and used as a weapon against Mozambique in a new aggressive strategy of destabilisation.

MNR activities spread in 1981 and 1982 to Tete, Inhambane and Gaza, whilst another group calling itself Africa Livre, comprising remnants of COREMO, a rival splinter group of FRELIMO, began operations in Zambezia from bases in Malawi.

The SADF used the 'armed bandits' to sabotage strategic infrastructure vital to SADCC, such as road and rail transport routes from Mozambique to Zimbabwe, bridges, electricity pylons from Cahora Bassa, the oil pipeline from Beira to Mutare, and Beira's port installations and navigational equipment. A more general strategy was to disrupt production in the countryside and to attack and terrorise the civilian population. In some areas the colonial chiefs were reinstated and whole villages fell under MNR for periods of time.

By 1982 it was clear that FRELIMO's army, the Popular Forces for the Liberation of Mozambique (FPLM), had failed to contain the rapid spread of the MNR. Evidently FPLM commanders, many of whom were newly-trained graduates of the Nampula military academy which taught conventional warfare, were unable to apply the lessons learned by FRELIMO in its ten-year guerilla struggle against colonialism.

Some of FRELIMO's most senior Politburo members were sent to take personal administrative charge of the provinces most affected by MNR activities. Popular militias were trained and armed for self-defence in a shift towards recreating the people's army that had been demobilised and replaced with a professional army after independence. FRELIMO veterans who had become marginalised after independence through lack of formal education were incorporated into the expanding army. In a series of meetings in 1982 with FRELIMO veterans, with religious leaders, and with 'the Compromised' — those deemed to have collaborated with the colonial state's repressive apparatus — Machel attempted to

broaden FRELIMO's base of support and appealed for national
unity in the face of growing disruption caused by the MNR.

The MNR's spread was contained in 1982, but at the cost of
diversion into the military of key personnel and resources which
Mozambique could ill afford. At the same time, the treatment by
FRELIMO of the peasant population in some of the affected areas
was reminiscent of colonial practice, and served to alienate further
vital support. The conduct of the war against the MNR threw into
sharp relief FRELIMO's policy towards the peasantry as the foundation of its revolutionary alliance, and it became clear that
FRELIMO had lost its base in many areas.

FRELIMO's Fourth Congress

FRELIMO held its Fourth Congress in April 1983, against the
background of the war with the MNR, an increasingly belligerent
South African neighbour, widespread economic disruption and
shortages of basic consumer goods, a burgeoning black market and
the worst drought in living memory which affected large areas of
Mozambique. The congress was an impressive display of
FRELIMO's mobilising capacities, and was preceded by many
months of careful preparatory organisational work aimed at widening and strengthening the party's base, and structuring debate
around key areas of social and economic policy.

The proceedings saw many criticisms from militants at the local
level about the impact of FRELIMO's policies on the rural areas.
The result was a move away from the stress on large projects and a
shift towards local, small-scale initiatives, although there was intense debate as to whether the new policy was a short-term tactical
expedient or a long-term strategic change. FRELIMO also enlarged
its central committee and incorporated many of its most articulate
critics, thereby giving greater weight to peasant and worker
interests.

The congress provided a vehicle for articulation of worker and
peasant demands, and this altered the balance of class forces within
FRELIMO to some extent. But such demands had then to be
translated into policy and implemented through the state apparatus, where there was considerable resistance from technocrats.
What was at issue, in fact, was the relationship between the party
and the state.

Following the congress, a government reshuffle sent two proponents of large projects to Sofala and Zambezia, in line with the directive to decentralise planning to the district level. Technical experts were also ordered out of their offices in Maputo and sent to the countryside. A new minister of agriculture, the fourth in five years, was appointed to head a bureaucracy still dominated by technocrats favouring large-scale projects. There was also an attempt to create a greater separation of party and state and to increase control of the former over the latter.

Hard times, harsh measures

Before the congress, FRELIMO declared war on the black market and introduced stringent penalties for infringements, including public flogging. The death penalty was reintroduced, and public executions of captured MNR men took place. From July to September, Operation Production screened people's documents, and deported thousands of Mozambicans from the cities back to the countryside. The government argued that food supplies and services in the cities were in a critical state and could not sustain thousands of unproductive marginals. It argued that there was an urgent need to reorganise rural production and to open up new underpopulated areas, especially in Niassa and Cabo Delgado.

The new measures to control *candonga* (black market trading) and deport the unemployed met with popular support initially, and investigative procedures were clearly laid down. However, widespread abuses became common. People were flogged for vague reasons, like showing lack of respect, or for minor black market offences, while large-scale operators went unchecked. In Operation Production people were shipped off without due process, families were split up and in many cases the receiving areas had been inadequately prepared.

All this generated a climate of fear and popular resentment. People began comparing FRELIMO's actions with the sjamboks and pass laws of South Africa. When the extent of the irregularities and illegalities committed in carrying out Operation Production became known, the FRELIMO central committee debated the issue and decided the operation could continue only if new safeguards guaranteeing the rights of citizens were introduced. FRELIMO's policies were emergency measures taken in response to crises which

had their origins in the rural areas. The shortages of basic consumer goods in the cities was intimately linked with agricultural
policy, as was the influx of people into the cities. The war, and the
severe drought which struck Inhambane, Gaza and Maputo in
1981, served to exacerbate the situation to crisis proportions.
FRELIMO's handling of the crises further undermined its popular
support.

In October 1983 the Organisation of Mozambican Workers was
created as a national trade union organisation under the control of
the party. 'Socialist trade unions' were conceived of as a force for
disciplining the working class and creating greater productivity in
the national interest, rather than as instruments of confrontation.
FRELIMO failed to mobilise the working class to restructure social
relations of production, and its policy towards workers remains
contradictory. It provided substantial material gains through
minimum wage legislation, social benefits, food subsidies and ration-
ing to guarantee basic minimum supplies. But the working class has
also borne the brunt of harsh laws on economic sabotage. Workers
from the ports and railways, traditionally militant, were the first to
be executed and flogged in 1983 for economic crimes.

Narrowing options

By the end of 1983 it was clear that the new policy directions taken
at the Fourth Congress had come too late to save FRELIMO from
some painful choices. The effects on Mozambique of South
Africa's undeclared war, natural disasters, the international recession
and what FRELIMO called the 'mistakes and failings of inexperienced managers and administrators' had produced a virtual
state of economic collapse. Tens of thousands of people starved to
death in Gaza and Inhambane because the worst-hit areas were
controlled by MNR, and the SADF ensured that the MNR was well
equipped to disrupt relief efforts.

Further, the provision of international relief aid was politicised
by the war, and donors who saw the US policy of 'constructive
engagement' as tacit approval for destabilisation were reluctant to
intervene, refusing requests from Mozambique to press South
Africa to allow relief columns in. However, Machel's European
trip in October 1983 succeeded in convincing Western governments
that Mozambique was pursuing 'genuine non-alignment' and food

aid was more forthcoming thereafter.

The Mozambican government, for its part, attempted to conceal the MNR's role in the problem when it first appealed to diplomats for aid, thus underplaying the seriousness of the situation. Indeed, its own communication channels had broken down and it took two months for Maputo to grasp the enormity of what was happening in Inhambane. A similar failure occurred in Tete, where drought killed thousands. Uncounted people starved in MNR-controlled areas; estimates of total deaths range between 30 000 and 100 000. In Maputo province the worst drought in memory ended in floods caused by Cyclone Domoina in January 1984, in which an estimated 350 000 people had their crops washed away and 50 000 were rendered homeless and destitute.

In January 1984 the Council of Ministers asked Mozambique's creditors to reschedule its debts, in what amounted to a declaration of national bankruptcy. The government circulated a document in which economic statistics were published for the first time in several years, and detailed the costs to Mozambique of war and national disasters.

FRELIMO had been aware for some time that the Mozambican economy could not withstand the damage caused by SADF-controlled MNR activity, and had been trying from mid-1982 to convince the United States and European governments to pressure South Africa to end destabilisation, but without much success. Inconclusive meetings with South Africa were held in December 1982 and May 1983. These left FRELIMO feeling that the South Africans were not negotiating seriously. Machel was able to convince European leaders of this during his October tour, but was unsuccessful in his objective of raising capital to help salvage the economy. The refusal of loans by European governments effectively precipitated Mozambique's declaration of bankruptcy, and it was clearly understood that an agreement with South Africa was a precondition for renegotiation of its foreign debts.

Nkomati and beyond: what price for peace?

The Nkomati Accord

The 'Agreement on Non-Aggression and Good Neighbourliness between Mozambique and South Africa' signed at an extravagant ceremony in March 1984 was the result of strategic bargaining on both sides. FRELIMO had succeeded in containing the MNR in late 1983 through a major military offensive, and calculated that an agreement with South Africa, coupled with a renegotiation of its debts, would provide the space it needed to revive the economy and rebuild its support base. A settlement had a certain attraction for South Africa, given its domestic recession and mounting defence budget. Western diplomatic pressure to cease military destabilisation and the interest of local and international capital in a stable and peaceful Southern Africa were additional factors. A further incentive was the prospect of translating its military dominance of the region into economic gains.

At discussions in Mbabane in December 1983, preconditions set by both sides were agreed. Mozambique refused to take action which could imply recognition of the bantustans. It insisted on maintaining diplomatic and political support for the ANC and it demanded that SA cease support for the MNR. The SA government called for a curb on ANC activities and demanded parallel talks on trade and investment, energy and tourism.

The key to the agreement was section three of the document, in which both parties agreed not to allow their territories to be used as a base or thoroughfare by other states, governments, foreign forces, organisations or individuals planning to commit hostile acts.

Both parties portrayed the agreement as a victory for their respective policies. In Mozambique rallies were held to celebrate another victory in the 'socialist policy of peace', but no debate was allowed amid the orchestrated approval. Mozambican commentators saw the Accord as a defeat for imperialism's regional strategy aimed at the destruction of the independent and progressive states in Southern Africa, and a failure of South Africa's military strategy aimed at overthrowing FRELIMO and diverting Mozambique from the path of socialism.

South African commentators saw the Accord as signalling that country's emergence as a fully-fleged sub-imperial power in the region. The Accord would be a potential vehicle for consolidation of regional economic and political dominance, and could provide access to markets not only in Southern Africa but further afield. The Accord would deny guerillas access to South Africa from Mozambique, and would allow political space for the internal 'reform' process to accelerate. The Accord was hailed as a major diplomatic breakthrough in South Africa's international rehabilitation. Ideologically, the Accord was held to provide the opening within which the superiority of capitalism and the bankruptcy of the socialist path to development could be amply demonstrated to the peoples of the region.

The ANC-in-exile was placed on the defensive both politically and militarily. Although FRELIMO had never provided the ANC with the full backing it gave ZANU, and had not allowed the creation of bases, it had recognised the ANC as the sole legitimate representative of the South African people, and had accorded the movement substantial diplomatic support. With the ANC's revival after 1976, and the intensification of the armed struggle by Umkhonto we Sizwe, Mozambique became a main point of departure for cadres heading for South Africa via Swaziland. FRELIMO's commitment to the ANC increased as the struggle developed in South Africa, reaching a high point in 1982 when the Frontline States promised to increase support for what now was termed a national liberation struggle from internal colonialism.

Destabilisation and the direct attacks on Maputo launched in January 1981 and May 1983 made it clear that the South African state was simply too powerful to be overthrown by military means alone, and the ANC was warned in late 1982 that FRELIMO would have to negotiate with South Africa and would be compelled to restrict the ANC's activities.

The relationship cooled very rapidly thereafter, and FRELIMO returned to its earlier line on the ANC — that apartheid is an internal problem and that the ANC is fighting an internal revolution. The ANC leadership was caught unprepared for the effects of the Nkomati Accord, despite Mozambique's warning, and reacted angrily to its new situation, denigrating FRELIMO for having negotiated with South Africa. FRELIMO for its part was critical of the ANC's failure to develop an adequate strategy for internal mobilisation against apartheid and for its over-reliance on a guerilla struggle.

FRELIMO was also critical of disinterest shown towards the Mozambican revolution by ANC members in exile, with a few very notable exceptions. Few members of the ANC had bothered to learn Portuguese or to keep themselves informed about major social issues in Mozambique. The arrogance of some ANC members offended FRELIMO, especially when they argued that Mozambique would never be truly liberated until South Africa was free, and that therefore the Mozambican revolution should be subordinated to the South African one. The passage of time since the Accord, its failure to end MNR activities and the growth of a militant internal challenge to the South African state may all have served to restore better relations between the ANC and FRELIMO.

The leaders of the Frontline States met at Arusha in April 1984 to consider the agreements reached by both Angola and Mozambique with South Africa and reaffirmed their understanding of the difficult circumstances which had led FRELIMO to sign the Accord. They also expressed the hope that the South African government would honour its commitment to stop destabilising Mozambique through the use of armed bandits. The heads of state used the occasion to reiterate their preference for a peaceful end to apartheid, to be achieved through free discussion between the South African regime and genuine representatives of the people of South Africa at present unrepresented in any government structure. The alternative to free negotiations within South Africa would inevitably be continued struggle against apartheid by other means, including violence.

Nkomati and the economy

The Mozambique government has placed heavy emphasis on obtaining capital investment from the West and South Africa since Nkomati, a trend likely to strengthen the hands of the technocrats and large project protagonists — the 'aspirants to the bourgeoisie' within the party and the state apparatus. In August 1984, a new Law on Foreign Investment was passed which guarantees security and legal protection to foreign investments, provides for tax exemptions for between two and ten years for certain types of business, and guarantees the transfer abroad of exportable profits. 'Free Zones' near ports and harbours have also been created where production can take place with a minimal tax burden.

In October 1984 the Organisation for Economic Cooperation and Development (OECD) agreed to reschedule some of Mozambique's debts to its members. This was interpreted as a clear sign that Mozambique's shift to the West was satisfactory to leading OECD members. In December, Mozambique officially signed the Lome Convention, which provides more or less free trade access to the European Economic Community. Mozambique thereby gains access to Lome aid and Stabex — a price stabilisation scheme covering a range of agricultural products. Mozambique has also joined the International Monetary Fund and the World Bank.

Since Nkomati, the Reagan administration has taken Mozambique off its blacklist and United States Agency for International Development (USAID) teams have investigated the possibility of providing aid to Mozambique via Portugal. The US administration has promised to step up aid, but is insisting on involvement of conservative American non-governmental agencies in its programmes.

Despite the obvious enthusiasm for the Accord in the South African business community, investors are not flocking to Mozambique in great numbers. Continuing uncertainty over the security situation and attacks on businessmen have acted as a deterrent to some extent. The main areas of interest have been tourism, agriculture and fishing. The South African Foreign Trade Organisation has been active in assessing and promoting the possibilities for South African investment in Mozambique — several visits by delegations took place soon after the Mozambican Reserve Bank governor outlined Mozambique's priorities for investment in agriculture, livestock, forestry, coal mining, oil, fisheries and tourism.

The South African Transport Services signed an important agreement with Mozambique in August 1984 to reestablish Maputo harbour as 'the Transvaal's natural gateway for imports and exports'. The agreement formed the basis of a plan which included a loan of R10-million to develop transport services, the repair of diesel locomotives in SA, assistance in running the Nkomati-Maputo railway line and the possibility of managerial and physical assistance for two of Mozambique's main marshalling yards, as well as extending cooperation between SA Airways and Linhas Areas de Mozambique.

With the disastrously evident failure of its agricultural policies, FRELIMO has turned to capitalist agriculture to take over some of the state farms. Eastern Transvaal lowveld farmers, whose labour supplies from Mozambique have been regularised since Nkomati, are interested in leasing farms on a commercial basis in Mozambique. In May 1985 the multinational Lonrho signed an agreement to invest in agriculture, tourism, mining, commerce and sugar production which made 'the unacceptable face of capitalism' Mozambique's largest foreign investor. The former CAIL, the Limpopo Agro-Industrial Complex — Mozambique's largest state farm in the Limpopo Valley — was on Lonrho's shopping list, and it is to establish a 3 000 hectare commercial enterprise with part of it.

Taken together, the shifts in economic policy since Nkomati are substantial, and will further redefine the relationship between various classes in Mozambique. The enlarged central committee elected at the Fourth Congress with greater peasant and worker representation did not meet for a year thereafter, and was not involved in the Nkomati Accord or in economic policy changes. The popular thrust of the Fourth Congress has been effectively buried for the time being.

War and politics: the looting continues

Since Nkomati, there has been an escalation of armed conflict with the MNR as it moved into Maputo province, isolating the capital by making access by road and rail from Swaziland and South Africa hazardous and disrupting power supplies. Some of FRELIMO's leaders argued that the South African government had never intended to honour the Accord, that it was simply a device to gain political leverage on Mozambique in order to displace or overthrow the government. Others were inclined to give South African president PW Botha the benefit of the doubt, claiming that he was not in control of elements within the armed forces who continued to give support to the MNR.

By August 1984 the Accord was under strain. FRELIMO had evidence that the MNR had been extensively resupplied and that 1 500 heavily armed men had been infiltrated into Maputo province while negotations prior to the Accord were in progress. Further evidence of supply drops and sea landings around Inhambane lent weight to the view that the South Africans had negotiated in bad faith.

Machel was increasingly hard pressed to defend the Accord in the face of growing disenchantment with its lack of results. A crisis point was reached in September 1984, when the Joint Security Commission set up under the Accord met in Pretoria. FRELIMO pressed for direct South African action against the MNR, while the South Africans attempted to initiate direct talks with an MNR delegation which was conveniently on hand.

Evidently there is a division within the South African state between interests represented by the Department of Foreign Affairs on the one hand and that of Defence on the other concerning stategy for neutralising whatever long-term threat FRELIMO is held to pose to the South African state. The MNR's handlers in South African Military Intelligence seem reluctant to allow their weapon to be disarmed, and maintain an interest in using it to cause maximum disruption in 'Marxist Mozambique'. Foreign Affairs practitioners, with their greater sensitivity to the international diplomatic and business environment, probably regard Machel's continued leadership of Mozambique as a stabilising factor in an increasingly unstable situation where the MNR does not constitute a viable alternative ruling force.

Between September and October 1984 intensive negotiations aimed at salvaging the Accord from collapse resulted in a South African declaration which acknowledged Machel as president of Mozambique and stressed that armed activity from 'whatever quarter' had to stop. The declaration was interpreted by South Africa as a ceasefire between the MNR and FRELIMO, neither of whom saw it that way.

Continuation of the war and the emergence of the MNR from the political shadows since Nkomati can be attributed to a successful shift in its strategic emphasis. This has seen the organisation of alternative supply routes, bases and training facilities — notably in Malawi — which make it less dependent on South Africa. The MNR's political connections in Europe have become increasingly evident, and the role played by former Portuguese colonial and *retornado* interests has become much more prominent. The MNR demands a role in the government of Mozambique whilst FRELIMO is not prepared to offer more than an amnesty to ex-combatants.

FRELIMO's refusal to make political concessions is based on its analysis of the MNR as an externally-led and financed movement with no political footing inside Mozambique. FRELIMO's strategy has been to stress the unacceptable nature of the external interests backing the MNR and to point to its *retornado* leadership. At the same time, it has attempted to persuade rank-and-file members in Mozambique that their best interests lie in reintegration within

Mozambican society rather than in the service of external neo-colonial forces.

Since the collapse of the South African attempt to open direct talks between FRELIMO and MNR, South Africa has taken some steps designed to gain credibility for its claim to have distanced itself from the latter. In March 1985 a Mafia-type crime syndicate supplying arms and finance to the MNR was 'uncovered', and the SADF took action against MNR sympathisers within its ranks — after FRELIMO supplied their names. The SADF has also declared the SA-Mozambique border area in the Eastern Transvaal a special restricted air space.

Recent information has emerged to provide more specific evidence of the nature and extent of South Africa's continuing support for the MNR. A diary written by the secretary of the MNR leader in Mozambique was found at its main base at Gorongosa when this was taken by FRELIMO in September 1985. Diary entries indicated that MNR leaders had been transported to and from South Africa by the South African Navy, and that there had been secret visits to the main MNR base by the South African Deputy Minister of Foreign Affairs. The diary also confirmed earlier FRELIMO allegations that SADF supply drops to the MNR had continued uninterrupted despite the signing of the Accord. All this supported speculation as to the rift between the SADF on the one hand and the Department of Foreign Affairs on the other, as a result of their differing policies towards the MNR.

South Africa's admission of continued support for the MNR in the eighteen months after the signing of the Accord is a further blow to its credibility. But it is no guarantee that South African politicians have the will or the means to halt the SADF's support for the MNR. Nor, despite South African violations, is FRELIMO likely to repudiate the Nkomati Accord. Important members of FRELIMO's leadership have too much political capital invested in it to be able to dispense with it. Rather, such elements are trying to use instances of its evident failure in order to mobilise international diplomatic pressure on South Africa.

In parallel with the continued war there has been an intensified struggle within FRELIMO and key organs of the state. In June 1984 two members of the Politburo were relieved of their posts as Ministers of the Interior and of Security, following criticism of widespread abuse of power by police, militias and the army. The situation had reached crisis proportions in Nampula in 1983, where forced villagisation and hut-burning had created widespread alienation, a precondition for the MNR to move into the province from Zambezia with no resistance from the local peasants. In addition, militia members had taken to robbing civilians, and there were reports of government soldiers attacking and robbing a train, claiming to be MNR.

The 'legality' issue and the conduct of the struggle against the MNR remain key factors in FRELIMO's winning or losing support. At issue is the relationship of the people to the state, and control over political power. The military apparatus is central to any power struggle, and the loyalty of its key personnel is vital. The army is now effectively divided between a professional army which emphasises modern conventional warfare, and the revived 'people's army' which has been expanded to meet the growing military crisis. Each of these wings represents to some extent the struggle being waged at various levels over the two lines now contained within FRELIMO.

The Agriculture Ministry has also been the site of intense debates since the Fourth Congress; a public campaign was launched by civil servants in Maputo in 1983 for the dismissal of the Minister. Planning policy and the failure of the Ten Year Plan have also been publicly criticised from within the planning ministry, indicating that FRELIMO's consensus style of leadership at the top level is under strain.

FRELIMO's response to the continuing war has been a 'war economy'. In April 1985 special measures were announced to increase agricultural production and to intensify the struggle against the MNR. No mention was made of the Nkomati Accord, which some observers read as an indication that it is no longer seen as the main factor in the combat against the MNR inside Mozambique, and that all FRELIMO expects from South Africa is that it should prevent aid to the MNR from its territory. Mozambique has been assured of military support from both Zimbabwe and Tanzania should the war escalate further, and was promised a base in Tanzania should FRELIMO be forced to abandon the capital.

When he spoke at the parade on 25 June 1985 marking the tenth anniversary of independence from Portugal, Machel's public optimism for the future was undiminished: 'Our country will be the grave of capitalism and exploitation', he said, and added, 'There is no force capable of bringing down the People's Republic of Mozambique, from whatever corner'.

Conclusion

Ten years after independence, Mozambique is in a state of crisis brought about by a combination of war and massive destabilisation, drought and natural disasters, as well as fundamental policy and planning errors. Any one of these factors on its own would have caused considerable damage and hardship, but taken together they have been catastrophic in their effects on FRELIMO's attempts at social reconstruction since it took power.

Mozambique's social capital at independence, in terms of its economic resources and level of skills and training, was meagre — the product of Portuguese colonialism. However, FRELIMO was able to tap vast resources of popular energy and initiative in the heady atmosphere following the collapse of the colonial regime. Much of this reserve has now been dissipated, to the point where it requires a man of Machel's courage to admit, as he did in Nampula in May 1984, that 'in all our cities, the police now act worse than the colonial police'.

That this should be so does not vindicate colonialism and its policies. Rather it is a profound comment on what can happen in an attempted transition to socialism in a society with a low level of productive forces, following a national democratic revolution led by a popular class alliance like FRELIMO.

The policy 'errors' that have helped to cripple Mozambique's economy, demobilise popular initiative, threaten FRELIMO's legitimacy and generate recruits for the MNR are the outcome of struggles within the party and the state apparatus waged for control over those organs of power.

In the absence of independent and democratic forms of organisation, the interests of the peasantry and the working class in Mozambique have been articulated by a party which speaks and acts 'on their behalf', but which is itself a site of struggle for leadership and control by contending classes contained within it.

The colonial state apparatus inherited by FRELIMO was only partially transformed, and the close links developed between party and state created the conditions in which the state, rather than being controlled by the party, came to exercise important influence within it.

FRELIMO's neglect of the peasantry has undermined its social base, reduced the country's ability to feed itself and hampered the creation of strong self-sufficient democratic communities, thereby rendering the countryside vulnerable to destabilisation. Social relations of production in the urban areas have been incompletely transformed. Early attempts at self-management by a small and disorganised working class were abandoned in favour of managerial control, which has now been supplemented by a party-controlled trade union structure.

FRELIMO's attempt to conquer underdevelopment within a decade through large projects modelled on the Eastern European experience has been a costly experiment in a situation where there may not be any second chance. It is not likely that the World Bank, the IMF, the EEC, USAID, the West or South Africa will adopt a benevolent attitude towards policies aimed at the reconstruction of socialism in Mozambique.

Real gains in social welfare, health and education are now under threat by the financial stringency measures Mozambique's creditors are likely to demand as a precondition for their aid in its economic rehabilitation. Nor is it likely that 'people's power' as a foundation for reconstruction will be encouraged by those internal class forces which stand to gain from socialism's burial.

The years of war and struggle have shown that 'the alternative civilisation' FRELIMO set out to build in Mozambique remains an elusive goal which is today endangered not only by external attacks but by forces and circumstances inside Mozambique itself.

Bibliography

Books

R First, *Black Gold: The Mozambican Miner, Proletarian and Peasant* (Harvester, Sussex, 1983).

FRELIMO, *Out of Underdevelopment to Socialism* (INLD, Maputo, 1983).
— *Building Socialism: The People's Answer* (INLD, Maputo, 1983).
— *FRELIMO Party Programme and Statutes* (INLD, Maputo, 1983).

J Hanlon, *Mozambique: The Revolution Under Fire* (Zed, London, 1984).

Mozambique: Seminar Proceedings (Centre of African Studies, Edinburgh University, 1979).

B Munslow, *Mozambique: The Revolution and its Origins* (Longman, London, 1983).

C Searle, *We're Building a New School* (Zed, London, 1981).

P Sketchley and FM Lappe, *Casting New Moulds* (Institute for Food and Development Policy, San Francisco, 1980).

JE Torp, *Industrial Planning and Development in Mozambique* (Scandinavian Institute of African Studies, Uppsala, 1979).

G Walt and A Melamed, *Mozambique: Towards a Peoples' Health Service* (Zed, London, 1984).

Periodicals

Africa Confidential (London)
Africa Research Bulletin (London)
AIM Monthly Bulletin (Maputo)
Mozambican Studies (Maputo)
Financial Mail (Johannesburg)
Tempo (Maputo)

Newspapers

Daily News (Durban)
Diario de Mozambique (Maputo)
Natal Mercury (Durban)
Noticias da Beira (Beira)
Rand Daily Mail (Johannesburg)
Weekly Mail (Johannesburg)

Namibia: A Future Displaced

Max du Preez

Seven years after all relevant parties formally accepted the Western Contact Group's independence plan for Namibia as embodied in UN Security Council Resolution 435, Africa's last colony does not seem any closer to that consummation. But there were several developments in 1984-85 that could seriously affect the pre-independence process, as well as the quality of eventual independence.

The first obvious but underrated development was the dramatic shift in focus of the international spotlight, from the Namibian independence struggle and the colonial power's refusal to let go, to South Africa's internal policy of apartheid and the violence it is generating.

The year 1985 was the twenty-fifth anniversary of SWAPO, but also the year of its most severe crisis. It became very clear that SWAPO's military wing, the People's Liberation Army of Namibia (PLAN), is past its peak and will probably never again be the formidable force it was in the late 1970s. This has serious implications for SWAPO's strategy that do not seem to be fully appreciated at Provisional Headquarters in Luanda.

But SWAPO has a bigger enemy: unprecedented apathy from the Namibian masses. SWAPO is suddenly faced with the harsh reality that time is *not* on its side despite what the books on revolutionary warfare say.

Adding to its headaches is the fact that the anti-SWAPO forces inside the territory succeeded in consolidating to form the Multi-Party Conference (MPC). Pretoria tried hard not to look pleased, and in June 1985 gave full governing powers (short of Defence and Foreign Affairs) to the MPC's 'transitional government of national unity'.

Granting self-government coincided with a new, aggressive regional policy by South Africa. The carrot of Nkomati-type benevolence after the stick of destabilisation was evidently becoming less attractive to Southern African states, so — more stick. The commando raids on Cabinda and Gaborone, and the Operation Treurwilger raid into Angola early in July are ample proof that Pretoria has fallen back on destabilisation, albeit on a more limited scale. Namibia certainly cannot escape the effects of this new policy.

Sudden deterioration in US-South African relations, despite the fact that a lot of it is probably public posturing, and the virtual breakdown in communication between Luanda and Pretoria after South Africa's blatant disregard for the Lusaka Agreement in attacking Cabinda, are other important factors that could influence Namibia's immediate future.

The Namibian internal situation remains as complex as ever, but at least the confusing days of 44 political parties are over: there are now only two significant political forces in the territory, namely SWAPO and the MPC.

SWAPO

SWAPO celebrated its twenty-fifth anniversay on 19 April 1985. But there was not much more to celebrate. Its armed struggle has been reduced to little more than an occasional small attack on a military base, acts of sabotage in Owambo and laying landmines on roads used mainly by the security forces. The annual high-profile rainy-season infiltrations into white commercial farming areas in the north have failed for three years now. In short, PLAN's main effect is to keep the South African Defence Force (SADF) and its surrogate force in Namibia, the SWA Territory Force (SWATF), present in large numbers in the northern war zone, and thereby cost South Africa a good deal of money.

There are several reasons for PLAN's weak position: South Africa's repeated raids into Angola ending with Operation Askari in December 1983 and starting again with Operation Treurwilger in July 1985; implementation of the February 1984 Lusaka Agreement between Pretoria and Luanda on the establishment of a Joint Monitoring Commission (JMC) and the phased withdrawal of

South African troops from Angola; the ruthless tactics of the notorious special police unit in Owambo, Koevoet; and the fact that about one-third of PLAN guerillas must fight with the MPLA's army, FAPLA, to contain the South African-backed UNITA rebels in central Angola.

As in most wars, truth is the first casualty. SWAPO still claims glamorous victories over the 'racist occupationist' forces, and the SADF counters that SWAPO's military back has been broken (for the umpteenth time).

On 18 June 1985, the officer commanding of the SWATF, General George Meiring, gave one of the fullest military briefings ever to foreign correspondents in Windhoek. According to him, there were no SWAPO guerillas left in the north-western area of Kaokoveld, and 'very few' in the north-eastern area of Kavango. There were an average of about 170 guerillas on any given day inside Owambo. In 1978, PLAN was 16 000 strong, but by early 1985 only 8 500 were left. Of these, only about 1 500 are used in the war against South Africa, while 3 400 are used to fight UNITA with FAPLA 'to pay for their stay in Angola'.

The security forces, said Meiring, are getting more and more information from the local population in Owambo on PLAN's movements and operations. In 1983, he said, the security forces lifted 70 landmines, in 1984 they lifted 111 and this increased to 216 in the period between January and May 1985.

Meiring said that 61% of all the soldiers in the Namibian war zone were Namibian members of the SWATF and they were almost all black. He gave the SWATF troop strength as 21 000, and said there were only between 6 000 and 7 000 South African troops deployed in Namibia. He believed that three or four battalions of UNITA guerillas had moved into the area in southern Angola cleared by the JMC. A battalion consists of 600 to 800 men.

Namibian Secretary for Finance Johan Jones said at the briefing that the Namibian war effort was costing South Africa in the region of R1-m per day and the Namibian authorities between R70-m and R80-m per year.

Meiring announced boldly: 'We are in the process of winning this war'.

There is another side to the story, obviously, although SWAPO rarely gives detailed information on its war effort. SWAPO president Sam Nujoma, in an interview with the author in Lusaka on SWAPO's twenty-fifth anniversary, reacted to statements like Meiring's:

> The war of liberation will continue as long as an inch of Namibia is occupied. Those racist South African soldiers simply failed to destroy SWAPO. They invaded Angola on several occasions, came back after the massacre of civilian refugees at Cassinga in 1978 and claimed to have broken SWAPO's backbone. And again after major invasions like Operations Protea, Smokeshell, Daisy and Iron Fist — all meant to destroy SWAPO. They all failed and they will fail in future to destroy SWAPO.
>
> SWAPO will live, and SWAPO will get stronger and stronger. They will feel the pinch of our bullets. We will raise the cost in terms of lives of South African soldiers and their mercenaries and in terms of money. They will have to continue to buy more jet fighters and helicopters and tanks. SWAPO is deeply rooted in the Namibian masses. We have been fighting for 19 years and the people are still with us. We will fight another 19 years to free Namibia. We will never surrender.

SWAPO's acting president inside Namibia, Nathaniel Mahuilili, was even more to the point when the author asked him during an interview in March 1985 in Walvis Bay about South African claims to be winning the war:

> If that is true, why must you now suddenly have a pass to go to the north? And why are all male Namibians now suddenly forced to join the South African Army? To fight the baboons? They fool no-one. We are prepared to suffer and we are prepared to die. And we will fight for our freedom until the day South Africa comes and says they want genuine freedom and Resolution 435. Then we will give them more peace than they require.

The political front is far more complex. It has become almost impossible to make a reliable assessment of how strong SWAPO's support really is. The best one can do is to look at some pointers.

Over the last few years SWAPO's once dense internal organisation has deteriorated to a few faithfuls holding positions that do not really mean much. The organisation had been crippled by repeated raids on its Windhoek offices, detentions of the internal leaders, and a ban on meetings of any organisation that 'supports violence as a political method'.

More: until 1984 the external leadership had virtually no contact with the internal leadership or the people themselves — and not only practical problems like passports and communication were to blame. Communication has improved slightly since the Lusaka Conference on Namibia in 1984, where most members of the internal SWAPO delegation met Nujoma for the first time.

The problem seems to be one that is not uncommon with other liberation movements: an external leadership may become so involved in fighting the diplomatic battle, addressing conferences and seminars and establishing itself in host countries that it loses track of the harsh realities back home. This is certainly true of some of SWAPO's top leaders, most of whom have been in exile for 15 years or more. The fact that SWAPO has never seriously been challenged in terms of mass support and was declared by the United Nations to be the 'sole and authentic representative of the Namibian people' probably contributed to this attitude.

Some internal leaders, especially the old guard like acting president Mahuilili and vice-president Hendrik Witbooi who have each built vast unwavering constituencies, feel the external leadership believes it is superior to internal leaders, while the men and women inside the country are the ones that really suffer.

In fact, the cream of the SWAPO leadership *is* outside. There are inside Namibia bright young men like deputy national chairman Daniel Tjongarero and secretary for foreign affairs Nick Bessinger, but they are members of Windhoek's black urban elite with little standing outside its Katutura township.

SWAPO's golden opportunity to reestablish an internal organisation was the release from Robben Island of SWAPO founder member Herman (now Andimba) Toivo ja Toivo. It was a calculated risk on the part of South Africa to free him — and SWAPO made it work for them. Toivo came out of jail stronger than ever, with a sharp mind and unmistakable presence and charisma. South Africa was in a difficult position, having made a major production of his release. The eyes of the world press were on him. He was virtually untouchable. But Toivo was never used by SWAPO inside Namibia. He stayed in Katutura and soon began travelling abroad — where he was very effective. He made one journey to the south of Namibia to meet Witbooi, but he never returned to his birthplace, the Owambo-speaking region in the north.

By mid-1985 it was clear that Toivo, who had since been appointed to SWAPO's Politburo, was not going to return home soon — perhaps not at all until independence. There may be some truth in the rumours, eagerly supported by the South African authorities and media, that the Nujoma leadership began to fear that Toivo could become too popular and powerful within Namibia if he stayed there, and so ordered him to leave.

When asked about this, an agitated Nujoma denied that he had ordered Toivo to leave.

> Toivo has the right to decide. If he thinks there is a threat, well, I have no right to force somebody to go to hell. Namibia today is hell for Africans and heaven for whites. I think it is just correct for Toivo to make his decision to leave the country. After all, he has spent 18 years in prison in South Africa. And it is his own decision whether he wants to go back.

One indication of SWAPO's support in Windhoek, and probably not a very reliable one, was when the parties opposed to the MPC 'government' held a protest meeting on the day the government was inaugurated. About 2 000 people assembled in Katutura, and more than half of them were dressed in the colours of the Damara Council or the other parties. The day was saved for SWAPO when camouflaged policemen savagely attacked some of the protesters on their way home and acutely embarrassed the new government leaders.

In loose alliance with SWAPO against the MPC and the interim government is the Damara Council, the South West African National Union (SWANU) dissidents, the Mbanderu Council and the Namibia Independence Party (NIP). At the time of writing this loose alliance was called the People's Consultative Conference (PCC), but it had no formal leadership, constitution or organisational structures. SWAPO's Tjongarero announced at a press conference on the day of the MPC government's inauguration that the PCC was about to become a formal organisation.

The Damara Council represents the majority of the Damara people and is led by one of the most respected politicians in Namibia, Chief Justus Garoeb. He was a founder member of the MPC, but pulled out shortly before the Lusaka Conference and attended that conference on SWAPO's invitation. It was a heavy blow to the MPC which was, and is, desperate for credibility in the eyes of black Namibians. Subsequently Garoeb has had several rounds of talks with SWAPO leaders, but there are no signs that he plans to disband his own party and join SWAPO.

The Multi-Party Conference

Namibia's first interim government, made up of parties that took part in the 1975 Turnhalle Conference, was disbanded by South Africa in January 1983. The administrator general who then took over, Willie van Niekerk, and his advisers tried very hard to create a state council made up of internal parties to replace it, but it was rejected by most parties.

The president of the SWANU, Moses Katjiuongua, the president of the SWAPO-Democrats, Andreas Shipanga, and the chairman of the Democratic Turnhalle Alliance who was also the 'prime minister' of the last interim government, Dirk Mudge, got together to work out their own plan, and on 29 September 1983 the MPC was formed. Other parties in the MPC are the white National Party (NP), the coloured Labour Party and the Rehoboth Liberated Democratic Party.

Ideologically, they are light-years apart. SWANU and SWAPO-D have constitutions very similar to SWAPO's, and their leadership consists mainly of black nationalists who spent most of their adult lives in exile. On the other hand there is the ultra-conservative white ethnocentric NP, and in the middle the tribalist DTA. About the only thing these parties have in common is their fear of SWAPO.

It took many long nights of debate and several threatened splits before the MPC produced the 'Windhoek Declaration of Basic Principles' of February 1984. In it the MPC 'reaffirmed that Resolution 435 is at present the only concrete plan on independence', but also stated that it 'accepts the challenge to lead our country to a nationally acceptable and internationally recognised independence', and to 'draft a permanent constitution'.

After many more long nights this was followed in April 1984 by a 'Bill of Fundamental Rights and Objectives'. In May the MPC scored its first victory. It was invited to the Lusaka Conference on

Namibian independence as a delegation separate from SWAPO and the South African representative, the administrator-general. This eroded SWAPO's status as the 'sole and authentic' representative. But the conference achieved nothing, and the MPC's behaviour did not endear it to the conference host, Zambian president Kenneth Kaunda.

The MPC followed this up with a visit to the United States and French Africa (the only part of Africa that would receive it): the Ivory Coast, Togo and Senegal. The welcome was warmest from Ivory Coast president Felix Houphouet-Boigny. SWAPO acknowledged that this was something of a setback by sending a delegation to all these countries shortly after the MPC to try and undo the damage.

On 27 March 1985, an MPC delegation presented a document to the South African state president with full proposals for a transitional government. It proposed a National Assembly of 62 members, a cabinet of eight ministers and eight deputies and a Constitutional Council of 16. The MPC proposals were contained in the South African state president's Proclamation No R101 of 17 June 1985. The new government has full powers, excluding the right to make laws that would change the international status of the territory, repeal or amend the provisions of R101 or diminish anyone's rights as laid down in the Bill of Fundamental Rights. It also has limited say over defence and security matters.

Compared with the restraint he was empowered to exercise over the previous interim government, the administrator general's power of veto is now very limited. The Proclamation states: 'When a law is submitted to the administrator general, he shall declare that he assents to it or that he withholds assent, but he shall not declare that he withholds assent unless he is satisfied that the law has not been dealt with as provided in this Proclamation, or that such law is contrary to the provisions of this Proclamation'. However, under section 38 of the SWA Constitution Act of 1968, the South African state president still has the power to amend or repeal any law passed by the administrator general.

The National Assembly has decided to create a Constitutional Council to be 'charged with responsibility for all constitutional matters and in particular, to draw up an independence constitution for the country'. The council will sit for a maximum of 18 months and present the draft constitution to the cabinet. Then, 'the cabinet shall, within a period of three calendar months after the date on which it receives the draft constitution from the council, arrange to have the draft constitution submitted to the electorate for its approval', the proposal states.

The question as to what will happen after this draft constitution is approved (or rejected) in a referendum has consistently been evaded by MPC leaders. However, in their Declaration of Basic Principles of February 1984 they state that the MPC 'accepts the challenge to draft a *permanent* constitution' (my emphasis). On 30 October 1984, the MPC declared that it was 'convinced of the need to adopt a constitution for the independence of this country before submitting the manifestos of the different parties to the electorate for the exercise of their democratic right of choice'.

From the start, MPC leaders strongly denied that they have their own kind of independence — outside of Resolution 435 — in mind. But in other statements they have let slip contrary indications. For example, the document handed to President PW Botha stated:

> The MPC is aware that the road to independence which the conference has selected by requesting the South African Government to instal a transitional government in Namibia, will be a difficult one. President Houphouet-Boigny's positive reaction to the MPC's proposal was encouraging and creates the impression that at least certain African states may be prepared to demonstrate understanding of the need for an indigenous Namibian effort to promote national reconciliation and stable and prosperous independence.

In different circumstances and at a different time in the history of Namibia, the MPC might have succeeded. It is indeed remarkable that after many decades of harsh apartheid repression, black and white nationalists and leaders from all tribes could come together in one organisation and compromise over policy on the most contentious and sensitive issues.

Further, it is in theory true that a 'transitional government of national unity' is needed while the independence process is being stalled by South Africa. Black and white communities and the different tribes do need to move towards a *modus vivendi*, the Namibian civil service must gradually be Africanised, the territory must be weaned from South African control, leaders do need political and administrative experience and the economy must be prepared for independence.

But the MPC government has several vital flaws: the most glaring one is that the national liberation movement, SWAPO, is not part of it and is continuing its war against South Africa. The MPC argument is that it has indeed invited SWAPO several times to take part but that SWAPO has rejected it. But this is simplistic: no-one ever seriously expected SWAPO to accept the offer. So the war continues, as do government attacks on SWAPO leaders and structures, and the economy and people in the north continue to suffer.

Now Namibia faces not so much a war for independence as war for a specific kind of independence. It has become a war for political power. The fact that the MPC government is a predominantly black and indigenous government determined to make fundamental changes to the socio-political scene in Namibia is eroding the very legitimacy of SWAPO's armed struggle, as perceived by African and Western eyes. This may well demand a dramatic shift in emphasis by SWAPO from armed struggle to political struggle — a shift that has only begun.

The MPC government's other weakness is that it is a government of the south. More than 50% of the people of Namibia live in Owambo, but a recent visit by the author to these parts indicated that ordinary people in this region do not even know that there is a new government. Those who do know see it as something that does not concern them. Not even the Owambo leader 'inside the system', Owambo second-tier authority chairman Peter Kalangula, and his Christian Democratic Action Party, are part of the MPC. Kalangula gave the impression during an interview in June 1985 that he is a bitter and isolated man whose main motivation for not taking part in the MPC is his bitter personal conflict with his old party, the DTA.

However, the DTA is making a strong bid to regain some support in the region and succeeded in persuading 16 Owambo headmen and 900 of their followers to attend the inauguration of the new government. Also, the SADF has formed an Owambo 'cultural' organisation with the name Etango (the sun), mainly supported by black members of the SWA Police and Territory Force and their families. This is fast becoming a political movement and could undermine Kalangula even more. Deputy Minister of Justice Katuutire Kaura told the National Assembly in July that Etango was an 'evil force aimed at undermining the activities of the transitional government'. He saw it as a South African effort 'to keep their options open'. Etango also has branches in Kavango and Caprivi.

The Caprivi is partially represented in the government through the DTA, but at the time of writing it was rumoured that the Caprivi African National Union (CANU) was also going to be drawn in. CANU leader and former vice-president of SWAPO Mishake Muyongo was released from jail in Senegal (probably through the good offices of the South African Department of Foreign Affairs) and was formally granted amnesty. SWAPO maintains that South Africa is secretly planning to allow Caprivi to secede from the rest of Namibia and will grant it independence as the 'Republic of Itenge', as CANU already calls it. While as yet there is no concrete evidence that this is indeed South Africa's intention, CANU would certainly be in favour of it.

All these factors contribute to the MPC's overwhelming problem: it has very low credibility in the eyes of most black Namibians. Mistrust is so strong that they see anything acceptable to the colonial master and to whites inside Namibia as against their own interests. And they have good reason to suspect that the establishment of the government could retard their dream of full independence.

The black leaders in the transitional government fully realise this and are determined to break down this image. With the exception of the white NP, Diergaardt's Baster party and two or three of the DTA leaders, the new government is committed to scrapping the unpopular ethnic second-tier authorities or at least reducing them to cultural councils; to scrapping mandatory racial classification; to working out some formula to open up white state schools to all; and to opening all hospitals to all races.

The MPC has already succeeded in getting the white ethnic government out of the traditional seat of administrative power, the Tintenpalast, a symbol for decades of white mastery. It is also trying to take over the prestigious and symbolically important campus of the white Training College in Windhoek.

The SWANU and SWAPO-D leadership in fact used the first few weeks of the first session of the National Assembly to prove that they were serious about making fundamental changes to Namibian society. They spoke out strongly against all remaining forms of apartheid, proposed drastic changes to the draconian security proclamations, AG 9 and AG 26, and asked that amnesty be granted to all political prisoners. The MPC government has another weapon to use in its fight for popularity: a development fund of some R300-m, made up mainly of money that the white second-tier authority and some third-tier authorities had quietly been hoarding.

But the MPC remains in a no-win situation: whatever it does that is popular with the black majority will be seen as a threat by the white community, and vice versa. It will essentially have to be a government of compromise — and black Namibians are more than a decade beyond compromise. What they want now is psychological liberation, a fair society and an end to the war. The MPC will find this very difficult, if not impossible, to provide.

One immediate demonstration of the new government's inherent weakness is its inability, because of inter-party squabbling, to agree on a cabinet chairman or prime minister. The chairmanship will now rotate every three months, and the first man to hdld the post was the weak and colourless (coloured) Labour Party chairman, Dawid Bezuidenhout.

This all presupposes that the MPC is going to stay in one piece. That will not necessarily be the case. At the time of writing, SWANU, SWAPO-D and the NP threatened to go to the Supreme Court on the issue of the second-tier governments. Parties in the MPC were acting like arch-enemies, and the rift between the two 'progressive' movements, SWAPO-D and SWANU on one side, and the rest on the other seemed to be growing. SWANU leader Katjiuongua and DTA leader Dirk Mudge nearly came to blows (literally) in the chamber over the issue.

Popular support

Objective assessment of popular support in Namibia is impossible without a free and fair election. Despite the unpopularity of ethnically based analysis, the fact needs to be faced that political support in tribally divided Namibia still runs mainly along ethnic lines. It seems that most whites, coloureds, Basters, Hereros, Tswanas and Bushmen support the MPC, while SWAPO seems to represent most Ovambos and Kavangos (who together form more than 60% of the population) and Namas. The Damaras are divided between the DTA and the Damara Council, and Caprivians between the DTA and CANU.

While this picture, if true, gives SWAPO still the vast majority of support, it must also be noted that the MPC support is based substantially on fear of tribal domination by the Ovambo, so that support is fairly secure. The same cannot be said of SWAPO's support among traditionalist Ovambo people or non-Ovambos.

The outlook for international negotiations

Pretoria's recent history of dealings with Namibia has been extraordinarily inconsistent. At present it appears that South Africa has no final blueprint for Namibia, but will do whatever seems in its interest at any given time.

There is no real pressure to implement the independence process now. International heat on South Africa at present has other causes than Namibia. The brewing revolution in the core of the region overshadows every other issue in the sub-continent. And as the civil war there hots up, more attention will be given to it by the international community and less to the Namibian issue. For years South Africa has successfully used Namibia as a lightning conductor to keep attention away from its internal policies. No longer.

Ironically, this could very well motivate a decision to let Namibia go: South Africa's internal situation is deteriorating so fast, and the external pressure is growing so rapidly, that Pretoria may well decide to steer the attention away from it by implementing Resolution 435. For seven months at least international attention would be deflected to Namibia, and Pretoria could pick up some goodwill. It could be a welcome breather for government. It is not even inconceivable that Pretoria could trade Namibian independence for a concession or two from Washington if the situation becomes desperate.

As things stand, South Africa is in a strong position to bide its time on Namibia and to wait and see what is in its interest. The transitional government is functioning, while options for an internationally acceptable solution remain open. It was Washington which initiated 'linkage' between Namibian independence and a Cuban withdrawal from Angola, and South Africa is quite happy to hold that up as an excuse. Chances of a Cuban withdrawal

diminished still more when South African commandos were caught
on a sabotage mission in Cabinda. And the next excuse is lined up:
Washington's and Pretoria's ally in southern Angola, Jonas
Savimbi's UNITA, which will be forced on Luanda as an ally
without which Angola cannot achieve peace and stability.

Of course, South Africa may still decide to make Namibia
independent outside of Resolution 435. There are several pointers
indicating that an 'internal solution' is very much in the minds of
both South African officials and the transitional government. Not
for nothing has the MPC government's new slogan become 'a
nationally acceptable solution'.

As PW Botha said at the inauguration of the government in
Windhoek:

> For as long as there is a possibility that the recent international negotia-
> tions hold any realistic prospect of bringing about the genuine withdrawal
> of Cuban forces from Angola, the South African government will not act
> in a manner irreconcilable with the international settlement plan.
> However, the people of SWA, including SWAPO, cannot wait indefinite-
> ly for a breakthrough on the withdrawal of the Cubans from Angola.
> Should it eventually become evident, after all avenues have been
> thoroughly explored, that there is no realistic prospect of attaining this
> goal, all the parties most intimately affected by the present negotiations
> will obviously have to reconsider how internationally acceptable in-
> dependence may best be attained in the light of prevailing circumstances.

A military intelligence colonel in Windhoek, who may not be
named, indicated that the old plan to force SWAPO to abandon
the armed struggle and come back as a purely political party to
negotiate with the MPC is still very much alive. He told a press
briefing in June that he had evidence that SWAPO and PLAN are
parting ways. PLAN's performance has become 'an embarrass-
ment' to SWAPO, and the political leaders are already beginning to
think of going back home as a political party.

This is certainly a distortion. Nonetheless, the recent increase in
contact between SWAPO leaders inside and outside Namibia,
coupled with the military stalemate, may see SWAPO taking
advantage of the MPC's promised cutback on political repression
to rebuild its internal structures and to mobilise its widespread,
though recently dormant, political support.

Pandora's Box: The Private Accounts of a Bantustan Community Authority

Jeremy Keenan

The Thaba y Batho Community Authority at Bosplaas is a few miles north of Hammanskraal and adjoins the Babelegi industrial complex in the Moretele region of Bophuthatswana. An analysis of the operation of its local authority provides a number of insights into the workings of bantustan repression and coercion.

Local authorities have a particular controlling role in the hierarchy of bantustan government. To understand this role it is necessary to detail how general administrative and 'control' functions of such authorities are mediated through the many and very specific local issues and structures which make each such authority in some senses 'unique'. These variables necessitate different forms and degrees of administration and control. The most notable factors are personalities, ethnic differences, differential degrees of incorporation into labour and other markets, different patterns of political resistance and incorporation, different principles and perceptions of the 'traditional' political and governmental system, and different class forces.

The Thaba y Batho Community Authority at Bosplaas should be seen in the wider context of Bophuthatswana's demographic/ethnic, economic and political problems, and of the 1982 Weichers Commission of Inquiry into 'local and regional government, the activation of tribal authorities and the political structure in the Republic of Bophuthatswana'. It should also be viewed against the specific background events at Bosplaas itself which led to the opening up of this Pandora's box.

Three aspects of Bophuthatswana should be borne in mind. Firstly, a very large proportion and perhaps even a majority of the de facto population resident in Bophuthatswana is non-Tswana. The 1980 population census gave the population of Bophuthatswana as 1 287 814. Today's official figure is somewhere around 1,7-million. Informal figures supplied by groups and organisations working in the area put the figure at closer to 4-million. Approximately 2-2,5-million of these live in the Odi-Moretele area of which Bosplaas is a part. Surveys of the area have also shown that about 80% of the region is populated by non-Tswanas. For the peddlers of Tswana nationalism this is an anathema with enormous political implications which go a long way to explaining the nature and necessity of 'control' in Bosplaas and many other parts of Bophuthatswana.

Secondly, Bophuthatswana is not the economic and human rights success story that government and media propaganda would have it appear. Resentment and resistance to the Bophuthatswana authorities is high. These authorities are seen by much of the population as an extension of what is usually referred to as 'central government', that is Pretoria. There is little support for 'independence' and Mangope's government amongst the non-Tswana population, and there is growing discontent amongst the Tswana population, especially working-class elements.

Thirdly, Bophuthatswana has to maintain an appearance of 'democracy' and the picture of itself as South Africa's 'separate development' success story.

With such widespread resentment to the Bophuthatswana government and its ruling Bophuthatswana Democratic Party (BDP), economic mismanagement (in agriculture for example) and substantive allegations of government corruption and nepotism, the opposition parties cannot be permitted access to legitimate platforms from which to expose cracks in the crumbling facade. So, at the second general election in 1982, the ruling party managed to get rid of the four Seopo Singwe opposition members of parliament. According to Bophuthatswana government officials this was done by distributing the 'urban' (South African) vote into those constituencies in which the opposition had gained a majority.

The authorities have taken a number of steps to secure the appearance of democracy, at the same time securing and strengthening the ruling party's grassroots organisation and 'control'. Youth and women's leagues have been formed; prominent members of the opposition have been discredited, smeared and actively harassed; there have been increasingly crude and jingoistic appeals to Tswana nationalism; more party branches have been established at local level where membership is fused as far as possible with membership of local administrative bodies. In turn these tribal and community authorities are given much more administrative power and control. 'Activating' these authorities was one of the main concerns of the Weichers Commission.

A National Assembly Select Committee, appointed to study the Weichers Commission findings and recommendations and to advise the Executive Council, came out strongly in support of Weichers's recommendations that tribal authorities not only be regarded as appropriate institutions to administer tribal affairs, but be revitalised and given responsibility for their own affairs, with their members being adequately remunerated.[1]

These 'activated' local authorities are necessary to control and repress the growing resistance to government. Not surprisingly the local authorities themselves have increasingly become the target of resentment. In November 1983 greater police protection for tribal and community authorities was announced. Government ministers explained this away in terms of the need to root out 'terrorists' and to protect citizens from increasing crime — which by implication was associated with the presence of non-Tswanas.

Bosplaas

Bosplaas is typical of many areas in the Odi-Moretele region. Like much of Winterveld it is African freehold land, sold off in 5-10 hectare plots under the 1936 Land Act. The purchasers of these plots were of totally diverse tribal origin. Subsequently, when people were removed or thrown off 'black spots' and overcrowded areas near Pretoria (Boekenhoutkloof, Wallman, Lady Selbourne, Marabastad to name but a few), many of them were resettled or driven into the Winterveld area where they became tenants or subtenants on plots. For many of these removed people, the Bantu Commissioner concerned went to great lengths to register their residency and passes — so they became legal residents.

In 1964 Bosplaas became an official Bantu Community Authority. Community authorities have very similar powers to tribal authorities except that community authorities, established in areas where there are two or more 'tribes' or portions of tribes, have

members who are elected five-yearly, while members of tribal
authorities are appointed, often through heredity. The first community authority elections at Bosplaas took place in 1964.

The current population of Bosplaas is estimated at 15 000. Most of
the population, both plot owners and tenants, have been legal residents
since before 1972 and many of them have been there since the 1940s.

Bosplaas, like most of the Odi-Moretele region, is predominantly
non-Tswana. At independence non-Tswanas were not forced to
take out Bophuthatswana citizenship. They were also theoretically
protected by the 'Bill of Rights' and by the reciprocal agreement
between Bophuthatswana and South Africa that each would process and pay social pensions of citizens of the other resident in their
country. After independence Bophuthatswana immediately reneg-
ed on this and refused (in nearly all cases) to grant citizenship to
non-Tswanas. Since independence in 1977 the Bophuthatswana
government has waged a relentless campaign against non-Tswanas.

This campaign has gone through three distinct phases. From
1977 to 1978 there were more or less continuous police raids against
non-Tswanas throughout most of Odi-Moretele. This was an
attempt to force these people out of Bophuthatswana since they
were such a large portion of the population and presented a threat
to the rulers.

The brutal treatment meted out to non-Tswanas during 1978 was
so well covered in the *Post* newspaper (15.12.78 — prior to its
banning) that a delegation of seven other rather embarrassed
'homeland' leaders sent a telex to Piet Koornhof, Minister of the
then Department of Plural Relations and Development, appealing
to him to stop the removals of non-Tswanas in areas of
Bophuthatswana.

South African and Bophuthatswanan authorities met in February
1979. Although it is not known what took place at that meeting, it
seems clear that no attempt was made to resolve the situation, but
rather to adopt less public methods of removing the people.

The second phase of the campaign from 1978 to August 1983 was
characterised by 'official harassment' of non-Tswanas. The most
common action was to deny non-Tswanas citizenship, residency
and work seekers' permits and to withhold pensions and other
forms of social security. Non-Tswana schools were harassed,
traders were threatened. Access to transport was impeded and
clinics in non-Tswana areas suddenly had crucial drugs and baby

formula withdrawn. Documents were also 'lost' and people were reduced to the status of 'illegals'. As 'illegals' they were subjected to further police raids. As a result a few were driven out of Bophuthatswana but most had nowhere to go. Rather than getting rid of people, the authorities generated massive resentment and hatred.

Since August 1983 Bophuthatswana has taken what its senior government officials term the 'Nigerian option'. Nigeria had recently expelled about two million migrants, mostly Ghanaians. Bophuthatswana tried to do this by amending the Land Control Act in such a way as to redefine non-Tswana residents as 'squatters' and thereby provide themselves with the legal means of evicting them from Bophuthatswana.

The first raids in Bosplaas under this new legislation began in May 1984. A group of 200 people decided to defend themselves in court. Their defence team successfully subpoenaed the minutes, receipts and financial records of the Bosplaas (Thaba y Batho) Community Authority. A detailed examination of these records revealed just how the Authority exercised control over the area and the role it played in the state's campaign against non-Tswanas.

Prior to the subpoena, the people of Bosplaas claimed they had paid taxes to the state; that the community authority had raised taxes illegally and had embezzled the money; that the community authority office had refused to allow them to apply for residency and/or citizenship on the grounds that they were 'illegals' or that as non-Tswanas they were not allowed to be in the area; that the authority had failed to call public meetings and that its members had not been elected as required by law, namely Act 23 of 1978 which replaced Proclamation R141 of 1968 and the Bantu Authorities Act of 1951.

Two allegations were crucially important to the defence 'team'. Firstly, if it could be proved that the Bophuthatswana authorities had wilfully and knowingly levied and collected taxes from non-Tswanas, the people whom the government was trying to evict would have a strong legal right to remain in the area. Bophuthatswana's constitution accepts that as a sovereign independent state the deepest root of its democratic government, as espoused by its own Weichers Commission of Inquiry, 'is the well-known principle of no taxation without representation'.

Secondly, if it could be proved that the authority had failed to

hold elections in 1979 as required by law, the authority would have
been a legal nullity since 1979. If that was the case then all actions
taken by the authority since 1979 would have no legal basis and the
residents of Bosplaas could not have legally applied for citizenship
or residency through the Authority. They could consequently base
their defence on grounds of impossibility. The subpoenaed records
confirmed both these allegations.

The Bosplaas Community Authority

After its inception in 1964 the Authority had elections each five
years as required by law, in 1969 and 1974. In 1974 the elected
chairman was Mhlolo Moses Mgiba who had won the first election,
but lost his seat in 1969.

Minutes from the first few weeks of 1975 indicate a campaign to
oust Mgiba. A certain SK Rafidile, who was linked to the ruling
Bophuthatswana Democratic Party, led the campaign. It included
accusations that Mgiba practised magic in the Authority's offices
and that the Authority had received a letter from the devil mention-
ing Mgiba by name. In February 1975 Mgiba was forced to resign
and Rafidile replaced him as chairman.

Since 1975, Rafidile, with a small but changing group of councillors appointed by him, and with the support of the chief
magistrate, kept a tight grip on the administration of the area, a
grip based on a growing spiral of corruption, embezzlement and
fear. Over the next ten years no proper records were kept concerning which councillors were in office at any one time. Some were
dismissed, some died and others were appointed by Rafidile.

It appears that Rafidile may have continued to draw salaries in
the names of councillors from the 1974 election. These names have
allegedly not been deleted from the official list of councillors in the
magistrate's office.

Evidently, four councillors who did not support Rafidile did not
attend many subsequent council meetings. This often made the
meetings non-quorate and therefore any decisions taken were
illegal. This problem was overcome when the Bophuthatswana
government changed the number required for a quorum in 1978
from half the members of an authority to the nearest whole number
exceeding one-third of the total number. In Bosplaas this reduced

quorum from eight to six.

In August 1975, Rafidile strengthened his position by appointing three councillors who appeared to support him. He also soon took over the finance portfolio from J Seropedi, against whom there had been accusations of fraud by both fellow councillors and inspectors from local government offices, and who was later to become the local chairman of the Bophuthatswana Democratic Party.

Bosplaas residents allege that financial irregularities increased under Rafidile's administration of the finance portfolio. One incident in January 1977 involved a government subsidy for school buildings which was not passed on to the school committee. Councillors queried the matter but were told by Rafidile that the matter was closed and that books could only be seen by 'inspectors'.

In September 1977, councillors again queried the books and instructed the secretary to investigate possible corruption over the previous year. When Rafidile refused to 'go back as far as that', it was suggested that the magistrate examine the books. This was evidently not acted on as there is no magistrate's stamp in the books. The minutes record that when a councillor persisted in demanding a financial statement Rafidile refused to say more than 'it had been given'.

Why was this embezzlement taking place? Most obviously it was seen as 'a perk of the job'. However, Rafidile, like many other leaders of tribal authorities in Bophuthatswana and other bantustans, was having to maintain more control and repression over an increasingly resentful and hostile population. This process seems to have been financed more and more from local rather than government resources. Also, tribal and community authority members, who were usually also members of the ruling party, viewed the embezzled funds for their personal use as part of the rewards proffered them by the state, believing that one way in which the state rewarded its bureaucratic functionaries and party workers was to allow them to get away with this sort of embezzlement. Certainly, when presented with serious and clear-cut evidence of such activities, the state often prefers not to make enquiries.

Rafidile's control over Bosplaas during his first period of office (1975-79) was by no means absolute. By 1979 there were still a few of the originally elected councillors who were not prepared to go along with Rafidile on all of these 'financial matters'.

The records also indicate that the Community Authority, or the councillors' pockets, were continually short of funds. Apparently dissident councillors were gradually dismissed or driven to resignation. Replacements were hand-picked by Rafidile himself.

Rafidile attempted to overcome the 'cash-flow' problem by continually increasing levies and introducing new ones. This was illegal although it is fairly obvious that the central government was happy to see a local authority taking such initiative. These taxes included a community tax, state levy, school building tax, wheel tax, dog tax, donkey tax, university tax, bridge tax, graveyard tax, bicycle tax and a number of independence day celebration levies.

It was also crucially important to the legal defence of the so-called 'squatters' that Rafidile had ignored repeated instructions of the senior magistrate at that time not to tax tenants as it would give them legal rights to be in the area. Not surprisingly both plot-owner and tenant residents resisted paying taxes.

In 1978 a group of school children, students, and youths, calling themselves the Bosplaas Youth Group, sent a letter to the Community Authority 'demanding an investigation into the history and state of the finances'. The council responded by 'calling on the young men and their parents', and residents say they threatened tenants' residency rights, and warned that they would not 'fix up' passes or issue work seeker permits. They also said that all meetings were illegal (which was not true) unless called by the Community Authority, the Party (BDP) or the magistrate.

These threats were not unique to Bosplaas, but were part of the intimidatory campaign against all non-Tswanas in Bophuthatswana. Rafidile had in fact told councillors not to help tenants to fix up their reference books. Resistance to taxation was so widespread that in 1979 Rafidile was forced to call a public meeting at which he pleaded with people to pay taxes.

By 1979 public resistance to Rafidile and his Authority was growing. It was also time for reelection of the council. He clearly could not allow an election as he was bound to be thrown out of office and replaced by a more popular and representative body. Just as clearly, such representative authorities could not be tolerated in Bophuthatswana as they would undermine the whole basis of control and repression in those areas. The government's fear of 'representative' local authority was epitomised by the Minister of Land and Urban Affairs, David Mokale, in his evidence to the Weichers Commission in January 1981. When asked about the absence of established and institutional forms of local government in areas such as Winterveld, the minister replied that he was opposed to establishing such local government as it could stimulate organised opposition to the government.

The problem of the pending election was overcome quite simply by not holding it. The senior magistrate for the region, seconded from Pretoria, appears to have known about and ignored this irregularity. After that the Thaba y Batho (Bosplaas) Community Authority ceased to have any legal existence.

Until 1979, an additional problem hampering Rafidile was that he had not been invested with powers of criminal and civil jurisdiction. Although he had fined people, he complained that his fundraising ability was hampered by the lack of these powers. He said that he needed powers equivalent to those of a chief or headman which would enable him to try cases and fine people with impunity.

The state obliged and in March 1979 the senior magistrate and administrator of the area, JM Vercueil, held a public meeting in Bosplaas at which he not only invested Rafidile with civil and criminal jurisdiction 'like a headman' but also told the assembled crowd that he was 'appointed for a further five years'. This procedure was illegal, as constitutionally elections should have been held. However, most members of the community believed that Rafidile was now an appointed headman with all the powers that entailed, for a further five years. The problems of legitimacy and cash inflow were overcome at least for the time being.

During the post 1979 period, membership of the community authority coincided more and more with local membership of the ruling BDP. A number of councillors began to sell BDP membership cards to both plot owners and tenants for R5 (membership was R1) telling them that as members of the party all their problems with residency and other permits would be taken care of. Bosplaas was apparently the fastest growing branch of the party at this time. Of course non-citizens, even if they were party members, still had no representation or additional rights. But the move to extend party membership to non-citizens, apart from temporarily dampening resistance to the authority and the Bophuthatswana authorities in general, provided certain councillors with an additional source of income. Party representation on the authority was so complete that in 1982 it 'unanimously agreed to join the BDP'.[2] Constitutionally it is not possible for a representative local authority to become a member of a political party.

The community authority's financial records indicate a substantial intensification of fraud and embezzlement of funds since 1979. The most common form of embezzlement was falsifying counterfoils of receipts issued to both plot-owner and tenant residents. Comparison of a random collection of receipts with subpoenaed counterfoils showed that 40% of all counterfoils were falsified. This practice was obviously condoned by the administrator of the area, JM Vercueil, as he approved numerous false and blank records for audit.

Conclusion

The authority's records reveal how the government assisted it in its illegal actions through both the direct intervention of senior government officials, such as the administrator/senior magistrate, and through its indemnification of such practices.

The nature and extent of the fraud, corruption and control at Bosplaas is very similar to that found in other tribal and community authorities in other bantustans. Resistance to this sort of control cannot be held in check for ever. In Bophuthatswana more and more police are needed in local authority areas which in turn has heightened resistance.

The fact that resistance is held in check for long periods is largely due to people's fear and resignation, and their lack of access to 'useful social knowledge'.[3] But as Goran Therborn has written:

> Fear cannot rule alone. Among the forms of fear are the fears of being excommunicated or of losing one's job. Resignation entails the belief that there doesn't exist a possible alternative to the existing order.[4]

In Bosplaas there is no fear of being excommunicated. But there is a very real fear of losing one's job, or being evicted, and of being beaten up and tortured by the police. There is also a terrible and pervasive resignation that has arisen from many years of such control, brutality and suffering, to the extent that organisation in the area, even in the form of establishing small committee structures to report on such events, barely exists.

The greatest fear is the fear of further reprisal. Police have raided the area almost weekly since May 1984. People known to have lawyers are often singled out. Others have concluded that it does not necessarily pay to challenge the system. Thousands have now chosen not to defend themselves.

At some point fear is overcome. This is now evident among the 200 Bosplaas tenants and plot owners whose trial has been postponed into its seventeenth month. The state cannot begin the trial because of the mass of evidence against it. With the sixth postponement the trialists' anger boiled over. They agreed that the Bophuthatswana government's achilles heel was exposure of how its 'Bill of Rights' actually worked. So they decided that details of their ordeal should be publicised.

Chief Magistrate Vercueil refused to answer a subpoena and the court issued a warrant for his arrest. He informed the court messenger to the effect that he had not come to Bophuthatswana to put up with this sort of thing and was resigning forthwith.

Notes

1 Report on the Weichers Commission from the Select Committee of the Bophuthatswana National Assembly to the Executive Council.
2 Thaba y Batho Community Authority minutes, 08.07.82.
3 RJ Haines, CP Tapscott, SB Solinjani and P Tyali, 'The silence of poverty: networks of control in rural Transkei', Carnegie Conference Paper 48, University of Cape Town, 1984.
4 Goran Therborn, *The Ideology of Power and the Power of Ideology* (Verso, 1980), 97.

'Banking on Discipline': The Development Bank of Southern Africa

Alan Hirsch

It is more frequently the closing than the opening of a bank that captures public interest. Banks are not the stuff of romance. The Development Bank of Southern Africa is no different in this respect, but it is an entirely new type of financial institution, with a great deal of financial power, and it is likely to play a very important role in shaping the nature and direction of economic (and political) development in South Africa during the remainder of the 1980s.

On 1 September 1983 the Development Bank of Southern Africa (DBSA) was formally opened, with authorised share capital of R2-billion, though only R20-million was paid up. Its stated purpose in terms of its Articles of Agreement is to develop economically the Southern African region by: reducing regional economic imbalances; financing the developmental objectives of participating governments; providing technical assistance in the formulation of priorities and projects; and promoting public and private investment 'that will contribute most effectively to economic development'.

The bank had been a long time coming. Two influential Pretoria economists, Jan Lombard and PJ van der Merwe, had, as early as 1972, proposed the establishment of a development bank which could take over the financing functions of the Bantu Investment Corporation (later the Corporation for Economic Development) to fund individual bantustan corporations, thus decentralising decision-making away from the Department of Bantu Administration and Development. By 1983 the process of establishing individual bantustan corporations had already taken place, but the Corporation for Economic Development (CED) still existed as a corporation, conflicting with the supposed autonomy of the decentralised corporations. The DBSA could be seen as a part of the rationalisation of these institutional relations as well as a part of the process of dismantling/restructuring the Department of Cooperation and Development.

But the stated intentions of the DBSA are broader than this. It is aimed at achieving 'greater effectiveness' in *mobilising* and *utilising* resources for development in the participating 'states', as well as 'extending the scope of development cooperation — both within and beyond the present participating states'.

The establishment of the DBSA

The DBSA was first formally mooted by the then prime minister, PW Botha, at the Carlton Conference between government and big business in 1979, but it had a protracted and difficult gestation. As early as March 1981, *Finance Week* reported that the Bank was due to open soon and would be 'all systems go by the year end'. Yet full operations began only in February 1984.

Difficulties stemmed from the 'multilateral' structure of the Bank. Participants were South Africa and the 'independent' and 'non-independent' bantustans, but though the former would be full members, the latter would be represented by South Africa. KwaZulu's chief minister, Gatsha Buthelezi, complained in a speech to the KwaZulu assembly that 'fundamental principles concerning the bank had not yet been sorted out to the satisfaction of the KwaZulu cabinet and should be resolved urgently'. He felt that the Bank's structure was pushing KwaZulu down the 'primrose path' to confederation in a constellation of states.

Professor Jan Lombard, designated chief executive of the Bank, also had difficulties with the structure the South African government was pushing for, apparently supporting Buthelezi's position and calling for less direct South African control. He resigned before the Bank was constituted, and was replaced with his former student, Dr Simon Brand, economic adviser to the prime minister.

Structure of the DBSA

Officially the DBSA is a multilateral, non-state body, controlled by a council of governors constituted by its member states. These members are South Africa and the TBVC 'states': the Transkei, Bophuthatswana, Venda and the Ciskei. Each member has a basic 300 votes plus an extra vote for every R500 000's worth of shares which it has subscribed to. Two thousand shares valued at R10 000 each have been issued. As South Africa has subscribed to 1 680 of the 2 000 available shares it holds 3 660 of the 5 500 votes, or 73,2%. Effectively, no major decisions can be made without South Africa's assent.

Beneath the council is the board of directors which consists of five nominated directors who are officials representing the member states, and five directors who are elected by the council. The latter are senior South African business executives, namely John Maree, formerly executive director of Barlow Rand, now MD of ESCOM; Dr Pieter Morkel, MD of Volkskas; Gerrie Muller, recently retired MD of Nedbank; Robin Plumbridge, MD of Gold Fields of South Africa; and Dr AP Scholtz, of the Noord-Westelike Kooperasie (a major agricultural cooperative). The board is chaired by the chief executive, Dr Simon Brand, who is appointed by the council and runs the Bank.

The Bank is divided into three divisions: the Research and Strategic Planning Division which attends to research into all spheres of development activity, but not direct project research; the General Manager's Division which administers the Bank and runs its advisory services; and the Programme and Project Division which researches and monitors all programmes and projects which the Bank finances.

The Bank as successor to the Corporation for Economic Development

Officials insist that the DBSA is not the CED in a new guise. Whereas the CED had fallen under the Department of Cooperation and Development (once 'Native Administration'), the DBSA does not officially fall under the South African government at all. The old political agenda of the CED has allegedly been abandoned, to be replaced with criteria of efficiency and utility. Whether or not this policy transformation has been achieved, the institutional changes are substantial and need to be spelled out.

The CED was at its establishment in 1959 named the Bantu Investment Corporation (BIC) and, alongside the South African Development Trust (SADT), was responsible for the economic development of the 'bantustans'. The SADT had been the first of the bantustan development agencies and remained responsible for its original functions, land purchases for bantustan consolidation, and the protection and development of forests. The BIC/CED, representing the second major phase of bantustan development policy, was meant to initiate and finance agricultural, commercial and, later, industrial development. In addition to these functions, the main activities of the CED were: running transport corporations and mining operations in the bantustans and, increasingly, financing the individual bantustan development corporations.

As initiator and controller of projects and funder of semi-autonomous corporations in the same regions, the operations of the CED were becoming increasingly conflictual. On the one hand, the CED ran commercial and agricultural projects in the bantustans, while, on the other hand, it funded corporations in the same bantustans to engage in similar, parallel, and sometimes competitive enterprises.

But the dissolution of the CED was clearly meant to be more than the rationalisation of function and form; it was part of the process of dismantling/restructuring the Department of Cooperation and Development which stood in the way of reform.

The functions of the dissolved CED devolved on the DBSA, the SADT and the individual bantustan corporations. Most of the agricultural and industrial functions and assets still held by the CED and SADT were transferred to the bantustan corporations, with the exception of land in the process of being transferred and disputed land, exploration and mining rights, and the transport corporations, all of which were held by or transferred to the SADT.

In addition to receiving project financing functions from the CED and SADT, the DBSA took over the bantustan financing functions from the Department of Foreign Affairs (which financed projects in 'independent' bantustans) and the Department of Community Development.

So officially, the DBSA is both narrower and broader than the CED: narrower in the sense that the scope of the DBSA is limited to financing, technical assistance and research, whereas the CED also undertook project initiation and control; broader in the sense that it engages with 'independent' and 'non-independent' bantustans and, potentially, with other independent Southern African countries. Officials indicate that talks with Southern African states may already have taken place, but that current political circumstances inhibit further developments.

The project cycle approach to financing

Following the practice of the World Bank and other development banks, the DBSA has, it is claimed, structured its financing around a project cycle system. In the Identification phase the client agency (bantustan corporation) submits project proposals to the Bank. If a proposal is successful it continues through the Preparation, Appraisal and Negotiation phases to the Implementation phase and, eventually, the Evaluation phase when the strengths and weaknesses of the finished project are assessed. In addition the Bank might provide 'technical assistance' to help the client draw up the proposal in the first place.

So, while it cannot initiate or control projects, the DBSA has a great deal of power, the power to support or reject a project.

The project cycle method of financing is meant both to depoliticise development funding and to establish sound economic criteria for loan policy. As we will see, neither goal is at all simple or easy to achieve.

In some cases decisions are straightforward. When the Ciskei applied to the Bank for financial support for its project to build an 'international airport', the application was rejected out of hand. The desire for political and economic autonomy could not justify an expensive and poorly conceived project which, at best, duplicated the under-utilised airport at East London.

Other cases, however, demand a balancing of political objectives with economic criteria. The decision to fund industrial development in the Ciskei, KwaZulu and Qwaqwa was not made because these are the most suitable sites for industrial development in South Africa, but because political objectives require it.

The project cycle approach is clearly also designed to attempt to police funding against corruption and fraud, omnipresent bug-bears of development funding in South Africa. However, as the funding process remains complex, with a large number of agencies involved, it seems unlikely that these problems will easily be overcome.

The practice of the Bank

As the Bank has been in operation for barely two years, and par-ticularly because the Bank has taken over most of its projects from other bodies, it is difficult to discern its precise impact on develop-ment funding. What is already clear, though, is that major goals of the Bank are contradictory and, consequently, difficult to implement.

In their 1984-85 annual report the directors argue that 'the emphasis [of funding] should gradually move towards agricultural and rural development projects, while in respect of industrial and infrastructural projects great care should continue to be exercised to avoid duplication of existing under-utilised facilities in the dif-ferent regions'.

In fact, on both counts, the practice of the Bank seems to con-tradict its policy.

By far the largest projects funded by the Bank during its first full year of operation were those to establish factories and industrial in-frastructures in KwaZulu (R80-million loan), the Ciskei (R40-million) and Qwaqwa (R24-million). Indeed, two-thirds of loans and commitments by the Bank are directed to industrial develop-ment.

It is clear that no shift in lending policy, away from industry and towards agriculture, has taken place. Two reasons can be sug-gested: firstly, policy shifts may not yet have had a chance to filter down to the lending operation of the DBSA; secondly, lending for large-scale industrial development remains a far more attractive accounting proposition.

Loans for industrialisation in the bantustans are attractive to the Bank because of the massive financial incentives provided by the South African government. In addition, large-scale industrial in-vestments are more predictable and are able to elicit a far shorter loan pay-back period. Whereas the maximum and minimum repayment periods set by the Bank for agriculture-oriented loans are seven and 20 years, the equivalent periods for industrial loans are three and 15 years.

Equally significant is the fact that the interest rates on industrial loans range between 8 and 17%, while the rates charged on agricultural loans range between a meagre 5 and 10%.

If profitability considerations are important to the Bank, and the Bank says they are, there must be an inbuilt tendency to favour industrial over other loans. This clearly gives rise to a contradiction between the goals of subjecting projects to 'strict economic criteria', and 'giving priority to those loans and guarantees that will contribute most effectively to economic development'.

A second noticeable area of contradiction in Bank policy is that in spite of intentions of avoiding duplication of infrastructure, one-quarter of all loans are going to the Ciskei where precisely that is taking place. While DBSA-financed industrial development takes place in Dimbaza and Mdantsane, across the border in Berlin prepared industrial sites have stood vacant for 15 years.

The Bank and political intervention

A senior official has indicated that the Bank may wish to intervene in the policies of borrowers. Manfred Reichardt, formerly of the International Monetary Fund, recently-appointed special adviser to the chief executive of the DBSA, has said that the Bank may engage in structural adjustment, non-project loans, which 'will allow the DBSA to promote important policy changes and economic reforms'.

While one of the chief rationales for the establishment of the Bank was the depoliticisation of the development process, the Bank seems ready to take upon itself an overtly political role, if in a new form. Instead of traditional CED-style authoritarianism, the new approach will be IMF-style paternalism.

What happened to BENSO?

Several institutions disappeared along with the CED, amongst which was the clumsily named Bureau for Economic Research re Black Development or BENSO (its Afrikaans initials). As its name indicates, the role of BENSO was general economic research into the bantustans. The products of the research were often published, at first in booklets devoted to each bantustan, and later in annual broad statistical surveys.

The research body has basically been transferred to the Bank as its research division. The division engages in research into broad economic issues relating to the bantustans and into areas which the Bank decides require attention, but does not officially do project-related research.

At this stage it appears that the division will be less oriented towards the *distribution* of Bank research data than was BENSO. If the division discontinues the BENSO function of distributing statistical data, it will become a good deal more difficult to obtain quantitative economic information on the bantustans (even if BENSO's was sometimes of dubious quality).

The cost of the DBSA

It is already clear that the Bank is a major drain on the South African treasury. The government has committed iself to providing R1 500-million for a Development Fund between 1984 and 1989. Of this only R400-million has been contributed over the first two years, which means that the state has an outstanding commitment of R1,1- billion to the Bank for the Development Fund between now and 1989.

The Development Fund is currently the major source of funds for the Bank, share capital amounting to no more than R56-million at the end of the financial year 1984-85.

In short, the South African government is committed to paying well over R1-billion to the DBSA over the next three years. This is a large sum by any standards and will seriously strain the state's fiscal resources.

Conclusion

It may seem trite, but one cannot avoid pointing out that it is early

yet to come to any profound conclusions about the Development
Bank of Southern Africa. What is already clear is that it is a significant and expensive institution which requires careful examination.
The Bank is the central development funding body in South Africa,
absorbing a very large proportion of state funds devoted towards
economic development.

Elsewhere in this *Review*, Cobbett et al argue that South Africa's
Regional Development Programme is designed to create a new geo-
political structure in South Africa, which would divide the country
into eight regions incorporating the bantustans, though not
necessarily dissolving the bantustan political structures. The
DBSA, a new institution which was linked to the Regional Development Programme initiative from the outset, is expected to play an
important role in the new strategy. So far it has done little, if
anything, to justify this expectation. Indeed, its very constitution,
as a 'multilateral' body on which the 'independent' bantustans
have ostensibly autonomous representation, is out of line with the
assumed direction of the new regional initiative.

The DBSA is a part of the reform process insofar as it takes
powers over the bantustans away from the Department of
Cooperation and Development, and insofar as it is claimed that old
apartheid determinants of development are being replaced with
conceptions of 'need' and 'efficiency'. But, at the same time, it is
the logical conclusion of apartheid in that it is a 'multilateral' institution in which 'independent' bantustans operate as
'autonomous states'.

July 1985

Reprieves and Repression: Relocation in South Africa

Laurine Platzky, on behalf of the National Committee Against Removals*

Forced removals in South Africa have not stopped. Despite the announcement of the Minister of Cooperation, Development and Education in February 1985 that removals would be suspended, six of the eight categories of relocation continue. They include and affect more than two million people.[1] When the Minister announced a review of removals, he was referring to only two of the eight categories — black spots and urban relocation. And even that suspension was heavily qualified by two conditions: that where leaders agreed to move, their communities would be relocated, and that squatters would not be tolerated.

Since the February announcement, four organisations comprising the newly-formed National Committee Against Removals (NCAR) have carefully monitored the situation. This overview of removals in South Africa is presented on behalf of the Association for Rural Advancement (AFRA), based in Pietermaritzburg; the Grahamstown Rural Committee (GRC), working in the Eastern Cape; the Cape Town-based Surplus People Project (SPP-Western Cape); and the Transvaal Rural Action Committee (TRAC), based in Johannesburg.

---

* The NCAR was formed mainly to coordinate research for its member groups and to continue to monitor and expose removals, bringing regional information together to compile a national picture. It will publish occasional papers and briefings on aspects of relocation, such as changes in government policy or tactics and community responses to removals.

The government's current policy on removals is at best confused and inconsistent, and at worst devious. Examination of even the suspended categories of black spots and urban relocation reveals the incoherence and contradiction of government action. This has caused severe strain and uncertainty in the affected communities, while providing breathing space to the government in the face of criticism.

Pressure on the government to end forced removals and thereby to restructure apartheid has continued from three sources: communities threatened with removal, enlightened local and international opinion, and conservative white farmers financially affected because their farms are to be consolidated. Each of these pressures affects different categories of removal in different ways.

The category with most potential for publicity and pressure is that of black spot relocation, as international protest about the forced removal of Mogopa on 14 February 1984 showed. The relocation against its will of the whole community of Mogopa to Pachsdraai in Bophuthatswana severely tarnished South Africa's reform image.

Eviction of farmworkers, the largest category of those removed and threatened, has received scant attention. Farmworkers are rarely able to resist because they are usually evicted as individuals. They have virtually no legal rights and no claim to compensation. They simply have to take their families and move to a bantustan, because influx control prevents them from moving to an urban area. Agglomeration and mechanisation of farms is in the interests of enlightened capital so the business community does not protest against this category of removal. And because ex-farmworkers are not entitled to land compensation, there is no pressure on the government's coffers. Evicted farmworkers and ex-labour tenants are therefore at the bottom of the relocation pile.

Over the past two years the call to end forced removals has grown both within South Africa and abroad. The demand has come from quarters as diverse as the Afrikaans press, the business community, and the United Democratic Front (UDF). This widespread call escalated as a result of the blatantly forced removal of the Mogopa people, which the Minister of Cooperation, Development and Education labelled 'voluntary' on an ABC Nightline programme in March 1985. He claimed that a headman (he did not reveal that this man had been democratically deposed by the community) had agreed to the removal.

Indeed, the government is still trying to persuade people to move 'voluntarily'. It is determined to find cooptable leaders. Words used by officials in the removal process do not reflect the people's reality — 'removal for development', 'urban renewal', 'the leaders agreed', 'voluntary removal'. There is wide difference between official and popular interpretation of the words 'consultation', 'negotiation', and 'agreement'. People may have been 'consulted' but that does not mean they were allowed to 'negotiate' and it certainly does not mean they 'agreed'.

A new bureaucratic language emerged with the appointment of the new Minister of Cooperation, Development and Education in September 1984. Instead of the 'cooperation' and 'development' of the Koornhof era, came the 'orderly urbanisation' and 'urban renewal' of the Viljoen era. Now everyone except for the extreme right wing has called for the abolition of influx control. The government, the PFP and the business community want 'orderly urbanisation' and an end to 'ideological removals'. But the people will settle for nothing less than complete freedom of movement.

'Urban renewal' will not simply be accepted as a reason for relocation. Too many communities have experienced urban and group area relocation undertaken in its name. Having frozen development, the government has declared certain areas slums as they deteriorated. For those moved from them, 'urban renewal' meant upheaval, dispossession, unemployment, high transport costs and, often, loss of South African citizenship.

Although the Orderly Movement and Settlement of Black Persons Bill was withdrawn in 1984, the penalty clause for 'illegals' in prescribed areas reappeared in the Aliens Act, which became law on 18 June 1984. The penalties are applicable to 'aliens', which means eight and a quarter million Venda-, Tswana- and Xhosa-speaking South Africans.

The government has responded to community demands and public pressure in some cases with piecemeal suspensions, moratoria and dubious concessions, and in others with direct violence and repression. There has been no change in policy. Relocation sites continue to be prepared. An examination of cases in all categories proves that the government has not abandoned its policy of forced removals.

Suspended categories

Black spots

While the government claims that black spot removals are suspended, sites continue to be prepared at Onderstepoort near Sun City, at
Vaalkop, Uitvlugt and Waayhoek near Ladysmith, and at Franklin
near Port Shepstone. On 27 November 1984 the authorities moved
over 250 people from the old mission farm of Stendahl (near
Weenen in Natal) to Waayhoek. They claimed it was a voluntary
removal. The people had been told to leave the farm before the end
of the year, but one month before the deadline they were taken by
surprise and moved by GG trucks. The mission farm had been sold
and the new owner evicted the people whose families had lived
there since 1860. They had no choice but to go 'voluntarily'.

Since Mogopa was moved, other black spot communities have
reaffirmed their determination not to move. Around the country,
at Matiwane's Kop, Mgwali, Driefontein and elsewhere, there is
strong resistance to being moved. Those communities which have
actively resisted for two or more years are strong and determined.
Others which have recently begun to organise against relocation are
experiencing problems.[2]

Mathopestad: In reply to a question in parliament as to whether the
government intended to move the people of Mathopestad in the
Western Transvaal, the Deputy Minister of Development and Land
Affairs said: 'Yes, in conjunction with the residents because it is in
the interests of all parties concerned (to move the people). The date
will be determined in conjunction with the residents of
Mathopestad'.[3]

This reply followed unsuccessful attempts to obtain the agreement of the chief of Mathopestad to move. It seems the local commissioner held secret meetings in the village, and was able to persuade a small number of tenants to agree to visit the proposed new
site at Onderstepoort on 11 March 1985. Most who agreed to move
appeared to be misinformed, believing that they would receive
compensatory land if they moved. Yet, by law, only landowners of
more than 17 hectares are entitled to compensation.

On 20 April the tribe held a meeting. (That day officials arrived
with buses to take people to Onderstepoort. This was arranged

after the local commissioner was informed of the Mathopestad meeting). At this meeting people declared their unwillingness to move and 291 adults, including the six headmen, the chief and sub-chief, all signed a petition against the removal. Since then many more people have signed: by early June signatories included 194 out of 230 household heads resident in Mathopestad, and 179 urban families who are descendants of landowners and hope to return to retire in Mathopestad.

During this period Deputy Minister of Development and Land Affairs Ben Wilkens reportedly stated to the SABC that the people of Mathopestad had declared themselves willing to move, and that a date for removal had been set. The Minister, Dr Gerrit Viljoen, echoed his own earlier promise to consult with the residents.

The tribe asked their lawyer to apply urgently for a meeting with Viljoen and the planning committee to discuss the removal.

The most recent government reply involved a letter from the deputy minister in which he stated that 'once a final decision had been taken by the government in connection with the future of, inter alia, Mathopestad, formal meetings and discussions will be arranged if necessary, on the basis previously agreed upon'.

The tribe's secretary replied to Wilkens, indicating its concern about his letter. He asked him and Viljoen to visit Mathopestad and speak with the tribe, and not to make a decision to move them prior to consultation.

It seems the government is unwilling to meet the residents of Mathopestad and witness their rejection of the removal. This may be an attempt to cause the community to lapse into uncertainty, while the government withdraws to think up yet another strategy to move the people and make it seem 'voluntary'.

KwaNgema: In 1984 this Eastern Transvaal black spot appealed to both Queen Elizabeth and the British prime minister to help them in their attempt to stay on the land granted to them by a former British monarch. The majority of the people there oppose the planned removal. Against their wishes, the government appointed a chief, Cuthbert Ngema, who said he was prepared to move. The elected Ngema committee applied to the Supreme Court to reverse the appointment of a chief, arguing that they were not a tribe. The application failed, because the Black Administration Act of 1927 allows the government to appoint whomever it wishes as chief of a black tribe, and the presiding judge ruled that the people of KwaNgema are a tribe. It appeared that, having set up a 'leader', the government would consult him over the 'negotiated' removal of the whole community. But in September 1985 KwaNgema was reprieved, along with Driefontein, in what appeared to be an unprecedented government concession designed to gain favourable foreign publicity.

Kwelera and Mooiplaas: During May 1985, the chief of these threatened black spots in the white corridor between Ciskei and Transkei told residents that houses were waiting for them at Kidds Beach. When the people suggested that the homeless squatters of Potsdam on the edge of Mdantsane would be better settled there, the chief replied that there were other plans for them; the Kidds Beach houses were for the people of Kwelera and Mooiplaas.

Mgwali: One government strategy may be not to move the communities physically, but to incorporate them under the administrations of the relevant bantustans. Mgwali, also situated in the white corridor, is contesting in court the Ciskei's right to administer it. Such administration may be the prelude to a 'reprieve' on removal but could involve constitutional incorporation of Mgwali under Ciskei authority. This would anger the residents of Mgwali and other black spots, because they do not want to lose their South African citizenship by being annexed to a bantustan any more than they want to move to Frankfort which is to be incorporated into Ciskei.

The democratically elected Mgwali Residents Association (MRA) tired both of pressures on them to move, and of Ciskeian control.[4] So the MRA applied to the Supreme Court to challenge the agreement between Ciskei and the Department of Cooperation and Development which empowered the former to administer Mgwali.

On 30 November 1981, according to the legal argument, the then Minister, Piet Koornhof, signed an agreement empowering Ciskei to administer pensions, school education, workseekers' permits, police power, land allocation and tax collection in four of the black spots in the corridor. The MRA challenged the agreement, arguing that the Black Law Amendment Act of 1978 only authorises South Africa and a 'national government' to make such agreement about an area which has been excised from South Africa. But the agreement was signed on 30 November, Mgwali was excised on 3 December and Ciskei took 'independence' on 4 December 1981. Yet Ciskei continued to administer Mgwali. This was a situation which could not have been created lawfully. Even if the agreement had been lawful and it had been converted into an international treaty via section 5 of the Ciskei Act, that treaty has never been incorporated into the municipal law of South Africa as legally required. Therefore the provisions should have no effect on Mgwali residents. Mgwali residents' affidavits handed in to the court describe the hardships suffered as a result of this administration.

The application was made in the Grahamstown Supreme Court. The South African government initially gave notice of intention to defend, but subsequently capitulated. On 5 September 1985 an order was made by consent in the Supreme Court, declaring the agreement between South Africa and the Ciskei to be invalid and without force. Mgwali is now under South African administration again. The court order is likely to affect the legal options open to Kwelera, Mooiplaas and Newlands.

Prospect Farm: Harassment of a resident of this Natal black spot was reported at a public meeting in Stanger on 26 May 1985. Mrs Thembani Dhlamini was told by a Natalia Development Board official 'to go and stay at Bulwer Trust Farm' when she complained that officials had demolished the walls of her home. Although she had not received an eviction notice, she had been told to move herself to a relocation area.

Urban relocation

On 9 May 1985, the Department of Cooperation and Development issued a list of 52 townships with more than 638 000 residents which were now no longer threatened with removal. The list included townships like Atteridgeville and Mamelodi outside Pretoria and the townships of Bloemfontein — much to the surprise of critics of removals, who learnt for the first time that these areas were threatened with relocation. Excluding these populations, a total of 354 587 people had until then been living under threat of removal from urban areas through 'disestablishment' or 'deproclamation' of townships. (The SPP had calculated only 157 000 people in this category, an indication of the conservatism of its figures).

The reprieve has not solved the problems of township residents. Development within reprieved townships is no longer frozen, but their size is still limited by the old borders. No houses have been built for so long that natural increase, not to mention new urbanisation, has caused extremely serious overcrowding which will not be relieved.

The reprieve of Huhudi outside Vryburg in the Northern Cape illustrates a more recent development in dubious strategies designed to cause people to move. When the government announced the reprieve, it said that the 'cooperation' of the people would be needed to develop Huhudi. The Huhudi Civic Association (HUCA) interprets this as meaning that residents will have to pay for development a second time; it argues that during the freeze on development between 1963 and October 1984 residents continued to pay rents and increases while receiving no township development in return. Now they are unwilling to pay again. If residents cannot pay, or refuse to do so, and are then evicted, their removal would be ascribed to 'economic' rather than 'ideological' factors.

Those people on housing waiting lists[5] will still have no choice but to move to townships built in the bantustans which were originally designed to accommodate the whole relocated township. Residents of Stanger, for example, are presently negotiating to have the borders of their township extended into nearby vacant land, rather than be forced to move to a bantustan township in order to get new housing.

Recent high rent increases constitute another pressure on residents to move despite the reprieve. This year, the people of Sibongile township outside Dundee successfully demonstrated against increases in rents, saying this was a tactic to get them to move to closer settlements[6] or townships in KwaZulu where rents are lower but distances to work much greater.

Despite the reprieve of townships, on 22 February 1985 the Deputy Minister of Cooperation, Development and Education, Sam de Beer, signed a deproclamation of Howick township in Natal. Residents are organising against the threatened removal.

Another 'back door' tactic to eject people to the bantustans is still in use. One example: for many years no new housing has been built in East Rand townships, and people were persuaded to move to Ekangala near Bronkhorstspruit, where housing was provided. On 9 February Viljoen announced that Ekangala would be incorporated into KwaNdebele, which is scheduled to take 'independence' in 1986. Residents are angry despite the Minister's assurance that they will not lose section 10 privileges. Not only are many of them not Ndebele, making them foreigners who would experience problems similar to those of non-Tswanas living in Winterveld, but South Africa will no longer be responsible for their social welfare. They are likely to lose such rights as being able to claim from the Unemployment Insurance Fund should they lose their jobs. Further, supporters of KwaNdebele 'independence' have formed gangs to harass those opposed to incorporation. Many people are talking of moving back to live in shacks on the East Rand.

Of course, the reprieve of the townships only affects those with section 10 rights to live there permanently. Thousands of 'illegals' are still threatened with eviction through influx control. For example, many Huhudi residents who qualify for the reprieve do not formally hold section 10 rights. Building at Pudumong, a township in Bophuthatswana, continues. HUCA feels that at some point these unregistered residents will be labelled 'illegal', evicted and forced to Pudumong. HUCA is working to get all residents registered and trying to bring back those who moved to Pudumong against their will.

HUCA continues to organise, not only against removals and for registration of section 10 rights, but also for old age pensions. It has started a brick-making project designed to help those who want to build since the reprieve.

On 27 February 1985 the remaining residents of the Northern Cape township of Valspan were told that they would not have to move from Jan Kempdorp to Pampierstad, in Bophuthatswana. However, those who 'chose to move' would receive 'all possible assistance and encouragement' from the government. Dr Viljoen went on to say that those who were locally employed would receive assistance in upgrading and development (*CT*, 28.02.85).

In 1984 urban removals included residents of Luckhoff in the Orange Free State who were moved to Onverwacht, due for incorporation into Qwaqwa. And at least 295 families were moved from Kleinskool to Motherwell outside Port Elizabeth.

It seems that the government will make a particular effort to move people where they are unorganised, or where there are divisions in the community. But it has had to back down on some of its more outrageous plans, such as the proposal to move all residents of Cape Town townships to Khayelitsha. Organised communities realise they cannot afford to relax their struggle, and are suspicious of government promises.

The unreprieved

Ex-farmworkers and labour tenants

These constitute the largest category both of those moved and those threatened with removal. Figures are extremely difficult to estimate, but at least one million ex-farmworkers, former labour tenants and their families ('squatters' in government terminology) have been moved over the past 25 years, and an equal number are threatened with relocation. As an indicator of the scale of this category of removal, the vast majority of those living in the OFS closer settlement of Onverwacht/Botshabelo, with its official population of 240 000, are from farms — families of redundant, disabled or aged farmworkers.

In the last week of May alone 67 families were evicted from Weenen farms. Forty-seven went to the closer settlement of Waayhoek, 45 kilometres from Ladysmith, where water has to be trucked in, where mosquitoes infest the toilets and where the rate of unemployment is very high. The rest of the families went to Compensation Trust Farm in the Impendle district where conditions are little better.

Farmworkers have no rights to compensation, although they may have been on the farms for generations. On eviction, they frequently have to move themselves, and find their own shelter in the bantustans, because the government does not assume responsibility for their relocation. They have no choice but to move to the bantustans. They have no right to organise and no possibility of resistance because they are evicted as individuals or small groups.

Consolidation[7]

The findings of the Commission for Cooperation and Development, which are to revise the 1975 proposals, have still not been announced. By the end of 1984, R930-m had been spent on consolidating the bantustans in terms of the 1975 plan.[8] More than one million people are threatened with removal in terms of the 1975 plan, although the Minister has indicated that the plans have changed. But until reprieved areas are gazetted residents will continue to feel insecure and anxious.

'Ethnic conflict' is rife over border adjustments being implemented in the consolidation of KwaNdebele, Venda, Lebowa and Gazankulu. For example, there has been serious 'faction fighting' in the north-eastern Transvaal around Tzaneen and Acornhoek. This occurred as Tsonga- and Sotho-speaking people who have lived together for generations suddenly found themselves having to use separate buses, hospitals, railway stations and even commercial facilities — because the central government had decided that one area shall be given to Gazankulu and another to Lebowa.

The Moutse section of Lebowa is another area of potential conflict, as the South African government has excised it from Lebowa to hand over to KwaNdebele. One hundred thousand people are threatened with incorporation into this soon-to-be 'independent' bantustan. Many Sotho people are leaving the area 'voluntarily' because they fear the Ndebele administration and they want to remain South African citizens.

Removals within the bantustans continue. They are difficult to monitor and virtually impossible to resist. People are seldom given more than two or three days' notice to move. They do not know whether they have any rights, and are generally too frightened and isolated to resist. It has not been possible to estimate the number of removals in this increasingly important category.

In the Eastern Cape, Oxton and Zweledinga have been moved to new sites within the Ciskei. People were moved from Bluerock to Potsdam in mid-1983. Many had moved to Potsdam in the vain hope of becoming eligible for housing in East London's Mdantsane township.

The people of Glenmore are no longer to be moved to Peddie. Instead, South African and Ciskeian authorities plan to move them about four kilometres away so that their present site can be used for agriculture.

Informal settlements

The concept of controlled squatting is not new. Throughout the 1950s and 1960s, stop-gap tactics like emergency site-and-service camps were permitted to some squatter settlements. But present policy involves shifting responsibility for most of this housing from the public sector to the private sector, in the interests of 'free enterprise'. This does not only mean that the business community will take more responsibility for the provision of housing: individuals will increasingly have to provide their own (approved) shelter.

The principle behind the present 'orderly urbanisation' and 'urban renewal' policy variants of influx control is that of 'werk en woon': that an individual's right to remain resident in 'white' urban areas should depend on his or her having either approved housing or employment in such an area.[9] This is directly in line with the recommendations of the Riekert Commission of Enquiry report on urban blacks, which was published in 1979. Riekert argued for the development of a stable privileged urban group ('legals') at the expense of the mass of rural 'outsiders' or 'illegals'. This principle was the basis of the now-withdrawn Orderly Movement and Settlement of Black Persons Bill, which is to be replaced by legislation controlling 'orderly urbanisation'.

This will result in a tightening of influx control, and potential displacement of people who currently have urban residence rights. At present, a person may be unemployed and/or waiting for a house, while retaining section 10 rights permitting residence in an urban area. In terms of the proposed changes, those who are unemployed and/or do not have approved housing will be endorsed out of urban areas.

An example from the East Rand township of Tsakane may illustrate the shape of things to come: in 1981, people were evicted from the old Brakpan township and allowed to build shacks in Tsakane while waiting for houses to be built. In early February 1985, a number of shack dwellers were subjected to 2 am raids in which their shacks were demolished. They were told to move to a site-and-service scheme where they would have to pay R150 per month to acquire approved housing. But the 'squatters' demand that the original promise of housing be fulfilled. If they cannot afford this 'urban renewal'/'orderly urbanisation' scheme, some may be forced to move themselves 'voluntarily' to a bantustan.

The government has made it clear that despite calls from the business community, it is not prepared to reform structurally. It continues to argue that it does not prevent urbanisation; that indeed, urbanisation is promoted in the form of closer settlements alongside decentralisation schemes in the bantustans. But essentially present government policy is set out in the Riekert report, which states:

> Control over the rate of urbanisation is, in the light of circumstances in South Africa, an absolutely essential social security measure. Even though . . . the abolition of such control would lead to faster economic growth, the price to be paid for it in terms of direct and indirect social costs would be too high.[10]

Crossroads and Khayelitsha[11]

Violence broke out in Crossroads on 18 February 1985 in reaction to a statement by the Minister of Cooperation, Development and Education that uncontrolled squatting in Crossroads would not be tolerated. At the same time a removal squad, which unlike Crossroads residents was not Xhosa-speaking, arrived from the Transvaal to move people to the controversial new township of Khayelitsha. During four days of conflict between residents of the Crossroads complex, Nyanga township and the police, 18 people were killed and more than 230 injured. This intensity of police reaction to those who resisted even a rumour of removal has not been seen since the 1960s, if ever, in South Africa.

On 22 February 1985, the government announced that 99-year leasehold would be extended to the townships of Langa, Guguletu and Nyanga, which meant that qualified residents were no longer threatened with removal to Khayelitsha. While this was a victory for those who had resisted the removal of the townships it was also an attempt to divide the united response of township residents and squatters.

On 27 February the government announced the upgrading of 3 000 sites for 'legal' Crossroads residents. Approximately three-quarters of the estimated 100 000 Crossroads and KTC residents would still be required to move. So while the government conceded that part of Crossroads could stay, this concession dividing the people into recognised Crossroads residents and 'newcomers' would force the majority to move.

Various concessions to Africans in the Western Cape have been granted since mid-1984, when a moratorium on demolition of shacks was announced. As a result, people streamed out of township backyard shacks to the Crossroads complex, hoping to qualify for rights and housing in Cape Town. Local control in Crossroads could not cope with the influx. Fights broke out between different groups as they competed for the same land which they each claimed had been allocated to them.

In September 1984, 99-year leasehold was extended to Khayelitsha, and legislation defining the Western Cape as a coloured labour preference area was abolished. Both these concessions angered right-wing whites who want the Western Cape free of a permanent African population. But they were on the other hand 'too little too late' for Africans — who demanded freehold rights (which on 19 April 1985 were extended to Africans in the rest of 'white' South Africa, but not those in the Western Cape) and the right to live and work where they choose.

Later the Urban Areas Act was amended to ease the process of qualifying for section 10(1)(b) rights, but this does not affect even migrants who hold section 10(1)(d) rights, let alone the 'illegals'.

The Minister of Cooperation and Development said in parliament that ' . . . the majority of the inhabitants of Crossroads will have to be settled elsewhere. I would be unable to deny this [that there would be settlement under some form of compulsion] categorically'.[12]

Representatives of three of the 'squatter' groups (from Nyanga Bush, Nyanga Extension and Portland Cement) unwilling to move to Site C of Khayelitsha finally met the Minister on 29 May (after he had told parliament on 21 February that he would be seeing them 'within the next few days'). He told them that he could not accede to their demands for rights to live and work in Cape Town because it was 'against the law'. This is the same argument used by his predecessor's secretary to the people of Umbulwane in 1981: 'It should be mentioned that the Honourable the Minister's statement that "no people must be forced to leave their homes" did not imply that the country's legislation could be disregarded'.[13]

The Minister 'advised' the people of Nyanga Bush to move to Site C. Their vault-type toilets were not cleared for more than a month. As the chairperson of the Nyanga Extension Committee said: 'We see that [refusal to clear toilets] as a subtle way of forcing us to Site C'.

Group Areas removals

These also continue, despite much talk of repealing the Group Areas Act. Early in 1985 Central Business Districts were opened to all races for trading purposes, but brutal responses to group areas victims still occur. In February 1985 police used batons and teargas to disperse Atlantis residents protesting against planned evictions. Wide-spread retrenchments have affected the ability of residents to keep up rent and bond payments. Those who have not paid their water bills have had their services cut.

In Natal at present African people are threatened with removal from Indian group areas land at Savannah Park, which is regarded by residents as part of St Wendolins. Although the rest of the area has been reprieved, some 2 000 people are threatened with removal in terms of Group Areas legislation. Forty-seven families were told to move from Indian-owned land, according to an answer to a parliamentary question.[14]

Infrastructural and strategic removals

Removals in these categories still occur, particularly in Natal, where AFRA estimates that up to 900 000 people may be threatened with removal from the catchment area of the Upper Tugela. Inanda Dam alone will dislocate more than 5 000 black people.

Conclusion

Since Piet Koornhof announced in 1981 that there would be no more forced removals, some 334 232 removals, or nearly 10% of the total implemented over the past 25 years, have taken place. Tactics have changed. Today fewer people are trucked from their homes and dumped *en masse* in the veld. More common now are the 'motivational efforts'[15] such as vague promises, ambiguous statements, announcements and retractions, rumours and harassment.

Nationwide, recent years have been a time of confusion and con-

tradiction, repression and reprieves. The apartheid structure is in
tatters. The bantustans are not viable. Even the highly-acclaimed
decentralisation plans of 1982 are a failure. For example, it was
reported that in at least two Ciskei factories workers only receive
between R40 and R60 of the R110 cash paid per worker per month
by the government (*CT*, 08.03.85). The economy is depressed. The
rand has fallen to a record low and the international community is
threatening disinvestment. The UN Security Council unanimously
condemned South Africa's handling of the Crossroads conflict.

Perhaps the most devastating and depressing aspect of forced
removals is that they are implemented and justified in terms of the
law. The desperate conditions to be found in South Africa's relocation areas are not a result of some tragic natural disaster, but of
carefully considered legislation intended to divide and control the
people in an attempt to maintain economic and political power in
the hands of the white minority.

Notes

1 Categories and numbers of removals are discussed in Laurine Platzky
and Cherryl Walker, *The Surplus People* (Johannesburg, 1985), 30-51.
The book was written on behalf of the SPP as a popular version of the
five-volume report, *Forced Removals in South Africa*, published in
June 1983.
2 *The Surplus People*, chapter 8.
3 *Hansard*, 09.04.85, col 944.
4 See *The Surplus People*, 428.
5 Only 11 902 houses were built for Africans in 1984, some 6% of the
estimated backlog of 196 000 (*Hansard*, 26.04.85, col 1287); some 500
of those were built in Khayelitsha, planned to accommodate the 'legal'
residents of Crossroads.
6 Closer settlement is the official term to describe a type of settlement
established for African people on reserve or Trust land that is for
residential purposes only. No agricultural land is attached, and facilities
in the settlement are rudimentary. People removed off black spots and
white farms are generally relocated to these settlements. They are provided with temporary accommodation and are expected to build their
own permanent houses. Facilities vary but generally (not always) include pit latrines and one or more communal water supply points.

7 Consolidation is the official term used to describe the policy developed by central government in the 1970s, and formalised by the 1975 Consolidation Plan. The policy aims to reduce the number of separate, isolated pieces of land making up each of the bantustans, and is part of the process of turning these areas into 'independent national states'.

8 Parliamentary question, *Hansard*, 12.03.85, col 510.

9 ABC Nightline programme and interview in *Leadership*, 12.03.85.

10 Quoted in *The Economist*, 21.06.80, 19.

11 In March 1983, the government announced that it planned to move the whole African population of Cape Town from the townships of Langa, Nyanga and Guguletu, and from the 'squatter camps'. Those who legally qualified to be in the Western Cape would be moved to Khayelitsha (meaning 'our new home'), and the 'illegals' would be deported to Transkei or Ciskei. In March 1985 an extension of Khayelitsha, Site C, was demarcated for a controlled site and service scheme.

The Crossroads complex includes at least ten groups of 'squatters' under different leaders.

12 *Hansard*, 26.02.85, col 1441.

13 *The Surplus People*, 276.

14 *Hansard*, 09.04.85, col 930.

15 *The Surplus People*, 157.